STRATEGIC AND OPERATIONAL DECEPTION
IN THE SECOND WORLD WAR

STRATEGIC
AND
OPERATIONAL
DECEPTION IN THE
SECOND WORLD WAR

Edited by
MICHAEL I. HANDEL

FRANK CASS

First published 1987 in Great Britain by
FRANK CASS & CO. LTD.
Gainsborough House, Gainsborough Road,
London, E11 1RS, England

and in the United States of America by
FRANK CASS & CO. LTD.
c/o Biblio Distribution Centre
81 Adams Drive, P.O. Box 327, Totowa, N.J. 07511

Library of Congress Cataloging-in-Publication Data

Strategic and operational deception in the Second
World War.

"First appeared in a Special issue on strategic and
operational deception in the Second World War of
the journal Intelligence and national security,
vol. 2, no. 3"—T.p. verso.
1. World War, 1939–1945—Campaigns.
2. Deception—History—20th century. 3. Strategy—
History—20th century. 4. Subversive activities—
History—20th century. I. Handel, Michael I.
D743.S72 1987   940.54'1   87–10316
ISBN 0-7146-3316-X
ISBN 0-7146-4056-5 (pbk.)

British Library Cataloguing in Publication Data

Strategic and operational deception in
the Second World War.
1. World War, 1939–1945—Campaigns
2. Strategy   3. Deception
I. Handel, Michael I.
940.54'012   D744

ISBN 0-7146-3316-X
ISBN 0-7146-4056-5 Pbk

This group of studies first appeared in a Special Issue on Strategic and Operational
Deception in the Second World War of the journal *Intelligence and National Security*,
Vol. 2, no. 3, published by Frank Cass and Co. Ltd.

Printed and bound in Great Britain by
Adlard & Son (The Garden City Press) Ltd

Contents

Preface

The essays in this book were presented during an international conference on 'Intelligence and Military Operations' held at the US Army War College at Carlisle Barracks, Pennsylvania, in April 1986. In organizing the conference and preparing the manuscript for publication, the editor received the support of Major General James E. Thompson, Brigadier General Richard L. Reynard, Colonel Charles Beitz, and Colonel Donald Lunday. The Chairman of the Department of National Security and Strategy, Colonel David Hansen, provided not only encouragement and support all along the way but also secured the editor the necessary time to write the introductory chapter for this volume. Colonel (ret.) LeRoy Strong, Executive Director of the US Army War College Foundation, has shown great interest in the subject and also provided some of the financial support for the conference.

Last, but not least, I would like to express my gratitude to my wife, Jill Handel, for her professional editorial assistance, sound advice, and constructive criticism. 'Who can find a virtuous woman? . . . she openeth her mouth with wisdom; and her tongue is the law of kindness.' The book is dedicated to her and to our children.

Carlisle Barracks,   *Michael I. Handel*
April 1987.

The views expressed in this book are those of the authors and do not reflect the official policy or position of the Department of Defense or the US government.

For
Jill, Yael, Benjamin
and Ethan

Introduction: Strategic and Operational Deception in Historical Perspective

MICHAEL I. HANDEL

... each surprise action is rooted in at least some degree of cunning.

The use of a trick or stratagem permits the intended victim to make his own mistakes, which, combined in a single result, suddenly change the nature of the situation before his very eyes.

But words, being cheap, are the most common means of creating false impressions.[1]

The invaluable ruse [Meinerzhagen's 'haversack ruse'] which has been described would not have worked the other way. The Turks could be confirmed in their belief that Gaza was the objective; they could not have been dissuaded from this belief by any faked plan of attack on Beersheba.[2]

What is or is not possible matters less than what the enemy believes possible.[3]

Deception has long been recognized as one of the most important elements inherent in warfare. In a nutshell, deception may be defined as: The process of influencing the enemy to make decisions disadvantageous to himself by supplying or denying information.[4] Sun Tzu concluded that 'All warfare is based on deception',[5] while Clausewitz, who did not assign a role of key importance to deception in his theory of war, nevertheless observed:

... it seems not unjust that the term 'strategy' should be derived from 'cunning' and that, for all the real and apparent changes that war has undergone since the days of ancient Greece, this term still indicates its essential nature. ...

No human characteristic appears so suited to the task of directing and inspiring strategy as the gift of cunning.[6]

Yet despite their recognition of deception as a very important – perhaps even decisive – dimension in waging war, strategists have never accepted it as one of the 'basic principles' of the art of war.[7] A special principle of deception has been omitted because deception *per se* has no value; it assumes significance only when used as a *means* of achieving surprise. In comparison, surprise is a decisive factor on all levels of warfare that has been duly acknowledged as an autonomous principle by all compendia of the maxims of war. Thus, deception is a valuable tool at the disposal of military commanders seeking to achieve strategic, operational and tactical surprise which may, in turn, provide them with one of the keys to victory.

DECEPTION IN HISTORICAL PERSPECTIVE

In classical antiquity, the use of stratagem in warfare was not only accepted – it was expected. Many accounts of war and battles in ancient epics, the Bible, the *Iliad* and the *Odyssey*, or Greek, Roman and Chinese histories abound with examples. The reason is obvious. During a time when almost all other factors were held as equal (there being minimal differences between the weapons available to adversaries), battles were primarily decided by either superior numbers or superior military leadership. Inasmuch as material changes evolved slowly, the 'cutting edge' of the battlefield was to be found in inspired ruses of war. Deception was consequently one of the few 'force multipliers' available that could lead to a decisive victory.

In medieval Europe, however, the inter-related influences of Christianity and chivalry caused the resort to deception to be considered a dishonorable and unfashionable course of action. Exerting an influence that endured at least until the First World War, the altruistic credo of the chivalrous knights was exemplified by their solemn vow 'to speak the truth, to succor the helpless and oppressed and never to turn back from an enemy.'[8]

> Christianity had a part in fashioning medieval warfare in both theory and practice. The central idea of a just Christian war for the sake of punishing evildoers was perhaps of little real significance for practice. But the same cannot be said of the military guild of knighthood with its strong individualistic moral code of chivalry shaped by a common Christian outlook. Widespread belief in the chivalrous virtues and in the Christian faith, the idea of common membership in the Republica Christiana, may have helped to prevent warfare from becoming the very bloody and total kind of activity that it had been among the ancients. Between medieval foes there was the bond of Christian conduct and gentlemanly behavior that tended to mitigate the nature of the punitive action resorted to by the victor. *This may account for the fact that medieval commanders did not make full use of the stratagems that had been a common part of the classical military leader's repertoire. Conversely, the medieval commander seemed particularly suscep-*

tible to the employment of deception and trickery by a ruthless and unchivalrous opponent.[9] [my emphasis]

The ethic of chivalry stressed a reverence for order that was regulated by commonly understood, formalized rules for combat. Preservation of honor and the demonstration of bravery were more important than victory in this type of warfare cum social ritual.[10]

Today the code of chivalry still forms part of the education of officers and gentlemen in some Western and Latin American countries; in fact, it may put them at a subtle disadvantage in confrontations with officers from either communist or Third World nations who do not feel bound by Western norms (examples include the US and Japan in the Pacific; the Germans and Russians on the Eastern Front; and the US in Korea and Vietnam).[11]

Even while chivalry was at its zenith, not all Christian states played according to the rules of the game. The Byzantine emperors were only too willing to take advantage of the attitude of the Franks, as illustrated by Emperor Leo's advice to his generals:

> The Frank believes that a retreat under any circumstances must be dishonorable; hence he will fight whenever you choose to offer him battle. This you must not do until you have secured all possible advantages for yourself, as his cavalry, with their long lances and large shields, charge with a tremendous impetus. You should deal with him by protracting the campaign, and if possible lead him into the hills, where his cavalry are less efficient than in the plain. After a few weeks without a great battle, his troops, who are very susceptible to fatigue and weariness, will grow tired of the war, and ride home in great numbers. . . . You will find him utterly careless as to outposts and reconnaissances, so that you can easily cut off outlying parties of his men, and attack his camp at advantage. As his forces have no bonds of discipline, but only those of kindred or oath, they fall into confusion after delivering their charge; you can therefore simulate flight, and then turn on them, when you will find them in utter disarray. On the whole, however, it is easier and less costly to wear out a Frankish army by skirmishes and protracted operations rather than to attempt to destroy it at a single blow.[12]

Charles Oman has commented on Byzantine strategy as follows:

> Of chivalry there is not a spark in the Byzantine, though professional pride is abundantly shown. Courage is regarded as one of the requisites necessary for obtaining success, not as the sole and paramount virtue of the warrior. Leo considers a cam-

paign successfully concluded without a great battle as the cheapest and most satisfactory consummation in war. . . . He shows a strong predilection for stratagems, ambushes and simulated retreats. . . . The Art of War as understood at Constantinople in the tenth century, was the only scheme of true scientific merit existing in the world, and was unrivaled till the sixteenth century.[13]

In stark contrast to the ethic of chivalry, the principles of Sun Tzu and Emperor Leo emphasized that the greatest skill a commander could demonstrate would be to subdue the enemy without fighting.[14] It is clear that strategists who prefer victory at the lowest possible cost or even without bloodshed also show much more interest in deception than those who see the acme of a commander's skill as being demonstrated in battle itself and are therefore continually searching for the decisive engagement.

The transition from the age of chivalry to the limited wars of the *ancien régime*, wherein the divine right of kings superseded Christianity as the highest moral guidance for the conduct of war, produced little incentive to resort to deception. When the stakes are relatively limited, adversaries who share common values and have a common interest in maintaining a general framework for order (in other words, the balance of power) are not as concerned by the search for a decisive victory nor do they fear total defeat. In such circumstances, the rules of the balance of power reduce military interest in deception by limiting the objectives and consequences of war. (There were, of course, always some individual leaders or states during each of these periods who relied extensively on deception thereby taking advantage of those who played by the rules.) Thus, to the influence of the *Republica Christiana* and the ethic of chivalry was now added the moderating effect of universal adherence to the rules dictated by the balance of power.

The French Revolution, however, gave rise to a revolutionary international system of total war in which no common rules were accepted by the opponents.[15] At first glance, it might seem as though wars between ideologically divergent groups whose pursuit of immoderate goals is fed by mass mobilization and backed by the whole of their industrial might would provide fertile ground for the use of deception. Yet this did not prove to be true from the outbreak of the French Revolution up to the end of the First World War. How can this be explained?

The experience of the Napoleonic wars seemed to bear out the effectiveness of the search for the decisive battle. Although Napoleonic warfare was largely based on maneuver, the purpose of maneuver was not so much deception, or even surprise, as the concentration of a larger number of soldiers ahead of the enemy on the battlefield. As Clausewitz and Jomini emphasized, superiority in numbers was the real key to victory. 'The best in strategy is always to *be very strong* first in general, and then at the decisive point. . . . There is no higher and simpler law of strategy than that of *keeping one's forces concentrated.*'[16] [Emphasis in the original.] 'An impartial student of modern war must admit that superior numbers are becoming more decisive with each passing day. The principle of bringing the maximum possible strength to the decisive engagement must therefore rank higher than it did in the past.'[17]

It is not surprising, therefore, that Clausewitz considered diversions a waste of strength since they reduced the number of troops available to the commander at the decisive point.

> To prepare a sham action with sufficient thoroughness to impress an enemy requires a considerable expenditure of time and effort, and the costs increase with scale of the deception. Normally they call for more than can be spared, and consequently so-called strategic feints rarely have the desired effect. It is dangerous, in fact, to use substantial forces over any length of time merely to create an illusion: there is always the risk that nothing will be gained and that the troops deployed will not be available when they are really needed.[18]

In circumstances in which victory was sought through firepower and attrition in the decisive battle and in which the ability to achieve surprise was limited – deception had no role to play.[19] The mobility and speed necessary to achieve strategic or operational surprise on a larger scale only became feasible during the First World War. Hence, the approach to strategic and operational success during the nineteenth century and the 1914–18 war emphasized the concentration of a larger number of soldiers at the decisive point on the battlefield – and ultimately, therefore, the superior concentration of firepower. Reinforced by the industrial–technological revolution, which supplied the weapons and ammunition required for superior firepower, this trend reached its most extreme manifestation during the First World War. It must again be emphasized that this describes a general trend not without some notable exceptions.

Paradoxically, deception and surprise appear to have reached their lowest ebb during the First World War even as the groundwork was being laid for their vital contribution during the Second World War. In the first place, new technologies such as the radio, the increase in speed and mobility, and air power created new opportunities for deception. Second, the lack of decisiveness combined with incredible losses led many to realize that more effective methods of waging war must be found. Third and on a different level, the experience gained from some of the deception operations in the Great War, in particular by Admiral Blinker Hall in the Admiralty and even more so by Wavell in Allenby's Palestine Campaign, proved to be of great importance in initiating deception operations during the Second World War.

Almost all the elements that made strategic and operational deception on a large scale possible in the Second World War already existed in the First. This is perhaps best demonstrated by Allenby's deception cover plans for the Third Battle of Gaza (November 1917) and the Battle of Megiddo (September 1918). Following two costly abortive attacks on Gaza in March and April 1917, the British government decided to send General Sir Edmund Allenby to command the Egyptian Expeditionary Force (EEF) in Palestine. It was hoped that a successful offensive in Palestine would not only ease the pressure of a possible Turkish offensive in Mesopotamia against Baghdad, but above all convince the Turks to abandon the war on the German side once Jaffa and Jerusalem were under British occupation.[20]

Soon after his arrival in late June 1917, General Allenby approved plans (August to October 1917) for a major offensive in Palestine. He decided to change the *Schwerpunkt* of the attack from Gaza to Beersheba (the Turkish left flank) in order to roll up the defenses of Gaza and defeat the Turks in central Palestine. Given the marginal superiority of the British (10 better-equipped British versus eight Turkish divisions), the difficult terrain, the obstacles to be overcome in providing logistical support, and the fact that the forthcoming attack could not be concealed from the Turks, the success of the offensive hinged mainly on the possibility of misleading the Turks as to the exact timing and place of the attack.

The overall deception plan was divided into two levels: strategic and operational. The strategic plan (much as the Palestine Campaign itself) was to pin down four to five Turkish divisions in Northern Syria in order to prevent them from serving as reinforcements in Palestine or taking part in Operation 'Yelderim' ('Thunderbolt'), the Turkish plan to reoccupy Baghdad. With this goal in mind, Allenby approved a scheme to convince the Turks that a large landing operation was going to take place in Northern Syria. Most of the deception activities supporting this notional threat of invasion focused on Cyprus, where new camp sites were set up and the small garrison force tried to give the impression of increased activity. The British also made extensive use of bogus wireless traffic in, to and from Cyprus, openly loaded equipment, soldiers and horses in the port of Cyprus; and entered into negotiations for the purchase of large quantities of food and other supplies. After being alerted to the possibility of suspicious activity, the Turks sent a special reconnaissance mission over Cyprus which apparently determined that there was no threat of invasion from that direction after all. Much like Operation Starkey (the subject of Campbell's article that follows), this deception operation failed primarily because there was not enough *time* for careful preparation of the necessary cover plan, and there were not enough real troops and other resources available to create a convincing notional order of battle.[21] Without the benefit of a pre-existing Turkish concept that such an invasion was quite possible, the time and resources at Allenby's disposal were simply not sufficient to convince the Turks that the threat was genuine.

The deception plan on the operational level, however, was very successful and made a major contribution to the success of Allenby's offensive. In many ways, this plan was the prototype for operational deception in the Second World War, for it incorporated elements later found in the deception plans preceding the battles of Alam Halfa and El Alamein, the invasion of Sicily, and the invasion of Normandy.

The scheme called for a *double bluff*, in which the forthcoming attack on Beersheba was presented as a diversion intended to draw attention away from the 'main objective' of Gaza. The great advantage of this type of deception is that even when the main attack has begun in earnest, the opponent still believes it is merely secondary. Expecting the 'real' blow to fall elsewhere, the opponent is usually reluctant to reinforce the attacked area and instead uses most of his troops to protect what he mistakenly perceives to be the true target. This often prolongs the effect of the deception plan even after the real attack has opened. During the Second World War, the Allies carried out a double bluff on a much larger scale when they presented Normandy as the planned site of a diversionary attack and the Pas de Calais as the main objective. This completely notional threat to the Pas de Calais was so convincing that the Germans believed in its veracity throughout the war. (See Cubbage's article.) Similarly, Operation Mincemeat presented the real invasion of Sicily as a diversion to cover the 'attack' on Sardinia and the Peloponnese. Since Turkish and German commanders had already surmised that Gaza was the most logical target for the British attack, it was relatively easy to reinforce their beliefs. A variety of active and passive deception means were used to achieve this.

The best known and most successful of these activities was the 'haversack ruse' of Major Richard Meinerzhagen, Allenby's intelligence officer. The ruse was so successful that in the Second World War it became the inspiration for similar operations such as the 'going map ruse' that preceded the battle of Alam Halfa and the more complex Operation Mincemeat ('The Man Who Never Was') that preceded the invasion of Sicily.[22]

After a number of unsuccessful attempts, Meinerzhagen finally managed to 'lose' a haversack containing carefully prepared documents in a staged encounter with a Turkish patrol. Among the documents were staff papers ostensibly prepared for discussion at Allenby's headquarters. From these it was possible to infer that the main operation would take place against Gaza supported by a landing from the sea, while the attack on Beersheba would be a diversion. Also included was an officer's notebook which discussed transport difficulties and the shortage of water and supplies necessary to support a large force in the Beersheba region as well as the fact that no solution to all these problems had been found. 'Private' letters from officers stationed near Beersheba implied that it was a mistake to choose Gaza as the main focus of the coming offensive. The orders of the day instructed officers and soldiers to complete the study of a detailed model of Gaza's defenses by mid-November; this, of course, suggested a later date for the attack, which was actually scheduled for 31 October. A central accomplishment of all major strategic/operational deception plans in the Second World War – from Sidi Barrani to El Alamein, Husky, Diadem and Normandy – was their convincing indication to the enemy that the attack would take place later than was actually planned. According to other accounts, the haversack also contained £20 in small notes and a cipher book which enabled the Turks to decipher British wireless traffic from Egypt. To lend credence to this *ruse de guerre*, an urgent signal was sent to GHQ ordering an immediate search for the lost haversack, while a second complained of Meinerzhagen's carelessness. A third signal ordered him to report to GHQ for a court inquiry and warned him to return in time for the attack on 19 November 1917.[23]

In the meantime, additional deceptive measures were set in motion. Misleading 'information', transmitted both in cipher and *en clair*, suggested that no offensive would take place before 19 November, for General Allenby had gone to Egypt on leave and would not be returning before 7 November. Moreover, most of the British formations were concentrated in front of Gaza in accordance with the rule that whenever possible all order-of-battle deception operations should be based on real formations. Just ten days before D-Day, the British gradually started to move the troops toward Beersheba under cover of darkness; at the same time, they made every attempt to maintain a façade of normal routine activity 24 hours a day in the now-empty Gaza camps. In other complementary deception activities, landing boats and troops were concentrated in the Deer el Balah area (south of Gaza); warships were sent to patrol the coast near Gaza, where they pretended to measure the depth of the water for a landing operation; and alarming rumors were spread concerning a landing in the rear of Gaza.

From August onwards, the British began an elaborate *acclimatization* program for the benefit of the Turkish forces in Beersheba.

About once a fortnight throughout the summer a reconnaissance was pushed close up to the defences of Beersheba by the cavalry division in the line. These reconnaissances served a double purpose. Their constant repetition suggested to the enemy that our efforts in this direction would be confined to demonstrations; it was hoped that the real attack on Beersheba would gain the advantage of surprise by being mistaken at first for another reconnaissance, an impression to which our Intelligence Service adroitly insinuated at the right moment by certain cipher wireless messages which were meant to be read by the Turk. *Secondly*, these periodical advances towards Beersheba provided a screen under cover of which commanders and staff became acquainted with the somewhat intricate ground towards Beersheba and worked out their arrangements for the approach to and assault on the Turkish works.[24]

The logistical infrastructure necessary to support the troop concentrations opposite Beersheba was prepared in great secrecy. The extension of the railway and water pipelines across the Wadi Ghuzze into no-man's land was postponed to a late stage of the program, while the stockpiling of stores was compressed into as little time and space as possible. All work was conducted at night after which the new sections of the railway and pipeline were carefully camouflaged. (This aspect of the plan closely resembles the cover and deception operations preceding the Battles of Sidi Barrani and El Alamein.)[25]

A week before the main attack on Beersheba was to take place, a large-scale artillery bombardment of Gaza from both the land and sea began. A day before D-Day, hundreds of Egyptian workers accompanying the EEF were marched in military formation during the day, embarked on landing ships, then disembarked during the night. To prolong the effectiveness of the deception and divert Turkish attention away from Beersheba even after the offensive had begun, the XXI Corps directly assaulted a portion of the Gaza defenses on D-Day.

In General Wavell's view, the achievement of air superiority in order to prevent the possibility of Turkish and German air reconnaissance missions was a key factor in the success of the whole deception operation.

All these devices to mislead the enemy would have been of much less avail had not the new squadrons and more modern machines received from home enabled our Air Force in the late autumn to wrest from the enemy the command of the air which he had enjoyed for so long in the theatre. After a few trials of strength had convinced the German aviators of the superior speed and performance of the Bristol Fighters, they came over only at a very respectful height, and by the beginning of the operations had been almost driven out of the skies.[26]

All the vacated camps behind Gaza had been left standing, and were lighted up at night. By day all troops were carefully hidden. To the enemy airmen, forced by the superior speed of the British 'planes and the antiaircraft artillery to observe at a great height, no change in the dispositions of the army was apparent. It is known from an order subsequently captured that on so late a date as October 29th the enemy believed *that six divisions* were still opposite Gaza, and that a movement by one division and one mounted division only need be apprehended against Beersheba.[27]

This was also his explanation for the success of the cover plan preceding the decisive battle of Megiddo.

> But it was above all the dominance secured by our Air Force that enabled the concentration to be concealed. So complete was the mastery it had obtained in the air by hard fighting that by September a hostile aeroplane rarely crossed our lines at all.[28]

This operational deception plan was as complex and meticulously prepared as any of the major deception plans of the Second World War. How effective was it?

Turkish intelligence estimates – documents and maps captured during the operation – clearly show that three days before D-Day the Turks had identified the changes in the British order of battle, discovered that many of the British camps opposite Gaza were in fact empty, and identified the general direction of movement of the British troops (towards Beersheba) with their true dispositions. It is also evident that the Turks were not misled by the bogus threat of landing in the rear of Gaza.

Nevertheless, these last-minute discoveries had little impact on the decisions of the Turkish-German high command. The reasons for this are not entirely clear, but may be, among others, an overestimation of the size of the British real order of battle; the existence of a powerful and rather rigid concept that the British would direct their major effort toward Gaza, and perhaps the inability of the German-Turkish High Command to digest the latest information in such a short time.[29]

General Kress von Kressentein had a fleeting suspicion concerning the genuineness of the haversack documents (much like Hitler's rhetorical question as to whether the documents provided to the Germans in Operation Mincemeat were not deceptive). (See Müller's article.)

> The success of the ruse to deceive the Turks as to the point of attack has been mentioned. It appears that the documents were examined with great care by Kress, and that, while not overlooking the possibility that they were faked, he inclined strongly to believe in their authenticity. At any rate, even after the attack on Beersheba had begun, he refused to believe the reports of the commander of the III Corps as to the British strength, ordered Beersheba to be held, and sent no reinforcements.[30]

Yet, in both cases, the documents fitted conveniently into the pre-existing concepts of the deceived, who were psychologically predisposed to accept them.

Even before the battle had begun, the British could observe that the Turks had reduced preparations on their left flank in Beersheba and significantly increased their work on the fortifications of Gaza. According to both the official history and Wavell's report, the Turks were completely surprised at Beersheba, not by the fact that an attack took place, but by its unexpected weight and direction.[31]

Even if the British somewhat exaggerated the success of their ruse, there is still no doubt that it succeeded with regard to the overall goal of achieving surprise, which in turn confused the Turkish–German defense and slowed down its reactions. As long as it is clear that the deception plan accomplished its principal objectives, one need not be over-concerned with the degree to which the success of the Third Battle of Gaza can be attributed to subterfuge as opposed to other factors such as the marginal British superiority or conflicts within the Turkish–German High Command. Suffice it to say that without deception, the Third Battle of Gaza might very well have ended in disaster like its two predecessors (and almost all other attacks on the Western Front).

A year later, Allenby once again relied on a major operational deception plan to conceal preparations for the battles of Megiddo (September 1918). Since the experience of the Turkish–German High Command in the Third Battle of Gaza had conditioned it to expect an inland attack, Allenby now reversed his deception cover to indicate that the next major British offensive would take place inland along the river Jordan and in Transjordan in conjunction with a 'diversionary attack' along the shore and in the Sharon valley. (A similar type of reversed conditioning deception took place in the Italian campaign during the Second World War. To begin with, the Germans were completely surprised by the Allied landing in Anzio (January 1944), for

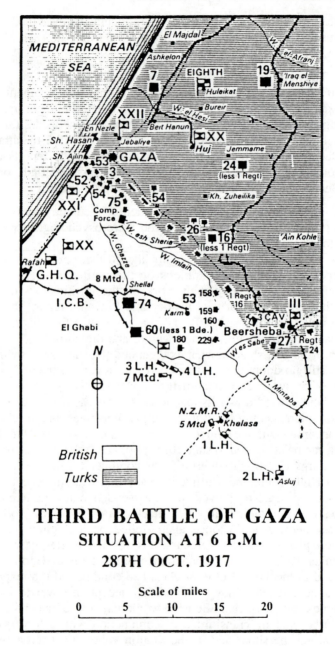

THIRD BATTLE OF GAZA
SITUATION AT 6 P.M.
28TH OCT. 1917

Scale of miles

0   5   10   15   20

MAPS 1 & 2: THE THIRD BATTLE OF GAZA. Note the concealed shift of

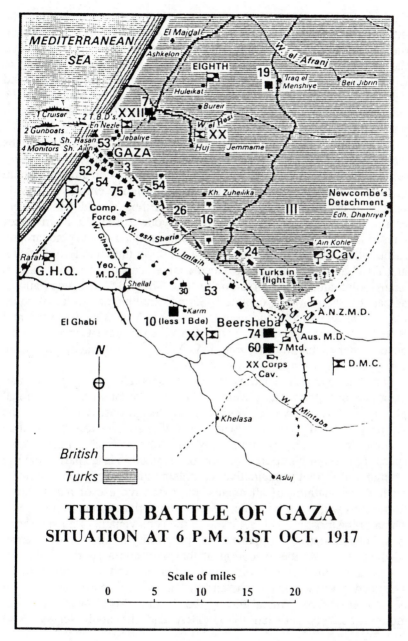

THIRD BATTLE OF GAZA
SITUATION AT 6 P.M. 31ST OCT. 1917

Scale of miles

0   5   10   15   20

British troop concentrations from Gaza on left to Beersheba on the right.

various Allied ruses had led them to anticipate an attack from the interior along the established front line. In the next phase of the attack on the Gustav line (Operation Diadem (May 1944)), the Allies tricked the Germans (Operation Nunton) into expecting another landing at Civitavecchia, whereas the main attack actually occurred on land and was directed against the Gustav line.)[32] There is no doubt that the susceptibility to conditioning is one of the most fundamental human proclivities to be exploited by deception operations.

As a result of thorough British preparations, the Turks and Germans were once again caught unawares when the 'major British offensive' turned out to be a diversion, and the supposed diversion along the shore quickly became a full-scale attack. Again Allenby employed a wide variety of complementary deception covers: bogus headquarters were established in a Jerusalem hotel for everyone to see; the main forces chosen for the offensive were secretly concentrated on the plain around Jaffa, while many empty camps were set up in the vicinity of Jericho; and T.E. Lawrence was sent to execute large-scale diversionary raids in Transjordan along the Deraa-Aman line. These detailed preparations, as can be seen from a captured German intelligence order-of-battle map, were completely successful. (Compare Map 3 showing the real British troop concentration, with Map 4, a captured German intelligence order of battle (OB) map.) As Wavell commented, 'the battle was practically won before a shot was fired'.[33]

For Allenby, unlike almost all other generals of the Great War, elaborate deception plans were a key element of every operational plan. As T.E. Lawrence remarked, 'Deceptions, which for the ordinary general were just witty *hors d'oeuvres* before battle, had become for Allenby a main point in strategy.'[34] The phenomenal success of Allenby's stratagems can be ascribed in large part to the use of many different imaginative complementary deception methods: meticulous planning of all details, the extensive use of real military formations whenever possible, adequate material support and secrecy. Three of the most critical factors were the achievement of air superiority in order to deny the opponent any possibility of air reconnaissance, adequate time for the execution of the plan, and a good intelligence system that could monitor the enemy's reaction to the deception baits. The need to know whether the enemy had 'swallowed the bait' which became even more crucial during the Second World War, was even more effectively satisfied by ULTRA and the double-cross (XX) system.

In their intricate preparations and exploitation of the opportunities provided by modern technology (in particular wireless deception and air superiority), Allenby's deception operations closely resemble the more complex schemes devised during the Second World War. Thus, Allenby's skillful use of stratagem represents a transition from earlier periods of either non-existent or *ad hoc* deception to deception at its zenith during the Second World War.

While the potential contribution of deception was generally ignored during the First World War, it eventually came to be appreciated as an essential part of strategic and operational planning in the Second. The principles of deception may not have changed in the interim but there is no doubt that its scope, means, organization and methods had.

It is interesting to note that there was a direct link between Allenby's imaginative use of stratagem in the Palestine Campaigns and the subsequent recognition of deception as an important source of support for all military operations during the Second World War. This link was provided by General Sir Archibald Wavell, the British Commander-in-Chief in the Middle East (1939–41), who had served in Allenby's headquarters and was personally acquainted with his deception operations. In his *A History of the Palestine Campaigns*, published in the late 1920s, Wavell strongly emphasized the contribution of deception operations to Allenby's achievement of victory. Having so closely observed the successful use of deception in military operations, Wavell was prepared to make extensive use of it when he became Commander-in-Chief of the Middle East. He once commented: '. . . I have always believed in doing everything possible in war to mystify and mislead one's opponent. . . '.[35]

In the fall of 1940, Marshal Graziani advanced into Egypt with close to a quarter of a million men under his command, while the Duke of Aosta in Eritrea and Abysinnia had another 100,000. In contrast, Wavell could field no more than 50,000 British and Commonwealth soldiers. Under such conditions, deception was really Wavell's only hope. Wavell therefore directly encouraged the extensive resort to deception in the Middle East. The first large-scale deception operation led to a brilliant British victory at Sidi Barrani by General O'Connor in Operation Compass. Two British divisions ultimately defeated ten Italian divisions by achieving complete surprise at the opening phase of the attack. In 10 weeks, two divisions under General O'Connor advanced over some 500 miles of difficult terrain and destroyed 10 Italian divisions at a loss of 500 killed, 1,373 wounded and 55 missing. The spoils of victory were 130,000 prisoners, numerous tanks, guns and other equipment.[36]

Although the British official history indicates that deception played a key role in achieving surprise, it gives no detailed account of how this was done. When the official histories first began to appear in the mid-1950s, the topic of deception was still too sensitive to be discussed

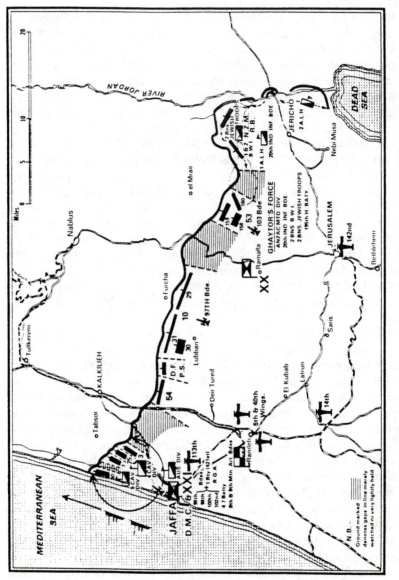

MAP 3   MEGIDDO, 1918. SITUATION AT 18 SEPTEMBER 1918

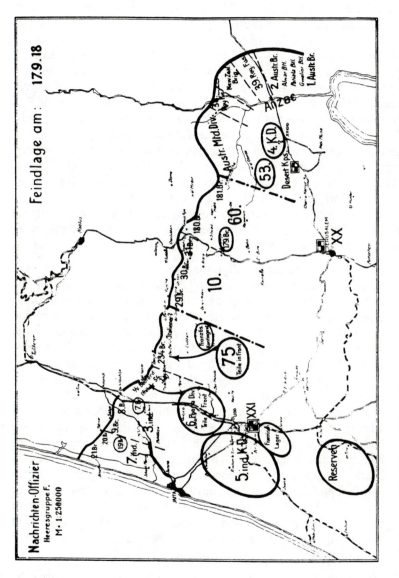

MAP 4   BRITISH DISPOSITIONS AS SHOWN BY ENEMY INTELLIGENCE SERVICE

in depth. Personal memoirs and partial accounts in other historical studies published in the 1970s only fragmentarily disclosed some of the stratagems and methods used in the Middle East in the second half of 1940. A comprehensive study of the evolution and history of deception in the Middle East and Mediterranean has yet to be written, though it is expected that much light will be shed on the subject after the release of the long-awaited official history of deception by Sir Michael Howard.

The circumstances under which Wavell established a special organization to develop deception plans in the summer of 1940 are still largely obscure. What is clear is that the cover plans before the Battle of Sidi Barrani called for the creation of a phantom army to threaten the flanks of Graziani's invasion force as well as for the extensive use of camouflage and other concealment techniques. In addition, Wavell's special deception outfit started to co-operate with SIME (Security Intelligence Middle East) in constructing a double-cross system to communicate deceptive information to the Germans and Italians.[37]

Despite their strenuous efforts to ascertain the truth through general intelligence gathering and air reconnaissance, the Italians were ultimately confounded by the British sleight of hand.

> Primed by alarming intelligence messages provided by the star network of his senior ally [i.e., German agents] Graziani sent his aircraft to photograph the area of the reported concentrations, where the British, in pursuit of their cover plan, had assembled about all the anti-aircraft guns they possessed. The Italian planes were greeted with a terrific volume of fire which in itself gave the impression of a lavishly equipped army and, moreover, kept the planes well up so that they could never take a close look nor photograph too accurately.
>
> The impact on . . . Graziani and his commanders was overwhelming. Here was confirmation of the alarming reports that he had reviewed. The British didn't just have reinforcements, they had an entirely new army encamped on his flank and ready to destroy him. In desperation he ordered his forces to create fortified positions along the Alexandria road in which they would prepare to defend themselves against the enemy on their flank. In these isolated positions they would be attacked and destroyed piecemeal. While the notional army was advancing, the factual contingent was concentrating for their attack.[38]

These are the oblique words in which the official history describes the deception cover for Compass:

> The fact is that in war, it is usually possible to produce some sort

of evidence in support of almost every course of action open to the enemy; the art lies in knowing what to make of it all. In this case the Italian Air Force had observed and reported movements and dispositions with fair accuracy – indeed, it was often intended by the British that they should. The important point was that these reports were consistent with what the 10th Army were convinced was happening. They themselves were very much occupied with their own preparations for renewing the advance, and were only too ready to interpret the air reports as indicating that the British were actively improving their defensive arrangements. The British attempt at strategic deception was therefore successful.[39]

The pattern of deception employed here was later refined and expanded in means, methods and scope for use in concealing preparations for the battles of Alam Halfa and even more so El Alamein. The outstanding results achieved in this deception operation led to the establishment of a special permanent organization under the Middle Eastern Command (Cairo) on 18 December 1940, while Operation Compass was still in progress. Referred to as 'A' Force, this special organization was to be headed by Brigadier Dudley Clarke, who had been hand-picked for the job by Wavell.

Following the campaign, Wavell probably personally briefed the military authorities in London on the methods and success of the deception plans in the Middle East. Dudley Clarke was sent by Wavell to report to the Chief of Staff in October of 1941.[40] 'A' Force soon became the inspiration for deception operations initiated in London on a much wider scale later in the war. Furthermore, it was Dudley Clarke's suggestion at that time which led to the appointment of a special controlling officer responsible for the co-ordination of all deception operations, a position that later developed into the London Controlling Section (LCS). In January 1944, Noel Wild, Dudley Clarke's deputy in 'A' Force, was sent to head Ops. (B) – the operational section in charge of all deception cover plans for the invasion of France (Fortitude).[41] Thus, the seed planted by Wavell in the Middle East bore decisive fruit in the victory over the Axis and the liberation of Europe.

The details of various other deception operations, their successes and their failures, are the subject of the essays assembled in this volume. At this point, it is useful to summarize some of the reasons for the success of strategic and operational deception in the Second World War, and how it differed from the type of deception practiced in earlier periods. These differences and unique characteristics can be grouped under two broad inter-related categories: (a) Means and Methods, and (b) Attitudes and the Environment.

The term 'means and methods' includes all mechanisms such as 'organizations' and 'special means' that were used to communicate the false information to the enemy. The further refinement of the radio in the First World War was a decisive factor in the renaissance of deception during the Second World War, for it provided the perfect means of listening in on an enemy's innermost plans, broadcasting 'valuable' information to an unsuspecting eavesdropper, and verifying the extent to which the proffered bait had been swallowed.

Environmental factors are primarily the general political and psychological attitudes which freed political and military leaders from any previous inhibitions they may have had concerning the large-scale resort to deception on all levels.

MEANS AND METHODS

1. *Organization.* Until the close of the First World War, deception was always left to the initiative and creativity of individual military commanders, who usually improvised *ad hoc* on the lower tactical and operational levels – that is, on the battlefield. Improvisation on the strategic level was rare indeed. Since deception was not a systematically continued activity, it required little or no co-ordination. All this changed during the Second World War, when deception became the focus of formally organized staff work. Dennis Wheatley noted that: 'organized deception was an entirely new development in World War II. From time immemorial ruses to mislead an enemy have been employed. But until the 1940s, force commanders had always given the job of making a cover plan to an individual'.[42] J.C. Masterman commented: 'Double-cross agents have been used since time immemorial but usually for short-time purposes and never, I believe, on the scale to which we developed the plan during the war'.[43] Special permanent organizations were required to manage this unprecedented deception effort which involved the complex co-ordination of activities among different commands and regions, as well as among different intelligence and military organizations; the control of double agents; and the use of ULTRA to monitor the impact of deception on the enemy.

On the regional level, or preceding each battle, a deception operation had to be co-ordinated among those who planned the operations and those who implemented them. Troop movements had to be carefully orchestrated and camouflaged while dummy forces had to be positioned. Co-ordination on the local level at each front had become a full-time occupation. Moreover, the complexity of strategic deception increased to such an extent that it required a high degree of co-ordination among different commands and regions.[44] In the words of the *Hesketh Report*: '. . . the control of a deceptive operation must be decided upon the self-evident principle that no people can safely tell the same lie to the same person except by closely concerted action'.[45]

For example, 'A' Force's creation of a notional threat to the Greek Islands and the Balkans in 1943–44 required the circumspect co-ordination of every move with other deception plans taking place simultaneously in Northwest Europe, the Western and Central Mediterranean, and India. For this complicated scheme, both real and notional Indian divisions stationed in Palestine, Syria and Iraq were used to build up the illusion of a threat directed towards Greece and the Balkans, though some of the troops were gradually transferred to fight against the Japanese. If the Allies had not exercised extreme care, collaboration between German and Japanese intelligence might have resulted in simultaneous identification of the same divisions (real or bogus) in two different areas and thus disclosure of the whole deception operation.[46] Acting in support of Operation Fortitude, 'A' Force later attempted to divert German troops and attention from the threat to the English Channel by creating large-scale notional threats in the Aegean and Balkans ('Zeppelin' and 'Royal Flush'). The implementation of this ruse again necessitated close co-ordination of details between the deceivers in London and the Middle East.[47] Fabrication of a threat to the Balkans as part of the cover plan for Normandy even led to unsuccessful attempts to co-ordinate deception with the Russians. The extensive co-ordination required by all this intricate strategic deception activity was considered so crucial that it was handled by the London Controlling Section (LCS) – a special organization created exclusively for that purpose. Flawed co-ordination risked exposure of the entire deception effort, and perhaps even jeopardized the whole intelligence system on which it was based (i.e., the double-cross systems and Ultra). As it turned out, efficient co-ordination combined with good fortune and the overall weakness of German strategic intelligence enabled the Allies to convince Germany that it faced substantial threats in Northwestern Europe and the Mediterranean. This, in part, prompted the German dispersal of troops to protect fortress Europe against non-existent forces. It appears that from 1943 to the end of the war, Germany consistently overestimated the size of Allied forces by about 100 per cent.

Although permanent because of security considerations, limited resources and the nature of the work, the specialized deception organizations were all quite small. (At its peak, 'A' Force, according to Cruickshank, included only 41 officers, 76 NCOs, and three units of company strength specially trained in the operation of visual deception devices.)[48] Given the organizational affiliation of Ops. (B) with SHAEF, it is more difficult to estimate the number of those participating in deception activities within England. If we consider those who played a more supportive role in the double-cross system and the XX Committee, the London Controlling Section (LCS), and B.1.A (the subsection of MI5 controlling the double agents) as well as the few who were *directly* involved in Ops. (B) activities – the number would be substantially larger than that of 'A' Force.

2. *Ultra.* In conjunction with the double-cross system which depended on it, Ultra was the single most important means of facilitating deception available to the Allies. Indeed, this revolutionary source of information provided the deceivers with *real time* access to the most closely-guarded plans, perceptions, wishes and fears of their enemy. It was the ideal tool for determining how to design a deception cover plan that would best reinforce existing German perceptions of the Allied threat. After implementing a particular ruse, the deceivers could rely on Ultra to monitor the degree to which it had been accepted by the Germans, then follow this up by fine-tuning continuing deception cover plans with the other means at their disposal. Ultra was therefore essential for the protection and growth of the double-cross system because it provided the corrective mechanism to cover up mistakes and carry on with this most reliable communications link to the enemy from one success to another.

Without doubt, Ultra gave the Allies an excellent picture of German strategy and the strategic decision-making process. The Allies were constantly a step ahead of the Germans not only because they were almost fully aware of German plans and strategy but also because they played a direct role in shaping them. Reading Masterman's *The Double-Cross System* and the *Hesketh Report* gives one the impression that the Allies were playing chess against themselves.

Yet the enormous strategic and operational advantages of Ultra and the double-cross system did not guarantee an easy victory at each stage. This is a tribute to the quality and tenacity of the German Army. It illustrates that no matter how good intelligence and deception may be, they can never replace combat and material strength. All they can do is reduce the cost and make the fighting somewhat easier.

3. *The Double-Cross System.* Developed in the Middle East by 'A' Force in co-ordination with SIME as well as in England by MI5's section B.1.A., the double-cross system eventually became the best means of communicating false information to the Germans,[49] although the original reason for turning around German agents was more to

prevent the Germans from learning what was going on (and so improve security) than to create channels for deception. Only gradually did the British realize that their control of German agents represented an excellent opportunity for deception. This could be achieved only when it was finally recognized that no *bona fide* independent German agents remained in England.[50]

The double-cross system was based on German agents who had been turned around after being intercepted by the British early in the war. The idea of using captured agents to pass deceptive information to the enemy is as old as spying itself, and was used quite extensively by Admiral Blinker Hall during the First World War.[51] While in the past the manipulation of captured agents took place on an individual *ad hoc* basis, through exploitation of opportunities that occasionally presented themselves, the use of double agents by the British during the Second World War was systematically organized on a large scale by a permanent organization that carefully co-ordinated its activities through the Twenty Committee (XX) in London and even earlier through 'A' Force in the Middle East. The success of the double-cross system was based not only on the existence of Ultra unit but also on the judicious management of the double agents. The guiding principle of the controllers was to supply their German counterparts with the greatest possible amount of accurate information in order to protect the deception plot with a bodyguard of truth.[52] Such information could be either correct but trivial ('chickenfeed' or 'foodstuff' in the controller's jargon) or correct and important but received too late to be of any use. For example, a few hours before the invasion of Normandy was to begin, Garbo sent his German controller an urgent warning. This seemingly important tip-off enhanced Garbo's credibility but was received too late to be of any practical use to the Germans.

Each double agent in turn mobilized quite a few sub and sub-sub operatives who funneled additional information through the original double agents who had been recruited directly by the Germans. In this way, British counter-intelligence was gradually able to develop and control a vast network of real and imaginary agents who virtually monopolized the German espionage effort. By 1943 the British could be reasonably sure (chiefly as a result of information supplied by ULTRA) that no important actual agents were independently providing the Germans with information either in the Middle East or in England. The double-cross agents' further expansion of their own notional network and the credibility they had established with their controllers in German intelligence apparently reduced the German incentive to create additional networks for corroborative purposes. Armed with the knowledge of German perceptions and fears provided

FIGURE 1
THE GARBO (ARABEL) NOTIONAL NETWORK*

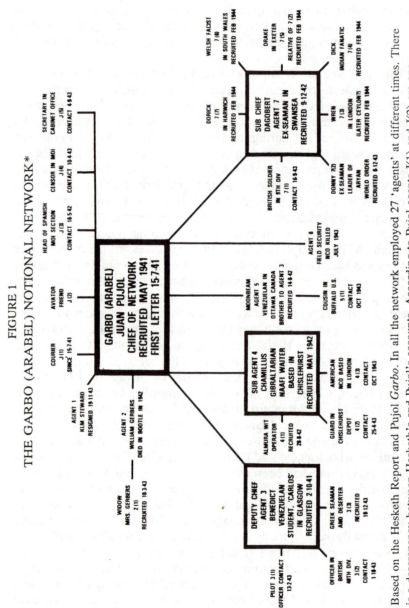

Based on the Hesketh Report and Pujol *Garbo*. In all the network employed 27 'agents' at different times. There is a descrepancy between Hesketh's and Pujol's accounts. According to Pujol agents J(1) and J(2) are one.

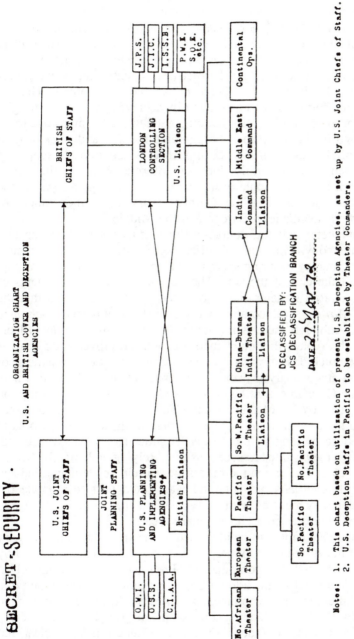

SECRET - SECURITY .

ORGANIZATION CHART
U.S. AND BRITISH COVER AND DECEPTION AGENCIES

Notes: 1. This chart based on utilization of present U.S. Deception Agencies, as set up by U.S. Joint Chiefs of Staff.
       2. U.S. Deception Staffs in Pacific to be established by Theater Commanders.

• Composed of one planner from each of the Army, Navy and Air Forces and a representative of Joint Security Control.
♦ No actual group under this name exists. Deception planning is accomplished by a sub-committee of the Joint Staff
  Planners; implementation by Joint Security Control.

DECLASSIFIED BY:
JCS DECLASSIFICATION BRANCH
DATE 27 Mar 72

by Ultra, these double agents continued to channel misleading information to the Germans until the end of the war. Some of them such as Garbo (Juan Pujol)[53] were even decorated by the Germans for their achievements. Descriptions of the double-cross system make it clear how complex this operation was and how much it depended on co-ordination between Bletchley Park (Ultra), counter-intelligence MI5-B.1.A, the deceivers in 'A' Force or Ops (B), and others. The co-ordination effort alone was a noteworthy achievement in its own right.

Most of the deceptive information passed to the Germans had to do with Allied intentions, primarily regarding the *time* and *place* of their planned offensives. This was accomplished by continuously supplying the Germans with carefully doctored information about the Allied order of battle in the Middle East and Europe. Through this system the Allies succeeded in doubling German estimates of the number of Allied troops available in Europe and the Middle East.

The uniqueness of the double-cross systems lay in their capacity to prepare convincing cover stories before, during and after each operation, thereby ensuring success on a continuous and uninterrupted basis until the end of the war. The outstanding accomplishments of the double-cross systems have prompted some to speculate that the German *Abwehr* collaborated with British intelligence (*Schwarze Kapelle*). Although there is no doubt that individual *Abwehr* officers *did* help the Allies, this devil theory cannot be proven. The truth is probably much less dramatic. The overall analytical weakness of German strategic analysis is one likely explanation, while another may be that the German controllers could not bring themselves to question seriously the loyalty of their agents. The controllers were too committed to the protection of their investment in the spying networks to admit failure as long as the British continued to supply them with information they wanted to accept as true. Relying on Ultra, the British operators carefully crafted their messages to suit the German mind-set. Finally, the Germans did not (and later could not) corroborate the information they received with the type of material evidence that could have been obtained from air reconnaissance.

If a single element is to be identified as the key to the extraordinary record of the Allied deception operations, it is the means provided by the double-cross/Ultra combination. From convincing Rommel to attack at Alam Halfa (much to his detriment), through the creation of a notional threat to the Peloponnese and Aegean in preparation for the invasion of Sicily, to achieving surprise at Normandy, the double-cross systems were decisive. Indeed, the Hesketh Report makes it clear that the work of double agents not only laid the groundwork for the Allied invasion of Normandy, but also prevented the Germans from mounting a major counterattack against the invading forces; a message from Garbo received precisely when the Germans were considering reinforcement of their troops at Normandy convinced them that Normandy was a mere diversion and that the real attack had yet to occur at the Pas de Calais. (See Figure 3, a facsimile of this document.) The double agents' influence on the direction of the war was usually much less dramatic; it consisted of an extended effort to supply the Germans with bits and pieces of misleading information. Each deceptive bit of information alone was almost trivial – yet when pieced together with the other tidbits it formed a beguilingly coherent though incorrect estimate of Allied capabilities and intentions. This painstaking process of course required time.

4. *Time.* Time is an essential ingredient in the preparation of complex deception cover plans. As mentioned earlier, such schemes depend upon the completion of a wide variety of time-consuming activities including co-ordination on many levels; the transmission of bogus wireless messages; the establishment of the necessary units; and the positioning of dummy aircraft, tanks, landing craft and depots. Rarely (such as in Garbo's message on 9 June 1944 to the *Abwehr* mentioned above) can a deceptive message be allowed to appear dramatic. The essence of deception is that it lets the enemy convince himself that the misleading picture presented is valid. Deception operations attempting to convey false information to the enemy over a short period of time without adequate material support were doomed to fail – not necessarily because the deception plan was exposed by the adversary but because there was not enough time at hand to make him convince himself. (See Campbell's discussion of Operation Cockade/Starkey.)

As Hesketh notes in his conclusions:

> Although there may be occasions when its [i.e., deception] services can be usefully enlisted to give immediate aid, it is generally more correct to regard it as a method which achieves its results by a slow and gradual process rather than by lightning strikes. Like the fly-wheel of an engine, it requires time to gain momentum and time again to lose it.[54]

During the shorter wars of the future, deceivers may not have the time to implement intricate deception operations; instead, cover plans will have to be prepared *before the outbreak of the war in order to be used in its initial stages and may be much more difficult to apply at later stages.*

5. *Allied air superiority.* When the Allies achieved virtual air superiority in both the Mediterranean and North-west Europe, their

FIGURE 3
FACSIMILE REPRODUCTION OF GARBO'S MESSAGE OF
9 JUNE 1944, AS RECEIVED BY THE OKW

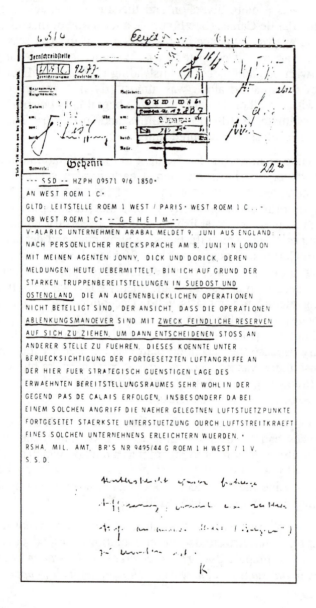

TRANSLATION

Garbo's message of 9th June, 1944, as received by teleprinter at O.K.W. and seen by Krummacher, Jodl and Hitler

Message received at 2230 hours on 9th June, 1944, sent by Garbo.

"V-man Alaric network Arabal reports on 9th June from England:—

After personal consultation on 8th June in London with my agents Jonny,* Dick and Dorick, whose reports were sent to-day, I am of the opinion, in view of the strong troop concentrations in South-East and Eastern England which are not taking part in the present operations, that these operations are a diversionary manoeuvre designed to draw off enemy reserves in order then to make a decisive attack in another place. In view of the continued air attacks on the concentration area mentioned, which is a strategically favourable position for this, it may very probably take place in the Pas de Calais area, particularly since in such an attack the proximity of the air bases will facilitate the operation by providing continued strong air support."

Krummacher underlined in red the words "diversionary manoeuvre designed to draw off enemy reserves in order then to make a decisive attack at another place," and added at the end—

"confirms the view already held by us that a further attack is to be expected in another place (Belgium?)."

This message was seen by Jodl, who underlined the words "in South-East and Eastern England." His initial in green may be seen at the top of the message. The green hieroglyph in the upper left-hand square indicates that Jodl considered it of sufficient importance to show to the Fuehrer, while the letters "erl" (erledigt) which appear in pencil immediately to the right indicate that it was seen by Hitler.

* Misprint for Donny.

Source: Reproduced from Roger Hesketh's unpublished 'Fortitude: A History of Deception in North Western Europe, April 1943 to May 1945'.

deception operations enjoyed a concomitant increase in effectiveness. From 1943 onwards, the Germans shifted most of their activity in the air to the Russian Front and to the defense of the Reich; air reconnaissance over the Mediterranean dropped to a level of sporadic rather than extensive and systematic activity. This neglect of air reconnaissance thus reflects the lack of co-operation between the Luftwaffe and the *Abwehr*, inter-service rivalries, a faulty order of priorities, and the reluctance to allocate equipment for air reconnaissance. Perhaps the Germans considered air reconnaissance to be of much greater use when on the offensive and less so on the defensive or perhaps the elaborate spy system in England and the Mediterranean was perceived as sufficient. Certainly, the Allied air superiority made it much more difficult to penetrate their air space (unless it was a case in which the Allies *wanted* the Germans to photograph certain areas).

This, of course, was a major stumbling block for German strategic and operational intelligence. If the Germans had chosen to allocate adequate resources to the matter, Allied deception might have faced some serious challenges. Air reconnaissance, or in today's world satellite reconnaissance, is one of the principal means of countering strategic and operational deception, while denial of air reconnaissance to the enemy (illustrated in Allenby's Palestine campaigns) is essential to the success of deception.

6. *The overall performance of German intelligence.* The consensus among experts is that the generally poor quality of German strategic intelligence contributed significantly to the success of Allied deception operations. As the Achilles' heel of the German war effort, this fatally flawed system reflected a variety of deep-rooted problems which deserve brief mention in this context. At the most fundamental level were German racism and a hubristic assumption that the German army would emerge triumphant regardless of the quality of German intelligence. True to his embodiment of this outlook, Hitler ignored intelligence estimates that he did not like and surrounded himself with an entourage of senior officers who furnished nothing but reassuring news; this, in turn, must have demoralized the German intelligence community.[55] Furthermore, career and recruiting patterns did little to encourage the most successful and ambitious officers to join the intelligence services, while the German educational system's emphasis specialization compared unfavorably with the more eclectic approach of the British. Nor was all well with inter-agency relationships. The high command lacked confidence in the *Abwehr*, while ruthless competition between the *Abwehr* and SS intelligence made co-ordination very difficult and wasted dwindling resources.[56] Finally, Germany's initial concentration on the offensive may have conditioned it to rely more on holding the initiative than on intelligence. In the end, as Hesketh remarked in a hand-written addendum to his report, the German High Command acted solely on the basis of evidence supplied by the controlled agents.

A more critical examination of the information and less wishful thinking might have changed the course of the war. Ironically, the very elements that brought about the initial success of Germany's political-military system – the Führer's leadership and the blind devotion of the German military – also precluded the establishment of an effective intelligence organization. The ideal function of intelligence is to ferret out the truth, yet the truth more often than not cannot be accepted by a totalitarian regime. Consequently, the short-run success of German might on one level contained the seeds of defeat on another.

ATTITUDES AND THE ENVIRONMENT

1. *Weakness and vulnerability.* History clearly demonstrates that an inverse correlation exists between strength and the resort to deception.

When states assume that they will win easily regardless of what the enemy does, they feel little need to resort to stratagem and deception; instead, they opt for the most direct way to attack and defeat the enemy. Such attacks often end in disaster. (The Soviet Union's attack on Finland in the winter war, Germany's attack on Russia, and the Arab attack on Israel in 1948 – which was announced in advance on the radio – are all cases in point.) On the other hand, the side which *a priori* recognizes its own numerical and material inferiority is therefore anxious to avail itself of all possible courses of action. Thus, even before the Second World War, the British were fully aware of their overall numerical and material weakness *vis-à-vis* Germany. Their early defeat in 1940 and the threat of invasion left the British no choice – they had to resort to deception. This argument may also explain why the British so rarely resorted to deception in the First World War. Then, the British Empire was at its zenith, the Royal Navy ruled the oceans, and the threat of air power to the British Isles was still small.

A similar observation can be made concerning the Israelis. While they perceived themselves as vulnerable and weak in 1948, 1956, 1967, they frequently and successfully resorted to the use of deception. By 1973 and 1982, they neglected stratagem in the hope of prevailing on the battlefield through superior firepower and technology. Only in those areas in which they felt weak or faced a threat such as the Syrian anti-aircraft missile and gun systems (1982) were they ready to resort to deception (though it was almost exclusively technological deception). Conversely, having been defeated three times by the Israelis, the Arabs in 1973 had a much stronger incentive to employ deception and indeed did so with success in the opening phase of the Yom Kippur War.

2. *The ideological environment.* When one is faced with an enemy who is completely ruthless and fanatically motivated by extreme ideology, religious fervor or racist doctrine, war acquires a zero-sum-game character. There is no room for compromise. In such conditions, both sides, particularly the more threatened one, will not recognize any constraints when the very survival of a state, religion or race is at stake. In a way, this is closely related to the preceding section, for war against a fanatical opponent creates a sense of vulnerability.

Hitler's Nazi Germany certainly posed such a threat to British survival. By 1939–40, German fanaticism and Hitler's complete lack of moderation had removed the scales from the eyes of the world. The British, however, did not threaten Germany in kind, so Germany did not contemplate the possibility of total defeat until late in the war. The British needed the best possible intelligence right from the start; the

Germans did not. By the time the tide had turned and Germany's existence was threatened, it was too late to build a high quality intelligence system or make extensive use of deception.

A homogeneous international system, a moderate environment and limited goals would not create the conditions for the wide scale resort to deception, while a revolutionary heterogeneous system, limitless goals and fanaticism would.

3. *Attitudes of leaders.* A sense of weakness and a threat to his survival would convince almost any leader to adopt those measures necessary to guarantee the survival of the state. Nevertheless, not all leaders are equally ready to engage in the widespread use of deception.

The British were fortunate to have such a leader as Churchill, who had always been interested in intelligence work and was fascinated by cloak-and-dagger stories. He was not only interested in deception – he was one of its sources of inspiration. His positive experience and familiarity with intelligence operations in the Admiralty during the First World War came in handy in the 1939–45 war, for the active interest and at times direct participation of leaders in deception operations was of critical importance. When England's fate hung in the balance, Churchill was ready and eager to open other gentlemen's mail.[57]

By virtue of a happy coincidence for the British, Wavell was Commander-in-Chief in the Middle East at a most critical time. Wavell's experience under Allenby during the First World War had left him with a deep appreciation of the decisive role deception could play in support of military operations. His readiness to resort to deception was unusual, if not unique, among military commanders. The early success achieved against the Italians in North Africa and Abyssinia (which may not have been achieved *even with* deception against a similar-sized German force) convinced Wavell that deception could work and ought to be regarded as an important force multiplier. Nothing, of course, as the saying goes, 'succeeds like success'. Had Wavell's early experiment with deception failed, it may have been viewed later on as an idle waste of time never to be repeated. The unique combination of an open-minded commander, a desperate situation, a weak enemy, and early success gave deception in the Middle East a good reputation, which helped in selling it to other commanders and to those in London.

In contrast, Hitler engaged in non-stop lying and deception only during the period following his rise to power, when Germany was still weak.[58] But after the Wehrmacht's spectacular early victories, deception became redundant. There was no time for reflection or carefully prepared deception operations – the blitzkrieg-style attack was the surest and quickest guarantee of victory. Unlike Churchill, Hitler had no need for intelligence – his intuition and will-power were enough. Those who take action for the sake of action do not need accurate intelligence reports, for sooner or later it will tell them that continued action will lead to inevitable defeat. At that point, intelligence becomes an obstacle to their policies and egos.

The combination of a leader interested in deception and intelligence and restrained from hyperactivity by his military staff, and a leader who often ignored intelligence and was restrained by no one, proved ideal for the Allies in the long run. While the British could direct all of their deception at a single man whose strategy they were well acquainted with, the Germans had to deal with intelligence organizations and military staffs, not ultimately with Churchill alone.

The following table puts deception in a historical perspective by comparing deception operations as they evolved in the Second World War with those of earlier periods.

DECEPTION PAST AND PRESENT

PAST	PRESENT
SIMPLE	COMPLEX
Initiated by individual leaders	Initiated by specialized organizations
Improvised, ad hoc, does not require long preparations	Requires extensive preparations, extensive coordination, material support, long lead time
Short ranged, 'one time shot'	Long range, continuous 'on going', not terminated by one operation
Primarily tactical operational less so strategic	On all levels
Did not depend on feedback from target; independent action	Requires continuous feedback and monitoring of enemy

THE FUTURE OF DECEPTION

'It is always unsafe to apply too literally the experiences of one war to the changed circumstances of another.'[59]

This is the opening sentence of the conclusions to the Hesketh Report. Stratagem will always remain part of the essence of war. The

basic principles and objectives of reinforcing the desires and perceptions of the deceived will not change, since human nature and the
psychological mechanism of human perception are ever the same. In
terms of its forms and the means employed, deception will, like war
itself, change as new weapons and technologies appear.

It is unlikely that strategic deception in future wars will resemble that
of the Second World War. The technological environment has radically
changed, and the unique conditions that facilitated the success of
strategic deception in that war are not likely to recur.

This can be explained in a number of ways. In the first place, the
lessons learned from the Second World War, the existence of Ultra,
and the double-cross systems, the influence of which on the course of
the war is widely recognized, might make it difficult to play the same
trick twice. (This very thought might encourage deception along
similar lines because deceivers like to manipulate the expectation that
something cannot happen again.) As I have stated elsewhere, the fact
that something is unlikely to happen greatly increases the probability
that it *will* happen.[60] Finally, the publication of the histories of intelligence and deception in the Second World War reveals a cautionary
tale.

Ultra was the most critical element in the success of the Allied
deception operations. It is not clear whether the deciphering of codes
leading to a similar large-scale penetration of the enemy's innermost
secrets on such a continuous basis will be possible again. Awareness of
the possibility ought to make all military organizations much more
careful. Moreover, the deciphering effort and development of a proper
distribution system require a great deal of time to perfect. Such time
may not be available in the future, although attempts to protect and
break codes will continue.

That this is still a real possibility was recently made clear by the
Walker spy trial, in which the defendant was convicted of supplying the
Soviets with the key to the US naval codes during the war in Vietnam
over a period of many years. It is quite possible that the information
gained from US message traffic was used by both the Soviets and the
North Vietnamese to deceive the US.

The double-cross systems managed by the British in the Middle East
and in London appear to have been unique. It would be extremely
difficult to replicate such an arrangement. The double-cross systems
themselves depended on Ultra which, as I have argued, may not always
be available. Yet again, the Soviet Union has more than once demonstrated its skill in penetrating the intelligence networks of the West
(including the one created by those who developed the double-cross
system).

Finally, the circumstances which allowed the Allies to gain control in the air and prevented the Germans from effective air reconnaissance may not recur. In the age of satellites, U-2s, SR-71s, infra-red sensors, radars, improved radio location equipment and a variety of other sensors, camouflage, concealment of troop concentrations, or the building of dummy weapon concentration will prove to be more difficult, though not impossible.

Deception, however, will continue to be as important as ever in all forms of warfare. It will require more attention, greater sophistication, and may become increasingly technological. Larger organizations will be required both to detect and implement it. In the end, even if in a different form, deception will always remain an integral part of all military activity.

CAN DECEPTION BE AVOIDED?

The evidence seems to indicate that even those who are well acquainted with the art of deception can be deceived as easily as anyone else. In theory, the deceiver's own use of stratagem should give him a heightened awareness of its existence and possible use aginst him. Yet, this very familiarity with deception can be used by an opponent to deceive the deceiver. This paradox has been described in the following way by Richard Heuer:

> Alertness to the possibility of deception can influence the degree of one's openness to new information, but not necessarily in a desirable direction. The impetus for changing one's estimate of the situation can only come from the recognition of an incompatibility between a present estimate and some new evidence. If people can explain new evidence to their own satisfaction with little change in their existing beliefs, they will rarely feel the need for drastic revision of these beliefs. Deception provides a readily 'available' explanation for discrepant evidence: if the evidence does not fit one's preconceptions, it may be dismissed as deception. Further, the more alert or suspicious one is of deception, the more readily available is this explanation. Alertness to deception also leads the analyst to be more skeptical of all the evidence, and to the extent that evidence is deemed unreliable, the analyst's preconceptions must play a greater role in determining which evidence to believe. This leads to a paradox: The more alert we are to deception, the more likely we are to be deceived.[61]

While deception often fails to attain its objectives, it rarely fails because the adversary has identified it as deception.

What counter-measures can be taken in order to reduce the possibility of being deceived? Some can be suggested, although their effectiveness cannot be guaranteed.

1. Avoid over-reliance on one source of information. 'Reliance on one source is dangerous, the more reliable and comprehensive the source, the greater the dangers.'[62] This statement by Donald McLachlan is based on the lessons learned from Germany's almost exclusive reliance on spy networks in England and the Middle East that were actually controlled by the Allies. (Perhaps it was also a warning not to depend on Ultra or similar systems in the future as the panacea for intelligence problems.) The Biblical words of wisdom, 'In multiple advisers you shall find safety' are as valid as ever.

The corroboration of any potentially valuable information by other independently verifiable sources such as air reconnaissance, radio and radars, and different sensors is imperative. In retrospect, Germany's readiness to rely so heavily on one (or few) sources is astounding.

2. A corollary of the last remark is that intelligence organizations should never rely exclusively on non-material evidence. As Clausewitz remarked, 'Words, being cheap, are the most common means of creating false impressions'. All information from sources such as agents' messages or radio traffic must be checked against material reality and positively verified.

3. Never rely on agents who have not been seen or directly interviewed. This simple advice is the only safe way to avoid reliance on notional spy networks that have been recruited indirectly.[63] Furthermore, even agents who were recruited directly in the past must be interviewed periodically in order that their continued reliability not be taken for granted. Controllers must be warned not to fall into the trap of identifying too closely with their agents: this might cause them to overprotect questionable agents whose activities should be examined with a critical eye. This rule should be even more strictly observed if the information obtained from possibly notional agents dovetails nicely with one's own preferences or needs, or when it fits without contradictions into the reports of other possibly notional agents.

4. Check and double-check all instances in which agents' reports that initially appeared correct turned out to be wrong on an important issue and yet always seemed to offer a good explanation for the discrepancy. Even more so, a special investigation should be made of any agents who supply first-rate information of the greatest importance *only when it is too late to be of any use* – even if it arrives before the action it warns against has taken place. As Hesketh, Masterman and Mure noted, this

was the most common device used by the British to build up the credibility of their agents in the eyes of the German controllers.

5. Controllers of agents should also be encouraged to heed more closely the opinions of lower-level intelligence analysts. To put it in a somewhat different way, deception (or a potential surprise) has a better chance of being detected by lower-level intelligence analysts, who are less wedded to any specific strategy or operations; wishful thinking is not as likely to sway their judgement. Less biased by political interests, the analysts' viewpoint is based more on narrower technological and professional considerations. As Dudley Clarke pointed out in a memorandum written for US military intelligence after the war, many deception operations are designed to appeal to the top intelligence and political leaders (see Appendix 1). It would therefore be easier to identify deception at lower levels, where the experts have different and narrower concerns and are therefore less likely to fall for specific deception baits.

Indeed, a lower-echelon German intelligence analyst who questioned the trustworthiness of an independent agent, Josephine, was simply ignored.[64] Had senior German intelligence analysts paid more attention to his analysis, it is quite possible that the entire doublecross system might have come under critical scrutiny in Germany.

As mentioned earlier, lower-echelon Turkish intelligence did manage to uncover some of the British deceptive measures before the Third Battle of Gaza. In much the same way, a junior Israeli intelligence analyst who warned of an impending Egyptian attack in a September 1973 memorandum was not taken seriously.

Following every realization that one has been surprised or deceived, the *post mortem* inquiry always reveals that there were those whose efforts to sound a warning were ignored. What makes sense in retrospect cannot necessarily be established as true before the event. Yet time after time, it appears that the 'negative' or unpleasant conclusions reached by those in the lower echelons have been given short shrift. It is therefore important to find a more formalized way of dealing with dissenting observations on lower levels and to encourage rather than ignore them whenever possible.

6. It is as necessary to know the enemy's limitations as his capabilities. With the 'aid' of deceptive information, German intelligence consistently overestimated the number of divisions available to the Allies, as well as their capacity to move troops, their number of landing craft, and the like. The Germans' most common perceptual mistake was to project not only their own preferences and fears on the enemy, but also their own military doctrine. As a result, they failed to understand that

air cover was in fact a necessary condition for each of the Allied landing operations. For the Allies, landing in Sardinia, the Bay of Biscay or the Peloponnese was out of the question because air cover could not be secured. Looking only through the lens of their own military doctrine, the Germans saw Sardinia – not Sicily – as the key to Italy; for them, the Balkans were the key source of raw materials, and the Pas de Calais was the most obvious direction of attack. Yet in each case, the Allies had totally different considerations: for them Sicily was the key to Allied communication in the Mediterranean while Sardinia was out of their fighter cover range; moreover, the Balkans were not viewed as an important source of raw materials. In fact, the Balkans were considered a dead end, a strategist's nightmare.

Most fundamentally, the Germans failed to understand the political dimensions of higher strategy because their attitudes and intelligence estimates incorporated too much of their own narrow military views. The principal motivation behind the Allied strategy was more often political than military. What makes sense politically often does not make sense militarily and *vice versa.*

Each year, the Allied political leaders were under pressure to show that they were making progress through decisive action. This political, not exclusively military, logic dictated the direction of operations and the implementation of deception cover plans. From a purely logical military point of view, the Germans were often right; in reality they were often wrong. The enemy's intentions must be estimated in accordance with *his* political and military needs – not one's own. This requires intimate knowledge of the enemy and a true interest in his problems. Since Germans saw their enemies as military objects, not as equals worthy of study and understanding, their capacity to expose Allied deception plans was severely undermined. High quality intelligence can be developed only when there is curiosity about and respect for the enemy, not an ethnocentric view of the enemy as a military object.

DECEPTION AND MILITARY OPERATIONS; OR DECEPTION AS A
FORCE MULTIPLIER

Sun Tzu's ideal victory, that is, victory achieved without the need to resort to force, is not a very common phenomenon in war. Clausewitz' view of the essence of war as a duel in which, through the physical use of force, the enemy is compelled to do one's will is more realistic. Yet the fact that war is as much an intellectual activity on its higher levels, as it is a material activity, cannot be denied (as Clausewitz would surely agree). While manpower, the number and quality of weapons, ammunition and other supplies are essential to wage wars – qualitative or non-material elements such as the quality of planning, organization, suitable military doctrines, morale, and intelligence are no less important.[65] Otherwise, the victory of larger armies over smaller ones would be a foregone conclusion. In war, however, there is no direct correlation between the size of armies and victory. As often as not, wars have been won by the numerically inferior side. The fact that bigger armies often fail to win may imply that the qualitative, non-quantifiable elements in war are usually more decisive.

Superiority in the qualitative dimension allows for a more efficient, more economic use of the material resources available. The non-material dimensions of war can thus be seen as force multipliers. (A material force multiplier, for example, would be the technological superiority of weapons.) One of the most important force multipliers available to the military commander is deception, which as stated earlier is primarily a means of achieving surprise on the battlefield.

Deception can provide the strategist and commander with effective answers to problems that are otherwise difficult to solve, or that could otherwise be solved only through material superiority. This indeed is the prime reason that real or perceived material superiority weakens the incentive to resort to deception. If a commander must launch an attack in an area where concealment of preparations would be difficult, passive deception (such as camouflage, and the use of decoys and dummies as was the case before the Third Battle of Gaza, Sidi Barrani or El Alamein) might be the best solution. The artful use of stratagem can also permit a numerically inferior army to concentrate superior forces at the decisive point through the device of notional threats. The enemy's perception of such threats as only too real will induce him to disperse his own troops, thus breaking the principle of the concentration of force and giving the weaker side an opportunity to achieve superiority at his point of choice. Furthermore, benefits flowing from the fabrication of illusory threats need not be limited to the weaker party. Even for the numerically superior side, the use of such a ruse facilitates the achievement of decisive results at a lower cost by reducing the opponent's resistance at the key point. (Good examples are the Third Battle of Gaza, El Alamein, the invasion of Sicily, Anzio, the Allied spring offensive in Italy (1944) and Diadem/Nunton or Normandy.)

Deception in such instances offers a solution primarily to armies on the offensive. In addition to facilitating the achievement of surprise in terms of place and strength, deception can also help the attacker to surprise his adversary in terms of timing: to launch an attack earlier than expected. This is borne out by the many cases in which the enemy commander was away when his forces were attacked. This was true of Rommel at El Alamein and Normandy, as well as General Vietinghoff, commander of the 10th German Army in Italy, who chose 11 May (D-Day for Operation Diadem/Nunton) to go on leave, while his own chain of command was in the midst of a complicated reorganization effort.[66]

Deception also provides operational opportunities for those on the defensive. It is always a rare but major achievement to lure the enemy into attacking at a point where one has a superior defensive position and is ready to meet the attacker. This is the best way to weaken the enemy at the lowest possible cost. In a classical example of this technique, the British succeeded in inducing Rommel to pursue his attack into Egypt long after he had passed the culminating point of victory and was running out of supplies, while the British, fully informed by Ultra, were dug in and waiting for his attack. Rommel's attack on Alam Halfa, which was the real turning point of the war in the Western Desert, might not have taken place without the aid of a carefully devised ruse.

Technological warfare is another area in which defensive operational deception has great application. In a brilliant, very successful scheme to divert the Luftwaffe bombers from their targets during their offensive against England, the British bent German navigational beams and induced them to bomb false targets. Another example was the use of the double-cross system to direct the German V1 and V-2 bombing attacks away from London.[67] This type of technological deception promises to become more important in the future.

While operational deception on a strategic or higher level requires time and elaborate preparations, feints and diversion on a lower level provide the commander with a simple though effective means of deception that can be improvised on relatively short notice. Clausewitz was mistaken in his assertion that feints and diversions were dangerous because they reduced the number of troops available for the decisive blow. A well-thought-out diversion will allow the deceiver to *increase* rather than decrease the number of troops at the decisive point. Again, the more that one learns about the enemy's expectations and fears from one's own intelligence, the more effectively real and notional diversionary threats can be designed.

Deception in war should be considered a *rational* and necessary activity because it acts as a force multiplier, that is, it magnifies the strength or power of the successful deceiver. Forgoing the use of deception in war is tantamount to deliberately undermining one's own strength. Therefore, when all other elements of strength in war are approximately equal, deception will amplify the available strength of a state – or allow it to use its force more economically by achieving victory at a lower cost and with fewer casualties. If opponents are unequally matched, deception (and surprise) can enable the weaker side to compensate for its numerical and other inadequacies. For this reason, the side that is at a disadvantage usually has the more powerful incentive to resort to deceptive strategy and tactics.

Although the tendency of powerful states to rely on 'brute force' can be understood, it certainly cannot be justified: the strong and powerful need not waste their strength or pay a higher cost simply because they are confident of victory. Strength unaccompanied by stratagem will become sterile and lead to eventual defeat. For that very reason, the more powerful military establishments must make a conscious effort to incorporate deception into their military thinking.

Unfortunately, while officers must be continuously reminded of deception's potential contribution to military operations, there is no systematic way in which deception can be taught. On its higher levels, deception by its very nature cannot be reduced to a simple set of principles set forth in an instruction manual. By definition, a manual deals with routine and standardized operations while deception can succeed only through deviation from the routine. Accordingly, the teaching of deception by manual would inevitably become so routinized and predictable that it would be self-defeating.

The art of deception can only be cultivated and learned through history, the experience of one's contemporaries, the encouragement of creativity and imagination in the military, constant emphasis on the need to reduce the cost and casualties of war, and an understanding of the enemy's own fears. Though deception is one of the more creative tools available to the commander in developing his grasp of the operational art of war, it is bound to remain an art. The recognition, in Clausewitz's words, that '. . . talent and genius operate outside the rules . . .'[68] is essential for developing the use and understanding of this tool.

THE CONTROL OF DECEPTION OPERATIONS

It is often asked whether deception operations should be controlled by the intelligence branch or operations branch. Operations provide the reason and rationale for deception while the intelligence experts supply the means. Should deception organizations have direct control over troops (as with 'A' Force), or should they operate through forces made available to them by regular army formations? There is no one answer to such questions, for there are certainly more than one or two legitimate, effective ways to organize and place units whose special task is to *develop, implement,* and *follow up* deception operations. (Despite their great differences, both 'A' Force and Ops. (B) were eminently successful.) Therefore, instead of searching in vain for a single perfect solution applicable to all situations, I will explore some of the conditions necessary for the formation of an effective deception organization.

'Broadly speaking, deception has three phases. First, the preparation of the deception plan; secondly, the execution of the plan in terms of movements of men, ships, etc.; and thirdly, measures to ensure that the movements become known for the enemy. . . .'[69] To these, a fourth stage can be added: following up the enemy's reaction to the deception and determining to what extent it has been accepted as reflecting reality. Success during each stage necessitates the closest co-operation and co-ordination among all concerned; those in the operations branch on the one hand and intelligence on the other must understand each other's needs, priorities, capabilities and limitations, and professional frame of mind. This is no easy task in view of the fact that operations and intelligence in many ways represent two very different cultures – two different mind-sets.

Deception is never an end in itself. It exists solely to support military operations by facilitating the achievement of surprise. In this sense, Brigadier Dudley Clarke was right in stating that, 'Deception is essentially a matter of the "Operations" Branch of the staff, and *not* the "Intelligence".'[70] This does not mean, however, that those directly in charge of leading deception organizations cannot or should not be primarily intelligence experts. There are a number of reasons for this.

Officers who are experts in operations are rarely as well-grounded in intelligence (and *vice versa*). Their training and experience are predominantly geared to battle and the planning of operations; indeed, most officers show relatively less interest in intelligence work and are not closely familiar with its potential and limitations. The consensus among those who have practiced and studied deception is that convincing most military commanders of its value on all levels has traditionally been a slow, uphill process. Had it not been for the early successes of 'A' Force under Wavell, it might have been impossible to convince the average commander of the importance of deception; those responsible for planning and executing military operations tend to view it as a last resort. G-3 officers are otherwise preoccupied with the minutiae of planning an operation, training the troops, and obtaining the necessary material support (ranging from soldiers and weapons to ammunition and food). The use of troops for purely deceptive operations strikes them as a waste of scarce resources. 'The reliance in deception operations on real troop movements . . . must inevitably interfere with normal training and movement.'[71] Other objections are raised by the fact that deception always entails the disclosure of some relatively important correct information. Those unfamiliar with deception often believe that the danger of selectively supplying accurate information to the enemy outweighs the potential benefits of misleading him, since exposure may result in betrayal of one's own real intentions and plans. Finally, the effectiveness of a particular stratagem is not always easy to assess or prove.

Being less familiar with the enemy, commanders with little intelligence-related experience may fall victim to the belief that what they know about their own problems and limitations is also known to the enemy. In *Beyond Top Secret Ultra*, Ewen Montagu explains why the Chiefs of Staff rejected the suggestion that the Allies create a notional threat to the Bay of Biscay. Even as Ultra, according to Montagu, indicated that the Germans feared such a development, the Chiefs knew that mounting this type of invasion was impossible since the Bay of Biscay was not within range of the Allied fighter cover. While the deceivers were interested in reinforcing German perceptions and fears, the Chiefs of Staff acted on the basis of reality *as it was known to them*. But what was known to them was not known to the enemy.[72] Therefore, it is the responsibility of intelligence officers to provide those in charge of operations with insights on enemy perceptions.

Once deception has proved itself, most commanders will quickly come to accept it as an indispensable part of all operational planning: the most common danger at this point is that the opposite problem of over-reliance may occur. 'There is a tendency on the part of those who are constantly at grips with compelling realities to regard deception as a swift panacea to be invoked when other remedies have failed.'[73]

Intelligence specialists are subject to a somewhat different set of problems. Having little experience in the planning of military operations, they may not know what is reasonable and what cannot convince the enemy. If unfamiliar with the details of the plans for which they must provide support, they may fail to perfectly synchronize the use of stratagem with the real plans. Such lack of familiarity with operational details may also inadvertently result in a deception plan that too closely resembles the actual one.[74] As Hesketh remarked,

> It may be mentioned in passing that the information most often required [by the deceivers] was about our own side and not about the enemy, a kind of inverted intelligence, for we were after all, posing as part of the enemy's Intelligence Service. That meant that our links with the Intelligence Division were slender as compared with those built up with Staff Duties, Training, Move-

ment and Transportation and other branches of the operational and administrative staffs.[75]

A thorough understanding of the operational commander's plans and problems is absolutely essential for the would-be deceiver, whose ultimate objective should be to make the enemy react in a specific way. Otherwise, a deception plan could easily backfire when the enemy, though persuaded by the false information, nevertheless takes action detrimental to the deceiver. Having learned this lesson the hard way, Brigadier Dudley Clarke recalled that 'it became a creed in 'A' Force to ask a General "What do you want the enemy to *do*?" and never "What do you want him to *think*?"'[76]

Major General de Guingand, General Montgomery's Chief of Staff, asked the right question when he gave the deception cover plan for Normandy its final twist in proposing that the Pas de Calais be presented as the real objective of the Allies. On 25 January 1944, General de Guingand raised the post-assault phase to a level of importance which it had not hitherto enjoyed. He said:

> I do not agree with the object which has been given for the attack on the Pas de Calais. If we induce the enemy to believe the story, he will not react in the way we want. I feel we must, from D-Day onwards, endeavour to persuade him that our *main* attack is going to develop later in the Pas de Calais area, and it is hoped that NEPTUNE will draw away reserves from that area.[77]

After this change was accepted, the final draft of Fortitude expanded the post-assault story to present Normandy as a mere diversion to the Pas de Calais. As a result, the Germans were persuaded that 'the operation in the NEPTUNE area is designed to draw German reserves away from the Pas de Calais and Belgium. . . . When the German reserves have been committed to the Neptune area, the main Allied attack will be made between the Somme and Ostend. . . .'[78] De Guingand's familiarity with Allied operational problems in planning the post-assault advance on Normandy forced him to search for a way to pin down the Germans in the Pas de Calais. At that time, no intelligence specialist was even in a position to recognize the need for such a solution.

In theory, those who head deception organizations ought to be equally familiar with the ins and outs of operational planning and intelligence. This is a demanding requirement which few officers can fulfill. Organizations must be kept relatively small in order to guarantee secrecy, and whether independent (like 'A' Force) or part of an operational staff (like Ops. (B) at SHAEF) they must be very close to the commander-in-chief and his planning staff. Such organizations do not necessarily need to control their own independent means, although a core of specialists in such areas as wireless simulation and camouflage would be useful. A better acquaintance with their own order of battle and resources makes it easier for those who prepare the operational plans to design a false order of battle. This arrangement may also make access to the requisite resources more direct.

A close relationship with operations is essential. It eliminates the need to differentiate between the real and deception operations or to depart from normal staff channels.[79] It allows the deceivers to remain in the operations picture and be in constant touch with the commander's thoughts. At the same time, the commander is able to be as well informed about his shadow armies as he is about his real ones.[80]

At the same time, a deception organization should try to develop the best possible rapport with all the necessary elements of the intelligence community. The deceivers must be thoroughly acquainted with all the capabilities of the intelligence community, which is the source of continuous, real-time insights into the enemy's reaction to their planned deception. In the final analysis, the ability to co-ordinate effectively the activities of several organizations is much more important than organizational independence, location and direct or indirect control over resources. Varying circumstances in different states and different wars will dictate unique solutions to the operation and control of intelligence. The order of battle deceptions so prominent in the Second World War may be less feasible for smaller states, whose war potential is well-known, than it is for great powers. Modern war may require more technological deception and less camouflage, while short wars will pose completely different problems and opportunities from long wars. In each case, the organization and location of deception planners within the bureaucracy may change to fit the circumstances.

John Campbell's article on Operation Starkey (1943) draws on extensive evidence from the German side to analyse an Allied deception operation that failed completely.[81] Operation Starkey was actually part of a general deception operation code-named Cockade, which was intended to pin down as many German troops as possible in north-west Europe (France and Norway) to prevent them from being sent to either the Eastern front or Italy. Cockade consisted of three operations: Starkey, which was supposed to create a notional threat against the north-west coast of France (targeted for 8 September, later postponed to the 9th), to be followed by other bogus threats; Wadham, which was designed to convince the Germans that an American landing in Brittany was imminent; and Tindall, which was intended to tie down

German troops in Norway by creating a limited landing and airborne threat to Stavanger.Only Starkey called for the movement of some real troops, landing craft and air bombardments while Tindall and Wadham were basically notional. Operation Starkey also had a secondary goal of trying to draw German interceptors into the invasion area in order to defeat them in an all-out air battle, similar to the one that occurred during the Battle of Dieppe.

This elaborate but immature deception plan was an unmitigated disaster. The Germans were not alarmed, no extra formations were tied down (in fact, von Rundstedt, commander-in-chief West, gave up seven of his divisions and two Corps HQs for deployment in the Mediterranean area), and the air battle never materialized. 'In the end,' according to Campbell, 'nothing made the slightest difference. . . . Hitler and the staff at *Oberkommando der Wehrmacht* (OKW) concentrated on events in the Mediterranean, so that Starkey was buried by Avalanche' (the landing in Salerno that occurred on the same day as Starkey.) Tindall 'completely failed to interest' the Germans,[82] while 'Wadham was so weak as to be laughable'.[83] In these three operations, the deceivers may have deluded themselves about the prospects for success; or perhaps they had no illusions at all but persisted through sheer inertia and a reluctance to admit failure. As Campbell puts it, '. . . there was an element of inevitability about Cockade, of deception for the sake of deception'. At this point it is useful to summarize some of the reasons for Cockade's failure and the lessons that can be learned from it. The causes of failure discussed here are not listed in order of priority.

1. The Germans had no preconception of a cross-channel attack as early as 1943. As mentioned earlier, it is always much easier to reinforce an existing concept than to create a new one.

2. At that time the Allies did not possess sufficient resources to construct truly convincing notional threats; nor were the Allied Commanders, particularly those in the Royal Navy and Bomber Command, ready to allocate their scarce resources to deception plans that *did not cover any real operation*. The navy refused to risk battleships for shelling German shore batteries at close range, while both British and American Bomber Commands saw their priority in bombing Germany – not unimportant targets in France. 'Of the 42 aerial operations planned, 14 were abandoned and only 15 were carried out in full'.[84] (For example, the original deception plans called for 3,000-day sorties of American bombers, although General Eaker agreed to only 300.)[85] In addition, there were not enough wireless operators to simulate the appearance of new formations, and there were not enough real

formations available to create a more credible notional order of battle. Finally, another important resource was missing: that is, ample *time* to allow for development of the deception plan and its gradual absorption by the Germans.

3. The plans were poorly co-ordinated with other agencies not directly taking part in the deception operations such as the BBC and news-papers or the *Political Warfare Executive* (PWE). A number of un-coordinated leaks on the BBC and other channels contradicted the scenario designed to be conveyed to the Germans. While it is not clear how it affected the Germans, it certainly did not help.

4. Lack of realism in the deception cover plans. As a prerequisite, any deception plan must in general make operational sense, that is, be feasible to the enemy. As Campbell quotes Colonel William Harris, 'Fortitude South succeeded because it was in scale with the facts, whereas Wadham was wildly out of scale'. The same can be said for Tindall.

The signals directed at the Germans were too obvious, too crude. As Campbell shows, because the Allies were trying to draw the Germans into an all-out air battle, they did not attack the German radars which would normally have been a target in a real invasion. In a powerful critique referring to the uncoordinated leaks mentioned above, David Mure stated:

> . . . If you are factually going to invade something, you do not announce it in the press and on the wireless, therefore, notional plans should not be announced either. . . . Plan Cockade and its constituents . . . broke every rule that had been laboriously formulated in the Mediterranean over a period of three years.[86]

The use of the press, or what we now call the mass media, for deception would be more productive not in telling the enemy one's intentions (positive deception) but rather for cover or negative deception.

5. The weakness of German intelligence was not properly exploited. While the Fortitude cover plans depended on the German failure (particularly of their air reconnaissance) to penetrate British secrecy, Operation Cockade was based on the opposite, *incorrect* assumption that the German Air Force would be able to detect the dummy concentrations of landing craft and aircraft prepared for them to 'discover' as part of the deception scenario. Apparently not up to the task, German intelligence never detected the intended bait. Thus, successful deception must always be carefully tailored to match the quality of the enemy's intelligence. As noted in the preceding para-

graph, it is dangerous to design a bait that is too obvious or crude; conversely, it is useless to devise a bait that is too subtle. Of the two types of failure, the former is more risky. A ruse that has not been picked up by the enemy, especially if this is known to the deceiver, is not too dangerous. In contrast, exposure of an attempt to deceive is extremely risky because it can lead to betrayal of the deceiver's means and methods as well as of his real intentions; worst of all, it can be turned against him.

The failure of Cockade gave rise to several dangers that were very narrowly averted. In view of the fact that the British conveyed so much information to the German *Abwehr* through their double agents, in particular Garbo (who later provided the decisive link for transmission of misleading information to the Germans in Fortitude) the entire network was placed in jeopardy. Had the Germans begun to suspect the authenticity of their agents in England, the most important means in the hands of the British deceivers would have been lost. Fortunately for the British, as Campbell proves, the Germans harboured no such suspicions, although they were aware that Starkey was possibly part of a deception plan.

Secondly, the failure of Cockade could certainly have discredited the potential contribution of deception in the eyes of many Allied commanders. Luckily, the arrival of Eisenhower and Montgomery and their staffs from the Middle East, where deception by 'A' Force had proved a great success, had already confirmed their belief in its value as a force multiplier. Moreover, the tremendous problems and risks involved in planning Overlord made it clear that there was really no substitute for deception. One danger that Campbell mentions seems to be fallacious. 'What,' he asks, 'if a twin threat to the Pas de Calais and Brittany persuaded them [the Germans] of the advantages of deploying their reserves in a central position, namely, Normandy?' This is a historical anachronism. For in such a case, the Allies may have decided to invade the Pas de Calais instead of Normandy and divert the Germans to Brittany. . . .

Ironically, the worst possible outcome for Cockade would have been success! Since no military operation followed the deception, the Germans would have been forced to recognize that they had been duped. Unlike the deception operation that had already been carried out by 'A' Force in the Mediterranean, Cockade was a sort of 'one-time', self-terminating ploy that neglected to supply the Germans with a proper explanation to conceal its existence. As David Mure observed:

> The most the cover plan, when it is aimed simply at containing
> enemy forces away from your chosen battle area, can do, is to

preserve a continual ever growing, changing and developing threat. It must never come to a climax and this should not be difficult to avoid as, in the case of a real operation, all security precautions exist for the specific purpose of concealing (1) that there is going to be a climax and (b) if there is, when is it likely to be. The same should apply in the case of a cover plan. The only way in which even a whisper of a climax should be hinted at is by finding a way by which over-elaborate attempts to cover up the possibility of one are leaked to the enemy. If the Archbishop of Canterbury called on the nation to pray for those 'about to invade the continent of Europe' as he did in the course of Plan Cockade, this means that no one was going to cross the channel.[87]

Whereas the failure of Cockade nearly exposed the double-cross system, its success would have almost certainly motivated the Germans to re-evaluate their intelligence sources and as a result discover British methods of deception. One possible lesson here is that deception operations not in support of real action may be counter-productive in that they could easily betray the whole deception system needed for the support of real operations.

In perspective, the failure of Cockade was a blessing in disguise. It probably convinced the Germans (certainly Rundstedt) that future Allied attempts to deceive would be equally inept and therefore relatively easy to detect. In the second place, the failure of Cockade impelled the Allied deceivers to refine their techniques and bring in new experts (such as Noel Wild, deputy of 'A' Force). By the time they began working on Fortitude many of these lessons had been learned. While Cockade is the paramount example of stratagem gone awry, Fortitude represents strategic and operational deception at its best.

A final lesson, simple but important, is that it is far better to relinquish a half-baked ruse with a high probability of failure than to carry it out to the bitter end and risk exposing the inner workings of one's entire deception organization.

Two articles in this volume explore the hitherto neglected subjects of strategic and operational deception during the Second World War as practiced by the United States in the Pacific and by the Soviet Union on the Eastern Front. Inasmuch as the use of deception on these fronts is barely mentioned in the existing body of literature, these chapters make an original and significant contribution to the historiography of the era and also serve as a starting point for further research. While it appears that the revelations concerning deception on the Pacific Front will not substantially change our observations on the course of the war in that arena, this is not the case with the war on the Eastern Front between Nazi Germany and the Soviet Union. David Glantz's detailed reconstruction of Soviet strategic and operational deception indicates that the scope of deception employed by the Soviet Union on the Eastern Front dwarfed even the largest Allied deception operations in Europe and the Mediterranean. His article may therefore prompt a complete re-evaluation of the war on the Eastern Front, especially since one critical dimension – *maskirovka* – has been omitted from all studies in the field.

First let us turn to a brief discussion of Katherine Herbig's chapter. According to Dr Herbig, the scope of deception as employed by the United States in the Pacific always remained small in comparison with that of similar undertakings in Western Europe and the Mediterranean, and on the Eastern Front. While they fared better than Starkey (i.e., did not fail), Operations Wedlock, Husband, Bambino, Valentine and Bluebird ultimately had no decisive impact on the course of events.

Unlike its European counterpart which had proved effective in the earlier phases of the war, deception in the Pacific never gained complete acceptance as a crucial dimension in the planning of military operations. 'To some extent,' Dr Herbig points out, 'deception remained suspect in American military circles throughout the war. . . .' Only with great reluctance did the US Navy begin to overcome its distaste for deception. 'No one, it seemed, had time in the fall of 1943 to develop strategic deception plans. . . . It was still considered an offbeat technique for many. . . . The American high command never granted its deception agency [i.e., the JSC] the access to top level commanders and the sweeping authority enjoyed by the London Controlling Section, a fact bitterly resented by US deception planners.' This can, at least in part, be explained by the fact that the British perceived themselves as extremely vulnerable and locked in a fight for their very survival, while the Americans were more inclined to believe that their victory was never in doubt but was merely a question of cost and time. As argued earlier, the essential point is that the incentive to resort to deception increases in direct proportion to the perceived gravity of the threat.

Even if fully successful, US strategic deception managed to pin down no more than 80,000 Japanese troops in the Kurile Islands. While this was a modest achievement, it was not critical relative to the scale of the Pacific war: the US would have won with or without it.

Moreover, it is not entirely clear whether the Japanese decision to station 70,000 to 80,000 troops in the Kurile Islands was a reaction to American strategic deception. The Japanese began to reinforce the Kurile Islands even *before* the US deception operation (i.e., it was an autonomous decision); the first Japanese reinforcement arrived in

March while the US wireless deception started in mid-April. Further-more, as Dr Herbig shows, the Japanese always considered the Kuriles as a secondary problem. Regardless of the picture that American strategic deception tried to present, the Japanese gave top priority to the southern threat to their oil and other minerals.

The Japanese also failed to change their behavior or call for a special alert before the US deceivers' notional day of invasion for Wedlock (15 June 1944). At best, it can be argued that the Japanese tied down more troops than were really necessary in the Kurile Islands and did not see through the American deception. It is worth noting that the US deceivers do not appear to have exaggerated their claims for success in this (and later) operations.

What were some of the major weaknesses of the US deception operations? As Dr Herbig shows, the American deception planners were far less familiar with Japanese perceptions than their British colleagues were with the German mind-set. This made it all the more difficult to design appropriate baits. To make matters worse, faulty co-ordination both among US military commands and with the British in the Far East (India in particular) generated even more friction for deception plans. US commanders and military branches (Army, Navy, Army Air Force) were much more jealous than the British in protecting their turf. Some of this may be attributed to the different organization of the US command structure and the greater independence of each branch of the armed forces compared with that of the British unified command system.

As in the failure of Starkey, much can be explained by the shortage of resources. 'Criticism of Wedlock later would note that there was probably not enough activity, especially not enough reconnaissance and bombing of the area to support the threat being portrayed by other means. Accordingly, actual operations were called "the weakest link" in the operation.' Other weaknesses discussed by Dr Herbig concern the lack of detailed attention given to wireless deception. Had the Japanese been more thorough in their traffic analysis, they might have detected serious anomalies between the patterns of real traffic and the simulated wireless traffic.

A major difference between deception in the European theater of war and that in the Pacific involved the means used to transmit false information to the enemy. In Europe the most critical link was the double-cross system. It was direct, fast and had a powerful impact on the Germans. In the Pacific, the double-cross system played only a marginal role and was used, in Dr Herbig's words, to pass 'tidbits' to the Japanese. The American deceivers were thus deprived of their most effective link. Other special operations (such as Mincemeat) which could have provided highly convincing evidence were apparently not carried out.

From an organizational point of view, it is interesting to note that the American deception planners were *never directly* incorporated in the planning of military operations. Although the Joint Security Control (JSC) was originally modeled on the British London Controlling Section (LCS), it actually acquired a very different character. The LCS was exclusively a clearing house, a co-ordinating body which did not plan deception operations; instead, it co-ordinated the deception operations of Ops. (B) or 'A' Force, organizations which were very close to or a direct part of operational planning. On the other hand, the US Joint Chiefs of Staff not only designated the JSC to co-ordinate all deception-related developments, but also agreed to a proposal that the JSC write deception annexes for all war plans. Approval of this proposal gave '. . . Joint Security Control its first official role in deception planning'. This alienated the JSC from various operational commands which probably resented an independent, remote deception agency. Consequently, the distance created between the deceivers and the operations people did much to undermine the potentially influential role of deception in the Far East. Dudley Clarke's insistence that 'Deception is essentially a matter for the "Operations" Branch of the staff and not intelligence' was apparently very wise and practical advice.

A final note must consider the quality of Japanese intelligence. Like that of the Germans, Japanese strategic intelligence was not very effective nor was it held in great esteem by the Japanese Armed Forces.[88] The inefficiency of Japanese intelligence, which depended primarily upon a single channel of information as discussed by Dr Herbig, made it quite vulnerable to deception, yet also less likely to pick up the baits dangled before it by US deceivers, for whom success was very uncertain in this respect. The fact that the Americans were forced to rely almost completely on wireless deception considerably limited their access to Japanese intelligence-gathering channels. In comparison, the British double-cross system guaranteed that all the messages which were supposed to reach German intelligence actually did so. In the Pacific many of the deceptive signals were probably never picked up and were simply ignored or lost. At times, the Japanese High Command seemed to plan its strategy and troop dispositions on the basis of its own autonomous judgement, evincing a disregard for intelligence which ironically rendered it immune to deception.

Paradoxically, it is as difficult to deceive an excellent intelligence organization as it is an inferior one. When the enemy's intelligence organization is extremely efficient and thorough, the danger is that a deception operation may be exposed and even turned against the deceiver (although I know of no such case). With a weak intelligence organization, the deception planners take the risk that their 'bait' will not even be noticed. This seems to have occurred with the Japanese, which may explain the rather limited impact of US strategic deception operations. Hence, it appears that mediocre or competent intelligence organizations are the most likely to be deceived.

David Glantz provides the first systematic survey of deception on the Eastern Front – the Unknown War, to use Churchill's phrase. While the average reader is probably familiar with deception operations in the north-west European and Mediterranean theaters of war, even the expert knows little about Soviet deception operations during the Second World War. After completing this article, Colonel Glantz continued his intensive research and concluded that his earlier work represents only a very small fraction of Soviet activities related to *maskirovka*. He is now preparing a full-length book on the subject.

Land warfare on the Eastern Front was, by a quantum leap, larger than all land operations in all the other theaters of war. This is also true of the scale on which the Soviets used deception. Colonel Glantz contrasts the success of Soviet deception operations with the enormity of the German failure to deal with the problem. In fact, despite one success after another, the Germans could never effectively pierce Soviet cover and deception operations. Glantz bases his pioneering essay on a careful study of Soviet and, to a lesser extent, German sources, including the comparison and corroboration of Soviet and captured German Order of Battle maps.

The weakness and desperation of the Soviets in 1941 left them with no hesitation whatsoever in resorting to deception on all possible levels – political, strategic, operational, and tactical. Through four fascinating case studies – the Battle of Moscow 1941, Stalingrad 1942, Belorussia 1944, and Manchuria 1945 – Colonel Glantz traces the evolution of Soviet skill in this art. Whereas Soviet deception was relatively crude before the Battle of Moscow 1941, it had improved considerably by the Battle of Stalingrad, was even more mature in the fighting in Belorussia, and had been perfected by the time the USSR invaded Manchuria. By 1943, as he shows, the Soviets were incorporating deception in every strategic and operational plan.

The magnitude of deception operations on the Eastern Front is staggering. Before the Battle of Moscow, the Soviets concealed no fewer than three complete armies from German intelligence; by the Battle of Stalingrad, using very sophisticated camouflage techniques, the Soviets managed to conceal the forward deployment of 160,000 men, 430 tanks, 600 guns, 14,000 vehicles, and 7,000 tons of ammunition across the Don. Before their offensive in Belorussia, German intelligence had identified 140 Soviet division equivalents and three tank corps facing Army Group Center. In fact the Soviets managed to concentrate in the same region no less than 168 division equivalents, eight tank or mechanized corps, and two cavalry corps (with significant armored strength). The Germans estimated Soviet tank strength to be somewhere between 400 and 1,100 tanks, when it was actually more than 5,000 tanks at the same front! The difference between the number of Soviet forces the Germans were able to identify and those the Soviets were able to conceal was as large as the whole invasion force that landed at Normandy. In Manchuria, the Japanese underestimated the strength of the Soviet forces confronting them by no less than 30 to 50 per cent.

In their major offensive in Belorussia, the Soviets capitalized on a German obsession with the south-eastern flank (the Balkans) when they 'helped' the Germans to convince themselves that the next attack would indeed come from the south and north. As Earl Ziemke suggested in a quote selected by Glantz, 'To a Soviet deception, the German commands added an almost self-induced delusion: "the main offensive would come against Army Group North Ukraine because that was where they were ready to meet it".' Following their attack against the Germans on the central front, the Russians proceeded to attack the Germans on both the northern and southern fronts in what I described earlier as reverse conditioning deception.

The means employed by the Soviets to conceal their troop concentrations, as Glantz points out, were simple and labor-intensive but effective. Measures such as strict secrecy, heavy use of camouflage, movement at night and in bad weather, as well as pretending to prepare for defensive rather than offensive operations, served them well. Colonel Glantz also mentions the extensive, though not always successful, use of bogus wireless traffic to mislead the Germans and the occasional use of disinformation and rumors.

This picture is undoubtedly incomplete, for Soviet deception is portrayed as relying mainly on passive means. While this may be true for the most part, no mention at all is made of Soviet decoding operations, agents, double agents and the like. Only the Soviet archives, which remain closed, may reveal some of the other means of deception used by the Soviet Union. Indeed, Glantz remarks at one point that 'One of the deadliest weaknesses of deception planning was lack of knowledge about what the enemy knew concerning one's own *maskirovka* techniques'. Perhaps so, but on the other hand, the Russians may have known much more than they have thus far been ready to disclose. It is possible that, like the British and Americans, they had their own Ultra system with which to keep track of German reactions. In fact, it would be surprising if they had not acquired such a capability in one form or another. Given their traditional skill in the development of spy networks, it may also turn out that the Soviet Union had its own version of the so-called special means. At present, though, these are only speculations which cannot be verified.

A comparison with other chapters in this book also shows that the overall weakness of German and Japanese intelligence was pivotal to the success of Allied deception operations. The difference in this case is, however, that while the Germans and Japanese consistently *overestimated* the Allied Order of Battle before each new landing campaign by as much as 80 to 100 per cent, they consistently *underestimated* the Soviet Order of Battle by 30 to 50 per cent. This accurately reflects the divergent aims of the deceivers on different fronts. Since the Soviets' main advantage was quantitative, they had the most to gain from concealment of their real capabilities. This they did with great success. Colonel Glantz's latest research (not reflected in his chapter in this book) indicates that while the Germans *overestimated* the size of the Red Army in the strategic sense, they *underestimated* the Soviet order of battle at each front before the Soviets launched a new offensive. On the other hand, the Western Allies, who did not enjoy a marked quantitative edge over the Germans, had to exaggerate their real strength in order to disperse German troops.

Glantz makes another interesting observation which was also true of the Allied experience in Western Europe and the Mediterranean. He argues that lower level German intelligence units were much more sensitive to deception and managed to detect developing threats much earlier than those at the highest OKH levels. 'There was a dichotomy between intelligence assessments at lower levels and high level headquarters, with lower level headquarters taking a more realistic view of the situation.'

Being closer to the front, Army Group intelligence is in a better position to observe material developments and troop concentrations; it is more alert because the threat is direct – not abstract and remote. Unlike those in the highest echelons, a lower level analyst may be less committed to certain strategies and therefore less prone to wishful thinking and self-delusion. In attempting to counter deception, then, greater attention should be devoted (in a prolonged large-scale war) to any discrepancies between the upper- and lower-level echelons of intelligence as well as to lower echelon intelligence reports. Most of the Allied deception efforts in north-west Europe and the Mediterranean were indeed directed at the upper echelons. Luckily for the deceivers,

German regional commands always accepted the OKW views, even when such views seemed to be contradicted by locally obtained evidence. Under the Nazi system, all critical decisions related to strategic intelligence were ultimately made by the Führer himself.

Colonel Glantz concludes his article with a look at lessons the Soviets learned from their extensive use of deception. Their spectacular success in using *maskirovka* against the Germans certainly convinced them to take deception seriously in the future. There is probably no other military organization in the world today whose military doctrine *on all levels* emphasizes the use of stratagem to such an extent. Yet contemporary Soviet deception experts face a task which has grown increasingly complex given the more sophisticated reconnaissance and sensor technology of today, the improved traffic analysis, the quality of Western intelligence organizations and the greater general awareness of the possibility that one's adversary might be using deception. From its own experience in the Second World War, the Soviet Union learned the importance of using deception to achieve surprise in the opening phase of every offensive. Having come full circle since the days of Stalin, who once claimed that in modern warfare objective economic factors – not strategic surprise – determined the outcome of war, the Soviet Union employed strategic and operational deception in its invasion of Czechoslovakia in 1968, which caught NATO intelligence off guard, and probably also in its invasion of Afghanistan. Its allies, Egypt and Syria, achieved a major strategic surprise in their October 1973 attack on Israel by basing their cover and deception plans on Soviet strategic and operational doctrine. Dealing with the Soviet *maskirovka* on all levels will always remain a major problem for the Western Allies and all other Soviet adversaries, even those within its own bloc.

This makes the Soviet Union an exception to the rule that weakness is the main incentive for the use of deception. Perhaps, in some ways, the Soviet Union still feels inferior, unable and unwilling to ignore a historical experience of vulnerability despite its current control of a formidable arsenal of nuclear weapons. Such tendencies may be re-inforced by Marxist ideology, which depicts a continuous struggle between capitalism and communism requiring eternal vigilance and guile. Finally, as noted above, *maskirovka* proved to be an immense success in the Soviet military experience. While the United States may consider deception to be an exclusively wartime activity, for the Soviet Union it exists both in peace and war.

Tom Cubbage contributes two inter-related articles to this volume: the first synthesizes a number of theories explaining intelligence failures in general and applies them to Germany's inability to anticipate the invasion of Normandy, while the second reviews Roger Fleetwood Hesketh's definitive account of Fortitude – the largest-scale Allied deception cover plan of the Second World War. Cubbage's first article includes a survey of much of the recent literature on the causes of intelligence failure. The bulk of this literature has focused on possible explanations for the better-known strategic surprises that launched a new war or opened a new front (e.g., 'Barbarossa,' Pearl Harbor, the invasion of Korea in 1950, and the Yom Kippur War). Less has been written on the differences between the type of strategic surprise that marks the onset of a new war compared with that which occurs during a war, where an attack is already expected although its specific time, location, or intensity are not known. Cubbage applies many of these theoretical observations in explaining how strategic surprise can be achieved even though the enemy is anticipating an attack. In a systematic analysis of intelligence problems that are largely psychological, he examines the nature of human biases and the impossibility of accurately perceiving reality. Distortions arise from factors such as preconceived ideas, wishful thinking, drawing conclusions from an unrepresentative sample of evidence, the human need for order, the need for consistency, and commitment to earlier analysis.[89] Cubbage also explains how the usual biases in combination with certain psychological, structural and organizational biases unique to German intelligence further aggravated the problems they faced in estimating Allied intentions.

As Cubbage has shown, the clever deceiver intuitively understands that he must take advantage of the enemy analyst's instinctive desire to reduce ambiguity and impose order on an uncertain environment. He must help the enemy to be quite certain, decisive and wrong. The deliberate introduction of deception by an enemy further complicates the intelligence analyst's work. The very fact that deception is an ever present possibility adds a question mark to every bit of information. Cubbage concludes that good intelligence can reduce, but never completely eliminate, the fog of war. To refrain from subterfuge is tantamount to simplifying the enemy's problems, though he will always deceive himself to some degree in any event. Deception simply convinces him to deceive himself in a way more conducive to one's plans.

Cubbage's second contribution is a review essay of Roger Fleetwood Hesketh's after-action report on Fortitude. While Masterman's *The Double Cross System* makes much easier reading, the Hesketh Report is a far more thorough and detailed account and thus of greater interest to the professional reader. Through close attention to minute details, Hesketh constructs a much more realistic view of how deception work is actually carried out and guides the reader through the development of a major deception plan, from its time-consuming inception and implementation to its adjustment according to information received from the enemy, including a follow-up of how it was absorbed at each stage by the enemy's intelligence and command systems. Cubbage's excellent introduction to this unusual document serves only to whet the appetite of those interested in this hitherto closely guarded information. Publication of the Hesketh Report, of Dudley Clarke's final report on the history of 'A' Force, and of Sir Michael Howard's official history of deception will be extremely helpful in putting the history of deception in the Second World War, and of course the history of the war itself, in a more accurate and complete perspective.

EVALUATING THE EFFECTIVENESS OF DECEPTION

> But in war, as in life generally, all parts of a whole are inter-connected and thus the effects produced, however small their cause, must influence all subsequent military operations and modify their final outcome to some degree, however slight. In the same way, every means must influence even the ultimate purpose.[90]
>
> It would however be disastrous to try to develop our under-standing of strategy by analyzing these factors in isolation, since they are usually inter-connected in each military action in mani-fold and intricate ways. A dreary analytical labyrinth would result, a nightmare in which one tried in vain to bridge the gulf between this abstract basis and the facts of life. Heaven protect the theorist from such an undertaking.[91]

An important but difficult question to answer is: How can we evaluate the effectiveness of a deception operation on any given level? In an after-action report, it is very difficult to isolate or separate a single variable from the extremely complex interaction of numerous variables. Attempting to determine the influence of each element may be convenient for analytical purposes, but it is still an artificial process. Recognizing this, Clausewitz warned against the danger of studying the various components of any type of military action in isolation. In *The Poverty of Historicism*, Karl K. Popper referred to this problem as '. . . a complexity arising out of the impossibility of artificial isolation. . .,'[92] while in his stimulating book, *Historians' Fallacies*, David Hackett Fisher analyses the issue as follows:

> The reductive fallacy reduces complexity to simplicity, or diversity to uniformity, in causal explanations. It exists in several

common forms, none of which can be entirely avoided in any historical interpretation. As long as historians tell selected truths, their causal models must be reductive in some degree. But some causal models are more reductive than others. When a causal model is reductive in such a degree, or in such a way, that the resultant distortion is dysfunctional to the resolution of the causal problem at hand, then the reductive fallacy is committed.[93]

In contemporary work on military strategy and technology, this problem is referred to as *synergy*, which is defined by the *Oxford English Dictionary* as increased effectiveness, achievement, etc., produced as a result of a combined action or co-operation. Even more relevant to our discussion is the definition of *synergism*: the combined activity of two drugs or other substances when greater than the sum of the effects of each present alone. *Webster's Dictionary* defines synergism as 'the co-operative action of discrete agencies . . . such that the total effect is greater than the sum of the two or more effects taken independently'. In certain actions, therefore, it is almost impossible to study each component separately and determine the relative contribution of each to the final process.

Similarly, while it is difficult to measure with any degree of precision the impact of deception on the outcome of a war, campaign or battle, we *can* assume that in its absence the final outcome would be very different.

One can evaluate the effectiveness of deception in two ways: either before and during a military operation (or implementation), or after the operation has taken place. Before a military operation has taken place and while the deception is being implemented, the only way to attempt to evaluate its success is by following its impact on the enemy's behavior. Has he changed his order of battle and dispositions as desired by the deceivers? Are his commanders aware of the time and place an operation will take place? The impact of deception can be assessed through such means as air reconnaissance, wireless interception, breaking the enemy's codes, and noting the extent to which surprise has been achieved at the location of the attack. For example, before the invasion of Normandy, the Allies knew through Ultra intercepts, special means, air reconnaissance and local agents, that the Germans had reacted as the deceivers wanted them to by concentrating their troops around the Pas de Calais without reinforcing the Normandy area. How much of this can be attributed to deception alone and how much to existing concepts of Hitler and the German High Command is difficult and unnecessary to determine because the two reinforced each other. Nevertheless, in this case the Allies knew in *advance* that their deception was working, or at least that the Germans had done nothing to negate it.

Before the Battle of El Alamein, British deception and camouflage operations obscured their concentration of forces from the Germans in order to conceal the *Schwerpunkt* of their attack. On the basis of information on German troop dispositions obtained through Ultra and air reconnaissance, the British could determine that the Germans had *not* anticipated where the main attack would fall. When the attack came earlier than expected, Rommel was away (as he was when the invasion of Normandy began).

By monitoring their deception measures before Anzio, the Allies knew that the Germans had not concentrated their troops at the landing area. As a result, the Allies subsequently achieved complete surprise and met no resistance at the landing area. This type of continuous assessment can give the deceivers a reasonable idea of how effective their deception is, though they can never afford to become complacent and assume – on the basis of such feedback – that their ruse will be completely effective.

The second way to gauge a particular plan's success is to interrogate the enemy commanders and examine captured documents after the battle is over. Only after the war did the Allies determine that Garbo's message of 9 June had been transmitted all the way up to the OKW and Hitler. In a post-war interrogation of Jodl, it became apparent that this message had a decisive impact on the German decision not to send reinforcements to Normandy. In this case, both documented evidence as well as German action (or lack of it) match perfectly, indicating beyond doubt that the deception worked. An examination of the diary of OKH *Lagebericht West* (OKH intelligence in north-west Europe) showed that out of 208 messages received and recorded in the *Üerblick des Britischen Reiches,* no fewer than 188 messages came from British-controlled agents.[94] Many more facts could be cited to make the point that Allied deception was highly effective. It is, however, not always so easy to prove the effectiveness of deception, as illustrated in the case of the 'going maps' ruse that preceded the battle of Alam Halfa.

As a prisoner of war, General Thoma in a conversation in Cairo admitted that Rommel had relied on a carefully doctored British 'going map' to plan and execute his offensive. Although the Germans never realized that the maps had been planted by the British (that is, they did not expose the deception), it is impossible to prove that this ruse had a direct impact on Rommel's planning and conduct of the offensive. Most authorities agree that he changed his plan during the battle as a result of a petrol shortage, and then may or may not have been misguided by the false 'going maps'. Basically, there are three schools of thought regarding the impact of this ruse on Rommel's division at Alam Halfa. Major General Sir Francis de Guingand, Sir David Hunt, Field Marshal Alexander (who participated in the deception) and Winston Churchill concluded that the 'going map' ruse was probably very effective and achieved its goal; whereas Liddell Hart was more skeptical, and more recently Hinsley, Carver and Barnett did not credit the ruse with any impact whatsoever. The original version of the story was recounted by Major General Francis de Guingand in *Operation Victory*.

> I will break off here to describe a ruse which we afterwards learnt had helped to defeat Rommel. We always produced 'going' maps which were layered in colours to show the type of desert in so far as it affected movement. We knew the enemy had captured many of our maps and was making use of them. At the time of the retreat to Alamein no 'going' maps existed of the area to the rear of our positions. These we produced after we had settled in. I, therefore, decided to have made a false 'going' map which would link up quite correctly with the maps already in enemy hands, and then to falsify a particular area to suit our plans. The area I selected, in consultation with our Intelligence staff, was one south of Alam Halfa. Due south of the highest point was an area of very soft sand. As we appreciated the enemy would make for this ridge I thought that by showing this bad area as good going, the enemy might be tempted to send his tanks around that way. It would also give him a shock if he were making for El Hamman, for instead of a 'good gallop', he would find himself wallowing in deep sand. We had this map secretly printed in very quick time by the energy of an old associate of mine in the M I Directorate in Cairo – Stuart-Menteith. Then we plotted with 13th Corps to have it 'captured' by the enemy. In the south, light forces were continually patrol-ling around the enemy's minefields, and so it was arranged that a scout car should get blown up on a mine, and that the crew would be taken off in another truck. Left in the scout car were soldier's kits and the usual junk, whilst stuffed away in a haversack was an old and dirty 'going map' (the fake) covered in tea stains, but quite readable. The car had been ransacked by the next morning, and the map had disappeared.
>
> The enemy certainly got badly 'bogged down' in this particular area, but how much the map was to blame I don't quite know. From interrogation of prisoners, however, we did obtain con-firmation that a falsified map led the enemy to send their tanks into this sandy terrain, which trebled their fuel consumption. We

MAPS 5 & 6
THE EL ALAMEIN 'GOING MAPS' RUSE

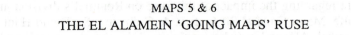

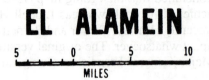

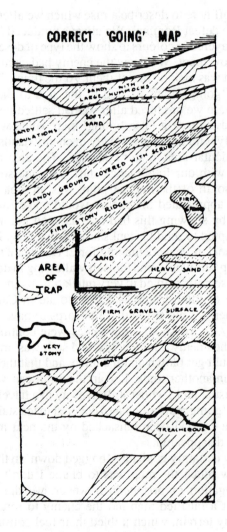

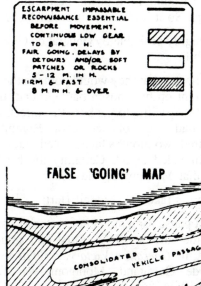

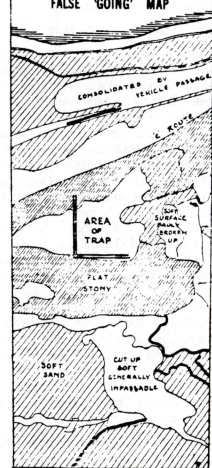

Source: Major-General Sir Francis de Guingaud, *Operation Victory* (London, 1947), maps 16 and 17.

also knew that Rommel put down the failure of his offensive to petrol shortage. So it looks as if it probably helped.[95]

What is seen as highly probable by General de Guingand is accepted as a fact by Churchill.

Montgomery hoped that they would not take the latter course. He preferred to fight on his chosen battleground, the ridge. A map which showed easy going for tanks in that direction, and bad going farther east, had been planted upon Rommel. General von Thoma, captured two months later, stated that this false information had its intended effect. Certainly the battle now took the precise form that Montgomery desired.[96]

A middle position is taken by Liddell Hart:

Here one must pause for a moment to refer to a striking story that has gained wide currency. It was first told authoritatively, soon after the war, in *Operation Victory*, written by Major-General Sir Francis de Guingand, Montgomery's chief-of-staff. He there described how he planned 'a ruse which helped to defeat Rommel' by luring the enemy forces into 'an area of very soft sand' just south of the Alam Halfa Ridge. He devised a map of the 'going' which showed this area fairly firm, and in conjunction with Horrocks, the commander of the 13th Corps, planted it on the enemy by leaving it in a scout car that purposely ran on to a mine. The story was repeated in a footnote to Alexander's Despatch, written in 1947, which stated that it had been subsequently learned from the captured General von Thoma that 'the enemy had intended to outflank the ridge to the north-east but had altered his plan on the basis of this false information'. But Thoma was in Russia when this battle took place, and it is clear from the records that Rommel had intended the Afrika Korps to drive eastward, on a line far south of this treacherous area, and only altered his plan because of the time lost in the passage of the initial mined belt. The most that can truly be claimed for de Guingand's clever ruse is that it may have led Rommel to imagine, when he changed course, that the Alam Halfa Ridge was more easily accessible than it proved. The soft sand area cramped the scope for local manoeuvre there.[97]

Professor Hinsley reached the following conclusions:

Deprived of the advantage of surprise, Rommel's thrust failed to make the quick penetration he had hoped for. In the afternoon of 31 August, Rommel, having been forced to abandon his original intention of trying to outflank the position to the south, turned north in an attempt to capture the Alam el Halfa ridge, consuming abnormally large amounts of fuel in this manoeuvre. ... A deception plan had been prepared by the intelligence and survey branches responsible for the production of 'going' maps. This was designed to lead Rommel up to the ridge by the route he eventually adopted. But the fact that this original plan would have sent the DAK overground marked on this map as bad 'going' suggests that he was not influenced by the deception.[98]

Correlli Barnett, in *The Desert Generals*, wrote:

> Now Rommel was seen to turn sharply north, a move forced on him not by a planted 'false-going' map, but by the delays in the mine-fields and by shortage of petrol.[99]

And finally, a similar conclusion was reached by General Michael Carver in his book *Al Alamein*:

> At the same time efforts were made to mislead the enemy. First of all he was to be led into deferring his attack altogether by an impression of great strength in the south. Two dummy tank battalions were moved into the area east of Himeimat, a dummy infantry brigade position was dug at Samaket Gaballa and dummy minefields were also laid. All this was completed by August 25th. If in spite of this Rommel were to break through, he was to be misled as to the nature of the 'going' by a false 'going' map deliberately lost on patrol in the forward area. There was in fact an area of very soft sand south of Alam el Halfa: this was shown as good hard 'going', and the good 'going' shown as bad in the hope of luring Rommel into that area. Unfortunately for those who planned to deceive, there is no sign that any of these measures had any effect on Rommel's plans or even came to his notice, certainly not the first.[100]

It seems as though the impact of the 'going map ruse' has been questioned more and more with the passage of time. Perhaps this trend confirms Cruickshank's observation: 'As a rule, the success of deceptive activities was overestimated, especially by those directly responsible for them'.[101] Sir David Hunt suggests that Professor Hinsley may not be right: 'In fact the map was planted between the making of the original plan and the adoption of the final plan. I don't contest [writes Sir David] the possibility that the change of the *Stoss-linie* was dictated by shortage of fuel and not by the deception; but that remains to be proved'.[102] In the end, this question will have to remain unresolved. What is important, however, is that the 'going map ruse' was only one of many other evidently more successful deception plans preceding the Battle of Alam Halfa. These included laying dummy (and real) minefields, creating a bogus threat on the southern flank of the German advance, and inducing the Germans to take action, despite their shortage of petrol, by the use of special means.[103] Although it may be difficult to try to assess the effect of one factor such as the 'going map ruse' in isolation from the much wider plan of deception, and further- more, to separate the impact of deception from that of other factors, one can nevertheless safely conclude that operational deception played a key role in the Battle of Alam Halfa one way or the other.

The methodological difficulties inherent in determining the effectiveness of deception are exacerbated by the fact that even if deception fails to achieve its intended objectives, it almost always fools the enemy – he is unable to identify the information he receives as false. While the impact of the 'going map ruse' will always be debatable, no one has ever argued that the Germans doubted its authenticity.

In 'A German Perspective on Allied Deception Operations in the Second World War', Professor Klaus-Jürgen Müller challenges the widely accepted idea that Allied deception operations were generally successful in influencing the decisions of the German High Command. He claims that much of what has been written on this subject – particularly by former practitioners of deception – has been based on the Allied point of view without due reference to, and corroboration with, the German decision-making process and related documentary evidence. By failing to undertake an in-depth study of the German perspective, many writers may have fallen prey to the *post hoc ergo propter hoc* fallacy. A closer examination, he believes, may persuade the historian that in many instances, German mistakes or moves previously attributed to the effectiveness of Allied deception were in fact the result of autonomous German decisions. He argues that simply because deception was not exposed does not necessarily mean that it was successful.

If anything, Professor Müller forces anyone interested in deception in general, and the Second World War in particular, to re-examine the evidence and take a critical look at the existing literature in the field. From a heuristic point of view, Professor Müller has certainly per- formed an important service for all students of deception by causing them to reconsider many methodological issues and ideas that may have been taken for granted.

The following quotations are representative of Müller's criticism and major arguments.

Reading books by former intelligence officers on the subject one often gets the impression that some authors are obviously inclined to overestimate the effects of the activities they were involved in. . . . [t]hey have obviously influenced more than one professional historian to adopt this evaluation without further scrutiny.

A closer examination, however, reveals that very often such an exaggerated evaluation of the effects of deception operations is not well founded, and therefore not very convincing. Even where these stratagems were 'bought' by those they were sold to, their effect at the strategic level was minimal in many cases. Deception at the tactical level, however, was very often successful. At the strategic level there are many examples of deception operations being less successful or even failures. In some instances deception is counter-productive.

Montagu, for example, came to his optimistic evaluation of Mincemeat's effects by analysing a small number of captured German documents he happened to find. . . . From the methodological point of view it is grossly inadequate to analyse enemy documents collected at random and to base one's conclusions on such a meagre sample of sources. . . . Yet this is how not a few of the memoirs and other books on deception have been written.

An account, and especially an analysis isolating deception operation factors, inevitably misses the point. Deception history cannot really be written by dealing exclusively with intelligence operations. This approach leaves out factors essential for understanding intelligence itself.

The German evaluation of the strategic situation and of the expected Allied operation, was not *decisively* influenced by Allied deception activities – even if some German authors also put forward this hypothesis. Quite the contrary, it was determined by a multitude of factors: military, psychological, political, geographical and economic. . . .

According to the German military tradition of strategic thinking . . . the planners aimed at a quick and decisive operation – the destruction of the enemy forces as quickly and as radically as possible by one decisive blow at the right place [my emphasis]. . . . No doubt, this specific pattern of thinking and perceiving reality decisively determined . . . the German evaluation of the strategic situation in the summer of 1943.

The German High Command was well aware that the Allies were doing everything to deceive and mislead them. In February [1943] the *Wehrmachtfahrungsstab* (WFst) issued a warning in this respect. *Nobody in the Führerhauptquartier could really distinguish between real or fictitious information. This contributed considerably to weakening the effect of Allied deception measures. The German analysts . . . therefore had to rely on their own strategic ideas when anticipating future Allied operations* [my emphasis].

Within this strategic context [i.e., at what location would the Allies invade in southern Europe] the two problems – securing the Balkans, and *keeping Italy in the war* – became the essential preconditions for the continuation of the war by Germany [my emphasis].

Sicily was where Hitler expected the next Allied landing operation to take place (not excluding secondary or diversionary operations elsewhere).

Germany's reactions in the Mediterranean were . . . predominantly determined by one single motive [Müller actually mentions two above] the fear of Italy's imminent collapse and/or defection.

At this point, it is useful to discuss briefly some of the problems raised by Professor Müller's methodology. In the first place, he relies on a very small and unrepresentative sample to make his argument.[104] This he does on two occasions; in his choice of authors representing those who wrote on deception, and in the sample of case studies from which he tries to prove his case.

Montagu's *The Man Who Never Was* is in fact a well-documented book for which the material was not chosen at random, but which represented important decisions and reactions of the German High Command. Furthermore, Montagu was writing a limited monograph that focused on only one episode of deception: Operation Mincemeat, which was actually part of a much larger deception cover plan, Barclay. Montagu may claim much for Operation Mincemeat (and rightly so) but he never suggests that Mincemeat was not complemented by many other deception operations (which at the time he wrote his book were all classified), nor would he deny that the German decision-making process involved an admixture of motives.

While David Mure's *Practice to Deceive* does contain its share of inaccuracies, it is nevertheless a generally reliable book based on first-hand knowledge and apparently also on advice from Dudley Clarke and Noel Wild. Unfortunately it is not an accurate or balanced account but documents released in the future as well as the official history will prove it to be largely correct. While Müller often chooses to argue over 'tangential' issues such as why Rommel was sent to Athens or whether the Panzer division sent to Greece was fully equipped, he conveniently ignores another very central matter – that of the notional order of battle created by 'A' Force in the Middle East and passed by special means to the German *Abwehr*. Implemented much earlier than Operation Mincemeat and never exposed by the Germans, this deception operation must have had considerable influence on the German decision to concentrate troops in the Balkans. Throughout the Second World War, the Germans believed that in addition to the British 8th Army there was also a 12th Army. This fictitious formation partially explains German fears of a threat to the Balkans. Similarly, he ignores the deception operation (as discussed by Mure and Cruickshank)[105] intended to convince the Germans that the British were considering an attack on the Balkans in co-operation with the Turks, who had become more and more sensitive to Allied pressure. Müller does mention possible plans of an Allied attack from Turkish territory, but he omits to mention that this threat, which was taken seriously by the Germans as he suggests, was primarily fabricated by the Allies.

While focusing on Operation Mincemeat, which was the object of much publicity, Professor Müller also omits to discuss the eastern Mediterranean order-of-battle deceptions which were less spectacular but far more important in diverting German forces to the Balkans.

As Sir David Hunt shows, other British deception operations started before, and continued long after, Operation Mincemeat had been terminated.

Already at the time of Husky the cover plan drew attention to a supposedly imminent invasion of the Peloponnese which caused, among other reactions, the precipitate move of 1st Panzer Division from France to the beaches of Kalamata at the southernmost extremity of the Balkans. S.O.E.'s operation in Greece, codenamed Animals, made a useful contribution. The next year [1944], the cover plan was even more elaborate, pointing to landings in Bulgaria on May 9. German susceptibility to these suggestions was increased by acceptance of the spurious formations continuously fed to their specialists in the Allied order of battle. This created a firm belief in the existence of strong forces standing ready in Egypt and North Africa to be used at the right moment in the Balkans; coupled with their ignorance of the essentials of amphibious warfare, this delusion gave them reason to suppose that landings almost anywhere in the peninsula were within Allied capability. On 10 June 1944, for instance, Foreign Armies West forecast an invasion of Albania and Epirus from Apulia commanded by the [fictitious] 3rd Polish Corps. At the same time the Operations Branch of OKW considered that an invasion of Istria was highly likely. These misappreciations multiplied the value of the forces in the Mediterranean theatre as an instrument for misdirecting the movements of German reserves.[106]

The most important works – that is, the British and American official histories and the official reports on deception like those by Hesketh and Masterman – make very modest claims for the success of deception. Apart from mentioning deception very briefly, the official histories tend to ignore its contribution to Allied strategy and military operations. Constrained by the need for secrecy, many were written in the 1950s and 1960s before disclosure of the existence of Ultra and the special means operators. Later volumes, such as Molony's Volume Six of *The Mediterranean and Middle East* published in 1984, unjustifiably continue to gloss over the role of deception. For example, the codename of the cover plan for Operation Diadem (i.e., *Nunton*) is not even mentioned in the British official history, perhaps because of the decision to concentrate the discussion of deception operations in a special volume being written by Sir Michael Howard.

Roger Hesketh, one of the foremost practitioners of deception and also one of its ablest historians, goes to unusual lengths *not* to exaggerate the impact of deception. Indeed the epigraph chosen for his account of Fortitude, the most successful of all deception operations, cautions the reader against the *post hoc ergo propter hoc* fallacy of assuming that simply because deception existed it was also decisive:

> It was prettily devised of Aesop: 'The fly sat upon the axle-tree of the chariot-wheel and said, "What a dust do I raise!" ' So are there some vain persons that, whatsoever goeth alone or moveth upon great means, if they have never so little hand in it, they think it is they that carry it.
>
> Francis Bacon, *Essay on Vainglory*

He mentions this again in the preface.

> It is always tempting for those who set out to deceive and who see their objects fulfilled, to claim the credit for their attainment when, in fact, the motive force lay in another quarter. Every effort has been made to complete the chain of cause and effect so that the reader can judge for himself to what extent the Germans were influenced by the action of Allied deceivers and to what extent they were impelled by other considerations. At all times the writer has kept before him the boast of Aesop's fly as he sat upon the axle-tree.[107]

The second fundamental problem with Müller's argument is the narrowness of the sample he uses to caution historians against over-emphasizing the importance of deception. Had he chosen as his sample deception operations Cockade, Starkey, Wadham, and Tindall as well as Fortitude North, it would have appeared as though deception does not work at all. This is what David Hackett Fischer refers to as 'fallacies of statistical sampling or generalizations which rest upon an insufficient body of data – upon a "sample" which represents the composition of the object in question'.[108]

The material presented in this volume and other cases not mentioned which took place in North Africa, Italy, Normandy, El-Alamein, and the Russian front, indicates that deception was often very effective and, even if not always successful, was only rarely counter-productive due to the overall incompetence of German strategic intelligence. In this book, for example, Colonel Glantz reveals for the first time the very successful and large-scale Russian deception operations on the Eastern Front. Not a single systematic study has yet been published on Allied deception operations in Italy (the best discussion so far is still in Sir David Hunt's *A Don at War*, a book not dedicated to the study of deception and intelligence operations), nor has the post-war report written by Dudley Clarke for the British Cabinet been published. While it is doubtful that any of those projects will lead to excessive claims, they will probably show that deception was practiced on a much wider scale than previously assumed.

A number of other methodological questions also merit discussion, for instance, complexity (or why deception and intelligence cannot be separated analytically). Professor Müller first suggests that deception must be studied in a wider context, that intelligence history must be studied in combination with other 'non-intelligence' issues, then proceeds to evaluate the influence of Allied deception on German strategy by discussing the German decision-making process in general and more specifically how independent strategic factors shaped German strategy. While this certainly is a sound methodology for his own discussion, Müller studies deception in isolation from one important dimension – the performance of German intelligence. Yet deception cannot be studied apart from intelligence, since intelligence is critical in designing and implementing deception operations as well as exposing them. In this last dimension of exposing deception, German strategic intelligence failed completely; worse still, it unwittingly became an important instrument in Allied deception. German strategic intelligence was unable to provide its high command with any useful clues on Allied strategy, intentions, capabilities or deception.

If the Allies intended to invade Sicily, Normandy, the northern

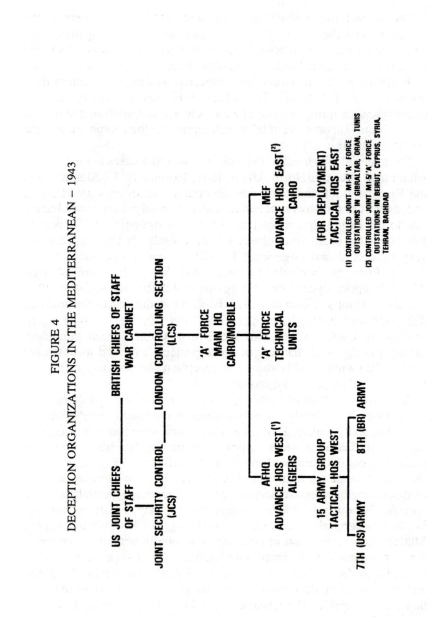

FIGURE 4

DECEPTION ORGANIZATIONS IN THE MEDITERRANEAN – 1943

sector of El Alamein, or land in Anzio, *good* operational and strategic intelligence ought to have given the German High Command a more specific warning. This does not mean the task was easy or even possible, but it is an ideal which good intelligence services aspire to reach. Allied intelligence was certainly not perfect and suffered from many failures, but its overall record was far better than that of the Germans. In this it was helped to a large extent by Ultra.

This discussion can be related directly to Professor Müller's example, the invasion of Sicily. German intelligence could at no time give the High Command a clear-cut answer to the question of where the main Allied thrust was to take place. Sardinia, the Peloponnese, and even Spain, Corsica and southern France were added to the list of possibilities. Even if, as Professor Müller claims, it was eventually clear that Sicily was the real target, such a warning came much too late to be effective. In addition, the warning did not discount major attacks in other locations and offered no clue as to where in Sicily the attack would occur. Be that as it may, the reactions of the German High Command most assuredly indicate its hesitation and inability to determine that Sicily was the target. The extent to which this indecision can be attributed to deception or poor intelligence is impossible and unnecessary to determine, for Allied deception and poor German intelligence reinforced each other.

It is clear in retrospect, but should also have been clear at the time to a high-quality intelligence organization, that the Allies could not have simultaneously invaded Sardinia, Sicily and the Peloponnese. They simply did not have the necessary landing craft. At no time was this recognized by German intelligence, which assumed the possibility of numerous simultaneous operations or at least of one major invasion in conjunction with two diversionary operations. A major achievement of Allied deception was the gradual construction of a notional order of battle accepted by and large as genuine by German intelligence. Discussed, for example, by David Mure in *Practice to Deceive*, this long-lasting, effective stratagem – *not* Operation Mincemeat – was the most important Allied deception operation preceding the invasion of Sicily, for it catered to the German perception of a threat to the Balkans at a much earlier time than Mincemeat. Mincemeat only reinforced German fears awakened earlier by a more important deception operation (such as the creation of the fictitious Twelfth Army). This is ignored by Professor Müller. The Allies repeated the same order-of-battle (OB) type of deception *before* the invasion of Normandy with similar results. In both cases, German intelligence overestimated the Allied OB by 80 to 100 per cent. (See Appendix 2 for OKW Estimates of the Allied OB in May 1944.) Incorrect identification of a few non-existent divisions as real would have been forgivable, but to make the same mistake with dozens of divisions, whose existence *should* have been corroborated by material evidence, was disastrous.

Even worse, German intelligence never properly understood that one of the Allies' cardinal operational principles was never to operate outside the range of air cover, particularly when one was planning a highly dangerous landing operation. This excluded Sardinia, Greece or Norway from any major landing operations. Yet the Allies themselves did not always agree on this principle right from the start. In 1941, 1942 and even later, Churchill seriously considered an invasion of Norway and was only dissuaded from this 'Gallipoli of the North' project by virtue of Alanbrooke's strenuous efforts. Sardinia was also considered as a target for invasion but in each case the impossibility of providing air cover was a major factor in the decision not to proceed. On the German side, Field Marshal Kesselring was one of the few to consider this possibility, which eventually enabled him to determine that Sicily was the Allies' true objective.

Müller also discusses two other factors that seriously undermined the quality of German intelligence as well as the German approach to strategic analysis in general. One can be described as German *ethnocentrism*, the other as the *whistling in the dark* syndrome. In the quotations cited earlïer, Müller repeatedly explains that the Germans tried to predict the course of Allied strategy on the basis of how they themselves might have acted. This approach would be rational only if the intelligence organization had absolutely no knowledge of the adversary. Otherwise, it is a poor substitute for good intelligence. Projection of one's own fears, procedures or expectations on an adversary is one of the cardinal sins of intelligence and strategic analysis in a world where strategy is neither purely rational nor symmetrical. The fact that Germany considered the Balkans to be a critical source of raw material did not mean that it was a top priority for the Western Allies. Germany may have been convinced that Sardinia was the key to victory in Italy, while the Allies did not necessarily consider it to be as important if it was out of range of their fighters or if their strategy in Italy was to divert and tie down German troops rather than seek a decisive victory. The fact that Norway was of critical value in Hitler's own mind did not bring it within Allied range of fighter cover or transform it into the most effective avenue of attack in north-west Europe. Similarly, to assume that the Pas de Calais would be the chosen location for the Allied invasion because that is how the Germans would have done it, is hardly a sound way to make intelligence estimates or strategic decisions. Just as almost every strategist can correctly determine the most obvious and rational course of action, he can also assume that the enemy will be equally aware of this possibility and prepared to counter it. While to a certain extent unavoidable, projection and ethnocentrism are very dangerous biases that must be overcome as much as possible. They facilitate self-deception as well as deception by the enemy. The combination of German staff methods, ethnocentrism, racism, and early victories rendered German intelligence and its high command very susceptible to the projection of its own strategic logic and preferences on others.

Müller mentions at least three times that the Germans knew they were the target of Allied deception. They circulated a memorandum by the *Wehrmachtführungsstab* to this effect; and at one point Hitler asked one of his military aides, 'Christian, couldn't this be a corpse they have deliberately planted on our hands?' This was 'whistling in the dark', because knowing that one is being deceived without knowing *how* is not always an advantage. Even if the police know that a crime is going to be committed every evening, they may not be able to prevent it unless more specific information is obtained.

A general warning to watch out for deception can be counter-productive because it places every piece of information in doubt, which may lead to paralysis and paranoia. The only constructive way to deal with deception is to unmask it – to find out how it is being implemented. This is the duty of intelligence and counter-intelligence. The Germans rarely succeeded in discovering deception. On occasions when deception failed to convince them, it was not because they had exposed it, but because they failed to pick up the bait. Mincemeat may not have been an important factor in determining German strategy but at least it was never exposed. Had the Germans recognized Operation Mincemeat as part of an Allied ruse, the results would have been quite different, for they would then have been able to identify Sicily as the Allies' true objective.

By dwelling on Operation Mincemeat and ignoring the more important notional order-of-battle deceptions, Müller appears to view deception as an *ad hoc* policy not as part of a continuing strategy; but since Mincemeat was only one scheme designed to reinforce the whole fabric of earlier deception operations, there is no justification for dealing with it in isolation. Viewing deception as a continuous policy may lead to a different evaluation of its worth. Indeed, after the invasion of Sicily, the Allies managed to protect and hence continue their deception operations in Italy (and elsewhere) with great success.

Professor Müller argues that because Operation Mincemeat was implemented only *after* the German strategy had already been formulated, those who credit this Allied ploy with so much success have fallen for the *post hoc ergo propter hoc* fallacy. This, however, is not a convincing argument. He cannot prove that it failed to have any influence simply because it came after the strategic decision had already been made. As is well known, a dog that does not bark can provide as much evidence as one that does. According to Professor Müller's line of argument, only a visible change in German strategy would constitute sufficient proof that the stratagem had succeeded. Yet the deceivers were not interested in bringing about any changes. Quite to the contrary, their deception was intended to *reinforce* – not contradict – existing German strategic concepts.[109] All that Müller can logically claim is that German strategy in southern Europe was decided before Operation Mincemeat. The evidence from German documents demonstrates rather convincingly that Mincemeat did indeed strengthen the existing German concepts and was therefore effective to at least some degree. The only positive way to prove that Mincemeat was a failure would have been to expose it as deceptive. Furthermore, Operation Mincemeat could only be effective because the Germans made earlier decisions that in turn were also influenced by Allied deception. It is very unusual and very difficult for deception to create new concepts for an enemy. It is much easier and more effective to reinforce those which already exist. For example, with or without deception, Hitler might have decided to identify the Pas de Calais as the Allies' chosen point for the invasion of Europe. All the deceivers did was to reinforce this concept and try their best to perpetuate it. How much of the success of Fortitude depended on Hitler's earlier decisions or on Allied deception is difficult to say. Without the kind of definitive proof provided by Garbo's 9 June message which was passed all the way up to Hitler and prevented German Panzer reinforcements from being sent to Normandy, Müller might have used the same reasoning to argue that deception was irrelevant because the Germans had decided long before to concentrate their troops in the Pas de Calais area; instead, he might have attributed the decision to Hitler's irrational obsession with the Pas de Calais and so on. In the light of the information acquired courtesy of the Allied deceivers, Hitler in fact made a very rational decision from his point of view.

Müller sets forth an array of independent strategic arguments to demonstrate that other factors, and not deception or Mincemeat, formed German strategy. Using his own arguments, it is possible to show why this is not convincing; had the Germans not been deceived or had their intelligence functioned better (two inseparable factors) they would have pursued a very different course of action! Effective strategy rests on a foundation of reliable intelligence. Had German intelligence warned Hitler that on 10 July at 0430 the Allies would invade Sicily from the south and southeast, he would have made very different decisions.

Müller himself supplies the best argument when quoting Wallach to the effect that German military planning always sought the most decisive battle of annihilation. If Hitler had known the place, time and date of the invasion, he could have decisively beaten the Allies on Sicily's beaches by replacing two weakened German divisions with four strong ones, thereby saving Italy, and significantly delaying the re-entry of the Allies to Europe. In a message to Churchill on 28 March 1943, Eisenhower warned of this risk:

> . . . if substantial German ground troops should be placed in the region (Sicily) prior to the attack, the chances for success become practically nil and the project should be abandoned.

In another message sent on 7 April 1943 he was more specific:

> . . by the term substantial is meant more than two German divisions.[110]

The validity of my argument is supported by Hitler's actions. This is how Sir Michael Howard commented on Hitler's actions immediately after the invasion of Sicily had begun:

> Hitler's own reaction was immediate. He ordered two more German formations, *1st parachute* and *29th Panzer Grenadier Division* to be hurried into Sicily to throw the invaders into the sea.[111]

The will to be decisive was surely there – but not the necessary intelligence to support it. The combination of Allied deception and poor German intelligence reduced Hitler's incentive to send more troops to Sicily before the attack started; indeed, as in Normandy, even after the invasion was under way, German planners at the OKH did not rule out the probability that it would be followed closely by another landing in Greece.[112] This is an excellent example of the decisive, if not always visible, role played by intelligence (and deception) in strategic planning.

Professor Müller argues that German strategy in southern Europe in 1943 was determined by the desire to secure the Balkans and keep Italy in the war. 'German reactions in the Mediterranean were . . . predominantly determined by one single motive, the fear of Italy's imminent collapse and/or defection'. The Germans should therefore have made it their first priority to defend Italy in Italy, not in the Balkans. After all, the occupation of Sicily or Sardinia was of more direct concern to Italy than the Balkans. It could be expected that the invasion of Sicily would bring about a more rapid Italian decision to defect. Why then did Hitler not send more troops to Sicily? This was not due to the consideration of Italian 'sensitivities' as much as it was a sign of uncertainty regarding the location of the Allied invasion. As long as Sicily did not appear to be threatened, Hitler could afford to consider Italian wishes. That the Germans viewed the Balkans as important for the defense of Italy makes sense only if they perceived no immediate threat to Italy itself. After all, invasion of Italy and Sicily was more of a direct threat to Italy's continued alliance with Germany. In sum, either Hitler and his generals made a mistake or they viewed a threat to the Balkans (and via the Balkans also to Italy) as more imminent. If the latter choice were correct, then their strategic priorities in the first half of 1943 would make more sense. In reaching such conclusions they were no doubt convinced in part by the Allied notional threat to the Balkans.

As Müller claims, Montagu may have analysed only a small number of documents. What matters, however, is the importance of the documents rather than their number. To begin with, Montagu selected two very important German Naval War Staff documents which unmistakably indicate the German reliance on Major Martin's documents. This led to changes in German dispositions and increased direction of attention to Sardinia and the Peloponnese with a corresponding reduction of troops in Sicily. Montagu also furnishes a facsimile of a document from the German Naval Archives in Tambach which evaluates one of Major Martin's documents that went all the way up to Dönitz. (The evaluation accepted the document as authentic.) Müller goes on to assert that the German Naval Command and the Naval Conferences with Hitler were not important. Perhaps this was so, although it is difficult to see Dönitz, the Führer's last heir, as an unimportant decision-maker. The Führer's Naval Conference of 14 May 1943 tells us that Hitler, having 'discovered the key to Anglo-Saxon order' (*sic*) did not consider Sicily as the target but rather Sardinia and the Peloponnese.[113] Even if he eventually changed his mind, as Professor Müller claims, he did not view Sicily as the target in mid-May 1943. Implementing strategy, building fortifications, laying minefields, transferring troops and the like are all time-consuming procedures. Therefore, even if by the first week of July Hitler had changed his mind and recognized Sicily as the main target (which is possible), the warning came too late. To be of value, strategic warning must be provided in time for the recipient to take appropriate action. Ironically, what may have finally given the Germans their first solid clue that Sicily was the real Allied invasion target, was the capture of Pantellaria on 11 June 1943. This operation appears not to have been co-ordinated with the deception cover operations and was not carefully evaluated as risking the disclosure of Sicily as the real target of the

Allies' next offensive. It was only after the seizure of Pantellaria that Kesselring ordered the Hermann Göring Division to move to Sicily. Sir David Hunt contributes the anecdotal, but apparently genuine, information that Lieutenant Colonel F.K. Von Plehwa, who served as the Assistant Military Attaché under General von Rintelen, said that, '. . . he well remembered listening in to a telephone conversation between his chief and Alfred Jodl, Chef der *Wehrmachtführungsstab*, some time in the second half of May 1943. Von Rintelen was talking about the imminent invasion of Sicily, when Jodl shouted impatiently, "You can forget about Sicily, we know it is Greece". Jodl was, of course, on the record to the same effect in OKH documents'.[114]

All of this evidence was discovered after the war in German archives. The Allies, however, knew at the time from Ultra intercepts that their bait had been swallowed, 'hook, line and sinker by the right people'. This is the Ultra intercept:[115]

REF: 779   MIL 1955 CO
REF: CX/MSS/2571/T4   IN TWO   Parts Part One
                          XX
INFORMATION FROM SUPREME COMMAND ARMED FORCES, OPERATIONS STAFF, ARMY TO AIC IN C SOUTH AND C IN C & C IN C SOUTH EAST ON TWELFTH. OPERATIONS STAFF OF SUPREME COMMANDS NAVE AND GAF & GAF INFORMED. QUOTE ACCORDING TO A SOURCE WITH [sic] MAY BE REGARDED AS ABSOLUTELY RELIABLE, AN ENEMY LANDING UNDERTAKING ON A LARGE SCALE IS PROJECTED IN THE NEAR FUTURE IN BOTH THE EASTERN AND THE WESTERN MEDITERRANEAN. ((MIL 1955 & 1955 CO 876 & 876 IN TWO PARTS PART ONE)) THE UNDERTAKING IN THE EASTERN MED & MED HAS AS ITS OBJECTIVE THE COAST NEAR KALAMATA & KALAMATA AND THE COASTAL SECTOR SOUTH OF CAPE ARAXOS & CAPE ARAXOS (BOTH PLACES ON THE WEST COAST OF THE PELOPONNESE & PELOPONNESE). THE LANDING NEAR KALAMATA & KALAMATA IS TO BE CARRIED OUT BY FIVE SIX INFANTRY DIVISION, AND THAT NEAR CAPE ARAXOS & CAPE ARAXOS
                          33
EMJ/   15//Z/15/5/43
KVB

BY THE REINFORCED FIVE INFANTRY DIVISION. IT IS NOT CLEAR WHETHER BOTH DIVISION [sic] WILL OPERATE AT FULL STRENGTH OR ONLY WITH ELEMENTS. ((ML 1955 & 1955 TWO/AND FINAL)) IF THE FORMER WERE THE CASE ABOUT TWO OR THREE WEEKS WOULD BE NEEDED BEFORE THE BEGINNING OF THE LANDING. SHOULD ONLY ELEMENTS OF

THE DIVISIONS OPERATE, THE LANDING COULD TAKE PLACE AT ANY TIME. THE COVER-NAME FOR THE LANDING IS HUSKY & HUSKY. A FEINT AGAINST THE DODECANESE & DODECANESE MUST BE RECKONED WITH UNQUOTE. COMMENT COLON KNOWS THAT FURTHER INFORMATION (PRESUMABLY DEALING WITH WESTERN MEDITERRANEAN & WESTERN MEDITERRANEAN) NATURE OF WHICH UNKNOWN THERE, WAS TOO [*sic*] BE SENT TO OTHER ADDRESSEES NAMED ABOVE, BUT NOT & NOT TO CHARLIE IN CHARLIE SOUTH EAST

1551Z/15/5/43

The documents cited by Montagu, Howard and others may not prove conclusively that deception was decisive in influencing German strategy in 1943, but they do provide strong circumstantial evidence that it worked. In the final analysis, Müller's evidence is not more direct.

What about Müller's Norwegian example? Here he is correct in the sense that the Allied deception, while again not exposed, failed to have a direct effect on German strategic decisions. This is evident from a German intelligence document of 4 March 1944 cited by Hesketh.

> Since the operations of the enemy command in the present stage of the war all mean the tying up of German forces on subsidiary fronts, or alternatively their removal from the decisive Atlantic front to subsidiary fronts, and as the enemy has already been successful in this sense in Italy, it seems thoroughly possible that he has come to a like decision in the Scandinavian area. The hitherto inadequate data do not allow us to call this certain or even probable.
>
> It seems nevertheless that henceforward enhanced preparedness on the Norwegian coast and above all on intensification of air reconnaissance over the whole of the North Sea area are indispensable. This measure appears to constitute the only means, which has any prospect of success, of avoiding surprises such as those of the Sicily and Nettuno landings.[116]

It is worth noting that even a German intelligence officer believed that the Germans had been surprised in both Sicily and Anzio.

Again, deception and intelligence work in general cannot be separated. Without air cover support and sufficient troops, the Allies had no intention of invading Norway. Good intelligence ought to have exposed the notional order of battle projected from Scotland. In the absence of adequate intelligence, however, the Germans could not afford to ignore the possibility of a diversionary threat to Norway, particularly given Hitler's obsession with the idea. In the end, Hitler and the German High Command deceived themselves and tied down an average of 250,000 soldiers in Norway.

What about the possibility that the Allies and some authors overestimated the contribution of Fortitude North? The most telling and relevant conclusions regarding this are in the Hesketh Report:

> Inasmuch as FORTITUDE NORTH aimed at convincing the Germans that certain forces were located in Scotland for a certain purpose when in fact those forces either were not there at all or at least were not there for the purpose stated, the plan, through the operation of Special Means, will be seen to have succeeded. The Germans accepted the danger of a diversionary attack against Scandinavia. They also accepted the presence of most of the formations which we had created or appropriated for the purpose of exercising that threat. To what extent did FORTITUDE NORTH succeed in tying down additional forces in Norway and Denmark? We have it from Jodl that Hitler had always been obsessed by the fear of an Allied attack on Scandinavia. It would not have required more than 100,000 troops to garrison the two countries and keep the native population in subjection. *In fact the average number of occupational troops had been in the region of 250,000 ever since Norway was first occupied.* The balance of 150,000 was to be regarded as an insurance against invasion. In these circumstances any minor troop movement that may have occurred in the spring of 1944 (and it is true that the garrison was increased at that time by one formation, the 89th Infantry Division) loses its significance, and one is thus forced to the conclusion, if one accepts Jodl's view, that FORTITUDE NORTH, though successful as a deceptive operation, had no influence upon the course of the war. It was, in fact, a case of the fly on the axle-tree.[117] [My emphasis].

Playing the role of devil's advocate, Professor Müller challenges his readers to reconsider much that has been written to date on deception as practiced during the Second World War. His argument that deception has almost always been examined with an overemphasis on the Allied viewpoint and that its success has often been taken for granted without a thorough study of the German decision-making process certainly merits very serious consideration. His methodological insistence on the fact that deception cannot be studied in isolation is well taken. The history of deception as well as the role of intelligence in general during the Second World War will require much more thinking by those seeking to determine its actual importance.

Throughout the history of warfare there has been no other period in which intelligence and deception occupied such a crucial position. Furthermore, the existence of detailed documentation on the Allied side regarding its total intelligence effort also makes it the first time in history that one can trace the role of intelligence in war with some measure of detail. Yet, as Professor Müller suggests, there is not always a direct linear connection between intelligence effort and success or failure in war. Such a methodological caveat should serve to provide the impetus for further detailed research and reflection on this subject.

The preceding detailed analysis which addresses Professor Müller's argument at length is the best tribute to its elegance and explanatory power. Professor Müller has made an important and stimulating contribution by causing those interested in the history and influence of deception in the Second World War to re-examine their views on the subject. After much thought, I cannot avoid the conclusion that, if anything, the role of Allied deception in the Second World War has been underestimated to date.

NOTES

1. All quotes are from Carl V. Clausewitz, *On War*, edited and translated by Michael Howard and Peter Paret (Princeton, N.J.: Princeton University Press, 1976), Book
3, Chapter 10, 'Cunning', p.202.
2. Cyril Falls, *Military Operations Egypt and Palestine* (London: H.M.S.O., 1930) Vol. I, p.32.
3. Quoted from R.F. Hesketh, 'Fortitude: A History of Strategic Deception in North Western Europe April, 1943 to May, 1945', unpublished after-action history of deception operations in north-west Europe, primarily those preceding the invasion of Normandy. February 1949, 259 pages, to be cited below as the Hesketh Report.
4. I have suggested elsewhere a somewhat different definition: 'Deception can be defined as a purposeful attempt by the deceiver to manipulate the perceptions of the target's decisionmakers in order to gain a competitive advantage.' Michael I. Handel, *Military Deception in Peace and War* (Jerusalem, Israel: The Leonard Davis Institute for International Relations, 1985, Jerusalem Papers on Peace Problems, Number 38, 1985), p.3.
5. Sun Tzu, *The Art of War*, translated by Samuel B. Griffith, (New York: Oxford University Press, 1982), p.66. Sun Tzu adds:

    Therefore, when capable, feign incapacity; when active, inactivity; when near, make it appear that you are far away; when far away, that you are near. Offer the enemy a bait to lure him; feign disorder and strike him. Pretend inferiority and encourage his arrogance. Attack where he is unprepared; sally out when he does not expect you (pp.66–7). Now war is based on deception. Move when it is advantageous and create changes in the situation by dispersal and concentration of forces. (p.106).

6. Clausewitz, *On War*, p.202.
7. For a comprehensive discussion of the principles of the art of war, see: John I. Alger, *The Quest for Victory: The History of the Principles of War* (Westport, CT.:

Greenwood Press, 1982). The basic principles of war differ from period to period and from army to army. A typical list of such principles will include: The Principle of the Objective; The Principle of the Offensive; The Principle of Mass; The Principle of Economy of Force; The Principle of Maneuver; The Principle of Unity of Command; The Principle of Security; The Principle of Surprise; The Principle of Simplicity (Alger, *The Quest for Victory*, p.XI.)

8. G.P.R. James, *The History of Chivalry* (New York: A.L. Fowle, 1900), p.28.

9. From the introduction of Neal Wood to Niccoló Machiavelli, *The Art of War* (Indianapolis: Bobbs-Merrill, 1965), pp.XXIV–XXV.

10. This attitude is reflected in a quote from Admiral De Roebeck's observance of the landing in Gallipoli. It is used by Liddell Hart in his book, *Strategy* (New York: Praeger, 1968). (Sec. Rev. Ed.) 'Gallant fellows those soldiers, they always go for the thickest place in the fence' (p.15).

   In Renoir's film, *La Grande Illusion*, the dialogue between the French and German commandants, who wish they could still continue fighting according to the old rules and agree that in fact they have more in common with each other than with their own soldiers, is also representative of the chivalrous ethic of war.

11. For ideological and racist tension that eliminates all the traditions of chivalry and moderation see, for example, John W. Dower, *War Without Mercy: Race and Power in the Pacific War* (New York: Pantheon, 1986). Also Omer Bartov, *The Eastern Front, 1941–1945* (London: Macmillan, 1986), and 'The Barbarisation of Warfare, 1941–1945', Ph.D. thesis, Oxford University, 1983.

12. C.W.C. Oman, *The Art of War in the Middle Ages A.D. 378–1515* (Ithaca, NY: Great Seal Books, 1963), p.34.

13. Ibid., pp.43–4.

14. 'Generally in war the best policy is to take a state intact; to ruin it is inferior to this. To capture the enemy's army is better than to destroy it; to take intact a battalion, a company or a five-man squad is better than to destroy them. For to win 100 victories in 100 battles is not the acme of skill. To subdue the enemy without fighting is the acme of skill'. Sun Tzu, *The Art of War*, p.77. See also *Maurice's Strategikon: Handbook of Byzantine Military Strategy*, translated by George T. Dennis (Philadelphia: University of Pennsylvania Press, 1984).

15. On the changes in the international system as a result of the French Revolution and the influence of ideological considerations on the level of tension and attitudes of states to each other see, for example: Kyung-Won Kim, *Revolution and International System: A Study for the Breakdown of International Stability* (New York: New York University Press, 1970), and Richard N. Rosecrance, *Action and Reaction in World Politics: International Systems in Perspective* (Boston: Little, Brown & Co., 1963).

16. Clausewitz, *On War*, p.204.

17. Ibid., p.282.

18. Ibid., p.203.

19. See Michael I. Handel, (ed.), *Clausewitz and Modern Strategy* (London: Frank Cass, 1986), pp. 51–95: 'Clausewitz in the Age of Modern Technology', by Michael I. Handel.

20. See Falls, *Military Operations in Egypt and Palestine,* Chapters I–II, pp.1–44. For an excellent article also Yigal Shefi, 'Stratagem and Deception in the Third Battle of Gaza', *Maarachot* (Hebrew) IDF Journal, Nos. 302–303, (March/April, 1986), pp.56–61.

21. For the importance of utilizing real troop formations whenever possible for the creation of a notional order of battle, see: the *Hesketh Report* and David Mure, *Practice to Deceive* (London: William Kimber, 1977).

22. For Operation Mincemeat, see: Ewen Montagu, *The Man Who Never Was* (Philadelphia: J.B. Lippincott, 1954); and *Beyond Top Secret ULTRA* (New York: Howard McCann, 1978), Chap. 13, pp.143–51. For a balanced account, see: Michael Howard, *Grand Strategy* (London: HMSO, 1970), Vol. 4, August 1942 – September 1943, p.370; F.H. Hinsley, *British Intelligence in the Second World War* (New York: Cambridge University Press, 1984), Vol. III, p.78; F.W. Deakin,

The Brutal Friendship (New York: Harper and Row, 1962), pp.346–57; Roger Morgan, 'The Man Who Almost Is', *After the Battle*, No. 54, 1986, 1–25.

23. On Meinerzhagen's 'haversack ruse' see: Falls, *Military Operations Egypt and Palestine*, Part I, pp.30–31; Colonel A.P. Wavell, *The Palestine Campaign* (London: Constable, 1936), (3rd ed.) p.106; Anthony Cave Brown, *Bodyguard of Lies* (New York: Harper & Row, 1975), pp.280–81; Meinerzhagen, *Army Diary, 1899–1926* (London: Oliver and Boyd, 1960); Sir, Major General George Aston, *Secret Service* (New York: Cosmopolitan Books, 1930), Chap. 16, pp.201–16; Shefi, 'Deception and Stratagem in the Third Battle of Gaza'.

24. Wavell, *Palestine Campaign*, pp.106–7.

25. See Charles Cruickshank, *Deception in World War II* (New York: Oxford University Press, 1980), pp.19–33; Mure, *Practice to Deceive* pp.130–47; David Fisher, *The War Magician* (New York: Howard McCann, 1983).

26. Wavell, *The Palestine Campaign*, pp.107–8.

27. Ibid., p.112.

28. Ibid., p.201.

29. Shefi, 'Deception and Stratagem in the Third Battle of Gaza'.

30. Falls, *Military Operations Egypt and Palestine*, Part I, p.43.

31. Wavell, *The Palestine Campaign*, p.124.

32. The best discussion on deception in the Italian campaign is still Sir David Hunt, *A Don At War* (London: William Kimber, 1966), particularly Chap. 15, p.252; Brigadier L.J.C. Molony, *The Mediterranean and the Middle East* (London: HMSO, 1984), Vol. 6, part I, Chap. 2.

33. See Wavell, *The Palestine Campaign*, p.203. Also B.H. Liddell Hart, *Colonel Lawrence* (New York: Halcyon House, 1937), new and enlarged ed., Chaps. 17–18, pp. 248–79; Falls, *Military Operations Egypt and Palestine*, Part II; W.T. Massey, *Allenby's Final Triumph* (New York: E.P. Putton, 1920), Chap. 8, pp.95–111.

34. Liddell Hart, *Colonel Lawrence*, p.249.

35. From General Wavell's introduction in Dudley Clarke's book, *Seven Assignments* (London: Jonathan Cape, 1948), p.7. Wavell's early deception initiatives and contribution to the use of deception in the Second World War have not as of now received the attention they deserve. Wavell issued a short order in July 1942 on 'Ruses and Stratagems of War' which can be found in General Sir Archibald Wavell, *Speaking Generally: Broadcasts and Addresses in Time of War, 1939–1943* (London: Macmillan, 1946), pp.80–83. See also his *The Palestine Campaign* and his biography by John Conell Wavell, *Scholar and Soldier* (London: Collins, 1964).

   David Mure goes so far as to suggest that: '. . . the General's lifetime conviction and mastery of the value of strategic deception of which he, and not Sir Winston Churchill as has sometimes been suggested, was the originator in World War Two' (*Practice to Deceive*, p.19).

36. Major General I.S.O., Playfair, *The Mediterranean and Middle East* (London: HMSO, 1954), Vol. I, p.362.

37. See Leonard Mosley, *The Cat and the Mice* (London: Arthur Barker, 1958); Major A.W. Sansom, *I Spied Spies* (London: George Harrap, 1965); Mure, *Master of Deception* (London: William Kimber, 1980), Chap. 7, also *Practice to Deceive*, pp.30–31.

38. Mure, *Practice to Deceive*, p.23.

39. Playfair, *The Mediterranean and Middle East*, Vol. I, p.274.

40. See Dennis Wheatley, 'Deception in World War II', *RUSI*, Vol. 121, No. 3 (September 1976), p.87.

41. Hesketh Report, p.17 (Noel Wild is not mentioned by name).

42. Wheatley, 'Deception in World War II', 87.

43. J.C. Masterman, *On the Chariot Wheel* (Oxford: Oxford University Press, 1975), p.22.

44. Insufficient co-ordination can lead to conflicts of interest and contradictions between different deception agencies in different regions – or with other interests

of other organizations and activities. In the winter of 1915, Admiral Blinker Hall and Lt. Col. Drake of MI5 initiated a notional threat invading the Belgian coast and Schleswig Holstein through a double agent system controlled by MI5. The information received and accepted as genuine by German intelligence led to German reinforcement of the threatened areas and to a large scale concentrated movement of the German Navy which was interpreted by British Military Intelligence – which was not aware of the original deception plan – as a possible threat of invasion of England. Better co-ordination between various intelligence authorities in England could have avoided unnecessary confusion and alarms. As was mentioned above, however, until the end of the First World War deception was still primarily an activity left to the uncoordinated initiative of individual commanders. See Patrick Beesly, *Room 40: British Naval Intelligence 1914–1918* (New York: Harcourt, 1982), pp.67–9. Also Admiral Sir William James, *Eyes of the Navy* (London: Methuen, 1955), pp.72–3.

45. Hesketh Report, p.174.
46. Mure, *Practice to Deceive*, Chap. 6, pp.93–104.
47. Cruickshank, *Deception in World War II*, Chaps. 6–8, pp.85–124.
48. Ibid., p.19.
49. The goals of the double-cross system were defined by Masterman as:
    1. To control the enemy system, or as much of it as we could get our hands on
    2. To catch fresh spies when they appeared
    3. To gain knowledge of the personalities and methods of the German Secret Service
    4. To obtain information about the code and cypher work of the German Services
    5. To get evidence of enemy plans and intentions from the questions asked by them
    6. To influence enemy plans by the answers sent to the enemy
    7. To deceive the enemy about our plans and intentions
    Masterman, *The Double Cross System*, p.XIV, pp.8–9, also *On the Chariot Wheel*, p.221. As can be seen from this list, the use of double agents as a major link in the deception process came only as a last priority and was not contemplated when the system was originally created.
50. Hesketh Report, p. 22.
51. Beesly, *Room 40*, pp.67–9.
52. Brigadier Dudley Clarke, quoted by Mure in *Practice to Deceive*, p.14.
53. See Juan Pujol, *Garbo* (London: Weidenfeld & Nicolson, 1986). See also, Dusko Popov, *Spy/Counterspy* (New York: Grosset & Dunlap, 1974).
54. Hesketh Report, pp.175–6.
55. See David Kahn, *Hitler's Spies: German Military Intelligence in World War II*, pp.523–47.
56. See Kahn, *Hitler's Spies*. Also Peter R. Black, *Ernst Klatenbruner Ideological Soldier of the Third Reich* (Princeton, NJ: Princeton University Press, 1984), Chapter 6, pp.176–217.
57. In his long political career, Churchill played a critical role in the founding and development of the British intelligence community. Of particular importance was his support of Ultra and all deception activities. A special study dedicated to Churchill as an intelligence consumer remains to be written. Much information can be found in his official biography by Gilbert and in books written by, among others, Andrew, Beesly, Roskill, and McLachlan.
58. Michael I. Handel, *The Diplomacy of Surprise* (Cambridge, MA: Harvard Center for International Affairs, 1981).
59. Hesketh Report, p.171. The conclusions of the Hesketh Report are also reprinted in Donald C. Daniel and Katherine Herbig, (eds.), *Strategic Military Deception* (New York: Pergamon Press, 1981), pp.233–45.
60. Michael I. Handel, 'Intelligence and the Problem of Strategic Surprise', in *The Journal of Strategic Studies*, Vol. 7, No. 3 (Sept. 1984), 229–81.
61. Richard J. Heuer, 'Strategic Deception: A Psychological Perspective', *International Studies Quarterly*, Vol. 25 (June 1981), 294–327.

62. Donald McLachlan, *Room 39: A Study in Naval Intelligence* (New York: Atheneum, 1968), p.366.
63. See Pujol, *Garbo*; Popov, *Spy/Counterspy*. See attached schematic chart of Garbo's notional network of spies 'recruited' by him in England. (Source: *Hesketh Report*, p.24 and *Garbo*.)
64. See Hesketh Report, Appendix 14, JOSEPHINE and FUSAG, pp.245–6.
65. Michael I. Handel, 'Quantity versus Quality: Numbers do Count', *The Journal of Strategic Studies*, Vol. 4, No. 3 (Sept. 1981), 225-70. Also in Samuel P. Huntington, *The Strategic Imperative* (Cambridge, MA: Ballinger, 1982), pp.193–228.
66. Hunt, *A Don At War*, pp.254–6.
67. On technological deception, see Michael I. Handel, 'Technological Surprise In War', *Intelligence and National Security*, Vol. 2, No. 1 (January 1987), 5–53.
68. Clausewitz, *On War*, p.42.
    LCS made the following comments on the teaching of deception in an answer to U.S. inquiries:

> Here we actually tried at the end of the war to write a manual and completely failed. The answer seems to be given in the first five chapters of the 'History'. Military deception is based on certain main principles, but the methods to be used in gaining the objective depend upon developments in warfare, the circumstances of each case, and the character and organization of your enemy. All these change, and all you can do is to study what was done in the past so that you may apply the lessons of the past to the problems that may arise. You may in fact have to devise entirely new methods. I think the comparison made by Brigadier Dudley Clarke when discussing this with Colonel Sweeney puts it best. You can study a masterpiece by Rembrandt to see how he deals with a certain subject, but nobody attempts to lay down firm rules based on Rembrandt's painting technique and materials as to how anyone should paint, shall we say, a street scene in New York today.
>
> The first thing in developing deception techniques must be a study of your potential enemy, his characteristics and the terrain in which you may have to fight him. As a result of this study you may come to certain conclusions and the lessons of the past will be valuable in showing how adaptation, improvisation and ingenuity can cope with the most baffling problems. One need only mention deception in the Middle East, North West Europe and the Far East. The methods were in many cases quite different, adapted to the different terrain and character of the enemy.
>
> From File RG 319 *Cover and Deception*, Folder 77, Box 4, entry 101, Modern Military Records, National Archives, Washington, D.C.

69. Hesketh Report, p.3.
70. Mure, *Master of Deception*, p.273.
71. Hesketh Report, p.3.
72. Ewen Montagu, *Beyond Top Secret ULTRA*, pp.140–41.
73. Hesketh Report, p. 173.
74. Mure, *Master of Deception*, p.274.
75. Hesketh Report, p.17.
76. Mure, *Master of Deception*, p.274.
77. Hesketh Report, pp.12–13.
78. Ibid., p.13.
79. Ibid., p.15.
80. Ibid., p.175.
81. See Mure, *Master of Deception* for a critical analysis of Cockade/Starkey, pp. 220–24; Cruickshank, *Deception in World War II*, Chap. 5, pp.61–84; *Hesketh Report*, Chap. 2, pp.5–6; Pujol, *Garbo*, pp.95–100.
82. Cruickshank, *Deception in World War II*, p.80.
83. Ibid., p.84.
84. Ibid., p.72.
85. Ibid., pp.62–3.
86. Mure, *Master of Deception*, p.222.

87. Ibid.
88. See Alvin Coox, 'Flawed Perception and Its Effect Upon Operational Thinking: The Case of the Japanese Army 1937–1941', in Michael I. Handel, (ed.), *Intelligence and Military Operations*, forthcoming in 1988 as a special issue of *Intelligence and National Security*.
89. Richard K. Betts, *Surprise Attack: Lessons for Defense Planning* (Washington, D.C.: The Brookings Institution, 1982).
90. Clausewitz, *On War*, p.158.
91. Ibid., p.183.
92. Karl Popper, *The Poverty of Historicism* (New York: Harper and Row, 1964), p.12.
93. David Hackett Fischer, *Historian's Fallacies: Toward a Logic of Historical Thought* (New York: Harper & Row, 1970), p.172.
94. From an additional typed introductory letter to the Hesketh Report, by Roger Hesketh, p.5.
95. Major General de Guingand, *Operation Victory* (New York: Charles Scribner's Sons, 1947), pp.146–7.
96. Winston S. Churchill, *The Second World War*, Vol. 4, *The Hinge of Fate* (Boston: Houghton Mifflin, 1950), p.546. See also John North, (ed.), *The Alexander Memoirs, 1940–1945* (London: Cassell, 1962), p.25.
97. Captain Basil H. Liddell Hart, *The Tanks* (London: Cassell, 195), Vol. II, p.219.
98. F.H. Hinsley, *British Intelligence in the Second World War: Its Influence on Strategy and Operations* (New York: Cambridge University Press, 1981), Vol. 2, p. 416.
99. Correlli Barnett, *The Desert Generals*, second edition, (London: Allen & Unwin, 1983), p.263.
100. Michael Carver, *Al Alamein* (New York: Macmillan, 1962), p.39.
101. Cruickshank, *Deception in World War II*, p.23.
102. Sir David Hunt, in a letter to the author, 21 January 1987.
103. See Mure, *Practice to Deceive*, pp.30–31 and *Master of Deception*, pp.118–23.
104. On the dangers of using a small sample in cases of deception see 'Deception Maxims: Fact and Folklore,' (Princeton: Machtech and ORD/CIA, April 1980), pp.9–11. 'The law of small numbers'.
105. Mure, *Practice to Deceive*, Chap. 6, pp.93–105; Cruickshank, *Deception in World War II*, Chap. 4, pp.50–61.
106. Quoted from a paper entitled, 'Military and Political Planning and Aims in 1944', presented by Sir David Hunt to a conference in December 1984 as a representative of the British National Committee of Historians of the Second World War, p.7.
107. Hesketh Report, Preface, p.VIII.
108. Fischer, *Historian's Fallacies*, pp.104ff.
109. See, for example, 'Deception Maxims: Fact and Folklore', pp.5–9. Magruder's principle – the exploitation of perceptions. This maxim has been chosen as the most important, i.e., number 1, by the authors of this monograph.
110. Michael Howard, *Grand Strategy*, August 1942 – September 1943, Vol. 4, (London: HMSO, 1970), p.368.
111. Ibid., p.468.
112. Ibid.
113. Führer conferences on Naval affairs in *Brassey's Naval Annual 1948*, ed. Rear Admiral H.G. Thursfield, (New York: Macmillan, 1948), p. 327.
114. Letter written by Sir David Hunt to Constantine Fitzgibbon dated 16 May 1977.
115. The original Ultra message can be found at the U.S. Army Military History Institute (MHI) at Carlisle Barracks, PA. Reel 127 5 to 15 May 1943 ML dated 15 May 1944. See also F.H. Hinsley, *et. al.*, *British Intelligence in the Second World War*, Vol. 3 (New York: Cambridge University Press, 1984), pp.78–9 (Chapter 3).
116. Hesketh Report, p.81.
117. Ibid., p.83.

APPENDIX I

From a letter written by Brigadier Dudley Clarke
to Major General Lowell Books of the U.S. Army*

The first concerns the scope of the organization's activities and, in particular, the directions in which they should be focused. Until this is properly understood there will be a tendency to muddle Deception with Psychological Warfare and even to suggest that the same instrument can serve both purposes. A moment's examination of the aims of the two will show this to be fundamentally unsound, and any attempt to mix both in practice will be highly dangerous. Nevertheless that danger is often present and is sometimes curiously difficult to dispel. The essential difference lies of course in the audience for whom the two organizations cater. Psychological warfare starts at the apex of a triangle and endeavours to spread its arms as wide as it can to embrace the broadest possible base. It matters little if many of its audience can detect the origin of their messages, nor if a privileged few can recognize distortion of the truth; its appeal is to the masses and it is unlikely to influence the thought or actions of the enlightened inner circles of the General Staff. Deception, on the other hand, works in exactly the opposite way. It starts at the base of the triangle and concentrates its influence towards a single point at the apex; its essential aim is to conceal the origin of its messages by directing them upon this single point from as many different directions as possible. It cares little for the thoughts and actions of the masses, but it *must* penetrate directly into the innermost circles of all. Its audience is narrowed down to a small handful of individuals, as represented by the senior members of the enemy's Intelligence Staff, and sometimes even to a single individual in the person of the Head of that Intelligence Staff. If they can influence him to accept as true the evidence they have manufactured for his benefit, then they have accomplished their entire aim, since it is only through the Head of the Intelligence that any enemy commander received the impression of his opponent upon which he has to base his plan of operation. It is necessary, therefore, that the single-purposeness of any deception machine should be recognized from the start and its shape dictated by the overriding need to concentrate every ounce of its diverse efforts upon that one ultimate target. As a corollary it follows that those who direct the deception machine must have an adequate knowledge of the small group of men on whom all their activities are focused, of their national characteristics, their languages, thoughts and professional methods with all their strengths and their weaknesses.

It is this note on personalities which leads to the next principle, which is a foundation stone in the successful application of deception. Deception is essentially an Art and not a Science, and those who practise it must be recognized as falling into the category of artists and not of artisans. This is difficult to accept in professional military circles where it is widely believed that the Art of War can be taught to the average educated man even though he may have little aptitude for it. But, nevertheless, it is true that frequently highly qualified and highly intelligent staff officers fail completely to cope with the work, although they do brilliantly

* File RG319, *Cover and Deception*, Folder 77, Box 43, Entry 101, Modern Military Records, National Archives, Washington, D.C. Letter from Lt. Col. E.J. Sweeney to Col. W.A. Harris, 18 December 1946.

afterwards on the Operations and other staffs. What they may lack is the sheer ability to create, to make something out of nothing, to conceive their own original notion and then to clothe it with realities until eventually it would appear as a living fact. And, since that is precisely what the Deception Staff must do all the time, it follows that the art of creation is an essential attribute in all who are charged with such work. To expect those who have not this art to produce the required results will lead to risks beyond that of mere failure.

If this thesis is accepted it is easy to see why one brain – and one alone – must be left unhampered to direct any one deception plan. It is after all little more than a drama played upon a vast stage, and the author and producer should be given a free hand in the theatre of war as in the other theatre. (Also, of course, in both they must have the necessary qualifications to justify that confidence.) It is not a bad parallel to compare a Commander in the Field with the Impresario who wants to mount a successful play at his theatre. He decides on the type of play he wants – drama, comedy, musical, etc. – and instructs an author to produce a script. Having accepted the script, he appoints a producer to mount the play. From that point onwards he may well leave everything else to those two, and look only to the results obtained. Provided these are satisfactory, the impresario who is not himself an author or producer wisely leaves them to rule the cast, scenery, costumes and all else that goes to make the play. The wise Commander-in-Chief will follow the same example. In his case the matter is simplified by the fact that the head of his Deception Staff doubles in the roles of author and producer. The Commander therefore tells him what sort of Deception he needs, examines the plans produced for him with the required aim in view, and, once the final version is approved, watches only the results and leaves all else to his specialist. In both peace and war, however, the Chief is the best judge of the results: in both cases he assesses them by the reactions of the audience (or the enemy), and should interfere in proportion to the degree in which they fail or succeed to achieve the object he himself has set. . . .

And it is this mention of the 'object' which brings me to the last of the principles I have tried to enunciate. For the theatrical impresario this presents no difficulty – all he wants is to see the audience moved to tears, laughter or rhythm in concern with the play – but to the General it is a problem which merits most careful thought. His audience is the enemy and he alone must decide what he wants them to do – to advance? to withdraw? to thin out or to reinforce? Whatever he chooses, the main point is that his 'object' must be to make the enemy do something. It matters nothing what the enemy THINKS, it is only what he DOES that can affect the battle. It is therefore wrong, and always wrong, for any Commander to tell his Deception Staff to work out a plan 'to make the enemy think we are going to do so-and-so'. It may be that the Plan will succeed but that the enemy will react to it in a totally unexpected way, upon which the Commander will probably blame the Deception Staff who have in fact produced exactly the results they set for. It is this boomerang effect which has made many people apprehensive of using the Deception weapon, and it cannot be stressed too strongly that, if used in the wrong way, it can prove a real danger. But there is one sure way to avoid any possible risk and that is to get the OBJECT right. Given a correct 'object' the Deception Plan may fail but it cannot in any do harm. Give it a wrong 'object' and it will invariably give wrong results. Our theatrical impresario after all will not attempt to dictate to the author the plot of the play, but that is precisely what the General does who tells his Deception Staff that he wants the enemy to be made to 'think' something. It assumes a knowledge of the enemy's likely reactions which the Deception Staff should know from experience very much better than the General. It is for the latter to say what he wants them to do, and for the specialists to decide what the enemy must be made to think in order to induce them to act in the manner required. Perhaps an illustration will explain this best. In the early part of 1941 General Wavell wanted the Italian reserves drawn to the South in order to ease his entry into Northern Abyssinia. He considered this might be done by inducing them to reinforce the captured province of British Somaliland, and he gave instructions for a Deception Plan to be worked to persuade the Italians that we were about to invade Somaliland. Deception was new then and on the surface that appeared to all concerned to be a perfectly laudable object. The Plan, innocently ignoring the real object of influencing the location of the enemy reserves, was entirely successful; but the results were totally unexpected. In face of the threatened invasion, the Italians evacuated British Somaliland. Not only had General Wavell to draw upon his own meagre forces to re-occupy the country, but the Italian garrison was freed to swell the forces in the North which were to block our advance at Koren. Had a different object been chosen, quite a different deception plan would have emerged and perhaps a quite different effect produced upon the actions of the enemy.

That concludes this brief review; and I will end by summarizing that to be successful any Deception Organization needs:

1. To be so organized that it directs the whole of its efforts to influence the enemy's Intelligence Staff – and that alone.
2. To be composed of senior officers with a real knowledge of the Intelligence Staff that is to become their audience.
3. To be directed, as specialists in an Art, by a Commander and Staff who tell them what results they require and who leave them unhampered to arrange the best means of obtaining those results.
4. To be given an object in terms of the manner in which the enemy is required to ACT in order to further the operational plan of their own commander.

Provided these four principles are faithfully observed, it matters little how the organization is shaped and it can best take the form most suited to the nationality concerned and the theatre of war affected.

APPENDIX 2

ANALYSIS OF ALLIED ORDER OF BATTLE
MEDITERRANEAN THEATRE
MAY 1944

	ACTUAL	BOGUS	OKW ESTIMATE
Divisions in Italy			
British	12	12	13
Polish	2	4	4
U.S.	7	7	7
French	4	4	4
	25	27	28
Western Med outside Italy			
British	1	4	3
U.S.	1	1	3
French	3	6	9
	5	11	15
Eastern Med including Persia and Iraq			
British	4	13	13
Defensive Formations			
British	0	8	10
French	4	5	5
	4	13	15
Grand Total	38	64	71

Operation Starkey 1943:
'A Piece of Harmless Playacting'?

JOHN P. CAMPBELL

After the Casablanca Conference in January 1943, it became clear that the only major Allied cross-Channel operation likely to be feasible that year was an uncontested landing in the event of a total German collapse. On 4 March 1943, the British Joint Planners decided that a landing force of 12 brigade groups with tactically loaded back-up would be required in face of *any* organized resistance. A force of that size was so far out of reach, however, that there was no point in attempting to remedy the situation even by curtailing plans for operations in the Mediterranean.[1] Nevertheless, at the insistence of the Prime Minister on 10 April, every effort was to be made to conceal the actual state of Allied weakness in England. One way to do so was by deception. The London Controlling Section (LCS) had already drawn up broad strategic plans based on decisions made at Casablanca. These plans called for steps to encourage German overestimation of Allied strength and capacity to undertake major operations on all fronts where such threats could plausibly be maintained. An appropriate disposition of forces and intensive invasion training in the UK, coupled with the exaggeration of the rate of American build-up (Bolero), were calculated to pin down German forces in the West.[2] With the appointment of Lieutenant-General F.E. Morgan as Chief of Staff to the Supreme Allied Commander (designate) or COSSAC, all cross-Channel operations, except for minor raids, became the responsibility of his combined staff at Norfolk House in London. Morgan's directive on 26 April charged him with the simultaneous planning of three operations: the actual invasion in 1944 (Overlord); the uncontested return to the Continent (Rankin); and thirdly, 'an elaborate camouflage and deception scheme extending over the whole summer with a view to pinning the enemy in the West and keeping alive the expectation of large-scale cross-Channel operations in 1943'. There was also some expectation of a bonus in the shape of an air battle over the Channel on advantageous terms for the Metropolitan RAF and Eighth USAAF.[3]

The Appreciation and Outline Plan for Operation Cockade – this 'vast scheme of cover and camouflage', as the British Chiefs of Staff (COS) referred to it in Churchillian terms on 30 April – was submitted by Morgan for their approval on 5 June.[4] Cockade was planned by the COSSAC cover and deception staff – Ops (B) – and embraced three subsidiary operations, Starkey, Wadham, and Tindall, the first two being inter-dependent. Morgan's staff appreciated that the raid on Dieppe on 19 August 1942 had likely led the Germans to the conclusion that their coastal divisions were capable of coping with even major raids without the assistance of a strategic reserve of mobile formations. To contain such a reserve in north-west France, accordingly, it was necessary to threaten the Germans with nothing less than a *Grosslandung* or Second Front. The same held true for air forces. The German Air Force's (GAF) growing number of first-line day fighter squadrons on the Western Front meant that they were in the position to put up a strong initial defense; but for lack of reserves this could not be sustained for long during intensive operations. The GAF would not be committed unless 'the High Command' was persuaded that a landing in strength to seize a permanent foothold was imminent. Starkey was to simulate preparations for such a landing on beaches between Boulogne and Le Touquet, with a projected D-Day between 8 and 12 September. But since it was also appreciated that the Germans must have concluded that the French Channel ports in an undamaged condition could still not provide logistical support for a force of more than about nine divisions, they would expect the landing of a follow-up force. Wadham was to provide this force, which would undertake a combined airborne and seaborne assault on the Brittany peninsula to capture Brest on or about 30 September, after Starkey had drawn off German reserves. Wadham was to be largely an American operation, with the assault force launched from England but the build-up force coming directly from the United States. The operation depended mainly on systematic leakage of information and would of course be closed down after Starkey D-Day.[5] Tindall, finally, was intended to contain German forces in Norway by aiming a threat at Stavanger. A large-scale airborne attack to capture the airfields close to Stavanger would allow a seaborne force of three divisions to come ashore under local fighter cover. Tindall was originally timed for 12 to 18 September but later postponed until November. This was done at the suggestion of the Controlling Officer, Colonel J.H. Bevan, so as to prolong tension; besides, the Germans were unlikely to credit that Starkey, Wadham and Tindall would all be feasible in the same month.[6]

So much for strategic theory. Planning for Starkey went ahead on as realistic a basis as possible, with the same attention to detail as for an actual operation. Indeed, the Air Plan called for actual operations, with a steady intensification of attacks on airfields and other military and transport targets in the Pas de Calais as the Preliminary Phase was worked up into the Preparatory and Culminating Phases. The Military Plan, on the other hand, amounted to a complicated movement exercise (Harlequin) to convey to the enemy the impression that some nine divisions were being concentrated and assembled for embarkation in south-east England. While the planners were at work, of course, the main events of the summer of 1943 – the start of the German offensive in Russia on 4 July, the invasion of Sicily (Husky) on 10 July, and the German decision at the end of the month to gather forces together in anticipation of a move into Italy (Alarich) – all took place without the staging of so much as a diversionary threat from England. Cockade, therefore, barely extended 'over the whole summer' and its only opportunity to contain German ground forces in France was missed when Field-Marshal von Rundstedt, Commander-in-Chief West, gave up seven divisions and two Corps HQs for Alarich. After that, there was nothing much left to pin down, since the immobile coastal divisions hardly counted, and Lieutenant-General G. Blumentritt, Chief of Staff to C-in-C West, took deception measures of his own to hide this fact.[7]

The most important reason for the inaction of July and August was the shortage of landing craft in the UK. Bevan had envisaged a July D-Day for the cross-Channel feint in the hope at least of diverting German air forces away from Husky. But, as Morgan explained to him early in May, there would not be enough landing craft left in July to mount anything resembling a plausible threat from the south of England. In July, in fact, the staff at Combined Operations was forced to concede that a minor raid to collect intelligence about V-weapons' sites being constructed behind Calais was beyond their resources.[8] These restraints were all part of the price paid for the provision of an additional assault division for Husky. Not only was the seizure of a permanent foothold on the continent (Hadrian) beyond all hope, but Combined Operations HQ had already been obliged to abandon plans drawn up in February for a raid on the Channel Islands in co-ordination with Husky. There were scarcely enough landing craft in the UK in the summer of 1943 to continue the training program on a reduced scale. Landing craft used in Sicily would not begin to arrive back in England until four months after Husky D-Day. Only in the second half of August could Morgan look forward to the concentration of an appreciable force of landing craft; even then there would be only about 500 craft on display for GAF reconnaissance, including 175 dummies, which came to just over double the number visible at the time of Dieppe, or about one-tenth of Husky's formidable armada.[9]

It is open to question, all the same, whether Starkey could have been ready before July even if sufficient landing craft had been available to stage a visual threat. Planning got off to a slow start and was of such scope and complexity that there was no question of inspired improvisation or speed-up. There was not enough time, for example, to implement a full W/T Deception Plan for Starkey. On top of that, the COS deferred decisions that Morgan considered crucial to the success of the entire scheme. On 12 July, he complained about the difficulty of planning the later stages of an operation for which the availability of essential components was in doubt.[10] He was well aware that whatever realism Starkey might enjoy depended on a number of props, the inadequate representation of any one of which threatened to undermine the whole set. For example, it took 18 Landing Ships Infantry (LSI) to launch a divisional assault. Nothing like that number would be available for Starkey. Therefore, a large force of assault landing craft would have to cross the Channel on their own on the night of D-1/D-Day. An assault south of Boulogne meant that Dover and Folkestone Harbors would have to be used for the final concentration of flotillas moving south from the Thames estuary. But Dover and Folkestone were within range of the German batteries at Gris Nez; therefore, those batteries must be neutralized by bombardment.[11] Two R class battleships were to engage the coast batteries at 23,000 yards on D-8 and D-5. These shoots would be co-ordinated with heavy raids the previous two nights by RAF Bomber Command, to fatigue and demoralize the gun crews and with simultaneous heavy bombing by the Eighth USAAF. The total bomber commitment estimated for Starkey came to no less than 6,000 sorties equally divided between night and day. There would also be minesweeping in broad daylight well within range of the batteries for a few days following 30 August.[12]

In the event, neither the battleships nor the heavy bomber sorties on anything like the scale originally requested were forthcoming. The Admiralty had no intention of risking even obsolete battleships in the confined waters of the Channel, least of all for a bluff. The loss of a battleship in such circumstances would hand the enemy an easy triumph and be difficult to explain to the British public. In this regard, at least, Morgan was told where he stood a day or two after his observation on 12 July.[13] It took longer to iron out the question of the heavy bombers. Air Chief Marshal Sir Arthur Harris, AOC-in-C Bomber Command, was openly scornful of COSSAC's proposals: 'just the sort of thing an idle army dotes on'. His staff pointed out on 11 August that it would require 11,000 sorties, or 15 full-scale raids, to neutralize such an unsuitable target as the defensive system protecting the long-range batteries. The fact that Air Marshal Sir Trafford Leigh-Mallory, AOC-in-C Fighter Command, was in charge of Starkey's detailed planning and overall direction simply made Harris all the more adamant.[14] He was supported by Lieutenant-General Jacob Devers, Commanding General ETOUSA, and Major-General Ira Eaker of the Eighth Air Force, both of whom attached a higher strategic priority to carrying out the Pointblank Directive from the Combined Chiefs of Staff than to joining in the deception. The Americans freely offered their medium and fighter bombers but drew the line at weakening their heavy bomber formations for forthcoming missions against targets in Germany.[15] Where Starkey's requirements ran counter to operational priorities, in other words, deception came off second best. The difficulty about deception lay not in devising plans or in passing the gist of them to enemy Intelligence: rather, it lay in implementation, in winning the commitment of scarce resources to provide the enemy with apparent confirmation of his Intelligence reports.

By the end of August there was a fairly conclusive case for closing Starkey down. Morgan came close to making this recommendation at the COS meeting on 28 August when he accepted Bomber Command's drastically reduced heavy bomber contribution.[16] Almost everything had so far gone wrong for deception that could possibly do so. The strategic situation was far more unstable than anticipated in the spring, with the Germans unexpectedly hard pressed in both Russia and the Mediterranean and signs of serious unrest in the occupied countries of Western Europe. Presumably the COS had considered that an operation to bail the Russians out would have had a better chance of attracting German attention than one to exploit German strategic embarrassment. On 11 August Reuters announced that an invasion was imminent; the British public reacted excitedly, or exactly as the COS would not have wished. The establishment of Restricted Areas along the south coast was widely publicized on 14 August, contrary to the Starkey Plan and to the rage of General Sir Bernard Paget, C-in-C Home Forces. The American press was alive with invasion rumors picked up at the Quebec Conference meeting that month, while the British press was publishing the texts of inflammatory Political Warfare Executive (PWE) broadcasts to France that were actually quite at variance with the Starkey PWE Plan. In the end, Fleet Street editors were urgently briefed in strictest confidence on 23 August to tone down speculation about a Second Front. Even the weather had been bad, appreciably curtailing the daylight sorties flown against the Pas de Calais and capsizing some of the dummy landing craft.[17]

Despite these setbacks, Starkey was allowed to continue to its dénouement on 9 September. There was always the chance that the Germans might be holding back until the invasion fleet actually set sail. Furthermore, it had now turned out that the landings at Salerno (Avalanche) were scheduled to take place on the same day as Starkey.

Leigh-Mallory was reluctant to disappoint the Americans, who had joined wholeheartedly in the fighter and medium bomber programs. The minesweeping, too, had yet to start on 28 August and there was no telling what effect such an unheard-of move so close to the French coast might have on the enemy.[18] When the sweeping did begin on 31 August, all it elicited were a few desultory salvoes from the coast batteries. In an Appreciation of Prospects on 2 September, Morgan considered that enemy reactions had not been enough to justify continuation. Nevertheless, a decision was made to carry on anyway and was soon bolstered by intelligence from Ultra. The Germans resorted to defensive mine-laying by aircraft on the night of 3/4 September. This step was so unusual because of the relative inaccuracy of airborne mine-laying as to entitle it to be considered the first hint that the Germans were taking Starkey seriously. Colonel Bevan reported to the COS on 4 September that German Intelligence had warned the 'General Staff' that a cross-Channel invasion was about to be launched. This information also came from Most Secret Sources and possibly for that reason was assigned special significance.[19] In the end nothing made the slightest difference. The coincidence with Avalanche would have been a classic example of bad timing had it in fact been planned. As soon as the GAF spotted convoys en route for Salerno on 6 September, Hitler and the staff at *Oberkommando der Wehrmacht* (OKW) concentrated on events in the Mediterranean, so that Starkey was buried by Avalanche. A scaled-down air raid on Boulogne on the night of 8/9 September killed one German soldier and about 200 French civilians. When the invasion force approached to within 16 miles of the coast the following morning, it was completely ignored, German R/T and W/T remaining 'singularly inactive'. One of four Me 109s on reconnaissance over the Channel was shot down. Apart from that, the only appreciable German reaction in the air was reserved for a force of American heavy bombers with fighter escort which struck at airfields near Paris and Beauvais. In fact the German documents give the impression that observers on the French coast first caught sight of the expedition only after it had already turned back for England at 0900 hrs.[20] German authorities were surprised when the British took the unusual step of announcing in a communiqué broadcast by the BBC that a full-scale exercise had taken place in the Channel. The draft communiqué had optimistically referred to defensive shelling and mine-laying, to say nothing of considerable enemy air and E-boat losses. Like so much else about Starkey, its final version was subject to abridgement.[21]

All things considered, it is tempting to join Bomber Harris in deriding what after all was intended as a major exercise in strategic deception as a major exercise in *opéra bouffe*. Almost everything about

Starkey was touched by irony. The small-scale raids on the French coast in July and August to simulate beach reconnaissance and capture a prisoner or two failed to yield more than a few strands of barbed wire. Some parties stayed ashore for several hours on the most heavily defended coast in the world without coming across a single German.[22] Morgan himself, not surprisingly, was defensive and apologetic in *Overture to Overlord* (1950). Later, he confessed, 'We found it mighty hard to believe that there could be any virtue in the plots we cooked up for our deception operations in 1943'.[23] Still, as he pointed out, it would be a serious mistake to suppose that no risks were attached to Starkey. The Germans, for a start, might have scored a major propaganda coup by representing it as a failed attempt at invasion. Or they might have deduced something from Starkey that would stand them in good stead for Overlord. What if a twin threat to the Pas de Calais and Brittany persuaded them of the advantages of deploying their reserves in a central position, namely, Normandy?[24] But COSSAC's greatest nightmare took the form of a premature uprising by the French Resistance. After such a calamity, there could be no hope of any assistance from the patriot armies when the real invasion took place. For that reason the Starkey PWE Plan underlined the importance of discipline and strict obedience to London, an injunction which, as earlier indicated, conflicted with some long-term PWE programs.[25] That none of those disasters ever materialized should not be allowed to alter the fact that Starkey was far from 'harmless playacting'. And if the maxim that more lessons are learned from defeat than from victory holds true for notional operations as well as for real ones, Starkey must have paid a rich dividend.

Any attempt to define that dividend in abstract or theoretical terms should be made with caution. It might be argued, for example, that Starkey proved that deception does not work in half measures any more than diffident deficit-financing does: half-hearted notional operations have no better chance of success than half-hearted actual ones. While there is some truth in this, it would none the less be a mistake to insist that deception in full measure in Starkey's case – battleships, heavy bombers and all – would have produced any better result. The Germans were clearly not prepared to react to anything short of an actual landing in sufficient strength to secure a permanent lodgement. The same need for caution applies to thinking about Starkey in terms of alternative models of deception. To borrow the terminology of strategic analysis, Starkey was an M-type deception, designed to reduce ambiguity by concentrating the enemy's attention on the wrong alternative. In 1942, by contrast, there was no formal exercise in deception where cross-Channel operations were concerned; instead, there was unlimited rumor and speculation about a Second Front. This might be taken for an exercise in the other main form of deception – A-type, designed to increase uncertainty and ambiguity.[26] Some point was seemingly given to invasion rumors in the third week of June 1942, when GAF photographic reconnaissance suddenly disclosed an unprecedented concentration of small craft along the English south coast. This revelation had considerable impact on Hitler, who issued an Order on 9 July to strengthen defenses in the west. At his insistence reinforcements were rushed to France from Russia, including some elite formations. Finally, on 19 August, just when the Germans had apparently come to terms with the presence of those landing craft and barges, came a second surprise – the raid on Dieppe, which was briefly mistaken for the initial stage of an invasion. The air battle that developed involved the entire available strength of Third Air Fleet, including night bombers from their Dutch bases. Their appearance in daylight was a welcome surprise to the RAF and seemed to prove that combined operations had found the key to inflicting attritional losses on the GAF in the west. Although the RAF lost 106 aircraft destroyed, the air battle over Dieppe was touted as its greatest victory since 1940. In 1942, in other words, all that Starkey was intended to achieve – and more – was actually achieved without any formally planned deception. As Liddell Hart later observed: 'It would seem that rumor was more effective than planned deception in playing on the mind of the enemy'.[27]

Before jumping to any conclusions about what should have been done in 1943, a few considerations should be borne in mind. First, the planners of wartime deception were supreme pragmatists who followed a few trusted guidelines based on experience rather than theory. In 1942, it need scarcely be pointed out, there was no thought of selecting an A-type deception. What evolved was the product of Anglo-American strategic uncertainty and the lack of planning machinery for large-scale deception. All this changed after Operation Torch, so that by the spring of 1943 deception was very much in vogue in London. There was so much talk about cover plans and the like as though they were some sort of secret weapon, observed Churchill in July, that he was concerned to put a stop to it. He himself, of course, was full of the subject. If word got about, he had suggested in April, that there would be no Sledgehammer in 1943, it must be insinuated that this was all part of a cover plan. Churchill supported Starkey to the extent of minuting on 23 July: 'I cannot feel that there is enough substance to this'. As a result, 20 MT ships were gathered in the Solent and actually set sail to a position ten miles south of Beachy Head on Starkey D-Day.[28] Once again, though, there was no deliberate choice, in favor this time of an M-type deception. Little or no thought was apparently given to any alternative to 'a vast scheme of cover and camouflage' whose success would largely depend on the enemy's being able to obtain visual evidence of the presence of adequate numbers of ships and landing craft. It is perhaps not going too far to say that there was an element of inevitability about Cockade, of deception for the sake of deception. It was as though the disadvantages of making such a choice months before the strategic circumstances in which the operation would unfold could possibly have been foreseen were outweighed by the promise of direction and control that a formal plan embodied.

Quite patently, Germany's strategic position by the late summer of 1943 was such that it would have made little difference which type of general deception was adopted. Nor was it likely that the Germans would over-react in the air a second time. Still, there was one aspect of Starkey that might inspire a general principle for inclusion in a manual on strategic deception. There was clearly a certain tension between the requirements for the overall deception and those for provoking the air battle. In Starkey's case, priority in some details of the Plan was given to the latter. The approach was timed for a putative H-Hour of 1100 hrs. to give the Germans time to appreciate what was taking place in the Channel, for the GAF had been very slow off the mark at Dieppe. Similarly, no attempt was made to destroy the GAF early warning radar chain or to subject it to technical interference, for fear of inhibiting German participation in the air battle. But GAF radar would have been a priority target in case of a real invasion, just as H-Hour for the real thing would have been set for much earlier in the day.[29] Notional operations, it might be proposed, should be planned to achieve surprise, or better still to appear to be attempting to achieve surprise; and the pressure to sacrifice realism for the sake of a conjoint but secondary purpose should be resisted.

Purely from a historian's point of view, theoretical principles of deception are of marginal interest – useful mainly to highlight aspects of wartime practice. More of a challenge to research are the still relatively unexplored features of Starkey, two of which stand out. One is the role of agents under MI5 control in passing intelligence about Starkey, Wadham and Tindall to the *Abwehr*. The second is the relationship between Starkey and Fortitude South, or between deception as practiced by COSSAC and then by SHAEF. These two features have remained unexplored largely for want of access to official files. Where the double agents are concerned, the records of MI5 remain subject to strict security classification, while the relevant German sources are often in a fragmentary state. On balance, it makes more sense to work from the German – or consumer's – point of view.

The whole point of using double agents was to encourage the

Germans to seek confirmation of their reports through other means.[30] The most trusted of those other means in the West was aerial reconnaissance. In 1942, Third Air Fleet made particular efforts to provide photographic coverage of the Southampton/Isle of Wight sector. Moreover, the initial discovery of the invasion craft came as a result of a request for reconnaissance from C-in-C West following an influx of invasion reports from agents.[31] Unfortunately for the planners at Norfolk House, the same pieces failed to fall into place in 1943. German reconnaissance was spasmodic in August; a slight increase was noticed between 2 and 6 September, after which surveillance decreased to normal. Tighter fighter and anti-aircraft defenses than in 1942 were not the sole explanation. The Germans obviously considered that there was no need for an exceptional effort to extend their overland coverage. On 7 September, an intercepted GAF signal revealed that some of the MT ships in the Solent had been spotted. Otherwise the elaborate visual effects laid on for Starkey and Wadham largely went for naught. The assembly and transit areas for Harlequin and the embarkation ports were photographed from the air all right – but by the RAF for the sake of security. The temptation experienced by Morgan almost to invite a German aircraft through without interception was resisted for obvious reasons.[32]

What went wrong in 1943? Did the Germans have doubts about their agents, or did they find the reports themselves unconvincing? Or was it simply that the strategic context had changed so much since 1942? It has been known since the publication of Sir John Masterman's book in 1972, that the principal agent selected to channel material relating to Starkey to the *Abwehr* was Garbo, a Catalonian exile in London who ran a network of notional sub-agents in the UK. Garbo was to play a decisive role in the cover and deception operations for Overlord. The whole XX system, it should be remembered, was being run to preserve it for use in what Masterman called this 'great final deception'.[33] How close was the Garbo network to being blown for the sake of something less than that in 1943?

To say that this area of investigation is full of pitfalls is surely an understatement. Quite apart from anything else, it is less straightforward than might be expected to pick out Garbo's handiwork in German sources. His reports were not singled out by use of his *Abwehr* covername (Arabal), as was done for the reports of at least two other agents at this stage of the war. For the months leading up to Overlord, many of Garbo's original reports were cleared for publication in Nigel West's biography (1984).[34] But for August and September 1943, West refers indirectly to only one message. The information it imparted supposedly came from a sub-agent employed in the NAAFI attached to a secret arms depôt in the caves at Chislehurst. Disappointingly, it has left no impression in the more accessible of the surviving German records.[35] It is not even safe to assume that apparently first-hand invasion reports from England are *ipso facto* Garbo's, or indeed the work of the XX Committee at all. It is difficult, too, to get a sense of the distribution of intelligence or of its variations in volume. Occasionally references are made to messages in the aggregate that rather contradict the impression given by individual examples appearing day-by-day in war diaries. C-in-C West evidently received reports from agents that never reached the Naval Staff, or at least that the Operations Branch rejected as unworthy of inclusion in their War Diary.[36] The *Abwehr* themselves compiled a list of incoming reports about a Second Front for the period from June to October 1943, yet even that was less than all-inclusive.[37] Furthermore, messages were coming in all the time from agents who were not under MI5 control, some of whom were evidently more highly regarded than Garbo.

Not surprisingly, then, the German Intelligence authorities never arrived at the appreciation intended by the planners at Norfolk House. No doubt the failure to follow through with aerial reconnaissance set the seal on Cockade's poor definition in German situation reports. The Foreign Armies West Branch of the Army General Staff missed altogether the interdependence between Starkey and Wadham; indeed they took little or no notice of Wadham at all, and certainly showed no sign of having been 'told' on or about 15 August that Wadham was contingent on Starkey's success. Foreign Armies West flatly credited the Allies with sufficient troops and tonnage to launch an invasion from England, most likely across the narrowest part of the Channel.[38] But that was only one of a number of possibilities. For much of August, reports tended to direct attention to troop movements in East Anglia and the north of Scotland, suggesting landings in Belgium or Holland and Norway respectively. One that was given wide distribution came from Lisbon on 17 August and was based on a Portuguese consular dispatch from London.[39] It is interesting to note that its forecast of a landing on the coast at the Franco-Belgian line was echoed in an *OKW Feindlagebericht* on 29 August.[40] This location was of course at the wrong end of the Straits of Dover for Starkey. Another well thought-of strategic notion featured landings in the form of pincers, one on the Biscay coast south of Bordeaux and the other on the Gulf of Lion in the Mediterranean. This strategy apparently appealed particularly to Hitler and was reported by a number of agents, including one who was currently considered especially reliable on the strength of having provided two days' warning of Husky.[41] There was also a recurrent theme that held that a cross-Channel invasion would only be risked if there took place a total collapse of German forces in Russia. The general idea that the forces in south-east England were merely at the ready to exploit such an eventuality was expressed by Ostro on 14 August.[42] Ostro was well known to the British as a gifted inventing agent based in Lisbon but esteemed by the *Abwehr* as the director of a worldwide network of informants. Ostro's standing was so high that a commotion took place on 1 September over the *Abwehr*'s delay until then in forwarding the report of 14 August to the Naval Staff (Operations).[43] Ostro concocted his own version of Cockade – Operations Viking, Black Prince and so on – which appeared twice, on 13 and 21 August, in the Operations Branch War Diary. It did little to sharpen Cockade's profile.[44] Nor should occasional snippets of reasonably accurate intelligence be overlooked. On 1 September Josephine, the other named *Abwehr* agent, announced that it had been decided at Quebec that there would be no decisive operation in France before the spring of 1944; the Anglo-American *Schwerpunkt* would remain in the Mediterranean for the time being.[45]

By a process of elimination it can be deduced what a Garbo original should look like. It should be an anonymous *Abwehrbericht* transmitted from London by way of the *Abwehr* station in Madrid and containing information that for the most part was accurate and verifiable by aerial observation or other means. Accordingly, a good bet was a message that appeared in the Operations Branch War Diary on 19 August. It was an eye-witness report from London 'über Madrid' describing developments in and around Southampton. A well-concealed tented camp for 40,000 troops had just been pitched, anti-aircraft defenses strengthened, loading hards for landing craft made ready, and new camps built north of the city.[46] This message was rather lost in the welter of other reports competing for attention in mid-August. But there was a noticeable change as Starkey moved towards its culmination. Just as the minesweeping began off Boulogne on 31 August, a series of remarkably explicit signals began to come in from London via Madrid, building up to what was clearly meant to be a climax on 9 September.

The minesweeping caused considerable concern at Naval Group West. Because of the promptness with which coastal waters could always be counter-mined, there was the strong implication of an imminent operation.[47] A report that von Rundstedt described as remarkably accurate announced the arrival of two flotillas of mine-sweepers at Dover on 1 September. Others told of the arrival of landing craft at Dover and Folkestone, the removal of barriers on the foreshore and so forth.[48] On 6 September, von Rundstedt found all this so overdone that he put it down to an attempt to divert his attention from the true point of attack – either Normandy or the German Bight. At the same time he could not entirely ignore the chance of a raid on the V-weapons' sites behind Calais. He had very shrewdly decided already that Allied air operations in August were not quite sustained enough to qualify as the preliminaries to a full-scale invasion.[49] There followed several messages little short of dramatic. One disclosed on 7 September that Southampton was sealed off; 25 transports were anchored in the Solent; 6 Commando had been at the ready in Brighton since 1 September. Another on 7 September from 'apparently the surest sources' predicted a landing in France the following morning, subject to a possible delay of a day or two because of bad weather.[50] Starkey, it should be remembered, had originally been scheduled for 8 September but then postponed for 24 hours on the strength of an inaccurate forecast. Another message divulged that 5 and 7 Commando were ready to embark at Dover. On 8 September a report from London by way of Madrid warned that troops had removed their badges; the center of action was likely to be the Straits because of the commitment of large numbers of small landing craft.[51] There was even an agent's report timed at 0100 hrs. on 9 September, according to von Rundstedt, about the issue of iron rations in anticipation of a take-off the following night. With this, he remarked drily, these messages reached 'einen gewissen Höhepunkt'.[52]

What conclusions can now be ventured about agents, their reports, and the strategic context? First, and not surprisingly, there are plenty of signs that intelligence provided by the *Abwehr* was treated with considerable circumspection. German staffs, like Naval Group West on 1 September, sometimes attempted to evaluate the situation on purely military grounds, by which they implied without reference to numerous *Abwehr* and other reports about impending enemy operations.[53] The *Abwehr* itself was well on its way to being discredited by repeated failures to guard against strategic surprise. Moreover, not only did the culminating reports from 6 to 9 September lead to no exceptional alerts on the Channel coast, but the most serious German invasion alarm in 1943 was self-generated, without benefit of messages from agents. Towards the end of October, the first evidence began to come in that the Allies had started to transfer landing craft from the Mediterranean to the UK. There had already been word earlier in the month of the arrival in England of growing numbers of ocean-going landing craft from the United States. Also, the Foreign Ministers were meeting in Moscow in October, and the Germans always took meetings with the Soviets far more seriously than meetings without them, such as those at Quebec in August.[54] The upshot was a sudden but quite serious alarm about an invasion in the West at a season of the year that would have given pause to the planners of even notional invasions. At OKW attention was focused on Denmark, though not as a result of any Tindall messages. Hitler was involved to a degree that was not evident in August and September. His Directive No. 51 of 3 November, after all, envisaged the possibility of an invasion in the spring of 1944 at the latest, but quite possibly sooner.[55]

The strategic context, therefore, clearly counted for far more than intelligence from agents. Deception, according to Brigadier Dudley Clarke, could never be successful if simply based on what it was desirable for the enemy to think. Instead, it should always be built on certain preconceptions of the enemy's. The COS had decided on 30 June deliberately to allow information regarding the development of British and American invasion organizations in the UK to reach the enemy. Yet this made little impression, because the Germans had no preconception of a cross-Channel invasion in 1943. In the absence of any kind of visual threat, there was next to no hope of altering the German perception of the war in the West by a surge of agents' messages at the end of August and early in September.[56]

This is not to say that the Germans regarded their agents as unreliable. If they found dependence on agents disillusioning at times, they could not readily escape it, at least in the West. Thus, even reliable agents were considered liable to pass on false information that had been put into circulation by the British and Americans. This allowance was made for none other than Ostro by German Naval Intelligence on 1 September.[57] The same misplaced confidence probably saved the Garbo network. There can be no question that the reports transmitted during Starkey's dramatic climax were the XX Committee's equivalent of sending two battleships into the Channel. The Appreciation and Outline Plan for Starkey spoke openly of allowing information about the sailing of the expedition to leak to the enemy by Special Means. It is impossible to say how calculated a risk that was without access not only to the messages sent by Garbo and the other double agents but also to the full range of intercepts and other intelligence at the command of the XX Committee and case officers. None the less, three observations are perhaps permissible. First, the Garbo network survived, but only at the cost of fairly severe surgery, sub-agents One and Six being the victims. According to West, Sub-agent Six had to be killed off in North Africa, much as a dead actor's part is written out of a soap opera.[58] Secondly, the most obvious conclusion for the Germans to reach was surely that a deception had been tried, all the more so considering the coincidence with Avalanche. Naval Group West lost no time in pointing to a 'Tauschungsmanover', with any purported 'exercise' playing a sub-sidiary role. The Naval Staff (Intelligence) carefully sorted through all messages received between 4 and 14 September, and reported on 18 September that they added up to a British cover operation, plausible enough as some of the individual reports might appear.[59] These findings should be read in the light of Bevan's opposition to any public description of Starkey as a 'deception' for fear of blowing any of the Special Means. It is hard to imagine, frankly, that he considered that the Germans would attach any credence to what the BBC or Reuters had to say. As it was, the last thing the Germans were prepared to believe was that an 'exercise' had taken place in the Channel.[60] Thirdly, the initial reaction in some German quarters, surprisingly enough, was to guess that an *actual* operation had been launched and then abandoned for one reason or another. On 9 September, Foreign Armies West thought it conceivable that a deterioration in the weather might have impeded the Allied air forces sufficiently to force a cancellation or postponement. On 12 September, they were still looking skeptically for independent confirmation that an 'exercise' had taken place. On 14 September, the most important evaluative Intelligence agency in this theater of operations came down against the idea of a '*Scheinoperation*' and in favor of an aborted one. This hypothesis had been taken seriously as well by the Naval Staff (Operations) on 10 September. Six weeks later, C-in-C West was still unable to make up his mind between a deception shrewdly timed to coincide with events in Italy and some sort of operation proceeding by stages that had come to grief for political (underlined) or military reasons.[61] From an Allied point of view, the German surmise of an abandoned operation had never really been bargained for – possibly was beyond what the planners at Norfolk House had dared plan for. But what is striking about the whole episode is the apparent rashness of putting such a valuable asset as the Garbo network at risk for the sake of what had become such a feeble strategic purpose.

Finally, there is the relationship between Starkey and Fortitude South. This was inevitably defined by the lessons learnt from Starkey. A close reading of documents now available at the National Archives suggests that Starkey had both a conceptual and an organizational effect on later cross-Channel deception planning. The conceptual is fairly clear-cut: a replay of Starkey would simply not do for the most important of Overlord's cover and deception plans. In July 1943, the Appreciation and Outline Plan for Operation Torrent, the earliest version of what was to become Fortitude South, called for a feint along the lines of Starkey to be staged against the Pas de Calais on about D-14. It was hoped as well that this operation would form part of the general air plan for the reduction of the German fighter force in the West. With decisive abruptness, Starkey put an end to thinking along these lines.

A Torrent draft of 16 September conceded that the GAF could not be brought to battle without an actual landing. There would not be enough landing craft to permit the mounting of a major diversionary landing at the expense of the main assault. At the most, such a landing at Dunkirk, or wherever, could not have been on a scale larger than a one-divisional assault. The Germans would soon realize that the landing of such a force without back-up was merely a preliminary diversion, freeing their reserves for redeployment in Normandy. There was nothing else for it but to shift the diversionary threat to the Pas de Calais from the pre- to the post-assault phase of the cover plan for Overlord. For months this concept did not amount to much – a one-divisional assault 14 days after D-Day, with one follow-up and four build-up divisions. Only in January 1944 was this minor threat transformed into a major one, to be posed by an entire Army Group and sustained for weeks beyond D-Day; and only then can Fortitude South be said to have evolved in all its 'elegance', as Masterman put it. Such an uninspired stratagem as the original Torrent plan may not in any case have passed muster for long, but it was with the failure of Starkey that the planners first altered course in the right direction.[62]

It was also stated once and for all that if a favorable air situation had not been attained by the target date by means of strategic bombing or other air operations, Overlord would have to be postponed. There would be no attempt to retrieve the situation by last-minute combined operations. The planners had at last shaken their thinking out of the rut into which it had fallen after Dieppe. Their efforts to replicate the great air victory of 19 August were in any case based on unsound strategic premises. GAF losses were only 48 aircraft destroyed, about half of the most modest claims made by Fighter Command. Attrition had been at the RAF's expense by a ratio of 2:1.63.

Starkey, then, sparked off some key conceptual changes. These would have been to little avail without the machinery for their implementation. This was largely the creation of Colonel Noel Wild, who had been Clarke's Deputy in A Force since August 1942. In December 1943 he was transferred to SHAEF Ops(B). In the face of some opposition but with the support of the Controlling Officer, Wild took steps to simplify and co-ordinate the work of various agencies in London involved with strategic deception. Perhaps the most significant change concerned control of Special Means. Following the A Force system, the deception staff at SHAEF took direct control over planting the Fortitude story on the enemy. From January 1944, close liaison was maintained between the case officers for Garbo and Brutus – the most important agents for Fortitude South – and the Special Means staff at SHAEF Ops(B) under Major Roger Hesketh. The actual planning of

Fortitude South was done by the deception staff at Twenty-first Army Group under Colonel David Strangeways. The G(R) section was run entirely along A Force lines and composed of officers transferred from its tactical echelon. There were other significant transfers. The problems endured by Morgan with PWE, for example, were solved by setting up an independent Publicity and Psychological Warfare Branch and putting it under the command of a Brigadier-General brought in from Allied Force HQ Algiers.[64] But it was Wild's appointment that really counted so far as the success of the key parts of Plan Bodyguard went. Was there a connection with Starkey?

A plausible case can be made that there was, starting with American skepticism about Cockade. This was muted but deep-seated. For a start, Devers quite rightly sided with Harris on the question of the heavy bomber sorties. Wadham was a flop, driving home for American officers the inadequacies of the arrangements and the urgency of setting up their own Special Plans Branch. Its first chief in March 1944 was Colonel William Harris, who later pointed out that Fortitude South succeeded because it was in scale with the facts, whereas Wadham was wildly out of scale. Cockade was condemned in virtually the same terms in a 12 US Army Group synopsis of the history of wartime deception completed in December 1944. This verdict was echoed at ETOUSA and in the War Department.[65] After Starkey, Devers objected to features of a proposal to put on a widespread but 'discreet' display in south-east England directed at the Pas de Calais. Such efforts to mislead, in his judgement, were not nearly discreet enough and would only give themselves away. He might almost have read von Rundstedt's mind in the first week of September. Devers's criticism was later endorsed by Montgomery's staff, and changes were made that led to a better balance between display in the south-east and concealment in the south and south-west. These American impressions may very well help to explain why the US Chiefs at first found Plan Bodyguard so ambitious as to cast doubts on its plausibility. Bodyguard, they pointed out in January 1944, could easily be overplayed; its success would depend on a considerable degree of reserve in its execution.[66]

The following pattern begins to make sense. Wild's was more than just another of the innumerable transfers following the appointment of the new Supreme Commander. To a certain extent it signified a rejection of the deception set-up in London and was at least partly the product of what might be termed the American connection. Eisenhower and his Chief of Staff, General W. Bedell Smith, were well aware of the value of A Force's work in the Middle East. Thanks to Devers, they were also aware that fairly drastic steps would be required before

deception could be made to work equally well in London.[67]
This, admittedly, is a sketchy oversimplification of an elusive turn of
events. But there is enough evidence to show that in this theater of
operations, deception was no longer a purely British speciality. Among
the repercussions of Starkey was a hitherto unacknowledged example
of the advantages of waging war by coalition.

NOTES

This paper was presented at the US Army War College Conference on 'Intelligence and
Military Operations', Carlisle Barracks, Pennsylvania, 22–25 April 1986. The views
expressed in this article are those of the author and do not reflect the official policy or
position of the Department of Defense or the US government.

Notes on sources: All British and American records cited are available at the Public
Record Office and National Archives respectively. German sources are available at the
Archives on microfilm (T 1022, T 77 etc.), including those unavoidably cited with
Imperial War Museum (AL 1704, AL 1740) and Freiburg (RH 19, III H) references.
Possibly the sole exception is MI 14/522/2, which was held by the Enemy Documents
Section of the Cabinet Office in 1976, but which may well have been transferred to the
Imperial War Museum by now.

1. JP(43)103 (Final), 4 March, CAB 84/53.
2. COS(43)194(0), 15 April, CAB 80/68. 'Deception Policy 1943: Part I – Germany
   and Italy' was adopted as COS(43)179(0), 7 April, CAB 80/68, after approval by the
   Combined Chiefs of Staff (CCS) as CCS 184/3, 2 April.
3. COS(43)215(0), 26 April, CAB 80/69. Lt.-Gen. Sir Frederick Morgan, *Overture to
   Overlord* (London, 1950), pp.64, 67.
4. The expression was indeed coined by Churchill – COS(43)202(0), 18 April, CAB
   80/69. COS(43)219(0)(Final), 30 April, CAB 80/69. COS(43)288(0), 5 June, CAB
   80/70.
5. Operation Cockade: Appreciation and Outline Plan, COSSAC(43)15(Final), 3
   June, copy in AIR 8/1202. COS(43)288(0), 5 June, CAB 80/70. COSSAC made
   weekly reports on cross-Channel operations to the COS which contain a great deal
   of information about Starkey.
6. Operation Tindall: Appreciation and Outline Plan, COSSAC(43)16(Final), 30
   June, copy in AIR 8/1202. COS(43)302(0), 11 June, CAB 80/70.
7. The operation was planned in detail and controlled by AOC-in-C Fighter
   Command, in collarboation with CG 8 USAAF and naval and military commanders
   nominated by C-in-C Portsmouth and C-in-C Home Forces. Joseph Schröder,
   Italiens Kriegsaustritt (Göttingen, 1969), p.244. P.E. Schramm *et al.* (eds.),
   *Kriegstagebuch des Oberkommando der Wehrmacht (Wehrmachtfuhrungsstab)
   1940–1945* (4 vols., Frankfurt, 1963), III(2), 933. These depletions were only
   partially offset by the deployment of 25th Panzer Division in France following
   Hitler's decision on 13 August to withdraw it from Norway (*KTB/OKW*, III(2),
   944). It was decided at HQ 21 Army Group that this move owed nothing to Starkey
   (General Sir B. Paget to AOC-in-C Fighter Command, 21 A Gp/00/12/10/ops., 7
   October 1943, AIR 37/228).
8. COS(43)253(0), 15 May, CAB 80/69. F.H. Hinsley, *British Intelligence in the
   Second World War* (3 vols., London, 1979/84), III(1), p.379.
9. Hadrian was the subject of a Paper by the Joint Planners at Casablanca (CCS/167,
   22 January 1943). COS(43)60(0), 17 February, CAB 80/67. Other planning papers
   for Operations Constellation, Concertina, and Metropole are in DEFE 2/458 and

DEFE 2/650A. JP(43)140(Final), 7 April, CAB 84/53. COS(43)249(0), 11 May, CAB 80/69.

10. COS(43)374(0), 12 July, CAB 80/71.

11. Operation Starkey: Appreciation and Outline Plan, COSSAC(43)4(Final), 26 June, copy in AIR 8/1202.

12. In the spring of 1943 the PM and his advisers were particularly interested in the effects of heavy bombardment on batteries encased in concrete. See, COS(43)51st Meeting(0), 22 March, CAB 79/60. Operation Starkey: Appreciation and Outline Plan, COSSAC(43)4(Final), 26 June, copy in AIR 8/1202. Minutes of the First Starkey Conference, 7 July, AIR 37/556. Leigh-Mallory to Morgan, COSSAC/RAF/363, 2 July 1943, AIR 37/228.

13. These difficulties were foreshadowed at COS(43)131st Meeting(0), 21 June, CAB 79/61. Leigh-Mallory to Morgan, TLM/MS 142, 14 July 1943, AIR 37/767. COS(43) 374(0), 16 July, CAB 79/62.

14. Harris to Portal (Marshal of the RAF Sir C. Portal, Chief of Air Staff), ATH/DO/4, 9 July 1943, AIR 8/1202. Group Captain Marwood-Elton to Morgan, BC/S 30324/ Ops., 11 August, added as an Annex to COS(43)477(0), 19 August, CAB 80/73. The quotation about 'harmless playacting' came from a Cypher Message, Harris to Portal, MS 17457, 25 August 1943, AIR 8/1202.

15. COS(43)344(0), 23 June, CAB 80/71. Eaker to Portal, 17 June 1943, AIR 8/1202.

16. COS(43)199th Meeting(0) – part of COS(43)137th Meeting, 28 August, CAB 79/ 63. It was finally agreed that Operational Training Units and Wellington squadrons would be used to the limit on the night of D-2/D-1, and the same force plus Stirling squadrons to a total strength of not less than 200 sorties on D-1/D-Day. On 8/9 September 259 bombers dropped 650 tons just south of Boulogne.

17. Paget to Leigh-Mallory, 21 A Gp/00/12/4/Ops., 21 August 1943, AIR 37/767. The Starkey PWE Plan was drawn up in consultation with Special Operations Executive and approved at COS(43)169th Meeting(0), 22 July, CAB 79/62. Publicity arrangements for Starkey are in Annex to COS(43)459(0), 10 August, CAB 80/73; and a copy of the statement to the editors is in AIR 37/767. Morgan summed up his difficulties in COS(43)521(0), 10 September, CAB 80/74.

18. COS(43)199th Meeting(0) – part of COS(43)137th Meeting, 28 August, CAB 79/ 63.

19. COS(43)507(0), 2 September, CAB 80/74. COS(43)206th Meeting(0), 3 September, CAB 79/64. COS(43)207th Meeting(0), 4 September, CAB 79/64. Most Secret Cypher Telegram, Concrete 736, Air Ministry to Quadrant, 4 September 1943, AIR 8/1202.

20. Air Vice-Marshal H.W.L Saunders, 'Operation Starkey: Air Commander's Report', 11 G/S 500/III/Ops., 16 September 1943, AIR 37/228. Vice-Admiral H.D. Pridham-Wippell to C-in-C Portsmouth, Dover Letter 00636a, 28 September 1943, copy in AIR 37/767. 'Tagesmeldungen Ob West 1.8 – 21.12.43', Ia Nr.4882/43 gKdos., 9 September 1943, III H 463/6.

21. At the suggestion of Portal, Starkey was not described as a 'rehearsal' for fear of encouraging speculation that it would shortly be followed by the real thing. COS(43)209th Meeting(0), 7 September, CAB 79/64.

22. Forfar Raids, DEFE 2/211.

23. Morgan apparently forgot that Starkey had been postponed until 9 September: Overture to Overlord, p.107. Morgan, Peace and War, a Soldier's Story (London, 1961), p.163.

24. Bevan to Morgan, CO 348/22, 14 July 1943: attached were Bevan's First Thoughts on deception policy for Overlord (13 July), in Plan Fortitude, Vol. I SHAEF, Office of the Chief of Staff, Secretary, General Staff, decimal file May 1943 to August 1945 (381/Eclipse to Freeborn), RG 331.

25. 'Effects of Starkey on Morale in Occupied Countries', COSSAC/18 DX/INT, 28 May 1943, copy in AIR 37/228. Morgan, Overture to Overlord, pp.109–10. COS (43)380(0), 18 July, CAB 80/71.

26. The terminology of A- and M-type Deception is borrowed from Donald C.

Daniel and Katherine L. Herbig, 'Propositions on Military Deception', *Journal of Strategic Studies*, Vol. 5, No. 1 (March 1982), 155–77.

27. John P. Campbell, 'Air Operations and the Dieppe Raid', *Aerospace Historian*, XXIII (1976), 10–20. B.H. Liddell Hart, *The German Generals Talk* – (New York, 1948), p.231.
28. COS(43)162nd Meeting (0) – part of COS(43)115th Meeting, 16 July, CAB 79/62. COS(43)202(0), 18 April, CAB 80/69. COS(43)174th Meeting(0), 28 July, CAB 79/63. JP(43)288(Final), 9 August, CAB 84/55, approved at COS(43)186th Meeting (0), 12 August, CAB 79/63.
29. Operation Starkey: Appreciation and Outline Plan, COSSAC(43)4(Final), 26 June, copy in AIR 8/1202.
30. Bevan to Major-General C. Bissell, AC of S, G-2, War Department, CO/560, 11 December 1944 in Army – Operations, General Administrative Files, 1943–1952, Cover and Deception, Box 1, Folder 1, RG 319 (declassified, November 1985).
31. Telegram, Ob West to OKH/GenStdH/Op.Abt., Ia Nr. 1744/42 gKdos., 27 June 1942, T 78/317.
32. Air Vice-Marshal H.W.L. Saunders, 'Operation Starkey: Air Commander's Report', 11 G/S 500/III Ops., 16 September 1943, AIR 37/228. Morgan, *Peace and War*, p.163.
33. J.C. Masterman, *The Double-Cross System in the War of 1939 to 1945* (New Haven and London, 1972), pp.142–3, 127.
34. Juan Pugol with Nigel West, *Garbo* (London, 1985), was published under the guidance of the Ministry of Defence's D Notice Committee. The texts of Garbo's messages are taken from Colonel R.F. Hesketh's unpublished study of Fortitude.
35. Pujol with West, op. cit., p.98.
36. 'Lagebeurteilungen durch Ob West vom 3.8.42 bis 18.10.43', AL 1704. These were sent weekly to the Operations Staffs at *OKH* (OKH/GenStdH/Op. Abt. (II)) and *OKW* (OKW/WFSt.). Kriegstagebuch Seekriegsleitung: 1 Abteilung, Teil A.
37. Amt Ausland/Abwehr, OKW/1697 (confidential reports on the probability of an Allied invasion: June to October 1943), T 77/1505. This collection, for example, contains a report based on two *Globusberichte* of 4 Sept. 1943 from Reading and Exeter, which are not mentioned in KTB/1 Skl., A; it does not, however, include Ostro's reports.
38. Operation Wadham: Appreciation and Outline Plan, COSSAC(43)24(Final), 15 June, copy in AIR 37/900. 'Feindlagebericht Nr. 14/43', OKH/GenStdH/Abt. Fremde Heere West, Nr. 3952/43 gKdos., 18 Aug. 1943, AL 1740.
39. KTB/1 Skl., A, 17 Aug. 1943, T 1022/1682; this message is also mentioned in Amt Ausland/Abwehr, OKW/1697, T 77/1505.
40. 'Feindlagebericht des WFSt. nach dem Stand vom Ende August', *KTB/OWK*, III(2), 29 Aug. 1943, 1024–5.
41. KTB/1 Skl., A, 14.8.43, T 1022/1682. Liddell Hart, *The German Generals Talk* –, p.230.
42. KTB/1 Skl., A, 31.8.43, T 1022/1682. A *V-Mann* report from Madrid a few days later that 'Col. Malaise' had assured him there was no danger of a cross-Channel attack if the German Army in Russia stood fast: KTB/1 Skl., A, 3 Sept. 1943, T 1022/1682.
43. Ostro was a Czech, Paul Fidrmuc. KTB/1 Skl., A, 1 Sept. 1943, T 1022/1682.
44. KTB/1 Skl., A, 13.8.43, T 1022/1682. The report was first received on 6 August and was supposedly based on the deliberations of the three British *Wehrmachtteile* on 30 and 31 July; diversionary landings on the Channel and Atlantic coasts had been put off for the time being until the situation had been cleared up in Italy; Black Prince was the *Kontinentalaktion*, to be decided upon by a special committee.
45. KTB/1 Skl., A, 7 Sept. 1943, T 1022/1683: 'Eine von 3/Skl als besonders zuverlässig bewertet Abwehrstelle (Josephine) meldete am 1/9 über Quebec-Konferenz'.
46. KTB/1 Skl., A, 19 Aug. 1943, T 1022/1682; this report was repeated in Amt Ausland/Abwehr, OKW/1697, T 77/1505, where it was described as a *V-Mann* report from London based on *Eigenbeobachtung*.

47. KTB/1 Skl., A, 2 Sept. 1943, T 1022/1682.
48. 'Lagebeurteilung durch Ob West', Ia Nr. 4797/43 gKdos., 6 September 1943, AL 1704. KTB/1 Skl., A, 31 August 1943, T 1022/1682 refers to earlier reports on 29 and 20 August 'aus beachtenswerten Quellen in England über Spanien ... Danach werden Landungsmittel in Dover und Folkestone gesammelt'. 'Ia Lagebericht West', OKH/GenStdH/Abt. Fremde Heere West, Nr. 1011 (Anlage), 3 Sept. 1943, MI 14/522/2.
49. 'Lagebeurteilung durch Ob West', Ia Nr. 4797/43 gKdos., 6 Sept. 1943; Ibid., Ia Nr. 5034/43 gKdos., 13 Aug. 1943, AL 1704.
50. KTB/1 Skl., A, 2 Sept. 1943, T 1022/1682. The report about a landing the following morning – 'Funk am 8.9 aus London' – is listed in Amt Ausland/ Abwehr, OKW/1697, T 77/1505 and in KTB/1 Skl., A., 8 Sept. 1943, T 1022/1683.
51. Amt Ausland/Abwehr, OKW/1697, T 77/1505: 'K.O. Spanien meldet aus London am 8.9: "Truppe legt Abzeichen ab. Infolge Verwendung von kleinen Landungsfahrzeugen Brennpunkt vermutlich an engster Stelle Kanals"'.
52. 'Lagebeurteilung durch Ob West', Ia Nr. 5034/43 gKdos., 13 Aug. 1943, AL 1704.
53. KTB/1 Skl., A, 2 Sept. 1943, T 1022/1682, quotes *Ob Marinegruppe West* on the minesweeping; like *Ob West, Ob Marinegruppe West* agreed there was a possibility of some sort of landing; 'unabhängig von den zahlreichen Abwehrmeldungen über Landungsabsichten'.
54. 'Feindlagebericht Nr. 20/43', compiled by 3 *Skl.*, KTB/1 Skl., A, 24 Oct. 1943, T 1022/1683.
55. *KTB/OKW*, III(2), 25 Oct. 1943, 1219–20. Concern about Denmark can be followed in the entries for the first half of November. H.R. Trevor-Roper (ed.), *Hitler's War Directives 1939–1945* (London, 1964), pp.218–24.
56. David Mure, *Master of Deception* (London, 1980). See, Appendix: 'Some Personal Reflections on the Practice of Deception in the Mediterranean Theatre from 1941 to 1945', by Brigadier Dudley Clarke (pp.273–5). COS(43)142nd Meeting(0), 30 June, CAB 79/62.
57. KTB/1 Skl., A, 1 Sept. 1943, T 1022/1682: Some of Ostro's intelligence could be traced back 'auf die Gewährsleute aus dem feindlichen und neutralen Lager ... wie das in Wesen derartiger Nachrichtendienst begrundet liegt'.
58. Operation Starkey: Appreciation and Outline Plan, COSSAC(43)4(Final), 26 June, copy in AIR 8/1202. Pujol with West, op. cit., pp.98–9.
59. KTB/1 Skl., A, 11 Sept. 1943; Ibid., 18 Sept. 1943, T 1022/1683.
60. COS(43)302(0), 11 June, CAB 80/70.
61. 'Ia Lagebericht West', OKH/GenStdH/Abt. Fremde Heere West, Nr. 1017 (Anlage), 9 Sept. 1943; Ibid., Nr. 1020 (Anlage), 12 Sept. 1943, MI 14/522/2. KTB/1 Skl., A, 14 Sept. 1943; Ibid., 10 Sept. 1943, T 1022/1683. 'Beurteilung der Lage', Oberfehlshaber West, Ia Nr. 550/43, gKdos. Chefs., 25 Oct. 1943, in RH 19 iv/i.
62. Operation Torrent: Appreciation and Outline Plan, COSSAC(43)39 (second draft), 16 September: the covername Torrent was dropped when the Bigot procedure was applied to the cover plans for Overlord at Morgan's suggestion towards the end of September; Torrent then became Appendix Y to COSSAC(43)28. See Plan Fortitude, Vol. I, SHAEF, SGS/381, RG 331. Masterman, *Double-Cross System*, p.158. Lt.-Col. James F. Barber to Supreme Commander AEF, 20 November 1944, in Fortitude (370.2), HQ 12 Army Group, Special Staff, Adj. Gen. Section, Administrative Branch, decimal file (370.2 Eclipse to Goldflake), RG 331.
63. Operation Overlord, COSSAC(43)28, Appendix Y, 20 November, in Plan Fortitude, Vol. I, SHAEF, SGS/381, RG 331. Campbell, 'Air Operations and the Dieppe Raid', *Aerospace Historian*, XXIII (1976), 10–20.
64. David Mure, *Practice to Deceive* (London, 1977), p.27. 'Cover and Deception, Synopsis of History', 12 Army Group, December 1944, Box 1, Folder 1, in Army – Operations, General Administrative Files, 1943–1952, RG 319. 'History of COSSAC', Historical sub-section, Office of the Secretary, General Staff, SHAEF, 8 – 3.6 CA cy 1, ACMH list.

65. 'Cover and Deception, Synopsis of History', 12 Army Group, December 1944, RG 319; in the same box there is a letter from Bevan to Major-General C. Bissell AC of S, G-2, War Department (CO/560, 11 December 1944), in which he criticizes several points raised in the Synopsis. It is clear from pencilled marginalia that Bissell (?) was not prepared to alter the critical evaluation of Cockade reached by 'ETO Staff'. Col. William A. Harris, Chief, Special Plans Branch, to Chief of Section G(R), undated, in Fortitude (370.2), HQ 12th Army Group, SS/Adj. Gen. (370.2 Eclipse to Goldflake), RG/331.

66. Memorandum from US Joint Chiefs of Staff to CCS, 18 January 1944, in Plan Bodyguard, Joint Chiefs of Staff, CCS decimal file 1942–1945, CCS 385(6-25-43), Sec. 1, RG 218.

67. Alfred D. Chandler Jr. (ed.), *The Papers of Dwight David Eisenhower: The War Years* (5 vols., Baltimore, 1970), III, p.1654, footnote 6: Eisenhower had wanted Major-General K.W.D. Strong, his G-2 at AFHQ, for his G-2 at SHAEF, but he had already moved so many other high-ranking officers out of the Mediterranean that the War Office at first refused; in May, however, Eisenhower did get Strong. Mure, *Master of Deception*, pp.231–3; Mure's source for Devers' views on Deception in the UK in 1943 was William Casey, OSS in 1943 and future Head of the CIA.

The German Misapprehensions Regarding Overlord: Understanding Failure in the Estimative Process

T.L. CUBBAGE II

From the German perspective, the D-Day invasion of Normandy on 6 June 1944 came as both a strategic and tactical surprise.[1] Within the context of the Second World War and the German intelligence analysis and command decision apparatus, this article seeks to examine the vital questions: what are the root causes of failure in the estimative process, and why does strategic surprise appear inevitable?[2]

Some popular historians have labeled the failure of German 'intelligence' regarding the Normandy landings as one of modern history's most extraordinary military blunders. In fact, there was nothing 'extraordinary' about the *Wehrmacht*'s apparent unreadiness for the main Allied assault, the *Schwerpunkt*. Rarely has a nation at war been more expectant of invasion. By late April 1944, Radio Berlin had broadcast to the German people that an enemy invasion in France would come at 'any minute, anywhere'.[3] On 18 May Radio Berlin announced that 'the ports [of England] are bristling – crammed to bursting point – with ... invasion equipment'.[4] The Germans certainly expected the *Grosslandung*; and yet, the critical details of their expectations simply were wrong. Though the Germans expected a diversionary attack to be made in Normandy, they were absolutely convinced that the *Schwerpunkt* would come in the Pas-de-Calais sector. Everything was set to await the arrival of the Allied forces north of the River Seine – where, in due course, Hitler and the *Wehrmacht* would destroy them. But, in their effort to build and man the *Atlantikwall*, the Germans made one critical mistake – one the French had made some years earlier. They forgot that a concrete and steel barrier with an exploitable weakness is no shield at all.

While this article is by no means a historical summary of the Normandy story, it does contain sufficient factual information to highlight the major threads of development and errors existing in the German pre- and post-invasion estimates.[5] As will become apparent, there is nothing unique about the factors that inhibited the German perceptive process; nothing to make the factors inapplicable outside the historical context of the war or the invasion. In fact, ten very common factors have been identified which, alone and in combination, formed significant blocks to the ability of the Germans to perceive correctly the Allied intentions. Stated in their simplest form, these are: 1) the human factor; 2) the bias factor; 3) the expectation factor; 4) the options factor; 5) the plausible interpretation factor; 6) the distraction factor; 7) the intelligence collection factor; 8) the deception factor; 9) the time factor; and 10) the organization factor.

GERMAN COLLECTION AND ANALYSIS CAPABILITY

Niccolò Machiavelli – who must have understood the concept of coincidence perfectly – believed that history proved that no great public misfortune occurred without being foretold, and that such prophets should be sought out and employed by the ruler.[6] In the Normandy story one-legged General Erich Marcks, who commanded *Armeekorps* 84 in the Normandy sector, played the part of 'Machiavelli's Prophet' – proving as always that it is hard to be a prophet in your own land. Inspecting the fortifications at Arromanches-les-Bains, on Thursday, 1 June 1944, he looked out to sea over what the British called Gold Beach, and told an officer with him: 'If I know the British, they'll go to church next Sunday one last time and then sail Monday. HGK B says they're not going to come yet, and that when they do come it'll be at Calais. So I think that we'll be welcoming them on Tuesday [6 June] right here'.[7] The problem then, as in the days of *Il Discorsi*, was that no one could recognize such casual observations as having historic significance until it was too late to matter.

By late 1943 the Germans understood that the Allies would invade the Western Front sometime in 1944. And yet, in spite of the fact that the Germans had a broad collection capability and a diverse analysis apparatus, Hitler and the *Wehrmacht* were never able to recognize and appreciate properly the key elements of the Overlord/Neptune invasion plan.[8] Nor could they deduce the correct time and place of the Anglo-American landings. At various times from between early 1943 and 6 June 1944, the Germans saw indications of, and gave credence to, the dangers of invasion in: the Balkans, Italy, Southern France, Spain, Portugal, and along the Biscay coast of France; also in Brittany, on the Contentin Peninsula, in Normandy, and the Pas-de-Calais; and even in Belgium, Holland, the Skagerrak, and Norway.

Asked by Japanese Ambassador Ōshima in January 1944 where he thought the enemy would land, the Führer answered: 'Beyond a doubt the most effective area would be along [the shores of] the Straits of Dover, but to land there would require much preparation and the difficulty would be great. I don't think the enemy would run such a risk'.

Hitler admitted to the Ambassador that it would be 'impossible' to prevent the enemy from landing 'somewhere in the West', but he declared that Germany would nevertheless 'absolutely stop any real second front'.[9]

Between 1941 and July 1944, the major German command and agency analysis centers had at their disposal a quantitatively if not qualitatively impressive volume of information relating to the Western threat from which they put together pre- and post-invasion estimates.[10] A brief review of how the Germans answered the four basic questions that faced them will aid in understanding their failure to anticipate correctly the Allied plan.

THE GERMAN ESTIMATES

• *The How of Attack.* By June 1944 the Germans had decided that the Allied invasion scenario called for several attacks. Hitler was firmly convinced that the enemy would stage several large diversions in addition to delivering the *Schwerpunkt* or main blow.

• *The Where of Attack.* Hitler believed that the first major diversion would come in the Normandy–Contentin Peninsula sector; the second diversion in the Brittany sector; and the main assault in the Pas-de-Calais sector.

• *The Date of Attack.* Initially the Germans decided that the invasion landings would begin on 18 May 1944. The exact date was established on the basis that the landings would be made on a high tide coinciding with dawn. When the expected invasion did not come in May, estimates varied as to the next most probable time. At first it was believed that the invasion would not come before mid-June. Bad weather developing over France on 3 June made an imminent attack appear very unlikely. *Heeresgruppenkommando* B (HGK B) and *Oberbefehlshaber West* (OB West) thought that the landings would be in either mid-July (Rommel's view at HGK B) or mid-June (von Rundstedt's view at OB West). Then, on the evening of 5 June, additional indicators pointed to an attack before 8 June. However, only the divisions subordinate to *Armeeoberkommando 15* (AOK 15) in the Pas-de-Calais sector were put on full alert.

• *The Strength of Attack.* Estimates varied of the size of the enemy forces in England and the number of divisions that could participate in the initial assault waves. Rommel's staff at HGK B believed that the Allies had about 65 combat-ready divisions in England (actually, of some 35 Allied divisions in England, 29 divisions were assigned to the Overlord plan). The staff at *Oberkommando der Kriegsmarine* (OKM) estimated that the Anglo-Americans were capable of simultaneous landing on a 25-division front. The *Oberkommando der Wehrmacht* (OKW) staff thought the enemy could land on a 15–20-division front, or make several strong diversionary landings in multi-division strength followed by the main blow.

When the landings began in Normandy, the Germans were at first uncertain whether it was a raid, a diversionary attack, or the main attack. By mid-day on 6 June, the Führer had decided that the landing was the strong diversion that he had predicted would come in Normandy, and not the *Schwerpunkt*. Hitler reminded his staff of his prediction, saying that his warnings had proved well-founded.[11] He then warned of the imminence of a second diversion in Brittany and of the main attack in the Pas-de-Calais sector. At the mid-afternoon Führer Conference, *Grossadmiral* Karl Dönitz argued that if there was to be a second seaborne assault it probably would not come in Brittany, but Hitler insisted that it would.[12]

As time passed, the *Wehrmacht* commanders in France became convinced that the Normandy invasion would be the only Allied landing; but Hitler – directing German war operations from his head-quarters 1000 kilometers to the east at Berchtesgaden – would not accept that view. As late as 8 July, the Führer was still warning of the danger of attacks in Brittany and north of the Seine in the Pas-de-Calais sector. On that day, in a new directive for the conduct of operations in the West, Hitler noted:

> the enemy probably will attempt a second landing in France in the *Armeeoberkommando 15* sector [which was the Pas-de-Calais area], all the more so, as public opinion [in England] will press for the elimination of the long-range [V-1 pilotless flying bomb] weapons firing on London. The disposition of the forces still available in England suggest attacks primarily against the sector between the Somme and Seine [Rivers], ... but [attacks] also [are possible] against [both] Belgium and Southern Holland. At the same time, surprise attacks designed to effect the capture of one of the large ports of Brittany cannot be ruled out. Similarly, an attack aggainst the French Mediterranean coast also may be expected.[13]

It was his belief in, and real fear of, a second attack which caused Hitler to hold back from the fight in Normandy all of the numerous strong divisions stationed in the Pas-de-Calais sector. If they had been committed immediately to the counter-invasion battle, these units well might have played a decisive part in the battle for the beachhead. It was not until 25 July that the Führer authorized OB West to move some of the AOK 15 units into the battle in the AOK 7 sector, but by then it was too late.[14]

THE ROOTS OF FAILURE

In the context of the times, and from the German perspective, there was no irrationality in the developing process that produced the pre- and post-invasion estimates concerning the impending June 1944 D-Day landings. Some writers have pointed to certain very specific indicators – the lines from Paul Verlaine's poem, *'Chanson d'Automne'*, in the *messages personnels* broadcast to the French resistance being the most popular choice – and characterized them as so absolutely unequivocal that as indicators they should have over-ridden any assumed level of wartime confusion in the analysis process. Nevertheless, on close scrutiny, each of the so-called clear warnings, in the context of January to June 1944, were not only ambiguous but often patently inconsistent with other apparently unequivocal information.

Consider, for example, the impact that the inclement weather during the first few days of June had on all the other 'obvious and unequivocal' warnings of an impending attack. On 6 June 1944 Admiral Theodor Kranke, *Chef, Marinegruppenkommando West* at Paris, noted in his *Kriegstagebuch*:

> The enemy has certainly succeeded in surprising to a certain extent the whole machinery of the German defense organization; and not the least by the clever choice of a period to land when the weather appeared to be [very] unfavorable, but kept improving.[15]

Much of the incompetence or wanton neglect imputed to the Germans and their several intelligence services has resulted from a suppression or ignorance of the many intelligence indicators that logically pointed to greater invasion dangers in every quarter except Normandy. Furthermore, many of the histories were written before the declassification and public release of the details of the Fortitude deception plan,[16] the Double-Cross agent operations[17] and the Ultra-Magic signal intelligence.[18] Indeed, when all factors are considered, it is hardly fair to say simply that there was a German 'intelligence' failure. To be sure, there were numerous notable intelligence collection failures. But, and of more significance, the Germans' 'failure' was also one of analysis and acceptance, i.e., product use; it involved both the German intelligence services and the command centers.[19] The 'failure' involved the Führer, *Wehrmacht* officers in Germany and France, and the men of *Abwehr* and the *Reichssicherheitshauptamt* (RSHA).

Any study of the intelligence process must accept that correct information, told in time yet not believed or not acted on, is no intelligence at all.[20] One of the most critical phases in the intelligence cycle lies in persuading the military and political leadership to make timely use of the information and analysis furnished to them.[21] The Germans never succeeded in this regard.

It must be understood that certain circumstances arise in the context of preparing military estimates which tend to form blocks to proper perception, and so make an already difficult intelligence task seem virtually impossible. While strategic surprise seems inevitable, it is too easy to allow that conclusion to follow merely from the difficulty of the task of analysis and acceptance. But, once the blocks that impeded the German perception capability are identified and their roots understood, it will be possible to appreciate better – if not understand fully – why the Germans failed to anticipate the Allied intentions. The ten perception blocks identified in this article are expressed in terms of blocking factors – factors which cloud men's minds when they try to see into the future.

1. *The Human Factor*

One very basic cause of the German inability to perceive the relevant indicators of an Anglo-American *Schwerpunkt* in the Normandy region was *the human factor*. If men are to perform the task of analysis and acceptance – for what machine can do the job? – then it must be accepted as inevitable that mistakes will be made.

An examination of the human factor means focusing on a few of the key people involved in the intelligence and command apparatus, for 'ultimately, the idiosyncrasies and personality of each leader play a definite rôle'.[22] In 1944 in Germany the key man was Adolf Hitler. As Führer, he was both the chief intelligence analyst and ultimate command policy-maker.[23] The important secondary figures were Rommel at HGK B, von Rundstedt at OB West, Jodl at OKW, Schellenberg at RSHA/SD, and Bormann at *Führerhauptquartier*. At the tertiary level, the cast is legion. In discussing the human factor it will suffice to focus on Hitler in particular, and the German officer corps in general.

In matters of intelligence analysis and command policy-making much depends on whether leaders are open-minded, especially to receiving unpleasant information, and freely encourage criticism.[24] As Michael Handel pertinently observes:

> Leaders in a democratic system are generally more inclined
> to consider a wider variety of options than those who have
> always functioned within authoritarian or totalitarian political

systems. In authoritarian countries, where the climb to the top is an unrelenting struggle for power, habits of cooperation and openness are usually less developed. The prevalence of ideology naturally restricts openness to variety, criticism, and consideration of contradictory ideas. Leaders in totalitarian countries ordinarily have little tolerance for ideas that deviate from the 'party line', since such ideas are seen as personal criticism – as a dangerous element undermining the existing ideology.[25]

As an example of totalitarian leadership, the Führer's attitudes and pattern of rule corroborate Handel's observations. Hitler was able to create and remain within his own closed and private world, from which the ugly and awkward facts of Germany's wartime situation were systematically excluded.[26] He simply refused to credit any report which contradicted his view of Germany and its role and position in the world, or its capabilities on the battlefield.[27] Hitler's staff at the *Führerhauptquartier* perceived their duty to their leader as to maintain his *Nachtwandlerische Sicherheit* – his sleepwalker's sense of security.[28]

> The power of Martin Bormann, Hitler's personal secretary, was built up on the skill with which he pandered to his weakness, carefully keeping back unpleasant information and defeating the attempts of those who tried to make Hitler aware of the gravity of the situation.[29]

With that view the RSHA/SD regulated the information forwarded for the Führer's attention – operating on the assumption that Hitler wanted reassurance rather than the truth.[30] In this cosmic isolation Hitler made most of his decisions without consulting anyone on his personal or military staff.[31] It is little wonder that in December 1943 *Feldmarschall* Rommel was moved to denounce the *Atlantikwall* and the concept of a *Festung Europa* as a cloud cuckoo land illusion: the figment of Hitler's *Wolkenkuckucsheim*.[32]

Klaus Knorr makes an especially important observation about the critical problem of interaction between the intelligence and the command decision staffs:

> While intelligence organizations are largely manned by professionals with expertise related to the warning function, top decision-makers are not, and have not been trained in the business of reacting to and acting upon warning. They have arrived at their positions on the basis of quite different skills, and their staffs have been selected on the basis of criteria that are for the most part indifferently or not closely related to the matter of responding to strategic warning.[33]

In this context, Hitler and his staff of sycophants can be viewed as merely the extreme case of a general mental disposition on the part of decision-making staffs.

In contrast to the situation today where large intelligence organizations and staffs are the rule, none of the major powers entered the Second World War with a trained, standing professional military intelligence corps. The *Wehrmacht* approached the problem as simply one of military staffing where one officer ought to be as good as another. However, in practice most *Wehrmacht* intelligence officers (*Ics*) were regarded as *die Mädchen für Alles* (maids of all work). That this could include war diary, morale, propaganda, and censorship duties as well did not make the *Ics'* position a distinguished one.[34] The RSHA/SD approach to military intelligence was not much different.

As Donald McLachlan has noted: 'Certain professions, certain kinds of university study, [seem to] develop just those mental skills that intelligence work requires; what is [much] more important, they encourage ... confidence in the making of [difficult] judgments'.[35] In other words, professional soldiers, it is implied, do not have the right attributes for strategic military intelligence. The need for obedience and subordination, and the rank consciousness in all uniformed services make it difficult for career military intelligence specialists to make bold assertions: the system does not tolerate what is often viewed as insubordinate behavior, and few career officers want to risk their reputation and advancement on a long-shot prediction.[36] Michael Handel has summarized what the 'gifted amateur' can bring to an intelligence service:

> Amateurs frequently bring with them new enthusiasm, a creative imagination, informality, perhaps some academic openness, and a somewhat more detached and objective search for *veritas* – all of which are intellectual qualities highly useful for intelligence work in general and deception work in particular. This fresh start allows them to reexamine old problems from a new point of view, unlike the pre-war professional intelligence bureaucrats: they were not obligated to commit themselves to earlier, not always fully rational, traditions or to old policies.[37]

A close look at those in the *Wehrmacht* and RSHA who were involved in the intelligence analysis and warning process does not reveal a strong cadre of well-trained or experienced intelligence officers.

Beyond the problem of training and experience is the issue of personal attitudes. How do the analysts and policy-makers view life in general? According to Michael Handel, the 'early and easily attained military successes caused the Germans to feel vastly superior to their adversaries, to feel that they were immortal ... [which], combined with their traditional nationalism, assumed racial superiority and ethnocentric view of the world, reduced their incentives to learn about others'.[38] Hitler had a particularly dangerous aversion to being on the defensive. His expansionist vision of Germany's destiny made him steadfastly refuse to retire voluntarily on any front,[39] even denying his frontline commanders freedom to maneuver when on the defensive.

Driven by his view of Germany and his historic rôle in creating the Third Reich, Hitler ceased to acquire and evaluate the evidence – intelligence or otherwise – available to him. All his judgements sprang from his belief that he was the leader of an irreversible historic movement. Accordingly, he had no need for intelligence, for if – as he believed – his was a divine mission, there could be only one outcome: total victory over Germany's enemies. For Hitler and the Nazi regime, there was no room for the notion that 'intelligence can and should be the voice of conscience of his staff'.[40]

The observation that Hitler made most of his decisions without consulting anyone implied that not even the intelligence staff at OKW/WFSt was consulted. Hitler disliked intelligence reports, partly because he believed they were only evidence of the enemy's deceits.[41] Most of all he distrusted signal intelligence, regarding it as an obvious vehicle for the practice of deception. The Führer also had an ideological bias regarding intelligence reports.[42]

John Campbell has put the intelligence situation *vis-à-vis* the Führer in the following perspective:

> Hitler's attitude toward intelligence was at best ambivalent. Intelligence at variance with his governing *Wunschbild* stood a good chance of rejection as defeatist; at times, according to [General] Warlimont, the clearer the information about enemy intentions the more Hitler was inclined to doubt it. [*Obserst* Alexis von] Roenne[, *Chef, OKH/Fremde Heeres West*] was summoned to [the *Führerhauptquartier* at] Rastenburg only two or three times a month and might then be granted only ten minutes of [General] Jodl's time. Hitler never saw him at all.[43]

Paul Seabury adds to the understanding of Hitler's bias:

> Hitler, for example, 'did not decide to occupy the Rhineland or Austria or to attack Czechoslovakia or Poland because any incoming information ... exposed an opportunity.' Instead the basic decision [to act] was made and then intelligence was gathered in order to determine the techniques to be employed.[44]

For Hitler, intelligence was not important, except at a tactical level or as a counter-intelligence tool. It was not seen as a policy-making or strategic planning tool.

Moreover, 'the more conservative German officer corps strongly resisted the integration of intelligence officers into the *Wehrmacht*. ... This conservatism, tradition and aversion to civilian intellectuals did not allow them to tap the enormous intelligence potential of civilian amateurs'.[45] When they were on the offensive – sometimes only in the Führer's imagination – Germany and the *Wehrmacht* simply neglected the strategic intelligence function.[46]

> This fundamental neglect of intelligence perfectly suited the elite of the German officer corps. They believed that aggressiveness from which [the neglect] ... stemmed protected Germany and thus their livelihoods from foreign dangers. Inside Germany, however, in the army, they did not merely ignore intelligence; they fought it. For intelligence threatened their jobs.[47]

To recognize the need for intelligence was simultaneously to acknowledge its importance. From that would follow the need to create a new kind of officer to deal with it. In the end, it would rob the traditional *Wehrmacht* officers of their power and *raison d'être*.[48]

The *Wehrmacht* officer corps was not unique in that regard; nor was Hitler's attitude about intelligence. Historical evidence supports Donald McLachlan's observation that 'men of action, [and] the commanders in operations tend at first to be suspicious or even contemptuous of intelligence unless they have experience of its methods'.[49]

Having good intelligence is one thing: being able to understand its significance and apply it to the conduct of battle is quite another. *Feldmarschall* Rommel, for one, knew how to make good tactical use of quality intelligence – when it was available, as, for instance, in North Africa. 'He never sent his troops into action without careful thought. Meticulous collection of information and reconnaissance, often carried out personally, always preceded an operation'.[50] In that theater he was well served by the tactical intelligence collection efforts of the combat Y-Service of the *Wehrmacht* which provided radio monitoring and radio direction finding information.[51] When Rommel went to France in December 1943 he discovered that he would have little reliable information for his use in defensive planning.

Much has been written about Hitler's uncanny intuition and amazing good luck. Throughout the 1930s and into 1941, Hitler acted on political hunches. Time after time his decisions turned out to be right. His many successes confounded friend and foe alike. It was the political successes that eventually encouraged Hitler to apply his intuitions to the battlefield as well.[52] Yet Hitler's 'good luck and uncanny intuition' was nothing more than an astute political appraisal of the timid leaders of France and England, and their unwillingness to call his bluff. When the bullets actually started flying that political astuteness counted for nothing.

Intuition is an interesting concept: 'the word implies that understanding can take place without the reason intervening. This may be true in the Arts and in religious experience, but in military matters it is nothing more than "hunch" '.[53] In the business of military intelligence there is no substitute for an analytical framework which allows for an orderly and objective arranging and weighting of the best evidence.[54]

To sum up, when the variety of individual preferences and prejudices are multiplied by the number of people involved in the German intelligence collection and analysis and decision-making systems, then the importance of *the human factors* becomes readily apparent. Sometimes men of diverse views and experience work well together and their diversity provides a complement, making for a better collective judgement. That did not happen in Germany and occupied France in 1943 and 1944.

Many German intelligence analysts did what they could to make proper use of the available intelligence. The *Wehrmacht* officers, particularly those serving in France, seemed to have paid due regard to the military intelligence information they received. It cannot be said that Hitler made good use of intelligence. But what is most interesting about the Normandy landings was that no one on the German side ever realized what the Allies were planning to do. Before the actual landings one does not see a situation in which Hitler believed one thing and the others something else. The fact that the Germans erred in their estimates cannot be persuasively explained by accusing Hitler, the *Wehrmacht* officers, individually or as a group, of conspiracy, neglect or simply stupidity.

Little care seems to have been taken by the Germans in the selection of their intelligence officers, or in training the commanders who made the final assessments of the situation. As a result the quality of their intelligence collection and strategic analysis was poor. Some may be tempted to speculate that if all the Germans who played a part in the development of the pre- and post-invasion estimates had been trained intelligence officers, better estimates *might* have been produced. Though the lack of a formal intelligence training may have derogated the intelligence analysis acumen of some of the key men involved, it was certainly not the whole cause of their failure. Consequently, there must have been, and indeed were, other important factors which influenced the German ability to perceive and act on the relevant indicators.

2. *The Bias Factor*

The bias factor opens new vistas in the study of the more general humanistic factors as they affect intelligence estimates. The central themes here are the patterns of erroneous perception and judgement, i.e. 'biases' or errors in judgement that are consistent and statistically predictable in the sense that in a large number of cases, most people will be influenced by such tendencies most of the time.[55] There are many biases, but most can be grouped into four general categories: cultural; motivational; cognitive; and perceptual.

• *Cultural.* Cultural biases − *arrogance* and *projection* − are rooted in the basic predisposition inherent in the analyst's cultural values and heritage.[56] Projection and arrogance are reciprocal cultural biases. Arrogance causes the analyst to think he and his party or nation are better than others; projection causes him to see other men as beneath or behind him. Both are cultural mental defense mechanisms. As Kenneth Booth points out, if the analyst knows too much about his adversary, the truth may be too frightening for him to comprehend, and a demoralization − the Hamlet syndrome − may result.[57]

Arrogance. As a cultural bias, arrogance has special relevance to the study of German intelligence estimates and command decision-making. Arrogance distorted the German view of the world into an unreal one, which, in turn, resulted in many harmful decisions.[58] National arrogance was echoed in Hitler's personal arrogance when he told his Foreign Minister, von Ribbentrop, that 'when he had to make great decisions, he considered himself to be an instrument of [divine] providence which the Almighty had determined. He [added] ... that before big decisions, he always had a feeling of absolute certainty'.[59]

In early 1944, at the age of 54, Hitler had no habits of co-operation or of orderly staff work, and was incapable of disciplined or systematic work.[60] He simply imposed his ideas on others. Early successes in the face of senior German military and foreign policy opposition convinced him that his intuition was infallible.[61] The Führer did not, in his own mind, need intelligence. He *knew* what would be the outcome of his decisions and had no need for intelligence estimates − particularly contrary ones.

Projection. The concept of projection relates to the tendency of human perceptions to be ethnocentric. That means seeing the external world inside out, which typically involves the projection of one's own belief systems, and, by definition, causes the underestimation, if not the denigration, of one's opponent's culture, motivations, intentions, material and technological achievements, and the capacity to identify with others.[62] The Germans' projection of their belief in 'Aryan superiority' made it appear to them that none of their adversaries would prove more than minor nuisances on the battlefield. Their experiences on the plains of Poland and the fields of France gave their new *Blitzkrieg* doctrine the appearance of the ultimate concept.

• *Motivational*. Motivational biases, such as *risk-taking* and *over-confidence*, result from the influence on judgement of ambitions and fears, and the need for men to perceive their past behavior as commendable and consistent.[63]

Risk-taking. Whenever decisions must be made in the face of uncertainty there is an element of risk, and a decision to go forward with a plan of action in the light of the risk involves an element of 'gambling'.

> When it comes to gambling, we must distinguish between *the considered gamble* and *the pure gamble*. A considered gamble is based on a calculated risk and is decided upon only after careful consideration of the pros and cons in the light of prevalent uncertainties. A pure gamble occurs when an actor is inclined to gamble as a matter of personality, or because he perceives viscerally that there is no acceptable alternative … and will plunge without a careful prior evaluation of the problem or when the calculated risk would be forbidding to the purely rational decision-maker.[64]

Practical experience confirms that in the real world *considered* and *pure* gambling occur in various mixtures. Without question, Adolf Hitler was predisposed to *pure* gambling. At no point – even after the most serious defeats – did the Führer ask for or encourage better intelligence analysis to aid him in making major decisions, for in his mind he had no need of it.[65]

In the late 1930s the senior officers of the *Wehrmacht* were generally disposed to be risk-averse. The early successes and Hitler's 'luck' changed all that. By 1941 the senior *Wehrmacht* officers at OKW were inclined to high-risk 'fuzzy' gambling – taking action where the frequency of the occurrence of low probability events is highly variable, and where the extent of the commander's control over the amount of reliable military intelligence about the combat environment is severely limited.[66]

This propensity is, and must be, in the nature of military line officers. To paraphrase Walter Warlimont:

> This was in the best tradition of the soldier. Such heroic determination in battle had given the Prussian–German army many a

victory and much more besides. But when it turned into a political code of conduct, as at the end of the First World War and during the Hitler period, it leads to irretrievable disaster. For what in the soldier is the height of courage, in the stateman is likely to be irresponsible temerity.[67]

It was this sort of unjustified arrogance which caused the senior *Wehrmacht* officers to lose touch with reality.[68] They were carried along with Hitler's pure gambling, and any need felt for good strategic intelligence simply disappeared. Thus, for them the strategic intelligence estimate became – if anything – simply a rationalization for what they were bound and determined to do; tactical intelligence was used after a decision was made.

Over-confidence. (Hubris). Over-confidence – that feeling that the other side would not dare – is said to be the most frequent cause of surprise.[69] Certainly it tends to breed vulnerability.[70] 'Swaggering tends to produce self-intoxication, and along with it an inflation of one's strength across-the-board', and such an enhancement of self-esteem tends to lead to even greater self-confidence, and produce even more aggressive attitudes toward an adversary.[71]

Hubris – the central theme in the Greek tragedies – is the zenith state of over-confidence, connoting a pride and insolence so extreme that in ancient times the infuriated gods would strike men down at the height of their success. One must understand the tremendous risks taken by Hitler in 1936–40, and appreciate his apparent good luck, in order to comprehend the hubris that prompted him to take even more impossible chances in his air attacks against England and land attack on Russia when his luck ran out.[72] When men like Hitler are being swept along in a hubristic state of mind, strategic intelligence becomes, at best, no more than an unnecessary distraction.

• *Cognitive.* The cognitive biases result simply from the way the mind tends to work and not from any intellectual or emotional predisposition toward a certain judgement.[73] The *attribution of causality*, the *estimation of probability*, and the *evaluation of evidence* all merit discussion.

Causality. This aspect of the cognitive bias affects the way the mind arrives at attributions of causality. An analyst can see a plane or a tank, but he cannot see causation. Instead, the analyst's individual perception of causation results only from a complex process of inference, and as with other forms of inference, his specific perceptions are subject to systematic biases.[74] For most people the events in the world are seen as part of an orderly, casually related pattern, in which chance, accident and error tend to be rejected as explanations for an observed event.[75] Moreover, the extent to which other people, ethnic or religious groups, or other nations pursue a coherent, rational, goal-maximizing policy is often overestimated.[76] The need to find order and not chaos or pure chance in the world is a powerful mental force; a bias that can lead to incorrect conclusions being drawn about causality.

The very real problem for the intelligence analyst is that, by definition, his task is to fit various intelligence reports into nice categories which can be explained. It is very hard to write an intelligence report on an observed event and conclude with an admission of ignorance as to the reasons for or implications of the event. Consequently, where the enemy is practicing some form of active deception, the analyst probably will find it much easier to accept and deal with the false data as true because he will find they fit better into an estimate that has good causal linkages. In the business of intelligence, if something is too good to be true, then it probably is not true; except, of course, when it is! The Germans were able to fit all of their evidence into one tidy package which pointed inexorably to a *Schwerpunkt* in the Pas-de-Calais sector.

Probability. This aspect of the cognitive bias affects the way the mind makes estimations of probabilities.

> Social, political, military and economic development are not rigidly determined but occur or fail to occur with some degree of probability. Decision-makers cannot be certain of the outcome of their actions, so they weigh the probabilities of alternate outcomes. The information on which these decisions are based also involves many uncertainties expressed in probabilistic terms.[77]

Nevertheless, there is much 'fuzziness' in defining the terms 'probable' and 'possible'.[78] More important than the linguistic problem (which is dangerous enough) there is a systematic bias which affects the very accuracy of the way that probability is measured.[79] In general, analysts will tend to overestimate the probability of future event scenarios that are constructed from a series of discrete and individually probable events.[80]

> The principle of representativeness dictates that the more detailed ... future scenarios become, the more likely they will seem – since the detail makes an account more strongly resemble the real world. But imagine a scenario involving seven such assumptions, each of which has a 90 per cent chance of being right. Its overall odds would be somewhat less than 50–50 ($\cdot 9 \times \cdot 9 \times \cdot 9 \times \cdot 9 \times \cdot 9 \times \cdot 9 \times \cdot 9 = 47.8$ per cent).[81]

Too many analysts and policy-makers never give a second thought to the fact that a multi-branch decision tree can produce a very low final overall probability factor.

If the bias in favor of giving so high a probability to a multiple sequence event is not bad enough, intelligence analysts often have even more difficulty in estimating the likelihood of low probability events even when they recognize that such events may have serious consequences.[82] In simplest terms, an analyst's estimate of an event's probability is directly influenced by its mental availability to him. If he can easily imagine or remember such an event, or something like it, then his probability estimate will be higher. Since many of the events that occur in war time are unique – and thus by definition low probability events – the likelihood of error because of this estimation bias looms large. For the German analysts, it was genuinely hard to imagine an Allied landing in the Normandy sector – with no ready access to a port and with the rocky shallows offshore – so it is not difficult to understand why they did not rate such a landing as a high probability event.

Evaluation. This cognitive bias affects the way the mind evaluates evidence in three different ways: the first is concerned with an over-sensitivity to *consistency*; the second with the *absence of evidence*; and the third with *discredited evidence*.

– *Consistency.* When preparing estimates, analysts routinely formulate alternate hypotheses and select the one which includes the greatest amount of the available evidence within a logically consistent scenario.[83] When very little information is available, serious problems of bias arise. Analysts tend to be over-sensitive to consistency. It is not uncommon for an analyst to have more confidence in the conclusions drawn from a very small body of very consistent information than from a larger body of less consistent data. Such confidence is misplaced because the conclusions drawn from very small samples are highly unreliable in a statistical sense.[84]

– *Absence of Evidence.* It is in the nature of military intelligence to have to assess situations in the recognized absence of evidence. In 1942 and 1943 the Germans were trying, with no objective evidence, to determine where the Allies would land in France before the Allies had decided. Most people in such situations have great difficulty in factoring the lack of evidence into their judgements.[85] There is a strong tendency mentally to sum all the variables in an equation to 100 per cent, and even the most experienced analyst finds it difficult to ascribe a high per cent factor to a single category called 'unknown information' or 'other unknown options'. Military officers, including those in intelligence, are constantly exhorted to 'expect the unexpected', but even when they do, they give it a very low probability factor.

– *Discredited Information.* Another critical bias phenomenon concerning the evaluation of evidence is that 'initial impressions tend to persist even after the evidence that created them is fully discredited'.[86] There is a natural 'tendency to interpret new information in the context of pre-existing impressions ... even after the new evidence authoritatively discredits the evidence on which it is based'.[87] Richard Heuer explains this: 'When evidence is first received, it is perceived within a context that implies [some] causal connection between the evidence and some antecedents that explain the evidence. The stronger the antecedents, the stronger the impression created by the evidence'.[88] Thus, even though early evidence is subsequently discredited, the original causal linkages remain plausible and may be seen by the analyst as sufficient to imply the existence of an event even in the absence of the discredited evidence.[89]

• *Perceptual.* The perceptual biases arise, as noted below in *Modeling, Plots and Narratives, Sagacity* and *Acumen*, from the nature of the process by which analysts perceive the world around them, and from the limits on the accuracy of perceptions.[90]

Modeling (Bounded Rationality). The world is a very complex place, yet man copes with the complexity.

> Over 20 years ago, Herbert Simon advanced the concept of 'bounded' or limited rationality. Because of the limits of our mental capacity, he argued, the human mind cannot cope directly with the complexities of the world. Rather we [all] construct in our mind a simplified model of reality and then work with this mental model. We behave rationally within the confines of our mental model, but this model is generally not very well adapted to the requirements of the real world.[91]

The mental models analysts construct as individuals are no more than 'simplifying strategies' which they employ to assist them personally when they mentally process information.[92] Since each of these models reflect individual needs – i.e., they are self-directed – they are dangerous models for use in viewing the world at large. The models an analyst must use when dealing with an adversary in a war-fighting context need to be sophisticated strategies, fine-tuned to the business of producing intelligence estimates. The German experience proved that even the personal models that are tailored to a professional military lifestyle are not well suited to estimating what an adversary will do.

Plots and Narratives. As an alternative to the use of simplifying models to deal with highly complex situations, Theodore Sarbin opines that human beings think, perceive and imagine according to a narrative structure. In other words, given two or three stimulus inputs, an analyst will connect them to form a story.[93]

> The narrative is a way of organizing episodes, actions and accounts of actions; it is a mode of incorporating not only accounts of actions but also accounts of accounts of actions; it allows for the inclusion of antecedent and concurrent events which guide action. In short the narrative is an organizing principle ... Gestalt psychology has demonstrated that organizing principles are at work in the patterning or structuring of sense data. The gestalt idea ... is incorporated by the aphorism: the whole is greater than the sum of its parts.[94]

The narrative as a perceptual device is well suited as a tool to deal with explaining the behavior of others in military situations involving unbounded complexity. The narrative device has all the properties of a lively metaphor, and calls to mind the images of a story, a plot, characters and a storyteller.[95] When using the narrative as an intelligence estimation tool, the analyst becomes kin to the historian, who, 'unlike the novelist, is expected to tell his stories so that they [truly] are consistent with chronology and reveal a 'truth'.[96]

Of course, the key to a good novel is the plot. The same is true when the narrative is used as an analytical tool. The analyst focuses on the plot as a device for penetrating the meaning of the actions of others. He looks beyond the story – the narrative flow – and reads the intentions of the adversary in the underlying plot. The use of the 'emplotment technique' of analysis is not a substitute for prediction by other methodologies; instead it is a supplementary concept necessary for dealing with the complex or unique case, or with counter-deception analysis.[97]

While it is a powerful analytical tool, the concept of plots and narratives is not without its limitations. The plot, once constructed, will dictate the best possible endings for the incomplete story: once established, the plot becomes part of the analyst's current expectations.[98]

> The problem for the counter-deception analyst is to construct a plot from antecedent events and predict the outcome. [He is] ... still concerned with predicting the actions of an adversary, but the foundations for [his] ... predictions are not chronologies of specific events, but the organizing principles that assign meaning to the happenings.[99]

Thus, if the analyst assumes that the adversary is practicing to deceive, and assumes that the enemy knows well the rules of the deception game, then the analyst's *a priori* question should be put immediately to the man who makes the policy – the man for whom the analyst is preparing the estimate.

The question for the policy-maker is simple: 'What makes YOU afraid?'[100] If the adversary is good at the deception game, then he will try to find out what makes the analyst's policy-makers nervous and play to that concern. Since the ultimate target of deception is the decision-maker, the adversary will use any means, fair or foul, to learn the fears of the enemy decision-maker or command apparatus. The analyst also must learn the same thing if he is to guard his policy-maker from the enemy's deception schemes. According to Brigadier Dudley Clarke: 'You can never by deception, persuade an enemy of anything not according with his expectations, which are not far removed from his hopes'.[101]

Sagacity. Sagacity relates to the ability to make keen discernments. It is a statistical approach to intelligence problem-solving.[102] Sagacity is simply a mental methodology which involves the making of predictions through the 'freezing' or 'holding' of a matrix of clues and inferences.[103] In using this statistical sort of approach, the analyst first establishes that particular pieces of information are part of a class of strategic actions and factors; he then predicts for the particular case from knowledge of the characteristic of the class – all of which assumes that the analyst first has inductively derived base rates available.[104] There are a number of intelligence judgements of this type which can be made with reasonable accuracy – but it is a 'bean counter' type of methodology.

The use of base rate statistical analysis is appropriate when occurrences are repetitive and when predictions are expected to be in error proportional to the probabilities contained in the base rate.[105] In wartime situations with extremely high stakes, where life-and-death issues must be decided, inferences derived solely from base rates are seldom acceptable; the cost of false positives is too high.[106] Thus, the sagacity technique should be used only to supplement other forms of analysis. It could have been, but was not, used by the Germans to develop more reliable information about the Allied assault landing capabilities. Instead, in determining the enemy's amphibious assault capability by counting landing craft, the Germans appear to have altogether ignored the so-called landing craft base rate – or other background data on sealift capability. The German intelligence staff at OKH, *Fremde Heeres West*, was more concerned with the details of the Allied Order of Battle. Accordingly, as FHW identified new units and added them to the OB charts, the Germans made the assumption that if a division was in England and was of the assault type, then, perforce, the landing craft for the units must also exist! The Allied deception planners knew of the 'bean counter' approach being taken by the OKH/ FHW intelligence staff and gave them plenty of fictional divisions to count.

Acumen. Acumen means superior mental astuteness. It is contextual in nature and involves the analyst 'moving with the experimental flow, and responding flexibly to change and novelty as the target person enacts his roles'.[107] It is the technique that relies solely on the particular analyst's training and experience. He must be possessed of instinct, imagination, or *Fingerspitzengefühl*, and be able to listen with the 'third ear' and for the 'still small' voice.[108]

Acumen is the most powerful mental tool of the gifted analyst. Experience shows, one either has it or one does not – and an analyst may have it for one type of estimation or target area, and not for another. Acumen is like common sense – only it operates on a more intellectual plane. To paraphrase Theodore Sarbin:

> Prediction by acumen is the stock in trade of the analyst who can penetrate the masks and expose the lies of the adversary. He does this not exclusively by verbal or nonverbal tip-offs or leakage but through emphathetic skills. Everyday experience confirms that some analysts have skill in taking the role of the other. What appears to be involved when one analyst consistently makes the correct predictions of the conduct of other? Various traits have been posited, such as *Einfühlung* i.e., an emphathetic under- standing, or a getting in the spirit of the thing, social intelligence, and so on. Such traits serve only as synonyms for acumen. Among other things, it seems that the ability to view the world from the perspective of another is related to the analyst's ability to 'decenter', i.e., to shift from an established mental anchor to a new position in perceptual and cognitive judgments. It may be inferred that the analyst who is successful in taking the role of another is able to construct a scenario, a story, and place himself in relation to the other features of the story, physical features such as geography and climate, and social features, such as role relationships with multiple role players.[109]

Sarbin asks and answers the pertinent question: 'Can acumen be learned? The literature of psychology contains a number of programs that in principle might serve as heuristic devices for the training of analysts of strategic interaction'.[110] But, more importantly, common experience teaches that those predisposed to reason well will work in areas requiring that talent – law, scholarly research, writing, etc. The Second World War experience of the British certainly seems to bear this out, whereas the military academies, whether Prussian pre-war or otherwise, do not produce this type of gifted individual in any significant number.

3. *The Current Expectations Factor*

The Germans clearly recognized that their estimates were probably anticipating the actual Allied decision-making process. To overcome that problem, the German analysts attempted to develop logically the plan of attack that they believed their adversaries in time might also develop. After cataloguing and analysing the advantages and disadvantages of many areas the Germans decided that the best coastal sector for invasion was in the Pas-de-Calais region of France – on which, interestingly enough, all the Allied plans up to mid–1943 had focused.[111]

The Germans began to prepare their defenses accordingly. At that point *the current expectations factor* began to interfere with the German perception capability. Having concluded that the enemy would land in the Pas-de-Calais, the Germans naturally tended to ignore or misinterpret indicators pointing to large-scale landings in other sectors. Inasmuch as the current expectations seemed logically sound – and they were the product of careful study – they carried with them their own self-proving persuasiveness.

Many experiments demonstrate the extraordinary extent to which the information obtained by an analyst depends on his preconceptions, expectations and even his assumptions.[112] An analyst's expectations have many diverse sources, including past experience, professional training and cultural and organizational norms; all of which predispose the analyst to pay particular attention to certain kinds of information and to organize and interpret this information in certain ways.[113]

Thus, the current expectations factor is a fundamental principle of perception: analysts tend to perceive what they expect to perceive. A corollary is that it takes more information, and more unambiguous information, to recognize an unexpected phenomenon than an expected one.[114] If an analyst is not expecting immediate trouble, or trouble of a particular kind, or trouble in a particular place, then his neutral expectations determine how he will read an intelligence report; even as he sorts the reports before him, an analyst will select what accords with his expectations.[115] Such patterns of expectation, rooted in past experience and training, subconsciously tells the analyst what to look for, what is important, and how to interpret what he sees; these patterns form a 'mind-set' that predisposes the analyst to think in certain ways.[116]

In dealing with a major target country, intelligence officers naturally approach their task with a set of expectations about the target's likely patterns of behavior.[117] It is practically impossible for an analyst to sift the relevant from the irrelevant and to perceive a pattern in a large volume of information unless he has some hypothesis to guide him, for it is the analyst's expectations, resting on his beliefs about what is likely to happen, that determine what information receives his attention.[118] Richard Heuer notes that 'mind-sets are neither good nor bad: they [simply] are unavoidable. There is no conceivable way of coping with the volume of stimuli that impinge upon our senses, or with the [total] volume and complexity of the information that we have to analyze without some kind of simplifying preconception about what to expect, what is important, and what is related to what'.[119] And analysts must recognize that objective analysis is not achieved by avoiding pre-conceptions but by recognizing the tentative nature of all knowledge and by devising means to test our perceptions and assumptions against reality.[120] Joseph Stalin is said to have warned his intelligence chiefs to keep away from 'hypothesis and equation with too many unknowns', saying that 'an intelligence hypothesis may become your hobby horse on which you will ride straight into a self-made trap'.[121]

Against this background of current expectation problems, Richard Heuer observes: 'As a general rule, we are more often on the side of being too wedded to our established views and thus too quick to reject information that does not fit these views, than on the side of being too quick to reverse our beliefs. Thus, most of us would do well to be more open to evidence and ideas that are at variance with our pre-conceptions'.[122] The problem with this advice, as noted by Michael Handel, is that 'open-ended ideas do not provide enough basis for action or longer planning, as continuous change [and conflicting information] can bring about confusion and paralysis'.[123]

Almost without exception 'human beings impose structures on the flow of experience'.[124] Scientists and engineers tend to impose more formal structures, and in doing so 'schematize the flow of experience, seeking structure and organization as abstracted schemata aided by mathematical, geometric, graphic ... or other models'.[125] They inevitably produce a regressive view of the world which over the long span of time accounts for the observation that 'the extremes move toward the average'.[126] Given a choice, this tendency suggests that artists and writers are better suited or mentally disposed, to be intelligence analysts.

While the current expectations of the analyst are important, so are those of the adversary. 'Intelligence prediction is the estimation of the likely actions or intentions of foreign nations, and its failure can be reduced ... to a misunderstanding of foreigners' conceptual frameworks − i.e., a failure to understand properly the assumptions or interpretations of the situation upon which the foreigners base their decisions.'[127] When the adversary's actions do not correspond with the analyst's current expectations, behavioral surprise results. Thus, when an analyst forms expectations about the enemy he must be sure that they correspond with the adversary's attitudes or predispositions, for both affect the behavior of the adversary government.[128] Attitudes, though powerful in shaping behavior, do not by themselves determine it: behavior depends upon the information on which the adversary in question acts and the value he places on the outcome of alternative courses of action; it is through a mediation of such calculations that attitudes are brought into play.[129] Accordingly, intelligence estimates are often wrong, not simply because the analyst does not know the information or basic values on which an adversary acts, but because he assumed the adversary would 'act on the basis of approximately the same information or values that the analyst possesses'.[130]

Intelligence analysts share information and ideas, formally in reports, or casually in conversation. Studies of group interaction show that an analyst's interpretation of a piece of intelligence information will influence those with whom he is in contact.[131] In a military environment, the rank of the intelligence officer will influence the weight given to information from him.[132]

Three concepts − *unconscious suppression, stubborn attachment, and psychological investment* − form a cornerstone theory that explains why the current expectations factor tends to cause intelligence analysts and commanders to become locked into certain mind-sets.

• *Unconscious Suppression.* When an analyst is processing new intelligence information he approaches it with 'a set of assumptions and expectations about the motivation of people and the process of government in foreign countries: events consistent with these current expectations are perceived and processed easily; those that contradict prevailing expectations tend to be ignored or distorted in perception'.[133] Accordingly, from time to time, all of the old information should be re-examined − for an analyst's current expectations may change − to see if anything was overlooked, albeit unknowingly.

• *Stubborn Attachment.* Sometimes the analysts' problem is one of not being able mentally to discard an expectation. 'Human beings have a stubborn attachment to old beliefs'.[134] In some instances the pattern of expectation are so deeply embedded that they continue to influence preconceptions even when the analyst is alerted to and tries to take account of the existence of data that does not fit his preconceptions; trying to be objective does not guarantee accurate perception.[135] This problem is often referred to as *mental anchoring*.[136]

• *Psychological Investment*. At some point in the normal development of every intelligence estimate, the analyst moves from having a tentative hypothesis to having a reasoned opinion, and, at that point, he subconsciously makes a psychological investment in his work product. The harder he has worked to get to that point, the bigger his psychological investment. As his work continues, the analyst will find the intelligence information he used first will support his initial theory more and more; he will also find more facts to support his view. Once his estimate is put down on paper – especially if it is disseminated – the analyst's psychological investment in the product will make a change of mind virtually impossible.[137]

4. *The Options Factor*

In their attempt to cast themselves mentally as planners in the role of their adversary, the Germans had to make certain basic assumptions about the expected Allied amphibious operations. Lacking reliable information about the enemy's developing doctrine, techniques and capabilities, the Germans assumed that their enemy would solve the problems in the same way that the Germans would. However, their only real experience in such matters was the invasion planning associated with Operation Seelöwe, the 1940 German plan to attack England.

Before the Allied raid at Dieppe in August 1942 there was considerable similarity in German and Allied amphibious assault theories.[138] The Dieppe raid and the invasion of French North Africa in November 1942 highlighted a number of serious problems, and the 1943 landing in Sicily and the landings on the Italian mainland allowed the Overlord planners to refine their amphibious doctrine.[139] The German understanding of the cross-Channel invasion difficulty remained primitive.

Computing the Allied sealift capability on the basis of their Seelöwe estimates, OKM overestimated it by 20 divisions. The Germans assumed that the Allied plan, like Seelöwe before it, would involve one or more large diversions in conjunction with or prior to the *Schwerpunkt*; that their enemy would land at dawn and at high tide in order to unload his vessels as close to the high water mark as possible; that the landings would be made when the seas of the English Channel were quiet, after the heavy caliber coastal guns were destroyed, and at a time of blue sky weather to allow for the most effective use of the Allied air forces. Finally they assumed that the initial object of the assault forces would be the capture of a port or ports. In addition, almost all of the assumptions made concerning Allied invasion logistics proved wrong which also contributed to the errors in the Germans' pre- and post-invasion estimates.

The Germans imputed a universality of options based on what they knew or thought they could do, or upon facts they assumed were true. The real danger in option projection is the likelihood that the analyst's catalogue of possible options is too limited. The Allies had far more options and capabilities than the Germans imagined.

For an analyst to be able to estimate what an adversary may do, his intelligence data base needs to mirror not only the information theoretically available to the enemy commander, but must also include the information actually known or believed by the enemy planner. 'What is or is not possible matters less than what the enemy's believes is possible.'[140] A determination of the enemy's capabilities must, of course, be based on real world data, but since intent is formed on the basis of a belief about capabilities – which may be wrong – the analyst needs a different kind of intelligence.

If an analyst is to formulate reliable current expectations about the enemy he must understand the enemy's total array of options, even those which appear to be beyond his known capabilities. Building a multi-option array is a useful exercise in imagination and helps to curb the tendency to make a hasty judgement both about the options the enemy believes he has, and about his actual intent. To have too narrow a list of enemy options, or to misunderstand them – the twin failings of German analysis – puts the analyst in a dangerous position.

• *Developing the Hypotheses.* The first step in developing the hypotheses is 'option building': the formulation of the widest range of options on the basis of the enemy's actual capabilities, and then adding all the options that would be possible if the facts were as the enemy believes them. This simple cataloging process will make these options 'available' in terms of recall if information is received later that bears on the original option hypotheses.

Availability. The real problem for the analyst involved in the development of a broad array options list – assuming that he does not have the convenient aid of MAGIC intercepts – is that it is very hard to imagine the unimaginable; to go beyond the readily apparent options to find new, clever or unexpected ones. The problem here, of course, is the availability bias. 'People judge the likelihood of something happening by how easily they can call other examples of the same thing to mind.'[141] Obviously then, if an analyst has little or no experience in operations, or his knowledge of tactical doctrine is out of date, he will produce a very short list of options.

All too often, the analyst considers only what his side would do and assumes that the other side would do likewise, as if military options had some sort of universality. To be sure, at the primary level of attack, defend, reinforce, counterattack or withdraw – which is a fine list for low-level tactical analysis – options do have a universality; at the strategic estimates level more imagination is required.

Consistency. A factor which impedes the formulation of good sets of possible options is the frequent assumption by analysts that enemies will always act as they have in the past. If analysts believe that their side learns from its mistakes and that real improvements come from experience, they should assume that the adversary also improves within the limits of its capabilities.

The consistency factor is made worse because analysts also tend to assume that the enemy will act in a certain way within the bounds of his presumed capabilities or limitations. Time after time the Germans tended to grossly overestimate or underestimate their enemy's capabilities. It is important for the analyst to know about the enemy's past actions, otherwise he may know too little about his total range of options. However, if he is to make consistency judgements, the analyst needs a more representative sample of what the enemy has done in the past.[142]

Alternative Hypotheses. Analysts tend to perform rather poorly at the task of formulating full sets of enemy options; they simply do not – or cannot – postulate a broad enough set of alternative hypotheses. The formulation of proper alternative hypotheses and the identification of the key indicators associated with each help direct an economical search for information. The hypotheses also serve as an organizational structure for the easy storage and recall of information in memory.[143] In this way, a wide variety of options can be examined over time as the evidence becomes available. It is never wise to discard an option too early in the search for information – the option you discard may be so secret that you have yet to get anything on it, or it may prove to be the solution to a problem that the enemy has yet to discover.

How fanciful a list of options should the analyst assemble? The Germans were sure that the key to the invasion strategy was the quick capture of a port. The Allies, believing the quick capture of a port would be impossible, brought their ports with them in artificial form. Accordingly, the wise analyst should remember these words from *Through the Looking Glass*:

'I daresay you haven't had much practice,' said the Queen [to

Alice]. When I was your age, I always did it for half-an-hour a day. Why, sometimes I've believed as many as six impossible things before breakfast.'[144]

How much easier it is to imagine only improbable things!

How does an analyst learn to do that? Some people certainly seem able to achieve an excited mental state that leads to insights which go well beyond the ordinary. Consider what the ramifications could have been if a German analyst had thought of the improbable option of the Allies bringing their ports with them; then tying that idea to the information the Germans actually had about the existence of the devices.[145] Had Rommel known the enemy had a method of avoiding the need to capture a port, he might have focused on the real danger to the Normandy sector.[146] What if Hitler himself – who imagined some pretty fanciful things – conceived that such an option existed?[147] The Führer was concerned about the Normandy sector, but failed to realize the seriousness of the threat because he linked the landing sites with the need to get to a nearby port: he was but a single option away from the truth!

In developing broad option lists, well stocked with alternative hypotheses, the analyst is probing the question of whether the enemy will actually end up doing the improbable. Doing the improbable is the very essence of effecting surprise. Therefore, a systematic worst-case analysis is necessary if a defender wants to guard against the happening of a low probability event.[148] The problem with the worst-case analysis, as the Germans found out, is that the defender may not have enough resources to be everywhere strong.

In thinking about the improbable, the analyst must remember that surprise results when the enemy is more imaginative than the analyst within the limits of his perceived capabilities. Progress in terms of the art of war is nothing more than the story of problems and solutions. The German *Blitzkrieg* was designed to avoid the stalemate of intractable trench warfare.

This brings up the issue of whether the list of options possibly open to the enemy should include only those which appear rational to the analyst. Certainly not. History is too full of examples of actions which at first appeared irrational, but on closer examination were quite logical to the actor. 'The behavior of people with a cultural difference from one's own often *appears* irrational when in fact they act rationally but evaluate the outcome of alternative courses of action in terms of value that differ sharply from others.'[149]

Helmuth von Moltke (the elder) cautioned: 'If there are four options open to the enemy, he is likely to choose the fifth'.[150] In other words, an analyst must never close his mind to the possibility that the enemy may have a greater than expected capability, or do something based on a mistaken appreciation of his capability of the situation, or simply analyse the situation from a different perspective. The deliberate conscious exploring of alternative hypotheses in regard to the enemy's options is a way for the analyst to examine these possibilities in a systematic way.

• *Testing the Hypotheses.* After the analyst has developed a broad spectrum of alternative hypotheses they are tested in an analysis process involving several critical aspects.

It is generally assumed that the only satisfactory basis for intelligence prediction is by the objective standard of estimating the actions of other states rationally in terms of their assumptions.[151] As often as not intelligence mistakes result from 'holding to an incorrect conception of how the [analyst's] opponent sees the situation'.[152] The analyst always must be ready to accept the view that the adversary is 'in the grip of a serious misconception'.[153] The analyst must be particularly sensitive to the adversary's view of risk-taking or his willingness to fight against what often may appear as seemingly overwhelming odds. The analyst must also be well versed in the enemy's tactical doctrine.

Still, the analyst must recognize that the art of war is not a new profession. Certain principles of war have proved to work best in certain situations. Accordingly, analysts must continually ask themselves: 'What are the most obvious and reasonable directions from which an adversary might attack, even if the available evidence contradicts such contingencies?'[154] Most often the obvious attack will come – at least at the tactical level – for often the defender is powerless to prevent it and sometimes the attacker does not have the time or capability to do anything else.

Thus, once the obvious attack – the school solution – is considered as an option, it can be examined to see if there are reasons which, though not apparent at first, will prompt the adversary to do something else. For example, there were many reasons why the Pas-de-Calais sector was the obvious first choice of a place to attack. But, upon careful examination, the Allied planners found that it was not the best place. The Germans never managed to get beyond the apparent school solution.

The concept of analysis through the enemy's viewpoint was not unknown to the Germans. *Oberst* Reinhard Gehlen, head of OKH *Fremde Heere Ost*, said that 'for many years my colleagues and I had trained ourselves to see through the enemy's eyes – to think as he would think and calculate his intentions'.[155] Still, the verdict of history is clear:

the German analysts failed miserably when they tried to apply the practice at a strategic level.[156]

Attribution. Analysts tend to attribute the behavior of others to the nature of the person and the behavior of their side to the nature of the situation.[157] This tendency leads to serious errors in analysis. 'Personal traits are not consistent determinants of behavior; which traits predominate at any given time is heavily dependent upon the situational context in which the behavior takes place.'[158]

Another attribution-type problem also bears mention. 'Attribution of behavior to national characteristics and the assumption that these characteristics are consistent over time leads to the perception of behavior as inflexible and unchanging. Conversely, to the extent that behavior is attributed to external circumstances, it is perceived as flexible and subject to influence by the actions of the adversary.'[159]

Risky Options. Michael Handel has noted the following paradox: 'The greater the risk, the less likely it seems, the less risky it actually becomes. Thus, the greater the risk, the smaller it becomes.'[160] In war, everything is risky, but some options are decidedly more risky than others. The decision of General Eisenhower to proceed with the D-Day landings in the light of the adverse weather conditions was a high-risk decision, but from the German perspective the weather made an attempt seem unlikely, so the Allied risk was lessened by the fact that the Germans were not on the alert – even though some signs suggested they should be. In order for the analyst to judge the degree of risk involved in any particular option he must first understand the concept of risk-taking.

In the 1960s Daniel Kahnemann and Amos Tversky determined that 'people tend to avoid risk when seeking gains, but choose risks to avoid sure losses'.[161] When analysing an adversary's risk-taking vs. risk aversion temperament, the analyst can assume that if the enemy is on the defensive and is being pushed back (the fight or flight situation) then he is likely to take greater risks to put the situation right – as Hitler tried to do at Stalingrad. However, as a guide to estimating the risk level acceptable to an adversary that is expected to attack, the theory is less reliable. To paraphrase Michael Handel:

> Assuming rational behavior on the opponent's part, the analyst may predict that a very risky operation, entailing very high costs and uncertain benefits, probably will not be implemented. Conversely, he also may assume than an operation involving low risks and high benefits will be selected.
>
> Although valid in theory, such assumptions are very unreliable

in practice. In the first place, a high risk in one culture may be acceptable in another. Second, what sometimes appears to be a great risk for an adversary may actually be less hazardous as a result of developments unknown to the analyst. Third, the analyst may underrate the readiness of the enemy to take risks assuming that the adversaries know as much as they do about the strength of the analyst's side as he does. Fourth, the assessment of a specific risk is complicated by the estimated impact of strategic surprise (will strategic surprise – as a force multiplier – redress an imbalance in forces). Finally, in many instances, the stronger defender, interested in perpetuating a favorable status quo, will not comprehend the potential attackers' desperate frame of mind.[162]

Thus, the attacker may choose what is, or appears to be, a high-risk attack option. And sometimes he may win doing so, although 'no rational connection exists between the degree of risk on the one hand and the choice of strategy on the other. The temptation to choose a high-risk/high-gain strategy always is present'.[163]

One of the problems in deciding whether a particular option is risky arises in assigning a probability to its success. Analysts naturally tend to have trouble dealing rationally with probability concepts. The old military planning rule, 'KISS' ('Keep it simple, stupid'), takes probability theory into account. So does the rule which states: 'The more things that can go wrong, the more things will go wrong'. Since these kinds of rules for planning operations are well understood, they ought to be applied when analysing enemy options. If an apparent option has too many chance events involved in it, then it may not be a real option, that is, one that a competent planner would choose if he has a better alternative. If the analyst simply keeps in mind 'that the likelihood of any two uncertain events happening [successfully] together is always less than the odds of either happening alone (it is easier to flip heads on one coin toss than to flip heads twice in a row)' then his chances of estimating the probability of risk associated with any given option will improve. By way of contrast, it appears that the Germans were perfectly content to accept the idea – their own pre-conception reinforced by the Fortitude deception – that the Allies would mount several large-scale diversions in France followed by the *Schwerpunkt* in the Pas-de-Calais, with a six-division sideshow thrown in for good measure in Norway!

• *The Unique Case.* History is full of random events; no vectoring of progress can be discerned in it.[164] Thus, why should the analyst suppose that an adversary's choice of options in time of war will be more ordered – for after all, is not the object of war controlled chaos? The problem becomes one of discovering which of a wide variety of options the enemy will actually choose in a particular situation. There are situations where the magnitude of the cost of failure is catastrophic and the benefit of success is stupendous (historic turning points); such events have unique properties so they become unique cases.[165] The D-Day invasion of Normandy certainly fits that definition. The Germans understood that an invasion was coming. They appreciated that, if the invasion was mounted successfully by the Allies, then the war would be lost.[166] It was not by inattention to the problem that they failed to estimate what was afoot. They simply failed to deal with the problem as a unique event and not a sand-table exercise with routine options.

5. The Plausible Interpretations Factor

The Germans had overestimated the size of the Allied force available in England for a cross-Channel deployment. They also overestimated the Allied sea-lift capability. To make matters worse, they assumed that the enemy would stage several diversions – some of division-plus strength – in addition to launching the *Schwerpunkt* in the Pas-de-Calais sector. Accordingly, the German analysts easily could, and did, accept reports of attacks at many far separated points as indicative of the diversionary targets.

It is not uncommon in intelligence work to have many bits and pieces of information which are subject to several equally plausible interpretations and may support several different theories. Not even all true intelligence information necessarily is mutually exclusive. The *plausible interpretations factor* facilitated increased confusion in the development of the German estimates.

In late 1943 and during early 1944 there were often several plausible alternative explanations of the significance of the intelligence information collected by the Germans, and it is not surprising that the German analysts were inclined to select the explanation that fitted the OKW expectation that the Allies would land in Pas-de-Calais. Moreover, at the same time the ambiguous information was coming in, the Germans had plenty of apparently good information pointing unequivocally to the Pas-de-Calais sector.

Although the phenomenon has been observed elsewhere, nothing satisfactory has been written to explain the phenomenon called 'unconscious finagling'.[167] This relates to intelligence information that is ambiguous, or apparently ambiguous, not to explicit data. In intelligence analysis there is a powerful tendency to make something out of all the information collected. Sometimes the analyst may conclude that some of the data is irrelevant or false and discard it. Or he may conclude that certain new information has value, in which case he is obliged to resolve the ambiguity. Common experience supports the view that analysts tend not to wait for further data that might clarify the issue but to resolve the ambiguity within the context of the existing data. There is a strong bias toward accepting the plausible interpretation which best fits the analyst's current expectations.

The longer an analyst is exposed to ambiguous data, the greater confidence he will develop in any initial – and perhaps erroneous – impressions he forms.[168] As that confidence increases, the resolution of the ambiguity – which the analyst increasingly will believe was only apparent – will become clearer, until he will finally conclude that there is no real contradiction between his expectation and the new information.[169] The ambiguity is subconsciously resolved so that it is perceived as a difference without a distinction. When this happens, 'the initial misinterpretation is maintained until the contradiction becomes so obvious that it [finally] forces itself upon our consciousness'.[170] But the problem does not end there:

> The early but incorrect impression tends to persist because the amount of information necessary to invalidate the [initial] perception is considerably greater than the amount required to form an initial impression. The problem is not that there is any inherent difficulty in grasping new perceptions or new ideas, but that the established perceptions are so difficult to lose. Thus, inaccurate perceptions generated by ambiguous data may persist even after additional information has been received to clarify the initial ambiguity.[171]

Richard Heuer suggests that 'one might seek to limit the adverse impact of this tendency by suspending judgment for as long as possible as new material is being received'.[172] The advice makes sense, but, practically, many analysts find it hard to do.

The tendency both to resolve ambiguity where possible, and to resolve it within the context of the analyst's current expectations can be explained in terms of a number of recognized *operative biases*. The following are but a few that play a role in the way analysts resolve the ambiguity of information that has several plausible interpretations.

• *Unconscious Suppression.* Since their current expectations determine what they are likely to see, analysts tend unconsciously to suppress any data that point away from the expected point of attack.[173] So strong is that bias that, if pressed to resolve what looks to be information strongly suggesting danger elsewhere, an analyst will often rationalize the ambiguous data as part of an enemy deception.

• *Stubborn Attachment.* Two of the most important characteristics of perception are that it is quick to form but resistant to change.[174] When the analyst has a current expectation based on some perceived likely enemy option, he will resolve new information, if ambiguous, in a fashion that will allow it to meld with his expectation. The process is like pouring water into a cup. There is no similarity between the cup (the expectation) and the water (the new data), but in the process of pouring the water takes the shape of the inside of the cup. By unconsciously dealing with information in this plastic sense the analyst can both use the new information and retain his expectation.

• *Assimilation.* In this corollary to stubborn attachment, the analyst becomes so desirous of using the new information that he simply incorporates it into the existing expectation, even if this produces some slight change in the original expectation. The analyst both changes the expectation, and denies that it is changed. This particularly deceptive bias explains why gradual change often goes unnoticed.[175] Richard Heuer notes that the 'tendency to assimilate new information to pre-existing images is greater "the more ambiguous the information, the more confident the actor is in the validity of his image, and the greater his commitment to the established view".'[176]

• *Consistency.* Another factor that prompts the analyst to resolve ambiguity in favor of the current expectation is the need to maintain consistency. If the ambiguous information is accepted as true, then it will either fit the current expectation or not. Because of the confidence the analyst already has in the current expectation, doubts will be resolved subconsciously in favor of accepting the new data as consistent with the existing expectation.

• *Rationality.* When an analyst initially forms his current expectations about the adversary he tends to use a rational process. Similarly, the analyst tends to resolve ambiguity in data in favor of the position which affords a greater sense of rationality. However, most analysts tend to overestimate the rationality of the decision-making process or apparatus they are analysing.[177] As Admiral Frank Fletcher reminds us: 'After the battle is over, people talk a lot about how the decisions were methodically reached, but actually there's a hell of a lot of groping around'.[178] For the analyst the problem also may be the reverse: what first appears irrational may be the result of a decision process which the analyst does not understand or had not anticipated.

• *Causal Illusion.* Because of our common tendency to impose order on our environment, we will often seek and see patterns that actually are not there.[179] In this regard the analyst may view apparently ambiguous evidence as either a causal precedent to or a causal result of his current expectation, ultimately seeing a relationship and connection that does not exist.

• *The Leading Question.* Sometimes an ambiguity is plausibly explained in terms of the current expectation because of the way the information came to the analyst. There are times when others may pass on information with a note saying that it may be important in regard to the current expectation. The implied question suggests the answer. The analyst may also get data in the form of a report he is asked to review for his superior officer who thinks that there is a 'fit' and wants a second opinion. There are several ways that information can be forwarded which may suggest a connection that the analyst might otherwise have missed. An analyst may give a different answer to the same question, when it is posed in a slightly different way.[180]

It is impossible to tell which one or more of these operative biases led the Germans to accept that the Allies had the capability to strike virtually anywhere in the West. But we know that they did; for that reason due regard must be paid to the *plausible interpretations factor.*

There is a useful heuristic – the fourteenth-century investigative principle known as 'Occam's Razor' – that will aid the analyst in resolving ambiguity while avoiding the snare of current expectations. William of Occam, born *c.* 1346 and a teacher at Oxford, is still remembered for his pragmatic approach to problem-solving. He believed in shaving away (thus the razor) all extraneous details related to the problem. Further, he postulated, where there are several apparent solutions to a problem, the correct one probably is the most obvious. Thus, the analyst who would follow the master's teachings will avoid unnecessarily multiplying hypotheses, or creating ones which are too complicated.

Some analysts do not find Occam's method an altogether satisfying form of analysis. It is a methodology that is neutral to consistency, causality and rationality, but works by cutting through to the very essence of the problem. It may lead to a conclusion that a chance or random event has occurred, which many will not like because 'people generally do not accept the notion of chance or randomness' – at least not in their lives.[181] Yet there are times when the intelligence information available to an analyst can, and should, be explained in no other way.

Some of the greatest confusion on the morning of D-Day was caused not by the parachute dummies dropped behind the enemy's coastline as part of the tactical deception plan, but by real live paratroopers accidentally dropped far from their designated drop zones. Local

German units reacted strongly to the reports of these parachutists as if they were part of much larger forces. Their accidental presence in the enemy's rear made it very difficult for the *Wehrmacht* units in the battle area to get a clear appreciation of what was actually happening. And yet, their presence was not part of any plan but the result of random chance in the form of transport pilot navigational error.

6. *The Distraction Factor*

One of the major problems associated with the implementation of elaborate cover and deception plans is the possibility that, under the close scrutiny of the enemy, one or more of the plans may be discovered to be a hoax. Working in the Allied planners' favor in 1944 was *the distraction factor: noise, work, fear, hope, self-righteousness* and *alert fatigue.*

• *The Distraction of Noise.* The concept of 'noise' was first used in the context of intelligence analysis in 1962:

> First of all, it is much easier *after* the event to sort out the relevant from the irrelevant signals. After the event, of course, a signal is always crystal clear; we can see what disaster it was signaling, since the disaster has occurred. But before the event it is obscure and pregnant with [many] conflicting meanings. It comes to the observer embedded in an atmosphere of 'noise', i.e., in the company of all sorts of information that is useless and irrelevant for predicting the particular disaster.[182]

'In terms of ... intelligence perception, noise is the buzz set up by competing information signals which prevents the essential message from being heard loud and clear.'[183]

Intelligence information is often divided into two types: correct and incorrect, or in intelligence jargon, signals and noise.[184] It may be more helpful to think of intelligence information as being of four types: true and false, relevant and irrelevant, all of which, in the sense of distraction, amounts to signals, noise, noise and more damn noise! The false indicators (relevant and irrelevant) tend to get just as embedded in the piles of true but irrelevant materials as the correct, real or actual indicators the analyst is seeking. Accordingly, in some instances, the noise generated by an abundance of high-quality but incompatible or irrelevant intelligence presents a formidable distraction – particularly where there is little evidence pointing to the real target, and a lot pointing elsewhere.[185]

The analyst must always remember that the false indicators always are more likely to be noticed than the actual ones, if the enemy is planting deceptive clues that correspond to the analyst's preconceived notion. Thomas Schelling has aptly noted that 'unlike movies, real life provides no musical background to tip us off to the climax'.[186]

Michael Handel has noted several paradoxes relating to the distraction of noise. First, 'as a result of the great difficulty in differentiating between "signal" and "noise" in strategic warning, both valid and invalid information must be treated on a similar basis. In effect, all that exists is noise, not signals'. Second, there are 'the sounds of silence. A quiet international environment can act as background noise which, by conditioning observers to a peaceful routine, actually covers preparations for war [or attack]'. Third, 'the more information [that] is collected, the more difficult it becomes to filter, organize and process it in time to be of relevant use ...', thus volume becomes noise.[187]

• *The Distraction of Work.* The commanders in France and Germany were subjected to the ever-present distraction of the normal daily functions in their sectors of command responsibility. For many of them, and *Generalfeldmarschall* Rommel in particular, time spent preparing for the expected invasion could not be spent in undistracted intelligence analysis. At the moment of the invasion, Rommel was in Germany preparing to see Hitler to argue the case once more for releasing the *Panzer* reserves to him so that he could position them well forward along the coastal front.

• *The Distraction of Fear.* The actual indicators – those pointing to a *Schwerpunkt* in Normandy – muted by the 'noise' of the false and the irrelevant indicators, competed for attention in the minds of Germans being subjected to the immediate distraction of fear arising from real concerns about the dangers of landings elsewhere in France, especially in the Pas-de-Calais. Anxieties about the course of events on the Russian and Italian fronts also influenced the thinking of some of the men responsible for preparing and acting on the estimates concerning invasion dangers along the coast of northern France.[188] This is not the sort of fear – the Cassandra syndrome – that paralyses men into inaction, but a real one that causes them to turn their mind from the problem.[189]

By the spring of 1944 the Germans were over-extended on every front. Reaction to the apparent threats on every quarter had thinned the defensive line in France to the point where it was comparatively strong only in the Pas-de-Calais sector. The other sectors could deal with large raids and division-sized diversions, but none could deal effectively with a large diversion or with the main landing. The over-commitment of forces and resultant weak defensive capability led to a very distractive type of fear. If the Germans accepted any new theory that predicted a large diversion or the *Schwerpunkt* outside the Pas-de-Calais sector, then the danger area would have to be strongly reinforced. With no strategic reserves available, any such reinforcement could come only at the expense of weakening another sector.

General Warlimont said that the OKW knew that the success of the enemy's invasion would be decisive for the outcome of the war, but neither Hitler or the OKW could bring themselves to make planned economies on the other fronts – in fact, on four occasions in 1944 before 6 June, units were moved out of the French coastal sectors. Pleas for reinforcements generally went unheeded.[190]

Most men have a natural, especially stubborn resistance to accepting and dealing rationally with unwelcome information.[191] Hitler and the other German analysts proved no exceptions to this rule; consequently, no unpleasant conclusions were accepted. The Germans initially opted to guard against every possible threat and, having reached the limits of their capability, opted to accept as real only those threats they believed they could defend with the existing deployments. Fearing the unpleasant conclusion, they simply ignored it.[192]

• *The Distraction of Hope.* Also working against the Germans in 1944 was the distraction of hope, sometimes called the Pollyanna Syndrome.[193] The Germans, especially Hitler and the OKW Officers, hoped that if the Anglo-Americans attacked in the Pas-de-Calais sector, where the Germans were the strongest, the invasion force could be destroyed or at least severely crippled and contained. Then a number of strong German divisions would become available for service on the Russian Front.[194] The Germans believed that the transfer of some 50 divisions to the Eastern Front could lead to the destruction of the Russian armies, or a bid for a separate peace from the Russians. That belief – and the hope it held for the salvation of Germany – made it difficult for the Germans, and Hitler in particular, to give credence to any estimate or report that did not predict the main assault would come somewhere in the Pas-de-Calais sector.[195]

The problem inherent in this type of thinking is that it focuses – according to the defender's view – on what would be most convenient for the enemy to do, and distracts from a proper analysis of what is is capable of doing and a determination of his best option if he seeks the most promising course of action in a given situation.[196]

• *The Distraction of Self-righteousness.* If an intelligence analyst is to perform at his best, he must be a dispassionate adviser and absolutely objective. However, in the heat of the action this is virtually impossible. In such situations, or those where there are moral or ideological overtones, the distraction of self-righteousness comes into play. Once an analyst becomes convinced that his side deserves to win – or simply must win – true objectivity is lost, and the analyst's perceptive abilities are distracted.[197] The same holds true for the policy-makers.

• *The Distraction of Alert Fatigue.* In the military action arena, warnings and alarms are part of standing procedure. A problem of frequent concern is the fact that alerts sounded far outnumber the successfully predicted attacks. Michael Handel cautions that the paradoxical predicament of intelligence organizations is that many alarms which are deemed false in retrospect may actually have been justified when issued: 'although the cause for the alarm is usually known, the defender's intelligence [organization] may find it much more difficult to produce a *timely* explanation (before the next crisis occurs) as to why the predicted attack failed to materialize'.[198]

This problem provides yet another reason why the Germans were unable to accept the relevant indicators pointing to anything other than a diversion in the Normandy region: the alert fatigue factor. Michael Handel has noted that a 'deceiver frequently tries to create the impression of *routine* activities by gradually conditioning the adversary to a certain receptive pattern of behavior'.[199] In this context, routine should not be equated only with a quiet and peaceful pattern of activities. Sometimes it is easier to use a prolonged period of heightened tension to create the required impression.

No military unit can maintain a maximum alert status for an extended period of time without its sense of danger becoming dulled.

> A single alert, let alone a series of alerts or a prolonged period of high alert which is not followed by war [or an attack] will have a decisively negative impact on future decisions. A series of false alarms [also] will undermine the credibility of the intelligence organization [or the command issuing the alert] (the so-called cry-wolf syndrome); and by the time subsequent [warning] decisions on similar matters have to be made, [all the] prolonged periods of mobilization and the routinization of alerts will have brought about 'alert fatigue' (i.e., condition the high command and troops to a state of alert and therefore progressively erode their readiness for action). A continual or 'permanent' state of alert can therefore be self-defeating.[200]

Consequently, military forces have multiple alert levels. For the *Wehrmacht, Alarmstufe* II was the highest alert status. Between the beginning of April 1944 and D-Day, there were no less than ten maximum alerts along the *Kanalküste*, not counting practice alarms.

With each new alert, the various commanders charged with the defence of the Normandy sector became less and less sensitive to the expected danger. AOK 7 staff had planned to hold a practice alert on the night of 5 June as part of routine training. When the AOK 7 commander decided to hold a *Kriegsspiel*, the alert exercise was canceled, giving the officers scheduled to assemble at Rennes for the map exercise the chance of a good night's sleep.[201] No one in AOK 7 expected that the invasion was imminent.

The dulled sense of danger was reinforced by the inclement weather conditions along the Channel coast in early June 1944. After receiving a weather briefing at 0600 hours on 4 June 1944, Rommel concluded that the invasion would not come until July. He believed that the enemy planned to use the usually inclement weather in June as a cover for the assembly of ships in the southern ports of England. He ordered all of the beach obstacle construction programs to be completed by 20 June.[202] At 0800 hours on 4 June Rommel left his headquarters at Château La Roche Guyon and began a trip that first would take him to his home at Herringen in Germany; he planned to rest, then go to Berchtesgaden on 7 June to plead with Hitler for permission to re-deploy certain OKW Panzer reserves and the LFK III FLAK units in the Normandy sector.[203] Before he left, Rommel told his naval aide, Admiral Ruge: 'It eases my mind to know that while I'm away the tides will be unfavourable for a landing. Besides, air reconnaissance gives no reason to think it's imminent'.[204]

When the invasion did come in Normandy, the officers at the *Führerhauptquartier* immediately labeled it as a diversion because a diversion in that sector had been predicted by Hitler since February. But once the local commanders became engaged in the fighting they quickly realized that the multi-division beachhead was no mere diversion. But Hitler – safely tucked away 1000 km to the east – could not be persuaded that the *Schwerpunkt* would come outside the Pas-de-Calais sector. Since 1943 he had believed that it would come in the Pas-de-Calais region and such an old established idea was not easily changed.

7. The Intelligence Collection Factor

The Germans simply failed to collect much of the vital information that might have indicated the danger in the Normandy sector. Analysts tend to be over-confident about how much they know.[205] Not only are they convinced that they know more than they do, but also that what they do not know must be unimportant – ignorance is bliss.[206]

Three types of information – weather data; naval reconnaissance data; and aerial reconnaissance data – if properly collected, might have produced the data needed to alert the units defending the *Kanalküste* during the night of 5 June 1944.

• *Weather Data*. During the period 3–5 June, the weather situation did more than any other single factor to relax the Germans to the threat of imminent invasion. The adverse weather, which they could see for themselves, led them to disregard the apparently clear warning of the attack conveyed by the broadcasts of the *messages personnels*.

The weather on the *Kanalküste* had been generally good throughout May but began to worsen at the beginning of June, and deteriorated significantly early in the afternoon of 3 June. The OKM forecasters predicted that it would remain bad – with rain, low clouds and a moderately high wind – for several days. The German meteorological stations on the Greenland coast were not operational in June 1944. The *Luftwaffe* weather aircraft operating out of Norway did not have the range to cover the gap in the weather intelligence collection program; and there were no *U-Bootes* operating in position to detect the oncoming small area of high pressure.[207] If the German weathermen had seen reports of the high pressure area, a higher state of alert might have resulted.

• *Kriegsmarine Patrols*. On the evening of 5 June, the northern sector of the English Channel was full of Allied ships; but the patrol craft of the *Kriegsmarine* were all in the French Channel ports. Because of the high winds and waves in the Channel, the usual night reconnaissance sorties were canceled.[208] On the one night when naval patrols were needed there were none, and the opportunity for a timely warning was lost.

• *Luftwaffe Patrols*. The bad weather on 4 and 5 June kept most of the *Luftwaffe* reconnaissance aircraft grounded.[209] Five reconnaissance sorties were flown on 5 June but none made contact with the vessels of the invasion force then at sea, and no unusual activity was noted in the ports of England.[210]

During the months of April and May the *Luftwaffe* had managed to fly only 120 reconnaissance missions over Britain.[211] Even then they saw or photographed little of value. On 24 May the *Luftwaffe* conducted overflights of the Dover, Folkestone and Thames River area. It was the first such coverage since 21 May, and would be the last until 7 June. The pilots' reports and aerial photographs indicated no build-up in the number of landing craft assembled. On 24 May the *Luftwaffe* failed to get any reports on the 14 harbors where the loading of hundreds of assault force vessels was actually taking place.[212] Criticism concerning the inadequacy of the coverage was repeatedly voiced, but to no avail.

Interestingly, both Rommel and von Rundstedt considered the meager results of the 24 May air reconnaissance very important. Believing that the main invasion danger was to the Channel coast north of the Seine River, they felt that the final warning of an attack would come in a report of increased enemy activity in the south-eastern ports of Kent. The small number of craft reported in the ports on 24 May indicated to them that the invasion was not imminent.[213]

Worse than their failure to collect the relevant information was the ignorance of the Germans in 1944 of the major gap in their 'agent operations' intelligence collection system. There were two principal reasons for that ignorance.

One was the large volumes of false information fed into the system by the Allies. In fact, the successful layout of the Fortitude South deception resulted solely from the false but credible messages of three British-controlled German agents.[214] By the start of 1944, too, the Germans were looking for information to confirm their invasion hypothesis, not to raise new fears. Much of the information they collected from the controlled agents confirmed what they already believed; consequently, they thought they were getting corroboration.

The Germans did not know, or even seriously suspect that all their agents in Britain were acting as double agents under the control of British intelligence, that the English were reading the German Enigma cipher machine transmissions, or that the Japanese Purple code had been broken by the Americans. The Germans never seem to have grasped the simple notion that sources as well as plans must be guarded.[215] Being able to read the enemy's mind – at least in the sense of Ultra, Magic, and the Double-Cross system – gave the Allied planners at SHAEF a tremendous strategic advantage. In this sense, the Normandy landings may have been unique in that for planning and deception purposes the Allies had a virtually perfect intelligence system.

8. The Deception Factor

• *Passive Deception.* The twin aspects of passive deception are *secrecy* and *cover* (or camouflage).

Secrecy. Secrecy is an important tool of strategic interaction.[216] In strategic interaction, secrecy performs the special function of concealing plans without the risk of using a distorted mirror, an ineffective mask, or a bare-faced lie. If the adversary is misled, it is because he has not been exposed to strategic information.[217]

While good secrecy is obviously desirable, perfect security is rarely attained, and yet, deceptions regularly succeed and surprise is achieved without it.[218] Indeed, Barton Whaley's study of 68 modern cases of strategic surprise revealed that in every case some sort of a warning or an indicator signaled the event.[219]

The Allied planners knew that the Germans knew that the big invasion was coming. They also knew that they could camouflage and conceal the deployment of men and material for the invasion, but not completely. The SHAEF planners believed that by stringent security controls they could keep the actual day, time, place and size of the attack secret, but that other information would eventually leak out. In spite of several potentially very dangerous security violations, the vital information, all protected by the BIGOT clearance, was never discovered by the Germans.[220]

Cover. Cover is synonymous with camouflage. What cannot be kept secret is disguised.[221] Cover also means to conceal or hide. The Allied cover efforts did more than just disguising and hiding things. In areas where the Allies did not want the Germans observing invasion preparations, special care was taken to keep the *Luftwaffe* aerial reconnaissance away. Because it proved easier for the enemy pilots to make 'snap and run' sorties over the Kent and Sussex counties German photo-interpreters were provided with reasonable coverage of the areas where the Allies wanted them to focus their attention.[222]

• *Active Deception.* Realizing that the Germans were bound to discover certain information about the invasion preparations, the Allies used the existing German collection system to advantage. To encourage and reinforce the German fears and expectations about the Pas-de-Calais region, the deception effort – Operation Fortitude – was mounted to ensure that there was no lack of palpable indications pointing to a large-scale attack in that sector.[223]

During the QUADRANT Conference held in mid-August 1943 at Quebec, the Allied invasion planners were directed to prepare a deception plan to support the invasion.[224] In addition to supporting the Overlord/Neptune invasion plans, it had to be in agreement with the Europe-wide deception plan, Operation Bodyguard.[225] The planners went to work and on 13 February 1944 promulgated Operation Fortitude.[226] It was:

A broad plan covering deception operations in the European theater, with the object (a) to cause the Wehrmacht to make faulty strategic dispositions in north-west Europe before *Neptune* by military threats to Norway, (b) to deceive the enemy as to the target date and target area of *Neptune,* (c) to induce [the enemy to make] faulty tactical dispositions during and after *Neptune* by threats against the Pas-de-Calais.[227]

In the broadest sense Operation Fortitude was designed to support Operation Overlord/Neptune simply by pinning down the *Wehrmacht* divisions. The deception plan was mounted, and it worked.[228] 'It was an impressive tribute to the success of the Allied deception plans that every key German commander greeted the news of operations in Normandy as evidence of *an* invasion, not *the* invasion' – the *Schwerpunkt*.[229]

A few points need to be made regarding implementation of the Fortitude plan. First, while the plan was elaborate, its central plot or theme was very simple. As Ewen Montagu has aptly pointed out: 'We had no illusions about the efficiency of the German *Abwehr*, so we had to make sure that the puzzle was not too difficult for them to solve'.[230] This brings up the second key point:

> One overwhelming conclusion stands out with respect to deception: it is far easier to lead a target astray by reinforcing the target's existing beliefs, thus causing the target to ignore the contrary evidence, than it is to persuade a target to change his ... mind.[231]

The target of the Fortitude deception was Hitler himself. Through the Ultra/Magic intercepts, the Allied planners knew what Hitler expected – a *Schwerpunkt* in the Pas-de-Calais, with several large diversions – and played to it. The same intercepts confirmed that Hitler had taken the bait – the third key point. The success of a deception plan depends on feedback from the target.[232] Thus, Fortitude kept Hitler's attention focused where he believed it should be focused.

9. The Time Factor

As it affects the acquisition, analysis and acceptance process, there are at least four ways in which time has a special importance.[233]

• *Time and the Event Horizon.* Every intelligence issue involves 'timing'. Is the problem one of explaining an event that has already happened, or of making a prediction about the future? It makes a difference whether the analyst is acting as a 'reporter' or an 'oracle'. It is in anticipating the event where most often the estimative process fails. If an event has not occurred, then it follows that the indicators that would flow from it do not exist and cannot be perceived. This fact is often overlooked by men who ought to know better.

Operation Archery, the raid of 27 December 1941 at the fishing port of Måloy on the Norwegian coastal island of Vågsoy by a British naval task force, focused Hitler's mind on the danger to Norway and to the whole coast in north and west Europe.[234] The Führer began to talk of turning Europe in an impregnable fortress – *Festung Europa*. Hitler visualized a belt of strongpoints and gigantic fortifications running from the Norwegian-Finnish border to the Franco-Spanish border.[235] Thus the German defensive building and the search for the relevant indicators of the Allies' true invasion intentions preceded by as much as 18 months the actual decisions. It was at the RATTLE Conference on *HMS Warren* at Largs, Scotland, from 28 June to 2 July 1943 that senior Allied officers decided that north-west Europe would be invaded in the Normandy sector and not on the Pas-de-Calais coast.[236]

Premature though their quest might be, in order to prepare the massive *Atlantikwall* structures that Hitler's coastal 'crust' defense doctrine envisaged, the Germans could not afford to wait until their adversary had decided upon a landing site or sites.[237] *Grossadmiral* Dönitz at OKM called the problem of prematurity the 'Defender's Dilemma'.[238] In order to know where and what to build the Germans literally had to know the unknowable. To make matters worse, once they began to prepare their defenses, they were at risk that the enemy might change their plans and shift the focus of the attack away from the fortified areas.[239] A self-negating paradox illustrates the point: warnings of an enemy attack may lead to a counterplan which, in turn, may prompt the enemy to delay or cancel his original plan.[240]

• *Time and the Perception Horizon.* Time impacts on the process of perception. Intelligence analysis and command acceptance are incremental processes. Seldom, if ever, do the facts bearing on a particular intelligence problem all arrive in one tidy bundle. Thus, the point at which facts are noted or an estimate is forwarded to a policy-maker has special relevane. Richard Heuer has aptly noted that 'if we consider the circumstances under which accurate perception is most difficult, we find these are exactly the circumstances under which intelligence analysis is generally conducted – dealing with highly ambiguous situations on the basis of information that is processed incrementally under pressure for early judgment'.[241] New information tends to be assimilated with existing data; thus the actual order in which information is received affects judgement because evidence received early has a greater impact than evidence received after first impressions are formed.[242]

As the Germans had earlier predicted that the *Schwerpunkt* would come in the Pas-de-Calais sector, new evidence – available only after the Allies actually had decided to land in Normandy – came as small and incremental additions to an estimate that had been finalized and was being acted upon. In this context, time and the organizational bias mixed:

[There are real] organizational pressures favoring consistent interpretation, for once the analyst has committed him- or herself in writing, both the analyst and the organization have a vested interest in maintaining the original estimate.[243]

It is hard enough to change an estimate once it is committed to paper and disseminated; it is virtually impossible to change one which figuratively is carved in stone in the form of concrete bunkers. Once the Führer himself had given his imprimatur to the estimate that the *Schwerpunkt* would be in the Pas-de-Calais, the *Organization Todt* began constructing on the basis of that belief. It was a case where early judgements were literally cast in cement.

• *Time and the Analysis Horizon.* The analytical process of distinguishing between signals and noise requires time.[244] In many intelligence matters there is simply not enough time to do a proper job of collection, analysis and dissemination. Time, in this regard, did not affect the Germans. However, having too much time can also degarde the analytical and acceptance process. It is clear that the Germans had more than enough time to collect and analyse the intelligence information they needed to make the required command judgments. But an early judgement can adversely affect the formation of future perception; once an analyst thinks he knows what is happening, such perception tends to resist change.[245] For the Germans the early judgement about the Pas-de-Calais sector was locked into the thinking of both intelligence and command analysts, and it did not alter with time.

Where there is ample time for analysis there may also be ample time for deception – and there certainly was time for an elaborate deception before the Allied invasion. This is a nice paradox: when the analyst has the most time for reflective assessment, he is most liable to be the victim of deception.

• *Time and the Warning Horizon.* One function of military intelligence is to give the commander early warning of the imminence of hostile action so that he, in turn, can warn his units.[246] An important question is whether all the *Wehrmacht* divisions guarding the *Kanalküste* should have gone to a partial alert on 1 June 1944 when the BBC broadcast part one of the *messages personnels* to the French. Another is whether all the units in the AOK 7 (Normandy) and AOK 15 (Pas-de-Calais) sectors ought to have gone to, and remained at, *Alarmstufe* II on the evening of 5 June when the second lines of the clear text alert-codes were broadcast. The AOK 15 units did go to a full alert, but those of AOK 7 did not.

Actually, the failure of AOK 7 to go to full alert on the evening of 5 June made little difference to the first 24 hours' fighting. Once the invasion scenario began to unfold around midnight on the night of 5/6 June, the local units implemented their prearranged defense plans. It seems clear that nothing short of moving the powerful Panzer reserves into forward positions immediately adjacent to the invasion beaches weeks before the landings – as Rommel wanted – would have helped much.[247] The lack of a tactical warning probably did not make a critical difference – the lack of strategic warning did.

10. The Organization Factor

From mid-1934 until very early in 1944, the two major German overseas intelligence collectors, the *Abwehr* and the RSHA were involved in an internecine bureaucratic competition,[248] resulting in the take-over of the *Abwehr* counter-intelligence and foreign agent operations by the RSHA.[249] This process started on 12 February 1944 and was completed on 1 June.[250] At a time when a smooth and efficient collection effort was most needed, the slow process of reorganization hindered such action and RSHA was not able to correct the other's faults before the invasion came.

Interesting as the ten-year struggle between the *Abwehr* and RSHA may be, the inter-agency rivalry did not amount to much in terms of actual intelligence production by the *Abwehr*, even during the February–June 1944 transition period. On balance, the end of the rivalry and the initiation of the absorption process did not materially contribute to the Germans' failure to appreciate properly the intentions of the Allied planners. The 'victory' of RSHA and the fusing of the two intelligence services was merely a chance event that coincided with the final days of Allied invasion planning. The *Abwehr* failed in 1939–41 as a foreign intelligence collection organization for reasons other than the inter-agency rivalry. Its problems resulted from a real failure of leadership by Admiral Canaris and his immediate staff.

The other major organizational failure of the Germans was in not coming to grips with what was to be the proper rôle of the strategic military intelligence estimate or appreciation. The traditional German view was that the ultimate responsibility for 'building the picture' of the enemy was that of the commander and not the intelligence analyst.[251] Hitler took this concept to an unnatural extreme, deeming himself alone 'qualified to make authoritative foreign assessments'.[252] Now this sort of rule of practice may have some merit when a tactical commander limits his judgemental combat visions to the tactical horizon of estimation and when the politician limits his estimates to the political arena. But neither the senior officers of OKW – trained to direct an 'in-contact land-battle' force – nor the Führer were capable of making reliable strategic military assessments without the assistance of a reliable intelligence organization. They tried to do it and failed.

Hitler made his decisions based on hasty appraisals of the situation while surveying a map table, and without taking into consideration the practical difficulties involved.[253] One officer at OKW, General *der Artillerie* Warlimont, described the Führer's decision-making style thus:

> Hitler grasps the operational idea without [ever] giving any consideration whatsoever to the necessary [military] means, the necessary time and space, troops and supplies. Those are the fundamental elements of strategy which are necessary for success, but Hitler rarely took them into consideration.[254]

If Hitler had no need for information about his own army and its capabilities, what need did he have for intelligence information about his enemy's capabilities or intentions? The answer was none.

Obviously the rôle of German strategic intelligence was not to serve the Führer in his decision-making task. In fact, it never had a mature rôle in the German war-fighting effort. Beginning in 1943, when the *Wehrmacht* went on the defensive, the German general officers began to ask OKH/FHO for more than just OB data, and the work at *Fremde Heeres Ost*, and later FH West, began to involve the preparation of strategic estimates. But by the time the 'fighting' officers of the *Wehrmacht* began to realize that they needed better intelligence – more than just tactical estimates – just to survive on the battlefield, it was too late to create either the professional staff to provide it, or the collection organization to support the analysts.[255]

At this point it must be emphasized that 'intelligence' had a rôle in Germany during the war, but it was one that the *Abwehr* and RSHA dealt with mainly in terms of internal defense – counter-intelligence and counter-espionage – and in that regard the *Abwehr* and RSHA were ruthlessly efficient.[256] The tactical aspect of intelligence was also generally good.[257] It was strategic military intelligence that never had a properly defined and workable rôle.

It is equally important to note that merely because the OKW and the Führer felt no real need for strategic military intelligence for decision-making purposes does not mean that it was not produced. It was simply produced on a decentralized basis. Under the German analysis system there could be, and usually were, as many as 14 different estimates at any one time concerning the potential threat to Western Europe. The same original information was viewed by each analysis center according to its own parochial interest.[258] More often than not, the resultant estimates reflected the reactions of the individual commanders to the unevaluated raw information as it tended to support their personal theories. The object was not to produce an agreed position; instead the various estimates were in the nature of *post hoc* rationalizations of what the particular command or agency was doing. This is an extreme example of multiple advocacy with no effective way to bring divergent views to the attention of the Führer. Only on rare occasions did Hitler see the various estimates. Schellenberg at RSHA/SD and Hitler's staff filtered all intelligence reports so that the Führer did not receive any of the disagreeable reports[259] except on rare occasions, like 17 June 1944, when the front-line commanders had personal conferences with him.[260] In the end, and by default, Hitler's opinion became – for better or for worse – the agreed estimate.

Even on so crucial an issue as the expected place of the invasion there was no agreement. Hitler, von Rundstedt and Rommel all believed that the enemy's main attack would come in the Pas-de-Calais region, but the three of them could never agree about where within the sector, with its 400 kilometers of coastline, the main blow would probably be delivered. Nor was the need to reach agreement on that point even perceived.

By 1944, the Germans simply did not have a realistic organizational structure capable of dealing effectively with the strategic intelligence problem. But by then it was too late to do anything about the organizational deficiencies – even if Hitler and Jodl had recognized a problem existed. There may be situations where a few changes in the organizational structure of an intelligence staff may improve the collection or analysis process, but that takes time. The Germans had neither the time nor the inclination to reorganize theirs.

SURPRISE

Because of the ten factors – and, in the sense of the Gestalt, their interaction and reinforcing effect – the ability of the Germans to collect, perceive, analyse properly and act on the relevant Normandy invasion indicators was weak and inefficient. Their analysis process developed pre- and post-invasion intelligence and command estimates which, while apparently rational and logical in development, simply were wrong. As a result, the Germans suffered both a tactical and a strategic surprise on 6 June 1944, and for some considerable time they continued to be the victims of strategic surprise. This, with the resulting confusion of the battle, caused them to make very serious mistakes in their counter-invasion planning. In the end they were unable to destroy the Allied beachhead. Thus, the D-Day invasion is one of the rare occasions where the attacking force achieved both a strategic surprise and the final victory.

The fact that an attacker achieves an initial surprise does not mean that surprise alone will carry the day. For, as Napoleon has said: 'Uncertainty is the essence of war, [and] surprise its rule'.[261] If anything, history consoles military men and political leaders with the observation that there is no direct correlation between an enemy achieving the highest degree of surprise at the outbreak of a battle or war and ultimately emerging victorious.[262] Michael Handel notes that 'one reason for this is that the attackers are often so amazed by the effectiveness of their own attack that they are caught unprepared to fully exploit the opportunities it presents'.[263] It is equally important to remember the corollary to this rule: 'To know your enemy's intentions is fine, but such knowledge does not always mean that you can stop him'.[264]

There is nothing very extraordinary in the German estimative failure. There is no credible evidence to support the proposition that the failure of the Germans to anticipate the Allied *Schwerpunkt* in Normandy was the result of any single instance of negligence, stupidity, treachery, or a conspiracy of silence. Rather, the roots of the problem lie in the circumstances which naturally tend to affect even honest, dedicated and intelligent man.[265] The surprise of D-Day all came to pass through a series of quite complicated but, nevertheless, extremely ordinary mistakes of decision analysis.

It is interesting to note that the Germans appear to have made every possible mistake. In retrospect it almost seems that they set out to be the textbook example of what not to do in war. In the context of the times, the men, the organizations, and the analysis methods combined to produce a situation which made strategic surprise inevitable *for them*. Though the surprise came like a bolt from the blue it was not the result of chance; instead it was deliberately planned for and skillfully attained. Accordingly, while some may contend that in the broad sense strategic surprise is inevitable, it is not proper to draw that conclusion from the Normandy experience. Since this study concerns but a single case, it would be inappropriate to project the findings here regarding the inevitability of surprise to a universal case.

IMPLICATIONS

The major reasons for the German intelligence and command failure in regard to the D-Day invasion of Normandy have been identified; it now remains to determine whether a knowledge of the causes of that failure in 1944 has any relevance to intelligence collection officers, or to intelligence analysts, or to commanders or executive decision-makers in the late 1980s and beyond.[266] Particularly important is whether such knowledge is of any value to the military intelligence officers and military commanders of the United States in the modern era. Clearly, such knowledge is both relevant and critical: it is vitally important now, and it will continue to be important for decades to come.

The German failure is by no means unique. It can be matched by many other examples of nations and their armies failing to perceive properly and react to military or terrorist threats.[267] In fact, current examples – in both the military and the political context – are virtually countless. The big surprise today is that so many people who ought to know better seem to be surprised by surprise.[268]

Strategic surprise in the opening phase of war is the most powerful force multiplier in conventional war.[269] The failure of the Germans, and many similar intelligence and command failures, underscore the hard truth that a nation at war, on the brink of war, or existing in a cold war or in a terrorist-sensitive situation cannot count on any strategic warning and may not even receive any sort of a local tactical warning in time to react properly to a threat. Accordingly, in order to increase the likelihood that a nation or its armed forces will receive adequate warning – and that is at least assumed to be an attainable goal – increased attention must be paid to the reasons for past failures.[270] If the factors that have caused other intelligence collectors, analysts and information users to go astray in their decision-making process are understood, then perhaps those charged with preparing future estimates may be able to avoid the analytical pitfalls.[271] Similarly, commanders and policy-making executives who must use intelligence estimates, or make their own, may better understand the likelihood of an estimative failure. Gaining a real and lasting sensitivity to the probability of an estimative failure may be the most valuable lesson to be learned from this type of historical case-study.

It is probable that no system of intelligence collection and analysis, and no system of command, control and warning, can be devised and staffed which will totally eliminate the identified perception inhibitors. While military technology has revolutionized almost every aspect of modern military doctrine and tactics, the one area in which it has made little progress is that of anticipating surprise attack; thus the 'far-reaching advances in the technical means of gathering intelligence information, and the greater awareness of political and perceptual mechanisms undermining the intelligence process has not yielded corresponding progress in the ability to anticipate strategic surprise'.[272] The reason why this is so is quite simple. Today, as in the past, intelligence collection and analysis, and command decision-making, despite access to all sorts of high-technology gadgetry, 'is still based on the human factor. As it is labor intensive, [all] intelligence work [and command decision-making] must reflect human nature, not technological excellence'.[273] The old saw that 'to err is human' packs a more fundamental truth than intelligence analysts and policy-makers care or dare to admit.

It is dangerous and probably wrong to believe that strategic surprise is inevitable – it only seems so. Indeed, the statistical evidence only supports the conclusion that it is highly probable. Many analysts and policy-makers have, at best, an imperfect understanding of the root causes of strategic surprise; i.e., a lack of understanding about how and why the analysis process fails. This article, if its purpose has been achieved, will shed some light on the reasons why strategic surprise has not been avoided in the past. It is hoped, too, that with understanding the effect of the ten 'fog factors' can be minimized and the process of estimative analysis – the real craft of intelligence – improved.[274] The goal of every analyst should be to improve his vital craft the better to serve those whose decisions must necessarily be based on reliable intelligence and estimates. For the real craft of intelligence, 'is to make the right deductions and present them to the commander in clear and logical form', with the object, in the midst of so much recognized uncertainty, that 'the so-called fog of war [is] ... seldom more than a mist'.[275]

NOTES

This is a condensed version of a paper presented at the US Army War College Conference on 'Intelligence and Military Operations', Carlisle Barracks, Pennsylvania, 22–25 April 1986. The views expressed are those of the author and do not reflect the official policy or position of the Department of Defense or the US government.

1. For 'out of the blue' see Michael I. Handel, 'Intelligence and Deception', *Journal of Strategic Studies*, Vol. 5 (March 1982), 149.
2. Several modern writers have concluded that strategic surprise 'comes close to being inevitable'. Michael I. Handel, 'Clausewitz in the Age of Technology' (Monograph, US Army War College, 1985), p.74, n. 29. Also, Idem, 'Intelligence and the Problem of Strategic Surprise', *Journal of Strategic Studies*, Vol. 7 (Sept. 1984), 229–82; Idem, 'Intelligence and Deception', 137; Klaus Knorr, 'Lesson in Statecraft', in Klaus Knorr and Patrick Morgan (eds.), *Strategic Military Surprise: Incentives and Opportunities* (New Brunswick, NJ: Transaction Books, 1982), p.256; Ronald G. Sherwin and Barton Whaley, 'Understanding Strategic Deception: An Analysis of 93 Cases', in Donald C. Daniel and Katherine L. Herbig (eds.), *Strategic Military Deception* (New York: Pergamon Press, 1981), p.179; Richard K. Betts, 'Analysis of War and Decision: Why Intelligence Failures are Inevitable', *World Politics*, 31 (Oct. 1978), 61–89.
3. 'World Battlefields', *Time*, 1 May 1944, 23.
4. *Army Times* Editors, *The Tangled Web*, (Washington: Robert B. Luce, 1963), p.144.

5. For a factual study, see T.L. Cubbage II, 'Anticipating Overlord: Intelligence, Deception and Surprise – German Estimates of Allied Intentions to Land Invasion Forces in Western Europe' (diss. Defense Intelligence College, 1969, retyped and edited 1985). See also Cubbage, 'Anticipating Overlord: Was Strategic Surprise Inevitable?' a paper presented at the Intelligence and Military Conference, 22–25 April 1986 (the longer version of this article).

6. Niccolò Machiavelli, *Il Discorsi,* I, 56 (1531); Walter Laqueur, *The World of Secrets: The Uses and Limits of Intelligence* (New York: Basic Books, 1985), p.305.

7. David Irving, *The Trail of the Fox* (New York: E.P. Dutton, 1977; New York: Avon Books, 1978), p.424.

8. Overlord was the code name for the overall plan for the invasion of northwest Europe in 1944, and Neptune was the code name for the actual operations plan within the Overlord concept.

9. 'Magic' Summary No. 677, 1 February 1944, A1, SRS 1198, Records of the National Security Agency, Record Group 457, Modern Military Records (MMR), National Archives (NA) Washington, DC.

10. A comprehensive collection of reports are contained in the War Diary of the Operations Division of the German Naval High Command. The intelligence section of that diary shows that reports, from all sources, got wide dissemination. See *Seekriegsleitung, 1 Abteilung, Kriegstagebuch, Tiele A, Heft 49–58, 1.V.43–31.VI.44,* Chief of Naval History Repository, Washington, DC.

11. Walter Warlimont, *Inside Hitler's Headquarters 1939–45,* trans. R.H. Barry (New York: Praeger, 1976), p.427; John Toland, *Adolf Hitler* (New York: Ballantine Books, 1976), p.566.

12. Chester Wilmot, *The Struggle for Europe* (New York: Harper & Brothers, 1952), p.248.

13. Lionel Frederic Ellis, *Victory in the West: The Battle for Normandy* (London: HMSO, 1962), p.322.

14. Jock Haswell, *D-Day: Intelligence and Deception* (New York: Times Books, 1979), p.184.

15. Samuel Eliot Morison, *History of United States Naval Operations in World War II: The Invasion of France and Germany* (Boston: Little, Brown & Co., 1957), p.13.

16. Fortitude' was the code name given to the plan outlining a part of the strategic deception policy for the war against Germany in conjunction with Overlord. See SHAEF/18209/Ops(b), 3 June 1944, Records of SHAEF, Record Group 381, File No. *Fortitude,* MMR, NA; and Plan 'Bodyguard', Combined Chief of Staff, C.C.S. 459/2, 20 January 1944, w/encl., Records of SHAEF, ibid. See also Roger Fleetwood Hesketh, 'Excerpt from *Fortitude*: A History of Strategic Deception in North Western Europe, April 1943 to May 1945, Conclusion', in Donald C. Daniel and Katherine L. Herbig (eds.), *Strategic Military Deception* (Elmsford, New York: Pergamon Press, 1981), pp.233–42; Barry D. Hunt, 'An Eyewitness Report of the *Fortitude* Deception: Editorial Introduction to R.F. Hesketh's Manuscript', in *Strategic Military Deception,* Ibid, 224–32; Cubbage, 'Anticipating Overlord', 52–60, 250–52; Cruickshank, *Deception in World War II,* pp.85– 205; and Jock Haswell, *The Tangled Web: The Art of Tactical and Strategic Deception* (Wendover: John Goodchild, 1985), pp.92–108, and 147–50.

17. 'Double-Cross' is the descriptive name given to the 'XX' or Twenty Committee, a group reporting to London Controlling Station, whose task it was to manage all of the double agent operations in England. For more on the clever work and methods of the Twenty Committee, see J.C. Masterman, *The Double-Cross System in the War of 1939 to 1945* (New Haven, CT: Yale University Press, 1972), *passim*; and Ewen Montagu, *Beyond Top Secret Ultra* (New York: Coward, McCann and Geoghegan, 1978), *passim.*

18. 'Ultra' was the British code name given to intelligence derived from decrypting German *Enigma*-enciphered radio messages. 'Magic' was the American code name given to intelligence obtained from decryption of the Japanese machine-

enciphered radio messages. The American radio station at Asmara, Ethiopia, intercepted the wireless messages from Japanese diplomatic and military attaché personnel in Western Europe. The message to Tokyo from General Hiroshi Baron Ōshima, the Japanese Ambassador in Berlin, and others, provided the Allies with valuable insights into both the intentions and capabilities of the Germans. The British intercept sites in England obtained information of a tactical and operational nature. For more on Ultra, see F.W. Winterbotham, *The Ultra Secret* (New York: Harper & Row, 1974), *passim*; Ronald Lewin, *Ultra Goes to War* (London: Hutchinson, 1978; New York: Pocket Books, 1980), *passim*; Ralph Bennett, *Ultra in the West: The Normandy Campaign of 1944–45* (London: Hutchinson, 1979; New York: Charles Scribner's Sons, 1980), *passim*; Thomas Parrish, *The Ultra Americans: The U.S. Role in Breaking the Nazi Codes* (New York: Stein & Day, 1986), *passim*. As regards the use of Magic in the European Theater, see Ronald Lewin, *The American Magic: Codes, Ciphers and the Defeat of Japan* (New York: Farrar Straus Giroux, 1982), pp.10, 12–13, 46, 204–17, 232–46.

19. Michael Handel properly notes that 'past failures in avoiding surprise cannot be blamed on a dearth of information and warning signals. Accordingly we must look to the levels of analysis and acceptance for an answer. Michael I. Handel, 'Strategic Surprise: Politics of Intelligence and the Management of Uncertainty', in Alfred C. Maurer, Marion D. Tunstall James M. Keagle (eds.), *Intelligence: Policy and Process* (Boulder, CO: Westview, 1985), p.245.

20. The essence of good intelligence is 'timely truth, well told'. Washington Platt, *Strategic Intelligence* (New York: Praeger, 1957), p.33.

21. Handel, 'Strategic Surprise', p.259.

22. Michael I. Handel, 'Strategic Surprise: The Politics of Intelligence and the Management of Uncertainty (First Draft)', (US Army War College, Photocopy, 1985), p.36.

23. Horst Boog, 'German Air Intelligence in World War II', paper presented at the Intelligence and Military Operations Conference, US Army War College, Carlisle Barracks, Pennsylvania, 22–25 April 1986, pp.3–4.

24. Handel, 'Strategic Surprise', p.259.

25. Ibid.

26. Alan Bullock, *Hitler: A Study in Tyranny*, abridged ed. (1964; reprint, New York: Perennial Library, Harper & Row, 1971), p.423.

27. Ibid.

28. Wilmot, *Struggle For Europe*, 161.

29. Bullock, op. cit.

30. Wilmot, op. cit.

31. Handel, 'Strategic Surprise', p.260. ('Members of his entourage were often as surprised as were the victims of his moves ... Such decisions, generally made on the spur of the moment, are very difficult to anticipate.')

32. Samuel W. Mitcham, Jr., *Rommel's Last Battle: The Desert Fox and the Normandy Campaign* (New York: Stein and Day, 1983), p.21.

33. Knorr, 'Lessons in Statecraft', pp.257–8.

34. Boog, 'German Air Intelligence', p.5.

35. Donald McLachlan, *Room 39: A Study in Naval Intelligence* (New York: Atheneum, 1968), p.344. According to McLachlan, the one thing that all the outstanding intelligence officers he knew had in common was 'common standards of exact scholarship'. He viewed the intelligence service as 'a new learned profession'. Ibid, p.346.

36. Klaus Knorr, 'Failure in National Intelligence Estimates: The Case of the Cuban Missile Crisis', *World Politics* 16 (April 1964), p.460. See also, David Kahn, *Hitler's Spies* (New York: Macmillan, 1973), p.533 ('they could ... express their opinions more forcefully').

37. Handel, 'Intelligence and Deception', 140.

38. Ibid, 141.

39. Arthur Bryant, *Triumph In The West: A History of the War Years* (Garden City, New York: Doubleday, 1959), p.142.
40. McLachlan, *Room 39*, p.343.
41. In February 1943 OWK/WFST issued a warning to all commands and staffs stating that the Soviet and Allied forces were trying to mislead and deceive the Germans. F.H. Hinsley, E.E. Thomas, C.G.G. Ransom, and R.C. Knight, *British Intelligence in the Second World War: Its Influence on Strategy and Operations*, Vol. III, Pt. 1 (London: HMSO, 1979), p.120.
42. Handel, 'Strategic Surprise', p.260.
43. John P. Campbell, 'D Day 1943: The Limits of Strategic Deception', *Canadian Journal of History* (1977), 234–5.
44. Paul Seabury, 'Knowing Who's Who', *The International Journal of Intelligence and Counterintelligence* 1 (Spring 1986), p.123; quoting from Michael Gayer, 'National Socialist Germany', in Ernest May (ed.), *Knowing One's Enemies* (Princeton, NJ: Princeton University Press, 1985), p.343.
45. Handel, 'Intelligence and Deception', p.140.
46. Kahn, *Hitler's Spies*, p.524.
47. Ibid, p.531.
48. To better understand the traditional *Wehrmacht* officer class, see T.N. Dupuy, *A Genius for War: The German Army and General Staff, 1807–1945*. (Fairfax, Virginia: HERO Books, 1984), *passim*.
49. McLachlan, *Room 39*, p.341.
50. W. von Mellethin, *German Generals in World War II* (Norman, OK: University of Oklahoma Press, 1977), p.82.
51. Harold C. Deutsch, 'Ultimate Consumers: Intelligence and the Operational Art in World War II (ETO)', paper presented at the Intelligence and Military Operations Conference, US Army War College, Carlisle Barracks, Pennsylvania, 22–25 April 1986, p.40.
52. McLachlin, *Room 39*, p.344.
53. Ibid.
54. W.D. Howells, 'Intelligence in Crises', in George R. Copley (ed.), *Defense '83* (Washington, DC: D&FA Conferences, Inc., 1983), p.349.
55. Richard J. Heuer, Jr., 'Cognitive Factors in Deception and Counterdeception', in Donald C. Daniel and Katherine L. Herbig (eds.), *Strategic Military Deception* (Elmsford, NY: Pergamon Press, 1981) p.32.
56. Ibid.
57. Ibid, citing Kenneth Booth, *Strategy and Ethnocentrism* (New York: Holmes & Meier, 1979).
58. Kahn, *Hitler's Spies*, p.141.
59. Handel, 'Strategic Surprise', p.259.
60. Ibid; Bullock, *Hitler*, p.6.
61. Handel, 'Strategic Surprise'.
62. Handel, 'Strategic Surprise (First Draft)', p.30.
63. Heuer, 'Cognitive Factors' in Daniel and Herbig (eds.), op. cit., p.32.
64. Klaus Knorr, 'Strategic Surprise: The Incentive Structure', in Knorr and Morgan (eds.), op. cit., p.176.
65. Handel 'Strategic Surprise', p.260.
66. Jesse Goldstaub, 'Risk Intelligence Analysis and Forecasting: Policy Gambling and the Catastrophic Event' (Occasional paper, University of Calgary, Faculty of Management, 1984), p.9.
67. Warlimont, *Inside Hitler's Headquarters*, p.587, n. 1.
68. Kahn, *Hitler's Spies*, p.524.
69. Roy Godson, 'General Discussion: Avoiding Political and Technological Surprise in the 1980's', in Roy Godson (ed.), *Intelligence Requirements for the 1980's: Analysis and Estimates*, (New Brunswick, NJ: Transaction Books, 1980), p.118.
70. Knorr, 'Lessons in Statecraft', p.249.
71. Michael J. Brenner, 'The Iraq–Iran War: Speculations About a Nuclear Re-Run',

        Journal of Strategic Studies, Vol. 8 (March 1985), 32.
 72. See Richard K. Betts, 'Strategic Surprise for War Termination: Inchon, Dien-
        bienphu and Tet', in Knorr and Morgan (eds.) op. cit., p.169.
 73. Heuer, 'Cognitive Factors', p.32.
 74. Ibid, p.56.
 75. Ibid, p.63.
 76. Ibid.
 77. Ibid, p.44.
 78. Ibid.
 79. Ibid.
 80. Kevin McKean, 'Decisions, Decisions', *Discover* (June 1985), 26.
 81. Ibid.
 82. Heuer, 'Cognitive Factors', p.45.
 83. Ibid, p.50.
 84. Ibid.
 85. Ibid., pp.51–2.
 86. Ibid.
 87. Ibid, p.53.
 88. Ibid, p.54.
 89. Ibid.
 90. Ibid, p.32.
 91. Ibid., pp.31–32, citing Herbert A. Simon, *Models of Man: Social and National*
        (New York, Wiley, 1957).
 92. Heuer, 'Cognitive Factors', p.32.
 93. Theodore R. Sarbin, 'Prolegomenon to a Theory of Counter-deception', in
        Daniel and Herbig (eds.), op. cit., p.157.
 94. Ibid, p.158.
 95. Ibid.
 96. Ibid, p.160.
 97. Ibid, p.161.
 98. Ibid, p.168.
 99. Ibid, p.168.
100. Goldstaub, 'Risk Intelligence Analysis and Forecasting', p.4. Questions being
        asked and information being accepted are subject to the ethno- and geo-centric
        predilections of policy-makers, their biases in terms of cultural perspective and
        logic, and both their doctrinal allegiances and political mind-set. This mandates
        that those who make decisions and formulate policy are asked 'What makes YOU
        afraid?'
101. David Mure, *Master of Deception* (London: William Kimber, 1980), p.101.
102. The statistical approach was labeled 'sagacity' by Karl E. Scheibe, *Mirrors,
        Masks, Lies and Secrets* (New York: Praeger, 1979).
103. Sarbin, 'Prolegomenon to a Theory', p.162.
104. Ibid, p.152.
105. Ibid.
106. Ibid. In such a situation, the analyst can use the case study (the intuitive or clinical)
        methods, where predictions from the available data allow for either tinkering with
        or ignoring the base rates.
107. Sarbin, 'Prolegomenon to a Theory', p.162.
108. Laqueur, *World of Secrets*, p.292.
109. Ibid. For more on 'empathy', see Ralph K. White, 'Empathy as an Intelligence
        Tool', *The International Journal of Intelligence and Counterintelligence*, 1 (Spring
        1986), 57–75.
110. Sarbin, 'Prolegomenon to a Theory', p.168.
111. See C.O. (R) 25, July 1943, 'Rattle', Record of a Conference held at *HMS Warren*
        from 28 June to 2 July to Study the Combined Operations Problems of 'Overlord',
        93, Records of SHAEF, Record Group 331, File No. 337/16 *Rattle Conference*,
        MMR, NA.

112. Heuer, 'Cognitive Factors', p.34.
113. Ibid, p.35.
114. Ibid, p.34.
115. See Wohlstetter, *Pearl Harbor*, p.390.
116. Heuer, 'Cognitive Factors', pp.35–6.
117. Knorr, 'Failures in National Intelligence Estimates', p.461.
118. Ibid, p.457, citing Wohlstetter, *Pearl Harbor*, pp.56, 390, 397.
119. Heuer, 'Cognitive Factors', p.36.
120. Ibid.
121. Angelo Cordevilla, 'Comparative Historic Experience of Doctrine and Organization', in Godson (ed.), op. cit., p.17.
122. Richard J. Heuer, Jr., 'Strategic Deception: A Psychological Perspective', a paper presented at the 21st Annual Convention of the International Studies Association, Los Angeles, California, March 1980, p.45.
123. Handel, 'Strategic Surprise (First Draft)', p.30.
124. Sarbin, 'Prolegomenon to a Theory', p.158.
125. Ibid.
126. Steven Jay Gould, 'The View of Life', transcript of the 18 December 1984 PBS television broadcast, NOVA 1118 (Boston, MA: WGBH Educational Foundation, 1984), p.11.
127. Benno Wasserman, 'Failure of Intelligence Prediction', *Political Studies* 8 (June 1960), 166–7.
128. Knorr, 'Failure in National Intelligence Estimates', p.464.
129. Ibid.
130. Ibid.
131. Sarbin, 'Prolegomenon to a Theory', p.169.
132. Ibid.
133. Heuer, 'Cognitive Factors', p.35.
134. Wohlstetter, op. cit., p.393.
135. Heuer, 'Cognitive Factors', pp.34–5.
136. Sarbin, 'Prolegomenon to a Theory', p.153.
137. See I. Nelson Rose, 'Litigator's Fallacy', *Litigation: The Journal of the Section of Litigation, American Bar Association* 3 (Spring 1985), 61. ('It is a normal human reaction to look for factual capital to support one's psychological investment.')
138. For the best account of the pre-Dieppe amphibious assault thinking, see Haswell, *D-Day*, pp.15–20.
139. Ibid, pp.22–3.
140. Hunt, 'Editorial Introduction to R.F. Hesketh's Manuscript – An Eyewitness Report of the Fortitude Deception', p.229.
141. McKean, 'Decisions, Decisions', p.26.
142. See Patrick Morgan, 'The Opportunity for a Strategic Surprise', in Knorr and Morgan (eds.), op. cit., p.219.
143. Heuer, 'Cognitive Factors', p.66.
144. Lewis Carroll, *Through The Looking Glass and What Alice Found There* (1872; reprint, New York: Avernal Books, n.d.), p.100.
145. The Allies opted to bring their ports with them. At a meeting of the Service Chiefs in late May of 1942 Admiral Lord Louis Mountbatten remarked that 'if ports are not available we may have to construct them in pieces and tow them in'. Dwight D. Eisenhower, *Crusade in Europe* (New York: Doubleday, 1948; New York: Avon Books, 1968), p.250.
146. Haswell, *D-Day*, pp.132–3.
147. In Louis Tracy, *The Final War: A Story of the Great Betrayal* (London: 1896), pp.78–80, a pre-First World War novel, the British used 'a great floating pier' to enable them to land on the coast of France far from the fortified port cities. In Tracy's book, the British land north of Le Havre.
148. Knorr, 'Lessons in Statecraft', p.253.
149. Ibid, p.459.

150. Haswell, *Tangled Web*, p.70.
151. Wasserman, 'Failure of Intelligence Predictions', p.163.
152. Morgan, 'Opportunity for Strategic Surprise', p.217.
153. Ibid.
154. Handel, 'Intelligence and Deception', 137.
155. Reinhard Gehlen, *The Service* (New York: Popular Library, 1971), p.99.
156. German tactical intelligence, on the whole, was quite good throughout the war. Haswell, *D-Day*, p.138 ('Gehlen could obtain accurate operational intelligence from units in contact with the enemy on the eastern front').
157. Heuer, 'Cognitive Factors', p.55.
158. Ibid, p.57.
159. Ibid, p.59.
160. Handel, 'Intelligence and Deception', 154, n.75.
161. McKean, 'Decisions, Decisions', p.28.
162. Handel, 'Strategic Surprise', pp.251–2.
163. Ibid, p.253.
164. Gould, 'View of Life', p.1.
165. Sarbin, 'Prolegomenon to a Theory', pp.154–5.
166. Warlimont, *Inside Hitler's Headquarters*, p.410.
167. Gould, 'This View of Life', p.19 ('Unconscious finagling'). See Wohlstetter, *Pearl Harbor*, p.393. The observation Roberta Wohlstetter made in 1962 concerning Pearl Harbor fits exactly with what was going on in Germany. The analysts simply resolved all ambiguities in favor with the 'party line'.
168. Heuer, 'Cognitive Factors', pp.39–40.
169. Ibid, p.40.
170. Ibid.
171. Ibid.
172. Ibid.
173. See Wohlstetter, *Pearl Harbor*, p.387.
174. Heuer, 'Cognitive Factors', p.36.
175. Ibid, p.37.
176. Ibid, p.38, citing Jervis, *Perception and Misperception in International Politics*, p.195.
177. Howells, 'Intelligence in Crises', p.351.
178. Lewin, *American Magic*, p.81.
179. Heuer, 'Cognitive Factors', p.56.
180. McKean, 'Decisions, Decisions', p.22.
181. Heuer, 'Cognitive Factors', p.56.
182. Wohlstetter, *Pearl Harbor*, p.387.
183. Lewin, *American Magic*, p.63.
184. Handel, 'Strategic Surprise', p.245.
185. Lewin, *American Magic*, p.64; Handel, 'Strategic Surprise', p.246.
186. Thomas C. Schelling, 'Forward' in Roberta Wohlstetter, *Pearl Harbor: Warning and Decision*.
187. All three quoted paradoxes are from Handel, 'Intelligence and Deception', 154, n. 75.
188. Richard K. Betts discusses this problem in terms of being 'preoccupied with other threats'. 'Strategic Surprise for War Termination: Inchon, Dienbienphu and Tet', p.160.
189. Laqueur, *World of Secrets*, p.270 ('the Cassandra Syndrome').
190. Speidel, *Invasion 1944*, p.59.
191. Wohlstetter, *Pearl Harbor*, p.393.
192. Compare, Klaus-Jürgen Müller, 'On the Difficulties of Writing Intelligence History: Some Reflections of an Old-Fashioned Historian', paper presented at the Intelligence and Military Operations Conference, US Army War College, Carlisle Barracks, Pennsylvania, 22–25 April 1986, p.14.
193. Laqueur, *World of Secrets*, p.270.

194. 'Magic' Summary No. 798, 1 June 1944, A5, SRS 1320.
195. 'Intelligence is the voice of conscience to a staff. Wishful thinking is the original sin of men of power'. McLachlin, *Room 39*, p.365. In 1962, Roberta Wohlstetter wrote that 'there is a good deal of evidence, some of it quantative, that in conditions of great uncertainty people tend to predict that events that they want to happen actually will happen. Wishfulness in conditions of uncertainty is natural and hard to banish simply by exhortation – or by wishing'. *Pearl Harbor*, p.397.
196. Earl F. Ziemke, 'Stalingrad and Belorussia: Soviet Deception in World War II', in Daniel and Herbig (eds.), op. cit., p.270.
197. For an illustration of the distraction of self-righteousness in regard to the French, see Douglas Porch, 'French Intelligence and the Fall of France, 1930–1940', paper presented at the Intelligence and Military Operations Conference, US Army War College, Carlisle Barracks, Pennsylvania, 22–25 April 1986, p.4.
198. Handel, 'Strategic Surprise', p.254.
199. Handel, 'Intelligence and Deception', 125; 'Strategic Surprise', p.263.
200. Handel, 'Strategic Surprise', pp.353–4.
201. Gordan A. Harrison, *U.S. Army in WW II – Cross-Channel Attack*, p.276; Ellis, *Victory in the West*, p.198.
202. Irving, *Trail of the Fox*, p.423.
203. Ibid, pp.435, 441; Max Hastings, *Overlord D-Day, June 6, 1944* (New York: Simon & Schuster, 1984), p.68.
204. Ryan, *Longest Day*, p.36; Friedrich Ruge, *Rommel in Normandy: Reminiscences by Friedrich Ruge* (San Rafael, CA: Presidio Press, 1979), p.169.
205. Heuer, 'Cognitive Factors', p.47.
206. McKean, 'Decisions, Decisions', p.26.
207. Morison, *History of United States Naval Operations*, p.49.
208. Wilmot, *Struggle for Europe*, p.229.
209. Ibid.
210. Wilmot, *June 1944*, p.63.
211. Ibid.
212. Friedrich Ruge, 'The Invasion of Normandy', in H.A. Jacobsen and J. Rohwar (eds.), *Battles of World War II: The German View* (New York: G.P. Putnam's Sons, 1965), p.329.
213. Wilmot, *Struggle for Europe*, p.217.
214. Hunt, 'Editorial Introduction', p.229.
215. McLachlan, *Room 39*, p.354.
216. Scheibe, *Mirrors, Masks, Lies and Secrets*; and 'The Psychologist's Advantage and Its Nullification: Limits of Human Predictability', *American Psychologist*, 33 (1978), 869–81.
217. Sarbin, 'Prolegomenon to a Theory', p.165.
218. Heuer, 'Cognitive Factors', p.60.
219. Ibid, citing Barton Whaley, 'Strategem, Deception and Surprise in War', (diss., Massachusetts Institute of Technology, 1969), p.164 and Appendix B.
220. The BIGOT procedures and the security scares are summarized nicely in Haswell, *D-Day*, pp.152–8.
221. Camouflage, in the sense of disguising an object, and cover, in the sense of hiding it completely, are forms of *passive* deception. On the other hand, the use of decoys – fake planes, tanks, ships and depots – involves an *active* deception effort.
222. Wilmot, *Struggle for Europe*, p.200.
223. For the theory of deception, see Haswell, *Tangled Web*, pp.19–20, 30–47; Handel, 'Intelligence and Deception', 122–54; Heuer, 'Cognitive Factors', pp.31–69; Sarbin, 'Prolegomenon to a Theory', pp.151–73; Sherman and Whaley, 'Understanding Strategic Deception', pp.177–94; Barton Whaley, 'Toward a General Theory of Deception', in John Gooch and Amos Perlmutter (eds.), *Military Deception and Strategic Surprise* (London: Frank Cass and Co., 1982), pp.178–91; and Donald C. Daniel and Katherine L. Herbig, 'Propositions on Military Deception', in Daniel and Herbig (eds.), op. cit., pp.3–30.

224. Albert Norman, *Operation Overlord: Design and Reality* (Harrisburg, PA: The Military Service Publishing Co., 1952), p.39.
225. Plan Bodyguard was approved by the Combined Chiefs of Staff on 20 January 1944, and sent to SHAEF for the purpose of planning on 22 January. C.C.S. 459/2, 20 January 1944, Plan 'Bodygurd', with enclosure, and Memorandum for the Supreme Commander, Allied Expeditionary Force, 22 January 1944, Subject: Overall Deception Policy for War Against Germany', Records of SHAEF, Record Group 331, File No. 381 *Bodyguard*, MMR, NA.
226. Wilmot, *The Struggle for Europe*, p.199.
227. SHAEF/18209/Ops (b), 3 June 1944, Records of SHAEF, Record Group 381, File No. *Fortitude*, MMR, NA. See also, Plan 'Bodyguard', Combined Chiefs of Staff, C.C.S. 459/2, 20 January 1944, w/encl., Records of SHAEF, Record Group 381, File No. *Bodyguard*, MMR, NA. See Charles Cruickshank, *Deception in World War II* (Oxford: Oxford University Press, 1979; New York: Oxford University Press, 1980), pp.85–205.
228. Compare Müller, 'On the Difficulty of Writing Intelligence History', p.9 ('The German evaluation of the strategic situation and, therefore, of expected Allied operations has never been decisively influenced by Allied deception operations.'). Admits Normandy deception was an exception. Letter to author, 12 December 1986.
229. Hastings, *Overlord*, p.77.
230. Montagu, *Beyond Top Secret Ultra*, p.61.
231. Heuer, 'Cognitive Factors', p.42.
232. Handel, 'Intelligence and Deception', 126.
233. See Handel, 'Intelligence and the Problem of Strategic Surprise', pp.237–39, particularly the Time Matrix at p.238.
234. Müller, 'On the Difficulties of Writing Intelligence History', p.25.
235. See Haswell, *D-Day*, p.78; Earl F. Ziemke, *The German Northern Theater of Operations 1940–1945* (Washington, DC: Department of the Army, 1959), pp.213–14.
236. C.O. (R) 25, July 1943, 'Rattle', Record of Conference, etc. to Study the Combined Operation Problems of 'Overlord', with *Strategic Background* C.O.S.S.A.C. (43) 29, 25 June 1943, 92–98, Records of SHAEF, Record Group 331, File No. 337/16 *Rattle Conference*, MMR, NA. See also, Haswell, *D-Day*, pp.109–10; Harrison, *Cross-Channel Attack*, p.72.
237. Unlike the 'Crust' concept, with the MLR at the high tide water's edge, normal *Wehrmacht* tactical doctrine called for the main line of resistance, the *Haupt-kampflinie*, to be from 7,000 to 9,500 meters behind the combat outpost line, and stressed the use of immediate and violent counterattacks. W.J.K. Davis, *German Army Handbook 1939–1945* (1973, New York: Arco, 1984), pp.57–8.
238. Karl Dönitz, *Memoirs, Ten Years and Twenty Days* (Cleveland, OH: The World Publishing Co., 1959), p.392.
239. If a defender waits too long to begin even the most general sort of defensive fortification work, then the enemy may take the activity to mean its plans have been compromised and change them. Walter Laqueur makes the observation – and by doing so, notes the paradox – that 'it could be argued that, almost by definition, intelligence is always bound to fail. If it correctly predicts the political or military initiative of another country, and as a result, countermeasures are taken and the [predicted] initiative does not take place, it will be blamed for making false predictions'. Laqueur, *World of Secrets*, p.4.
240. Handel, 'Intelligence and Deception', 154, n.75.
241. Ibid, p.40.
242. Ibid, p.50.
243. Heuer, 'Cognitive Factors', p.41.
244. Handel, 'Strategic Surprise (First Draft)', p.11.
245. Heuer, 'Cognitive Factors', p.41.
246. See Lawrence J. Edwards, 'Discussion – Avoiding Political and Technological

Surprise in the 1980's', in Godson (ed.), op. cit., p.112.
247. Irving, *Trail of the Fox*, pp.411–12.
248. For a detailed account of the *Abwehr*/RSHA rivalry and the eventual downfall of Admiral Canaris, see Heinz Hölne, *Canaris (Canaris: Patriot im Zwielicht)*, trans. J. Maxwell Brownjohn (Munich: Bertelsmann, 1976; New York: Doubleday, 1979), pp.163–554 *passim*. Shorter accounts include: Peter R. Black, *Ernst Kaltenbrunner: Ideological Soldier of the Third Reich* (Princeton, NJ: Princeton University Press, 1984), pp.176–217 *passim*; Lauran Paine, *German Military Intelligence in World War II* (Briarcliff Manor, NY: Stein and Day Publishers, 1984), pp.181–8; and Gehlen, *The Service*, pp.93–5.
249. It is interesting to note that Hitler's decision to fuse the *Abwehr* into the RSHA was not prompted by a failure of the *Abwehr* collection or analysis effort. Instead it was prompted by a bomb in a crate of oranges! Hitler had forbidden the initiation of any acts of sabotage in Spain. Contrary to his orders, the *Abwehr* station in Spain planted a bomb aboard a British freighter that was bound for England with a cargo of oranges. The incident infuriated the Führer. Black, *Kaltenbrunner*, p.194.
250. Ibid.
251. Cordevilla, 'Comparative Historical Experience', pp.25–6. See also, Boog, 'German Air Intelligence', p.4 ('The Army Manual H. Div. 89 g of 1941 ... stated that it was the commander who prepared the situation estimate with his Chief of Staff or Operations Officer').
252. Ibid.
253. Walter Warlimont, 'From Invasion to the Siegfried Line', in *MS ETHINT-1* (19–29 July 1945), p.30, MMR, NA.
254. Ibid, pp.30–31.
255. Cordevilla, 'Comparative Historical Experience', p.26.
256. Paine, *German Military Intelligence*, pp.116–17.
257. Haswell, *D-Day*, p.138.
258. Cordevilla, 'Comparative Historical Experience', p.25; Haswell, *D-Day*, p.51.
259. Haswell, *D-Day*, p.51.
260. Mitcham, *Rommel's Last Battle*, pp.108–10.
261. Handel, 'Strategic Surprise', p.265.
262. Ibid.
263. Ibid, p.240.
264. Lewin, *American Magic*, p.93, citing Samuel Eliot Morrison's account of the Battle of Midway.
265. Roberta Wohlstetter noted in regard to the failure at Pearl Harbor, 'we have found the roots of this surprise in circumstances that affected honest, dedicated, and intelligent men'. Wohlstetter, *Pearl Harbor*, p.397.
266. We are mindful of R. Fleetwood Hesketh's warning that 'it is always unsafe to apply too literally the experiences of one war to the changed circumstances of another'. Hunt, 'An Eye-witness Report of the *Fortitude* Deception: Editorial Introduction to R.F. Hesketh's Manuscript', p.233, citing 'Fortitude: A History of Strategic Deception in North Western Europe, April 1943 to May 1945' (February 1949), Conclusion.
267. The Allied landings in North Africa, Sicily and Italy add to the list of disasters for the Germans in the Second World War. There are numerous other examples involving Soviet forces on the Eastern Front. See Ziemke, 'Stalingrad and Belorussia', pp.243–76.
268. As Roberta Wohlstetter noted: 'In view of all these limitations to perception and communication, is the fact of surprise at Pearl Harbor, then, really so surprising?' Wohlstetter, *Pearl Harbor*, p.395.
269. Handel, 'Clausewitz in the Age of Technology', p.26.
270. It may be that in today's high technology intellience collection environment, where information is compartmented into numerous categories of secrecy, the study of recent instances of surprise is practically impossible outside a small circle of people in the government. Consequently, detailed examinations of historic

instances of surprise, such as the D-Day event, must serve to instruct a wider audience both within and without the government and the armed services.

271. In 1962 Roberta Wohlstetter concluded that 'the possibility of ... [strategic] surprise at any time lies in the conditions of human perception and stems from uncertainties so basic that they are not likely to be eliminated, though they might be reduced'. Wohlstetter, *Pearl Harbor*, p.397.

272. Ibid, pp.244, 265: 'On this account, understanding but not being able to avoid the phenomenon has led to a certain futility'.

273. Ibid, p.244.

274. But even here a word of caution is in order, for as Pascal Lainé has so wisely noted: 'Sphinx, your great power is not in the solution of enigmas, but in the appearance of one who offers this possibility'. David Hamilton and Pascal Lainé, *Tender Cousins* (New York: Quill, 1981), p.87.

275. According to Field-Marshal Earl Alexander of Tunis; his quote, which I have modified, is from McLachlin, *Room 39*, p.338.

The Red Mask: The Nature and Legacy of Soviet Military Deception in the Second World War

DAVID M. GLANTZ

INTRODUCTION

As students of war and believers in dialectical materialism, modern Soviet military theorists appreciate the accelerated pace of contemporary war, and the potential impact of modern weaponry on its course and outcome. They realize the importance of time and the broadened spatial dimensions of global war. Most important, they understand the increased importance of surprise, particularly at strategic and operational levels, and the decisive effects it has on friend and foe. As a leading Soviet military theorist, Colonel V.E. Savkin, wrote in *The Basic Principles of Operational Art and Tactics* (1972):

> The ways and methods of achieving surprise are very diverse ... Depending on the concrete conditions of the situation, surprise may be achieved by leading the enemy astray with regard to one's intentions, by secrecy in preparation and swiftness of troop operations, by broad use of night time conditions, by the unexpected employment of nuclear weapons and other means of destruction, by delivering a forceful attack when and where the enemy does not expect it, and by employing methods of conduct and combat operations and new means of warfare unknown to the enemy.

Savkin's remarks, although based on history, reflect recent conclusions of Soviet military science regarding the importance of surprise in war.

Few nations have suffered as greatly from the consequences of surprise and deception as the Soviet Union. Few nations have labored so intensely to reap the benefits of surprise on the battlefield. The experience of surprise and deception has come to play a key role in contemporary Soviet military thought and practice.[1]

This article surveys Soviet experiences with deception while attempting to achieve surprise during the Second World War. Because the means, deception (*maskirovka*), is closely connected with the end, surprise (*vnezapnost*), it is impossible to deal with either topic without the other. While focusing on concrete deception measures, I will also be surveying changing Soviet attitudes toward success with surprise. The growth and development of Soviet military art and science has been evolutionary, and heavily dependent upon experience. The structure and focus of this study reflect the extensive dimensions of Soviet military experiences in general with particular emphasis on surprise and deception. In the Second World War the Soviets conducted nearly 50 major strategic operations and over 140 front (army group) offensive operations. The fronts ranged upward to 500 kilometers with depths to 650 kilometers – each involving between 300,000 and 2.5 million men. In virtually all of these operations the Soviets attempted, with varying degrees of success, to achieve surprise through deception.

The scope of these efforts reflected the magnitude of those military experiences. As early as December 1941 at Moscow, the Soviets were able to mask the offensive employment of three armies totalling over 200,000 men. In the summer of 1944, in Belorussia Soviet deception measures concealed from German eyes the redeployment and subsequent offensive employment of two armies, a tank army, and several tank corps numbering over 400,000 men and 1,500 tanks. On the eve of Vistula–Oder operation (January 1945) German intelligence failed to detect the presence of six Soviet rifle armies and one tank army and only tentatively detected another rifle army and two tank armies, a total force of almost one million men and over 2,000 tanks (about 40 per cent of the Soviet force used in the January offensive).

Since such a scale of conflict precludes comprehensive coverage, I have focused my study on representative cases. The first section surveys Soviet deception measures throughout the war. The four subsequent sections deal with specific operations, each representing the state of Soviet military theory and practice of deception during particular stages of the war. To restrict length, I have focused only on the successes. The failures (which the Soviets also candidly discuss) I leave for inclusion in a future work.

In my methodology I have relied as much as possible on Soviet sources, which are available, extensive and accurate. Since the Soviets rely on experience to teach their officers, and are wedded by ideology to scientific methodology, they must for political feasibility treat their operations objectively. Thus, self-criticism operates in the military as elsewhere, and is a motivating force for accuracy in Soviet military studies.

Despite overall Soviet candor, I utilized German sources to validate Soviet claims. For this I have relied on some secondary accounts and the operational records of German army groups, the high command in the east (OKH) and *Fremde Heeres Ost* or German military intelligence (Foreign Armies East). These records generally confirm Soviet claims, and at times reflect more success than even the Soviets realized.

As in any general survey, this study leaves many important questions unanswered. I have not mentioned to what degree the Germans exploited Soviet deceptive measures to prepare their own operational plans. I have covered only lightly the art of playing upon opponents' misconceptions, prejudices and attitudes, which was certainly exploited by both Soviets and Germans. The most important question not addressed here is to what degree the Soviets were able to monitor the success or failure of their deception plans. We know the results of operations and the degree to which the Germans were deceived. We do not know to what degree the Soviets were able to detect and assess German response, enabling them to alter and adjust their deception measures and operational plans accordingly. Such questions and many others offer fertile ground for future research and will be the focus of subsequent studies.

This study, then, introduces the subject of Soviet military deception and provides a basis for further, more extensive research. It demonstrates the extent of Soviet experiences of military deception and the degree to which the Soviets have studied them. Most important, however, it emphasizes the importance the Soviets attach to military deception in a contemporary and future context. It would be folly for American military specialists to accord less attention to the subject.

I

THE THEORY OF MASKIROVKA: GENERAL

On 22 June 1941, German forces, spearheaded by four Panzer groups, crossed the Polish–Soviet boundary and thrust deep into the Soviet Union. Capitalizing on surprise, in six months they had inflicted a shattering defeat on Soviet armies, and advanced over 800 kilometers along three strategic axes to the very outskirts of Leningrad and Moscow. By the time the offensive ground to a halt in the face of stiffened Soviet resistance and deteriorating weather, the Germans had destroyed a large portion of the peacetime Red Army, disrupted the Soviet military command structure, and forced the Soviets to initiate a drastic restructuring of their armed forces.

The devastating consequences of this surprise offensive left an indelible imprint on the work of Soviet military theorists. Although they had long appreciated the value of surprise in war, this was not enough to prevent the catastrophe of 1941. Consequently, they again focused their attention on the role of surprise in combat, and the techniques an army must master to achieve it. The wartime education was effective. By the last two years of war the Soviets had clearly mastered surprise at all levels. As a result, German armies experienced the same devastating effects of surprise that the Red Army had suffered in June 1941.

The lessons of the Second World War were not lost on Soviet military theorists in the post-war years. Intense investigation of surprise dominated Soviet military thought, particularly after Stalin's death. Improved communications, weaponry and the prospect of nuclear war placed a premium on the timeliness of offensive and defensive war preparations. Thorough Soviet study of the nature of the 'initial period of war' has focused first and foremost on surprise, and taught the Soviets that the achievement of surprise by friend, or the denial of surprise to the enemy, is indeed a major factor in achieving victory or avoiding defeat.

Among the many factors contributing to the achievement of surprise, deception is undoubtedly the most important. The Soviet term for deception, *maskirovka*, is often translated into the simple English term camouflage.[2] This definition, however, belies the complexity of the Russian term. In fact, *maskirovka* covers a host of measures ranging from disinformation at the strategic level to the skillful masking of an individual soldier's foxhole. Officially the Soviets define *maskirovka* as:

> The means of securing combat operations and the daily activities of forces; a complexity of measures, directed to mislead the enemy regarding the presence and disposition of forces, various military objective, their condition, combat readiness and operations, and also the plans of the command ... maskirovka contributes to the achievement of surprise for the actions of forces, the preservation of combat readiness and the increased survivability of objectives.[3]

Characteristically, the Soviets categorize *maskirovka* as strategic, operational and tactical. At the strategic level *maskirovka* 'is conducted by the high command and includes a complex of measures to protect the secrecy of preparations for strategic operations and campaigns, as well as disinformation of the enemy regarding the true intentions and operations of armed forces'.[4] At the operational level *maskirovka* 'is conducted by front, army, and fleet commanders and is undertaken to secure the secrecy of preparations for operation'.[5] Also, at the tactical level *maskirovka* is 'undertaken by divisions, regiments, and battalions and on separate objectives in order to hide preparations for battle or the presence (disposition) of objectives'.[6] Thus, by definition, *maskirovka* includes both active and passive measures designed to deceive and surprise the enemy.

Deception, in the Soviet view, permeates all levels of war. Since by Marxist–Leninist definition war is but an extention of politics, deception also transcends war into the political realm – specifically into the period preceding the outbreak of war. Thus, 'experience demonstrates that to secure surprise blows, the government and military control organs of the aggressor states mobilize all methods and means of influencing the enemy, including political, diplomatic, and military acts, in order to hide from them the secret concept and timing for unleashed aggression'.[7] Although written about hostile powers, this quote encapsulates Soviet belief in the all-encompassing nature of deception. Since the state of war is a logical, if not inevitable, extension of peace, then the outcome of waging war depends in part on how a nation exploits conditions existing in the pre-war period. To be effective, deception designed to ensure victory or forestall defeat must be of constant concern in peacetime as well as wartime. This all-encompassing attitude is as much a product of Marxist ideology as of military theory.

Marxism–Leninism is founded upon the truth of inevitable and predictable dialectical change.[8] The dialectic is deterministic. Based on economic, social and political realities; the dialectical method describes a process of inevitable change, resulting in the state of communism. To one who accepts the nature of the dialectical change, any and all measures that accelerate the process are desirable, if not essential. War, in its various forms, is a natural element of that process. Thus, deception is a legitimate tool to hasten change both in peace and war.

The dialectic, and the role of deception in it, assumes a moral character somewhat alien to Western democratic concepts, which view deception as immoral, akin to lying. As a result, Americans either resort to deception reluctantly, or do it poorly. Marxist–Leninist theory defines morality differently. Simply stated, morality is measured by the degree to which an action impels the dialectical process to its logical and desirable end. What assists in the achievement of socialism is moral. What does not is not. Hence, deception in peacetime is a valid, if not an imperative, means for achieving political aims without resort to war. It is likewise a valid means for securing advantage in wartime.

Coexisting with this overall attitude toward the morality of deception and its relationship to historical changes is the Soviet attitude toward the morality of war in general. To the Soviets, there are 'just' and 'unjust' wars, and their justness is measured against the same scale as for measuring morality. Simply stated, 'just' wars contribute to progress toward Socialism while 'unjust' wars do not. The use of deception is justified in both cases, either in achieving 'just' goals, or in thwarting the actions of the 'unjust'.

II

PRE-WAR THEORETICAL VIEWS

The scope and sophistication of Soviet deception has evolved with the changing nature of war. Before the Second World War the Soviets were more concerned with the physical, rather than the intellectual, aspect of deception at the strategic level. This attitude was derived from the nature of the Soviet military establishment and the technological level of the Soviet state. Some nations (for example: Japan in 1904 and Germany in 1941) have been able to use strategic deception at the onset of war, because their sophisticated military establishments permitted hasty but efficient mobilization and rapid implementation of complex war plans in the opening phase of hostilities. It was beyond the capability of the Soviet Union, however, with its ponderous peacetime military establishment and a cumbersome mobilization process inhibited by the immense size and the relative technological backwardness of the Soviet state. Certainly the Soviets realized the potential benefit of strategic deception. In their Civil War they had, on occasion, enjoyed its benefits;[9] but that was with small forces employing limited weaponry. To do likewise against the most efficient military machines of the more technologically advanced Western powers was impossible.

This attitude was reflected in Soviet military regulations and war plans. They focused on operational and tactical deception, but paid only scant attention to strategic deception. However, as we shall see, in their military theoretical writings of the inter-war period, the Soviets displayed a growing realization that technological changes, particularly the development of air and mechanized forces, offered prospects for the conduct of more meaningful deception on a higher level.

Soviet military writings during the 1920s concentrated on the, by then, classic realm of deception involving concealment of location and strength of offensive operations. They conceded that offensive intent and the timing of an offensive, were more difficult to conceal.[10] Regulations and directives adopted a similar focus by limiting the impact of deception primarily to the operational and tactical levels of war. Thus, 'in Soviet military art during the 1920s the theory of operational maskirovka [deception] was developed as one of the most important means of achieving surprise in operations'.[11] The 1924 directive, 'Vyschee komandovania', (Higher Commands), emphasizing the importance of operational maskirovka, was 'based on the principles of activnost' (activity), naturalness [sic], diversity, and continuous conduct of [maskirovka] measures'.[12]

In a more concrete vein, the 1929 Field Regulations of the Red Army enunciated the role of deception in achieving surprise:

> Surprise has a stunning effect on the enemy. For this reason all troop operations must be accomplished with the greatest conceal-ment and speed. Rapidity of action combined with organization is the main guarantee of success in combat … Surprise is also achieved by the sudden use for the enemy of new means of warfare and new methods of combat.[13]

While underscoring the importance of concealment, the regulation gave hints about the impact of further technological developments in the realm of deception. For the first time the Soviets put forward the often ignored idea of achieving surprise through the use of new combat methods unforeseen by the enemy. The remainder of the regulation referred only tangentially to deception by detailing the role conceal-ment played in the successful conduct of maneuver. Concealment is achieved by:

a. confusion of the enemy by active operations of the covering force;
b. adaptation to the terrain and camouflage;
c. performance of the maneuver swiftly and properly, particu-larly at night, in fog, and so forth, and;
d. keeping secret the preparations for the maneuver and its goal.[14]

The Soviet mechanization program undertaken in the 1930s widened the horizons of deception by increasing the speed and maneuverability of combat units and the importance of the time factor in the preparation and conduct of operations. Soviet military theorists first developed the theory of deep battle (glubokii boi) and subsequently operations (glubokaya operatsiya). As a corollary for these theories the role of deception, as defined in regulations, expanded in scope and importance – but still only at the operational and tactical levels. The 1935 Instructions on Deep Battle and the 1936 Field Regulations emphasized the growing importance of deception within the confines of the battlefield. While repeating the 1929 statements on the importance of surprise, the 1936 regulations added:

> Surprise constitutes one of the essential elements of maneuver and success in battle. The present-day implements of war which combine great fire and striking power with high mobility make it possible for the commander of larger units by skillful sudden maneuver to place his own forces in a favorable position with respect to the forces of an adversary and to force the latter to accept battle under unfavorable conditions.[15]

More importantly, the regulation emphasized the role of new weaponry and the potential for achieving technological surprise:

> Surprise action depends on concealment and speed, which are achieved by swift maneuver, *secret* concentrations of forces, concerted perparation of artillery concentrations, opening of surprise artillery fires, and *by launching unexpected infantry (cavalry), tank, and air attacks* ... Surprise is also achieved by the unexpected employment of new military weapons and new combat tactics.[16]

Yet while recognizing the importance of operational deception, theorists continued to discount the utility of deception at the strategic level, particularly deception designed to conceal the intention to launch an offensive. Illustrating this trend, M.R. Galaktianov pointed out in 1937 the difficulty involved in covering major troop movements and hostile intentions. He hinted that it was only possible to mask the scale of such movements and stated, 'the higher the mobility of the maneuvering mass, the more the effect of strategic surprise'.[17]

Events in the Far East, Poland, Finland and France in 1939 and 1940 were a vivid reminder to Soviet theorists of the role and importance of deception in war. The Soviets themselves had success with deception measures in September 1939[18] at Khalkhin Gol where they assembled a large force under the future Marshal Zhukov and inflicted a disastrous defeat on a Japanese force of two divisions. By using strict concealment measures the Soviets succeeded in concentrating a force double the size expected by the Japanese and containing a large armored contingent. The Soviets also used disinformation in the form of false troop concentrations and false defensive work to deceive Japanese planners about the location of the main Soviet attacks. Then, using the secretly assembled armored forces, they succeeded in rapidly enveloping the Japanese defenders and destroying them. The events at Khalkhin Gol accorded with contemporary Soviet military doctrine regarding deception. The deception measures at Khalkhin Gol were essentially only tactical in scope, although they were imaginatively implemented.

In late 1939, however, when the Soviets attempted to launch a surprise war against the Finns to secure territories necessary to improve the defense of Leningrad, their tactics failed. Hastily mobilized, the Soviet forces planned a massive attack along multiple axes to catch the Finns by surprise. But the mobilization was chaotic, the attack poorly co-ordinated, and the forces were unprepared to perform their assigned tasks. Not only did the Soviets fail to achieve surprise, they suffered stunning and often disastrous defeats on virtually every axis of advance. Learning from this massive failure, the Soviets in 1940 carefully prepared a new offensive incorporating more imaginative use of forces. This achieved the desired aims.[19]

The German campaigns in Poland and France in September 1939 and May 1940 clearly demonstrated the potential for successful deception on a strategic scale, especially in the initial period of war. The lessons were not entirely lost on the Soviets. A critique of these German operations written in early 1941 noted that:

> The Allied command did not expect that the German army's main attack would be inflicted on the left flank through Luxembourg and the Ardennes. Their intelligence was not able to discover in time the concentration of two German shock armies (sixth and ninth) in the Ardennes Forest ... the French command, while expecting the offensive of the German Army, mistakenly calculated that, as in 1914, the main attack of the German army would be inflicted on the right flank.[20]

The Soviet assessment was that 'German disinformation and unsatisfactory intelligence work of the Allies led to this mistake'. The German army, true to recommendations of Soviet regulations, 'having benefited from the factor of surprise', developed the blow by massive use of aviation, armor and airborne units, the new types of forces previously mentioned in Soviet regulations.[21]

Reflecting on operations in Poland and France, the Soviet military theorist, S.N. Krasil'nikov noted that:

> the rapid and hidden concentration of the army is a mission of first degree importance, since it hinders the enemy in undertaking operational countermeasures and consequently helps us secure the operational-strategic initiative.[22]

He also displayed a new realization of the strategic possibilities of deception, stating:

measures for the operational masking of them [movements] have special importance in the period of concentration and deployment. External indicators along the front and in the sector of army concentrations must not display any kind of change noticeable to the enemy.[23]

Krasil'nikov outlined specific measures designed to effect the rapid and secret concentration of forces, including:

1. Air reconnaissance must be conducted with accustomed intensity and on usual directions.

2. Divisions located at the front must, in no circumstances, be changed with new ones before the completion of an operational deployment.

3. Radio transmissions must remain normal and can conform sometimes to the radio deception of the enemy (disinformation of a plausible character).

4. Secrecy of upcoming operations is maintained from forces and staff.

5. Regrouping and transfer of forces at night, gradually and in small columns.

6. Operational deception of forces in the forward region is organized by means of creating false orders about the arrival of forces in the forward area and the covering of the real disposition of forces and by a series of other *maskirovka* measures.

7. The starting positions for the offensive are occupied not earlier than on the eve of the offensive.[24]

Krasil'nikov's study anticipated many of the methods and techniques the Soviets would learn during wartime. Significantly, it captured the essence of changing warfare characterized by the introduction of large motorized and air forces. Thus Krasil'nikov concluded:

The high level of motorization of modern armies creates a very real threat of sudden and rapid appearance close to the region of army concentration of large combined arms enemy formations, designated to disrupt the systematic character of our operational concentration of fresh forces, if it is discovered by the enemy.

Therefore higher commands, undertaking an operational concentration of a new army on a direction not secured by a dense combat front, are obliged to put under strict observation all approaches from the enemy side to the concentration area ... with the aim of operational *maskirovka*, all movement of enemy forces in the concentration area must occur as far as possible only at night, and in the daytime there must be a strict routine in the region of deployed forces.[25]

III

THEORY AND WAR EXPERIENCES

Despite the writings of Soviet military theorists on *maskirovka*, as the Second World War approached there remained a significant gap between the theory and practice of deception. As the events of June 1941 proved, the Soviets still lacked a serious appreciation of the nature and potential impact of strategic deception. Moreover, the shock and chaos produced by Germany's surprise invasion ruled out constructive Soviet use of deception during the opening months of war. At the operational and tactical level, ineptness and technogical backwardness hindered Soviet attempts to implement deception measures.

Remedies to Soviet problems soon began to flow from the very top of the command structure in the form of a series of instructions or directives. At first these were randomly aimed at specific ills in fighting techniques. In November 1942, however, the Soviets devised a system to gather, assess and capitalize on war experiences in more organized fashion.[26] In subsequent months orders appeared pertaining to the planning and conduct of battle across the entire spectrum of war. By mid-1943, the techniques these orders mandated were absorbed by operating units and incorporated by the high command into more substantial regulations.

During the early years of the war, the Red Army underwent a costly education, of which the learning of deception techniques at every level was but one aspect. Red Army units soon learned that successful *maskirovka* was only one means of survival, an absolutely essential one in the light of Germany's early dominance in armored and air warfare. The main early weaknesses, which persisted into the mid-war years, were an inability to master radio discipline and maintain communications security, and the adverse effect of individual security problems on the secrecy of operational planning. On the positive side, the Soviets quickly learned camouflage techniques and were able to mask the movement of large forces when radio transmissions were not required. In addition, the Soviets severely limited the size of planning circles to provide a more secure planning environment. While this procedure improved the security of Soviet operational planning, it also had a negative impact on the performance of lower-level units with limited planning time.

The first wartime instruction concerning *maskirovka* was passed to Red Army units only four days after the German invasion. On 26 July 1941 the Red Army Military Engineer Administration repeated the contents of the 1936 regulation and exhorted Soviet commanders to undertake such operational measures as 'conducting a series of secondary blows on a wide front before beginning operations on the main axis' and 'strengthening the reconnaissance activity of all types of forces on secondary axes'.[27] In addition, it instructed commanders to mask important operational objectives and create false objectives to confuse enemy air reconnaissance, making the performance of such tasks the responsibility of the unit chief engineer. Later, in September 1941, the STAVKA (High Command) issued a directive reminding higher level commanders to mask their reconnaissance efforts and, more importantly, to hide preparations for main attacks by their forces.[28]

In the first year of war Soviet successes with deception were as much a product of the chaotic combat conditions produced by the rapid German advance as of improved Soviet security. During the German advance from June to October 1941 the Soviets were able to mobilize and commit to combat a series of new armies. Initially, German intelligence generally kept up with the formation and commitment of these new forces for they were in accordance with pre-war estimates. By the late summer and fall, however, the scale of Soviet mobilization began to surprise the German High Command. In addition, German intelligence began missing the scale and location of large Soviet operational deployments (although German tactical intelligence was quite accurate). The failure of German intelligence, and the corresponding success of Soviet deception, was manifested by the Soviet Moscow counter-offensive which was spearheaded by three armies, undetected by German intelligence. Although it ultimately did not achieve the desired end (the destruction of German Army Group Center), it did establish a future pattern for deception. By virtue of strict secrecy, the Soviets were able to conceal the movement and deployment of large army formations (aided by the depth of the German advance, bad weather and – perhaps most important – German over-confidence).

Despite the success of Soviet deception at Moscow, throughout 1941 and 1942, the German High Command was able to identify the primary geographical area of Soviet strategic concern while masking their own priorities. In the summer of 1942, the renewed German offensive in southern Russia caught Soviet planners by surprise, although the Soviets adjusted well to this unpleasant reality. Throughout 1942 German strategic offensive Soviet planners repeated their performance of late 1941 by marshalling under strict security measures a new array of reserve armies which they ultimately committed to battle in the Stalingrad region.

During the summer campaign Soviet deception measures improved in another regard, the secret formation and deployment of new type units.[29] In the spring and summer of 1942, the Soviets created 15 new tank corps and later five new tank armies. The *maskirovka* measures were so successful that German intelligence failed to note the creation of these forces. In the abortive Soviet offensive at Khar'kov in May 1942, the Soviets used two of their new tank corps, which German intelligence identified as brigades rather than corps. The same situation occurred in June and July when the Soviets committed to combat the first of their new tank armies. Again the Germans identified them as brigades. Regardless of these intelligence failures, however, German forces were able to deal effectively with these new Soviet formations.

By the fall of 1942, growing Soviet numerical superiority over the Germans and more effective security improved Soviet operational *maskirovka*.[30] Marshal Zhukov wrote, 'Our superiority over the Germans was manifested in the fact that the Soviet Armed Forces began to keep secret their intentions, to conduct large-scale disinformation, and to mislead the enemy. Hidden regroupings and concentrations permitted surprise attacks on the enemy',[31] such as the launch, in November 1942, of the Stalingrad Counter-offensive. Although there had been indicators of a future Soviet offensive, its scale and location and the nature of units available came as a surprise to the Germans. For the first time, the Soviets had undertaken a major effort at the highest level to mislead the Germans about their strategic intentions. This effort included STAVKA orders directing only defensive preparations around Stalingrad and orders for offensive operations elsewhere. Although the Germans were not totally misled, operationally the Soviet *maskirovka* measures succeeded. The encirclement of the German Sixth Army at Stalingrad resulted.

Throughout the winter of 1943, as Soviet armies advanced across southern Russia toward the Dnepr River, Soviet commanders continued to attempt to use deception. It took the form of attacks of a persistence and abandon which amazed the Germans. Actually, the frantic nature of these efforts was conditioned by a belief that German forces were actually hastening to withdraw from their over-extended position in the south.[32] Consequently, renewed German counterattacks inflicted serious (though temporary) defeats on over-extended and over-optimistic Soviet commanders.

There was little deception about Soviet operational planning mid-1943, during the German Kursk offensive. Soviet forces were clearly and deliberately on the strategic defensive. However, unknown to German intelligence, the Soviets included in their defensive planning plans for a large-scale counter-offensive scheduled to begin when the German offensive tide began to ebb. The Soviets engaged in large-scale *maskirovka* measures to cover their intentions, including radio deception (the establishment by radio of false large-scale concentrations) and camouflage measures for troop concentration. While the radio deception failed, the active measures succeeded, and the Soviet August 1943 Belgorod–Khar'kov offensive came as a surprise to the Germans.[33] Again, although the Germans accurately assessed future Soviet intentions, they wrongly estimated the timing and scale of the attack and paid for this mistake by suffering a major defeat which forced German forces to withdraw westward to the Dnepr River line.

In the autumn of 1943, while Soviet forces advanced along a broad front from Smolensk in the north to the Black Sea coast in the south, German intelligence correctly assessed that the Soviet main effort would be in the Ukraine. Consequently, German forces contained Soviet armies along the Dnepr River and in limited bridgeheads south of Kiev and south of Kremenchug. After a month of stalemate, a major Soviet deception operation produced a break. By utilizing a variety of deceptive measures including dummy radio nets, mock-up tanks, and night movements, the Soviets secretly shifted an entire tank army (3rd Guards) from the Bukhrin area south of Kiev into a bridgehead across the Dnepr River in the Lyutezh area north of Kiev.[34] There 3rd Tank Army joined 38th Army in launching a surprise operation which drove German forces from the Kiev region. The Germans had insufficient forces available, and were unable to parry the Soviet offensive thrust before it had established a major bridgehead west of Kiev.[35]

Along with these successful examples of operational deception, the Soviets also suffered failures, most notably in the Donbas (July 1943) and Chernyov–Pripyat region (August–September 1943) where poor Soviet radio security undermined their aims. In both instances the Germans adjusted their forces and halted the Soviet offensives after only minor gains.

By the end of 1943, Soviet deception operations had progressed from random attempts to a comprehensive and more active program. By late 1942, specific staff agencies within each headquarters were required to prepare specific deception plans to accompany normal operational plans.[36] Soviet deception successes during this period occurred primarily at the operational and tactical level. Attempts at strategic deception were still crude and largely unrealized. Cumulative operational successes did produce some positive strategic results, in particularly at Moscow, Stalingrad, Kursk and Kiev.

During 1944 and 1945, the strategic initiative fell clearly into Soviet hands, permitting the Red Army to select the form and means for conducting the war. Consequently, the scale and scope of Soviet deception expanded to encompass overall offensive intent, the region of operations, as well as the form and timing of the attack. Improved technology (principally armor and communications equipment), growing Societ domination of the air, and improved Soviet technical expertise made possible large-scale strategic deception and more efficient deception at all lower levels of command. Growing sophistication of deception became evident in early 1944.

Simultaneously the Red Army incorporated lessons learned in deception into a wide range of regulations. The 1943 *Field Regulation* (Proekt) addressed the planning, conduct, security and control of deception measures.[37] It ordered the creation of deception plans at every level of command and required those plans to include: the objectives of deception in the various steps of preparing for battle and in the separate stages of battle; the nature of deception measures and the place and time of their implementation; and responsibilities for fulfilling these measures. The regulation made all commanders responsible for passive deception (such as camouflage) within their units. The 1944 *Regulation for Penetration of a Positional Defense* stated:

> The difficulty of securing the concentration of large masses of forces in the penetration sector and the requirement of fulfilling a large volume of engineer work, demands the safe protection by military aviation and the most careful working out of measures for operational and tactical *maskirovka*.[38]

The 1944 *Field Regulation* demonstrated the expanded understanding of *maskirovka* derived from wartime experiences. The opening section of the regulation declared:

> Surprise dumbfounds the enemy, paralyses his will, and deprives him of an opportunity to offer organized resistance.
> Surprise is achieved:
>
> - by leading the enemy astray and by keeping the plan of up-coming actions in strictest secrecy;
> - by the concealment and swift regrouping of forces and of the concentration of overwhelming forces and weapons in the decisive locations;
> - by the surprise [unexpected] attack of aircraft, cavalry, and motorized tank units;
> - by surprise [unexpected] opening of annihilating fires and the beginning of swift attacks.
>
> Surprise is also achieved by employing methods of fighting that are new for the enemy and weapons unknown to him.
> The enemy will also strive for surprise.[39]

The regulation then outlined specific measures for deception, underscoring the importance of those measures for achieving operational and tactical success, specifying the contents of deception plans, and delineating the staff responsibilities for implementing those plans. It declared:

> *maskirovka* is a mandatory form of combat support for each action and operation. The missions of *maskirovka* are to secure concealment of the maneuver and concentration of troops for the purpose of delivering a surprise attack; to mislead the enemy relative to our forces, weapons, actions, and intentions; and thus force him to make an incorrect decision.[40]

Unlike previous regulations, that of 1944 specified that an enemy was to be misled:

- by concealing real objects from enemy reconnaissance and observation;
- by changing the external appearance of objects;
- by setting up dummy objects and by feints;
- by spreading false rumors;
- by sound discipline and by artificial noises;
- by masking the operations of radios, by setting up dummy radio nets, and by radio deception.[41]

The regulation reiterated that successful *maskirovka* was based on the principles of 'naturalness, diversity, continuousness and activeness *(actvnost)* and *maskirovka* measures'.[42]

Drafting the overall plan of *maskirovka* was the responsibility of appropriate staff, in accordance with the commander's concept of the operation. The plan was to articulate general missions by planning each phase of the operation; specific *maskirovka* measures by time and location of their execution; and officers responsible for the execution of the plan. However, planned feints and the spreading of false rumors were to be accomplished only under the direct orders of army and front headquarters as outlined in the army and *front maskirovka* plan.

Guided by their experience of three years of war, the Soviets were more capable of carrying out effective deception in the final two years.

From late December 1943 into early 1944, the Soviets concentrated their offensive efforts in southern Russia as they drove to clear the Ukraine of German forces. There was little attempt by the Soviets to mask their strategic intentions, but what surprised the Germans was the Soviet intention and ability to operate right through the period of thaw *(razputitsa)*. Previously, as if by mutual consent, both sides had halted operations in late February and March as the soil turned to a deep gluey mass which inhibited effective operations.

In late February 1944, however, the Soviets launched a series of simultaneous *front* operations from Korosten (west of Kiev) to the Black Sea. To the Germans' consternation, the Soviets committed six tank armies and a cavalry-mechanized group to spearhead these operations which endured through early June, pushing German forces toward the Polish borders and into Bessarabia. While abstaining from the use of *maskirovka* as a strategic means to achieve surprise, in this period the Soviets relied instead on deceiving the Germans regarding the form and timing of their offensives. In addition, the Soviets did resort to extensive *maskirovka* at the operational and tactical levels with mixed success. In early December 1943, west of Kiev, while Soviet forces struggled in the waning stages of the Kiev operation, they successfully masked from German view the assembly of two full rifle armies and one tank army, armies which then in late December unexpectedly penetrated the German defenses (see maps 1–2).[43] In February the Soviets conducted a major deception operation designed to mask the redeployment of 5th Guards Tank Army before the Korsun–Shevchenkovsky operation, with only limited success (see map 3).[44] In the early spring as the thaw set in, examples of operational deception diminished in number and effect.

As the spring offensive ebbed, the Soviets undertook one of their most successful strategic deception operations, one which was disastrous for the Germans. Using a variety of active and passive *maskirovka* measures, the Soviets sought to convince German planners that Soviet offensive efforts would continue against German forces in south-eastern Europe and in the Baltic region. In reality, the Soviets intended to conduct a major strategic redeployment of forces and then strike German Army Group Center defending in Belorussia. The ensuing deception operation, orchestrated by the STAVKA, involved extensive radio deception, rumors, false orders, feints, and massive movement of forces under cover of extensive passive *maskirovka* measures. As a result of these efforts, the Germans concentrated all available operational reserves in south-eastern Poland, thus depriving the real Soviet target, German Army Group Center in Belorussia, of virtually all of its armored and mechanized forces.

The Soviet offensive destroyed the three armies of German Army Group Center. Then, having advanced all the way to Riga, East Prussia, and Warsaw on the Vistula River line, the Soviets suddenly shifted their strategic emphasis southward in August. In rapid succession they delivered devastating blows against German Army Northern Ukraine defending south-eastern Poland (July) and against

Army Group South Ukraine, defending Romania (August), both of which had just dispatched a significant portion of their armies' reserves northward to assist the remnants of Army Group Center. In both operations the Soviets made extensive use of operational *maskirovka* with good effect.[45]

In early 1945, as Soviet forces operated on a narrowing front from the Baltic Sea to the Danube River, it became increasingly difficult for the Germans to detect which sector posed the greatest danger. In fact, the Soviets deliberately sought to remain active on all fronts. Soviet strategic *maskirovka* was effective enough to attract German attention to Hungary and the critical Danube Basin where it appeared the Soviets would continue their drive into Austria and the soft underbelly of the German Reich. Consequently, as German forces concentrated their defensive (and offensive) efforts in Hungary, Soviet forces prepared and unleashed devastating offensives against German forces in East Prussia and Poland. They crushed three German Army Groups and propelled Soviet forces to the Baltic Coast and across the Oder River to within 60 kilometers of Berlin.[46]

As the incessant series of Soviet offensives in early 1945 moved toward final defeat of German forces around Berlin, the Soviets were already contemplating a strategic offensive of even grander scale against Japanese forces in Manchuria. Acting in their own political interests and coincidentally responding to US requests for assistance, the Soviets planned a major strategic redeployment of forces into the Far East after the final defeat of Germany. The reinforced Soviet Far Eastern Command would then strike at the Japanese Kwantung Army, occupy Manchuria, and prepare for possible joint US–Soviet operations against Japan. Soviet planners realized the operation had to be a rapid one, in their view complete within 30 days.

The severe time constraints on the operation, the size and terrain in the projected theater of operations, and the number (700,000) and dispositions of Japanese forces in Manchuria dictated that maximum deception be used by the Soviets both during the strategic redeployment of forces and during the operation itself. The Soviets faced the same problem as Germany faced in June 1941, the necessity to win quickly in an 'initial period of war'.

The Soviets used extensive *maskirovka* measures: false orders, night movement, and a host of passive concealment and camouflage techniques. They also took maximum advantage of poor weather conditions and planned large-scale attacks in terrain considered unsuitable by the Japanese. These deception measures achieved their object. Japanese planners underestimated Soviet strength by over 30

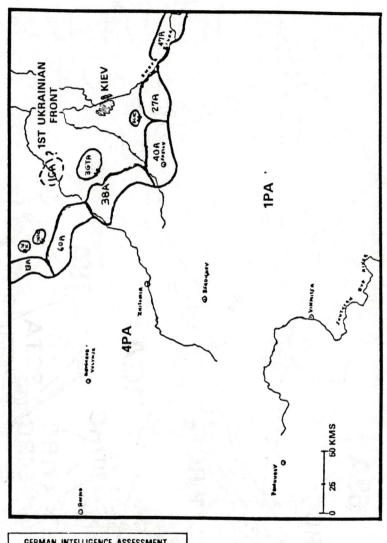

. GERMAN INTELLIGENCE ASSESSMENT
(4TH PANZER ARMY), 22 DECEMBER 1943

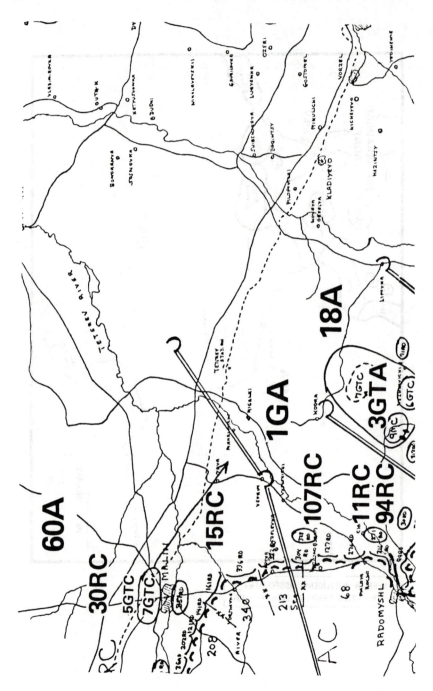

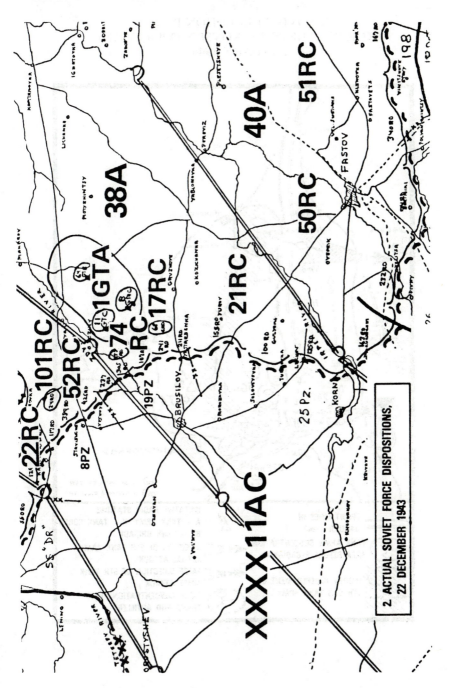

2 ACTUAL SOVIET FORCE DISPOSITIONS, 22 DECEMBER 1943

3. SOVIET DECEPTION PLAN
(KORSUN-SHEVCHEVKOVSKY OPERATION)
JANUARY 1944

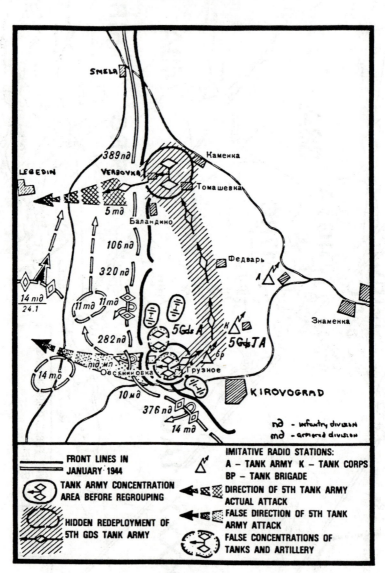

per cent and assessed that the Soviet invasion would take place at least a month after it actually occurred. The Soviets completed destruction of the Kwantung Army and occupied Manchuria in just over 15 days.

At the war's end, the Soviets had extensive experience with *maskirovka*, both as victim and as employer of deception. The complexity of those experiences reflected the difficulty and vast scope of operations on the eastern front as a whole. To judge the efficiency of Soviet planners and operators in this shadowy form of war, it is necessary to look in some detail at a number of specific examples, a limited number for reasons of space, of the use of *maskirovka*. These exaamples provide an indication of the maturing Soviet appreciation and talent for such measures.

IV

THE PRACTICE OF MASKIROVKA

Moscow, 1941

The first major attempt by the Soviets to employ large-scale *maskirovka* to cover preparations for offensive operations occurred in November and December of 1941, while German forces were straining to overcome Soviet resistance and seize Moscow. Accordingly, the Soviet planners were driven as much by desperation as by a conscious well-planned effort to deceive and defeat German forces. They were unwittingly assisted by the German commands maintaining an optimistic tone and continually depreciating the Soviet ability to generate and deploy fresh reserves. On 18 November the German Army Chief of Staff General Franz Halder wrote:

> Field Marshal von Bock shares my deep conviction that the enemy, just as much as we do, is throwing in the last ounce of strength and that victory will go to the side that sticks it out longer. The enemy, too, has nothing left in the rear and his predicament probably is even worse than ours.[47]

This typified German attitudes through the end of November and into December 1941. On 2 December Halder again wrote, 'Overall impression: Enemy defense has reached its peak. No more reinforcement available'.[48] Meanwhile, between three and seven days before, elements of three new Soviet armies had been deployed into the Moscow region.[49] Just three days before Halder's comment, the STAVKA, in co-ordination with the Western Front, had approved a plan to use these and other Western Front armies in a general counter-offensive against the advance spearheads of German forces lying exhausted on the northern and southern approaches to the Russian capital.

The Soviet counter-offensive, ordered by Stalin and planned by General Zhukov, commander of the Western Front, envisaged the use of these three new armies as shock groups to spearhead the new offensive. Deployment of the new armies into the forward area had begun on 24 November and continued until early December, ready for the designated attack date of 5 December.[50] Soviet *maskirovka* measures associated with the Moscow counter-attack in general, and the movement of the three armies in particular, were not systematically planned, nor part of any well-organised strategic deception plan. Yet specific aspects of planning and deployment did have seemingly positive results, in particular an improved Soviet ability to cover large troop movements, and poor German intelligence. The Moscow counter-attack came as a distinct surprise for German Army Group Center and the German High Command.

Soviet planning for the Moscow counter-offensive was completed in only six days and with the utmost secrecy. Even army commanders knew only their portion of the plan. Soviet resort to sequential planning (step by step through various levels of command), which endured in the future, improved the secrecy of operational planning but limited the preparation period of subordinate headquarters. In the Moscow operation, however, it prevented disclosure of the plans to German intelligence.

Deployment of 1st Shock, 10th, and 12th Armies; as well as other units into their attack positions, took place in strict secrecy (see map 4). The troops were required to observe strict light and camouflage discipline, and all movement occurred at night under absolute radio silence. The Soviets made every effort to camouflage supply depôts, rail lines, and roads along deployment routes. Weather made the task of covering forward movement much easier.[51] These measures, plus the preoccupation of German forces with their own increasingly over-extended situation, prevented German detection of Soviet redeployment.

German intelligence was, however, not entirely unaware. On 27 November, three days after the Soviet reserve armies began their redeployment, Halder wrote:

> The Right flank of Second Panzer Army is confronted with an enemy concentration; similar concentration is reported by Second Army. New forces have made their appearance in the

direction of the Oka River, at which Second Panzer Army is aiming its thrust. The situation is not clear . . .

The enemy is apparently moving new forces also against the attacking wing of A Gp Center northwest of Moscow. They are not large units, but they arrive in an endless succession and caused delay after delay for our exhausted troops.[52]

Two days later Halder noted questioningly, 'On the front of Fourth Army . . . there is some talk that the enemy is preparing for an attack? . . . Further east [of the Second Panzer Army], the enemy movements to Ryazen from the south are continuing'.[53] The casual note of Soviet troop movements, however, was lost in the general optimism of Halder's notes.

Meanwhile Army Group Center evinced similar optimism on 4 December: 'The combat power of the Red Army cannot be so highly regarded to consider that the enemy presently located in front of the army group can launch a major counter-offensive'.[54] The following day Army Group Center and the German High Command noted on their intelligence maps only seven Soviet armies operating on the Soviet western front. Nowhere on the maps did the 1st Shock, 10th or 20th Armies appear (see maps 5 and 6).[55]

On 5 December the new Soviet offensive began, spearheaded by the three undetected armies. Within a week German forces were hard-pressed to withdraw from the Moscow region in good order. Belatedly, on 8 December Halder noted, 'Northwest of Moscow, Twentieth Russian Army has been in action since 6 December'.[56]

Though the German forces were surprised by the ferocity of the Soviet counter-attack, it is by no means clear that the surprise was the result of an efficient Soviet *maskirovka* plan. Certainly the Soviets did not engage in cohesive strategic planning. Attacks in the Leningrad area to the north and around Rostov in the south, although the Soviets cite them as planned distractions for the Moscow counter-offensive, were actually a response to local conditions and in no way weakened the German intention of seizing Moscow. Additionally, the haste and secrecy in planning the Moscow operation mitigated against the creation of a comprehensive *maskirovka*. Radio discipline, light discipline, and night movement masked the scope of movement and ultimate destination of relocating Soviet forces. So did the bad weather and German distraction with the distressing situation at hand.

At best, Soviet experiences at Moscow partially indicated what could be done with *maskirovka*. It also indicated what needed to be done. The Soviets' ultimate frustration was their failure to achieve their strategic objectives. This spurred the High Command (STAVKA and

4. SOVIET REGROUPING OF FORCES IN THE MOSCOW REGION, NOVEMBER–DECEMBER 1941

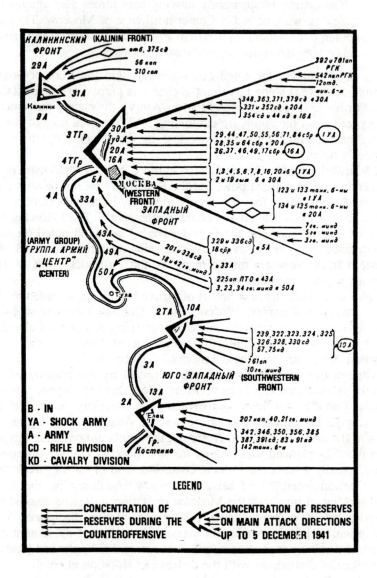

General Staff) to consider a broader range of *maskirovka* measures that could contribute to even greater success in future operations. Moscow was only the first lesson in a long combat education.

Stalingrad, 1942

In June 1942, following a series of operational failures resulting from Soviet attempts to seize the offensive, the German Army started a second strategic offensive across southern Russia. Its forces swept forward to the Don River at Voronezh and then swung south toward Stalingrad and past it into the Caucasus. The Red Army resisted the German advance with a series of counter-attacks in the Voronezh region, along the upper Don River, and on the approaches to Stalingrad proper. It also adopted a deliberate defensive strategy involving the systematic withdrawal of forces before they were threatened with encirclement and a conscious decision to conduct a deliberate defense in the city of Stalingrad, preparatory to launching a strategic counteroffensive. Unlike the 1941 situation, in late 1942 the Soviets retained the planning initiative. By November 1942 German forces were locked in a bitter and costly struggle for Stalingrad, a struggle which consumed German operations reserves, forced the Germans to deploy extensively allied forces, and rely on those forces for protection of the long German flanks extending into the Stalingrad area.

As in late 1941, in the summer and fall of 1942 the STAVKA carefully raised and deployed reserve armies and formed new armored forces (tank armies and mechanized corps) for use in a major counterstroke in the Stalingrad region. It also undertook a concerted attempt to capitalize on war experiences (by now systematically collected, analysed, and converted into orders for every level of command among which were directives for more thorough *maskirovka* measures). A directive of Red Army engineer forces dated 9 November 1942 spoke of recurring operational-tactical deficiencies in Soviet *maskirovka* practices and recommended a series of remedies. This directive specifically stated:

– false objectives and concentrations of forces are seldom used and are unsystematic, and during the erection of false objectives matters are often limited to the construction of only one type of dummy and no reserves are used to animate them, a consequence of which reactive measures of the enemy are absent, aside from scattered reconnaissance flights, which established the fact of false objectives;

– of all rear area objectives only command posts of *front* and army staffs are well camouflaged;

5. GERMAN INTELLIGENCE ASSESSMENT
(ARMY GROUP CENTER) 4 DECEMBER 1941

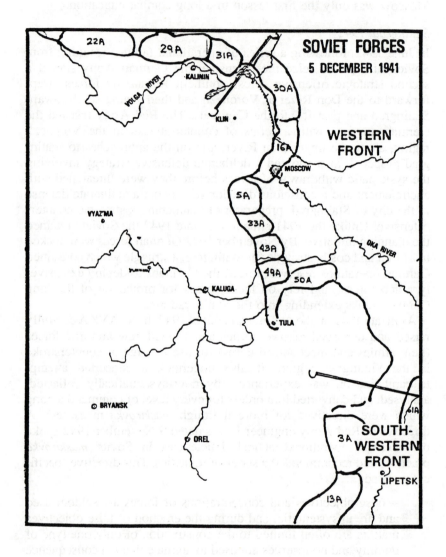

6. ACTUAL SOVIET FORCE DISPOSITIONS
4 DECEMBER 1941

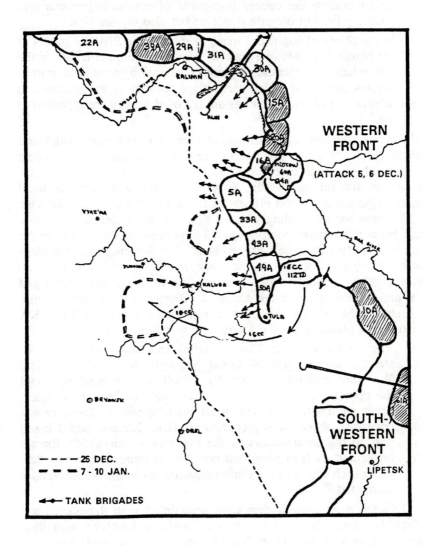

– roads, used as the basic routes for transport and evacuation, are in no fashion masked by vertical covers from ground observation, and therefore the enemy is capable of conducting mortar and artillery fire not only on transport but also on vehicles;

– the chiefs of engineer forces, in spite of the *STAVKA* orders of 28 November 1941 in a majority of cases do not participate in the formulation of operational plans conducted by *fronts* and armies, a consequence of which camouflage security of the operation is absent and camouflage units are not used as they are supposed to be.[57]

The directive went on to demand that units take corrective action and made chiefs of engineers, individual *front* and army commanders responsible for such corrections. It also specifically required greater efforts at disinformation. The November directive became the focal point of Soviet deception efforts for the Stalingrad counter-offensive.

Planning for the Stalingrad operation was more deliberate than it had been at Moscow. Starting on 13 September it intensified as the attack date (19 November) approached.[58] The Soviets conducted planning in the greatest secrecy and integrated into the strategic plan measures both to deceive the Germans about the location and timing of the attack, and to cover the scope of offensive preparations. Future Marshal A.M. Vasilevsky, then a representative of the STAVKA involved in planning for the Stalingrad operation, wrote:

The Commander in Chief [Stalin] introduced conditions of strictest secrecy into all initial preparations for the operation. We were ordered categorically to tell no one anything about the operation, even members of the State Defense Committee. Stalin gave notice that he himself would speak to whomever was necessary about such preparations. G.K. Zhukov and I could pass to the commanders of the *fronts* only that which directly concerned each of them and not a word more. I dare say that, under such conditions, a similar measure of caution would be fully warranted.[59]

Only the *front* commanders were acquainted with the operational plans, but even they did not become actively involved with their development until November. The General Staff also sought to restrict the size of the planning circle. It forbade correspondence relating to the operation between the General Staff and the *front* and between *fronts* and armies. All co-ordinating for the offensive was to be accomplished personally through contact of STAVKA representatives (G.K. Zhukov, A.M. Vasilevsky, and N.N. Voronov) with *fronts* and armies. Voronov wrote:

With the purpose of keeping offensive preparations secret, it was forbidden to publish any written printed, and graphic documents. At first, a very limited number of generals and officers were acquainted with the new combat missions. This, of course, made preparation for the operation very difficult, and made us plan our work by each *front* and then by each army. In my case, the number of officers who could be entrusted with such an important secret were also quite limited.[60]

Within corps and divisions all instructions were verbal and directed only to those who would carry the orders out.

The STAVKA attempted to deceive the Germans as to the location of the Soviet counter-offensive. In mid-October 1942 it ordered the *fronts* in southern Russia to engage only in defensive operations. Detailed written instructions specified the establishment of defensive boundaries, construction of engineer obstacles, and the preparation of populated areas for all-round strongpoint defense. Simultaneously, throughout the summer and fall of 1942, the STAVKA ordered the Kalinin and Western Fronts in the Moscow region to prepare active offensive operations against German Army Group Center in what they hoped the Germans would perceive as a renewal of Soviet actions that had terminated in April 1942. As a result, the Soviets launched the Rzhev–Sychevka operation (30–23 August) which achieved only limited gains but drew 12 new German divisions into Army Group Center. The Soviet feint and subsequent build-up west of Moscow had the desired effect. An August 1942 assessment of the Eastern Intelligence Branch of the German Army High Command (OKH) concluded that the Russians would have considerable offensive potential in the fall in both Army Group Center's and 'B's' sectors, but

> that the Russians would be more eager to remove the threat to Moscow posed by the forward elements of Army Group Center and would therefore most likely exploit the salients at Toropets and Sukhinichi for converging attacks on Smolensk, with the objective of destroying the Ninth, Third Panzer, and Fourth Armies.[63]

In the following two months OKH noted the Soviet build-up west of Moscow and judged that a Soviet offensive would begin after the rains projected to occur two to three weeks after 16 October.[64]

Strenuous Soviet *maskirovka* measures within the *fronts* and armies of the Stalingrad region contributed to the confounding of German intelligence assessments. The chief intention of Soviet *maskirovka* was to cover the forward deployment of the immense forces needed to conduct a successful offensive, complicated by a limited transport network and restricted bridgeheads south and west of the Don River. *Maskirovka* would have to cover the forward deployment of over 300,000 men; 1,000 tanks; and 5,000 guns and mortars with ammunition, fuel, and other supplies.

A 25 October directive by A.M. Vasilevsky to the commanders of the Don and Southwestern Fronts set the standards for the *maskirovka* effort:

a. All marches will be conducted only at night, placing the units in concealed positions for day time rest;
b. Movement will be covered by aviation and anti-aircraft units ... the necessity of camouflage of each operation will be assigned to the Military Council of the front (army), and development and execution of a decision will be achieved for the camouflaging, based upon the utilization of operational and engineering camouflage measures and misinformation of the enemy; separate commanders, who will be personally responsible for camouflage on a *front* and army scale, will be allotted from the personnel of the staffs of the engineer troops of the *fronts* and armies ...[65]

Following these instructions, the South-western Front began masking the forward deployment of the Fifth Tank Army and Twenty-first Army restricted bridgeheads south of the Don River at Serafimovich and Kletskaya. It built 22 bridges (five false) across the Don, concealing the approaches with vertical covers. They also camouflaged the crossings, command points, *front* and army headquarters. German aircraft bombed the false bridges but left the functional bridges intact. As the attack date of 19 November neared, the Soviets used smoke to cover armor units crossing the Don. On 19 November extensive smoke screens covered the crossing by 26th Tank Corps into the Serafimovich bridgehead.[66] At army level, engineers constructed simulated concentrations of artillery and tanks to deceive German artillery and air observation. With the assistance of road guards and traffic controllers all movements within armies was carried out at night under strict light discipline. Skillful camouflage and the use of loudspeakers to cover engine noises facilitated the secret forward deployment of three Soviet tank corps (1st, 26th, 4th) into the bridgeheads.

The Stalingrad Front conducted active offensive operations between 29 September and 4 October to secure enlarged bridgeheads for the future offensive and to distract German forces from the defensive actions at Stalingrad proper. Subsequently the Stalingrad Front moved two mechanized corps, one cavalry corps, five air defense artillery regiments, a tank brigade, two rifle divisions, and seven artillery divisions into its bridgeheads west of the Don. The night movements here and at Stalingrad proper involved the passage across the river of 160,000 men; 10,000 horses; 430 tanks; 600 guns; 14,000 vehicles; and 7,000 tons of ammunition, most undetected by German intelligence.[67]

The forces of the Don Front undertook similar extensive measures to cover preparations. Front commander K.K. Rokossovsky recalled:

> Much was done in order to deceive the enemy. We tried to convince him that we were about to attack in the area between the rivers and conducted more operations here. In the remaining sectors of the front, intensified operations for the erection of foxholes, fortifications, etc., were simulated. Any movement of troops into those regions, from where they were to operate, was carried out only at night, with the observance of all camouflage measures.[68]

65th Army Commander General P.I. Batov wrote:

> Concentration and regrouping of forces was conducted exclusively at night. Some formations and units of the troops even moved in an opposite direction to deceive the enemy. At the Kletskaya bridgehead, in spite of intensified reconnaissance flights by German aviation, we managed to concentrate the basic mass of our troops and equipment in time. In this region, the rumble of mortars was not audible in the daytime, movement of ground forces was forbidden, and everything died down.[69]

Similar camouflage measures occurred in the air forces supporting all three Soviet *fronts*.

As well as using disinformation on a strategic scale and extensive operational and tactical *maskirovka*, the Soviets used more subtle methods to cover their intention to attack and create an impression of defensive intent. Front, army and divisional newspapers echoed the by then familiar slogan, *Ne shagu nazad* (not a step back) and added a host of exhortations to Soviet troops to hold fast in every sector and make the Germans pay a heavy price in blood for every offensive effort. At the same time, the newspapers talked of plans to seize other objectives elsewhere and periodically mentioned the feats of fictitious units and commanders.

These extensive Soviet *maskirovka* measures achieved considerable success. The greatest feat was in masking the scale of the offensive. While numerous indications of Soviet offensive intent surfaced, they did not convey to German intelligence the magnitude of the Soviet attack. As at Moscow, German optimism and even overconfidence tended to distract intelligence officers from the actual evidence.

German intelligence reports in the last two weeks of October 'indicated that the buildup opposite Army Group 'B' was limited to the Serafimovich bridgehead opposite the Romanian Third Army'.[70] Romanian concern was, in fact, growing. On 29 October, General Dmitrescu of Third Army reported to Army Group:

1. Marked increases in the number of Don crossings in the Russian rear;
2. Statements from deserters;
3. Continuous local attacks, the sole object of which must be to find the soft spots and to pave the way for the major attack.[71]

On receiving this report, General Paulus, commander of German Sixth Army, recollected:

I went myself to Army Group Headquarters in Starobielsk on November 9 and submitted a report with the following details: three new infantry formations with some tanks had been identified in the Kletskaya area, and one new armored, one new motorized, and two new infantry formations were thought to be concentrated in the same area; and in the Blinov sector the presence of two new infantry formations with a few tanks had been definitely established. A major enemy attack, it was considered, could be expected at any moment.[72]

Army Group responded by moving a support group and the weak XXXXVIII Panzer Corps to back up the Romanians and by ordering intensified air reconnaissance and direct air attacks on Soviet concentrations. However, on 31 October, Eastern Intelligence Branch (OKH) reported, 'The level of activity in the bridgehead did not presage a major attack but rather appeared more and more to indicate that only local attacks were expected'.[73]

Indicators of a Soviet build-up against Army Group 'B' mounted in early November to a level sufficient to raise concern within the Army Group. By 10 November two rifle divisions of Soviet 5th Tank Army were identified in the Serafimovich area, although the parent unit was still assumed to be further north. In addition, German intelligence detected a new *front* headquarters (the South-western) to go with the already detected Don Front north of Stalingrad.[74] Meanwhile XI Army Corps, Fourth Panzer Army and XIV Panzer Corps reported Soviet movements into and concentrating at bridgeheads facing their positions.[75] While Army Group 'B' had concluded by mid-November that an offensive was in the offing against Third Romanian and Fourth Panzer Army, the Eastern Intelligence Branch of OKH clung to its optimistic view, noting on 6 November that the Soviet main effort was certain to come against Army Group Center and that the offensive on the Don would come later. It reiterated this view on 12 November in an assessment claiming conditions were too obscure for a definite prediction, but qualified the assessment by stating:

> However an attack in the near future against Romanian Third Army with the objective of cutting the railroad to Stalingrad and thereby threatening the German force farther east and forcing a withdrawal from Stalingrad must be taken into consideration.[76]

The branch added that, 'There are not sufficient forces available for the enemy to develop broad operations'.[77] Chief of the German General Staff, General Zeitzler, echoed this view:

> The Russians no longer have any reserves worth mentioning and are not capable of launching a large scale offensive. In forming any appreciation of enemy intentions, this basic fact must be taken fully into consideration.[78]

Despite these predictions, on 19 November Soviet forces launched an offensive which penetrated Romanian and German defenses, encircled Sixth Army, and inflicted the most disastrous defeat on German forces since the creation of the Wehrmacht (see maps 7–8).

To the Soviets, Stalingrad represented a turning point (*perelom*) in their military operation in the Second World War, first and foremost because they achieved their first unqualified strategic success on the battlefield. Their success with *maskirovka* was even more remarkable, for their record of deception before November 1942 was generally a poor one.

At Stalingrad the Soviets first experimented with rudimentary techniques for strategic deception. They made conscious efforts to simulate offensive preparations in other sectors of the front. While German troop adjustments in reaction to this attempted deception were minimal, the German OKH became transfixed by Soviet intentions in Army Group Center's sector. This, plus high command preoccupation with the bitter fight for Stalingrad proper, distracted them from undue concern over the vulnerable flanks of Army Group 'B'. If Soviet strategic *maskirovka* measures were rudimentary, they certainly indicated the potential value of such activities if carried out on an even larger scale. Soviet planning in 1944 was to demonstrate that increased Soviet appreciation with more devastating effects for the Germans.

In the operational and tactical realm, Soviet *maskirovka* feats reaped even greater harvest. The virtually airtight planning secrecy and extensive camouflage measures successfully covered the forward

7. GERMAN INTELLIGENCE ASSESSMENT
18 NOVEMBER 1942

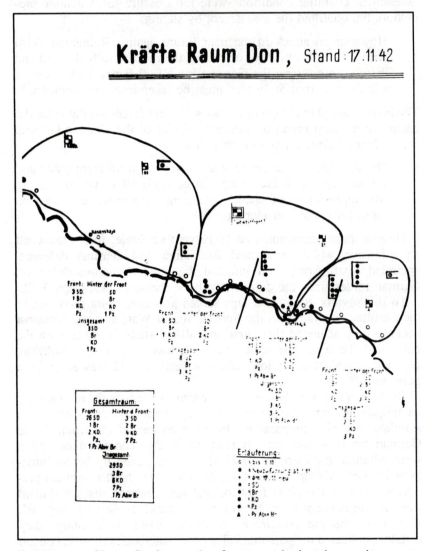

deployment of large Soviet combat forces producing destructive, para-
lysing surprise to the German and Romanian forces when the assaults
began. Before the Germans could regain their balance, the major
damage had been done, and could not be repaired. Although Soviet
maskirovka did not eradicate all indicators of future offensives, it
blurred their overall intention, obscured the timing and form of the

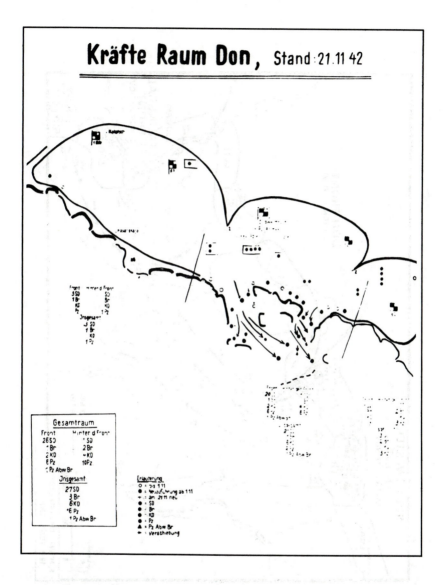

attack, and certainly masked its scope. By virtue of these experiences, the Soviets learned the relative importance of the latter two effects which, if achieved, almost negated the necessity for concealing ultimate intention. In subsequent operations, while the Soviets continued to attempt to hide intention, timing, form and scope of offensives, they would concentrate on the latter three with increasing success.

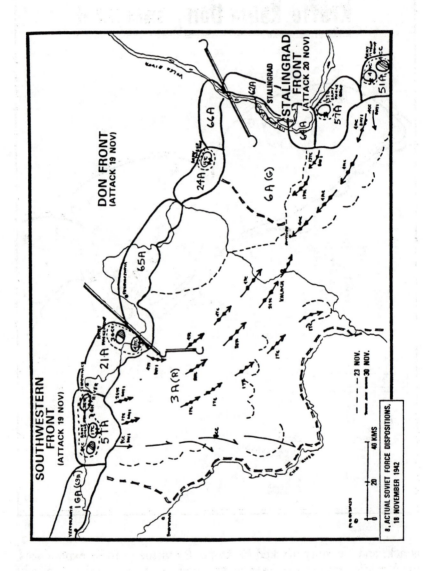

8. ACTUAL SOVIET FORCE DISPOSITIONS, 18 NOVEMBER 1942

Belorussia, 1944

During the spring of 1944, the Soviets conducted a series of simultaneous and successive *front* operations across southern Russia which together ultimately drove German forces from the Ukraine to the Polish and Rumanian borders. By late April, the Soviet planners were considering where to focus their next strategic offensive. There were several enticing options. They could continue their offensive southward into the Balkans and reap considerable political as well as military rewards. This option, however, would extend Soviet forces and leave large areas of the Soviet Union under German control which would threaten the flanks of potentially over-extended Soviet forces. The Soviets could also launch a major offensive from the northern Ukraine across central and eastern Poland to the Baltic Sea entrapping both German Army Groups Center and North. But that option would involved maneuvers of strategic scale, perhaps beyond the capabilities of Soviet forces. It would also leave large German forces on the Soviet flanks. As a third option, the Soviets could crush German Army Group Center in the so-called Belorussian balcony (jutting westward north of the Pripyat region); penetrate into Poland and East Prussia; and, perhaps, reach the Baltic Sea and isolate Army Group North as well. This would clear German troops from Belorussia and create conditions conducive to future operations in Poland on the direct route to East Prussia and, ultimately, Berlin. The Soviets selected the third option, but in their strategic planning sought to capitalize on the deception potential of the other options.

The destruction of Army Group Center was no small task. In late May elements of four Soviet *fronts* (1st Baltic, 1st, 2nd, and 3rd Belorussian) confronted the four armies of Army Group Center (3rd Panzer, 4th, 9th, and 2nd). Approximately one million Soviet forces confronted about 850,000 Germans, a ratio not to Soviet planners' liking. To establish requisite ratios necessary for success would involve a massive strategic redeployment of forces to reinforce the four Soviet *fronts*. Specifically, it was necessary to move into Belorussia five combined arms armies, two tank and one air armies, the First Polish Army, plus five tank, two mechanized, and four cavalry corps, a force of over 400,000 men, 3,000 tanks, and 10,000 guns and mortars, as well as 300,000 tons of fuel and lubricants, and 500,000 cans of rations (see map 9).[79] Hiding such a massive redeployment from German view posed serious problems and required extensive *maskirovka* at the strategic as well as operational level. The Soviets drew upon their vast wealth of experience in their attempts to deceive German planners.

9a. SOVIET REDEPLOYMENT OF FORCES PRIOR TO THE
BELORUSSIAN OPERATION, MAY–JUNE 1944

Перегруппировка войск 1-го Прибалтийского и 3-го Белорусского фронтов

Even so, the scope of redeployments necessitated measures exceeding those used before. In his memoirs Marshal Vasilevsky noted:

> Measures associated with forthcoming regrouping and the shifting from the depths of the country of all necessary for the Belorussia operation demanded great work and attention of the Party Central Committee, the General Staff, and the central administration of the People's Commissariat of Defense. All that colossal work had to be conducted in conditions of strict secrecy in order to hide from the enemy the huge complex of preparatory work for the forthcoming summer offensive.[80]

To guarantee secrecy, the Soviets, drawing upon the lessons of the

9b. SOVIET REDEPLOYMENT OF FORCES PRIOR TO THE BELORUSSIAN OPERATION, MAY–JUNE 1944

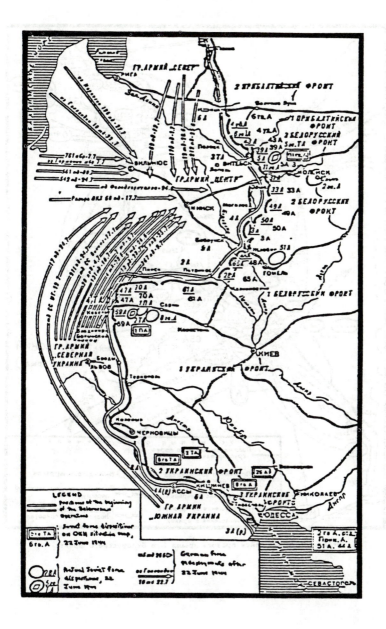

9c. SOVIET REDEPLOYMENT OF FORCES PRIOR TO THE BELORUSSIAN OPERATION, MAY–JUNE 1944

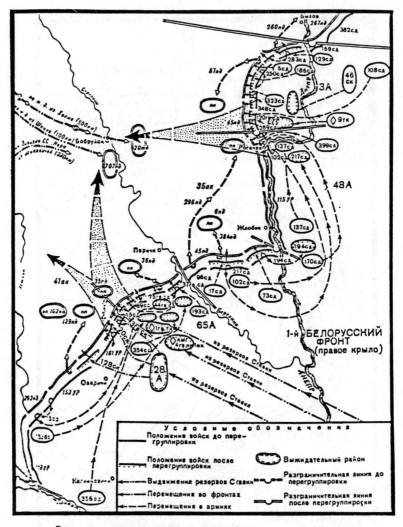

Перегруппировка войск правого крыла 1-го Белорусского фронта

Stalingrad operation, limited the number of persons actively involved in planning, and severely controlled the production of written documents. The immediate planning circle included only the Deputy of the High Command and the Chief of the General Staff and his deputy. Only these figures knew the full scope of the plan. Two or three staff officers in each *front* headquarters developed the *front* operational plans. As at Stalingrad, documents were not reprinted, but rather reported personally to the respective commanders.[81] Virtually no correspondence relating to the attack was permitted. The required planning documents were revealed only to those who would sign them. The Soviets prohibited all wire and radio communications and carefully monitored the operations of all communications centers. Although the Soviets again engaged in sequential planning, the longer duration of the process permitted lower headquarters greater preparation time for this segment of the plan. Even so, the time of the offensive was kept secret until virtually the last moment. The Military Councils of the *fronts* announced the major offensive to troop units only hours before the attack began.

Earlier successes of Soviet forces and the strategic positioning of those forces in early May facilitated Soviet use of strategic deception on an unprecedented scale. Ultimately, its success depended on the ability of the Soviets to effect a secret regrouping of forces. Thus, all segments of the overall *maskirovka* plans, those pertaining to disinformation and those pertaining to the masking of movements and deployments, were irrevocably interdependent.

Very simply, the Soviet strategic deception plans sought to play on Germans fears for future Soviet offensive operations against central and south-eastern Europe. Capitalizing on the situation which had persisted from January to May 1944, the Soviets actually displayed an intent to continue operations along previous lines into southern Poland or Rumania. Deputy Chief of the General Staff, General S.M. Shtemenko, wrote:

> During the preparations for the Belorussian operation the General Staff wanted to somehow convince the Hitlerite command that the main Red Army attacks in the summer of 1944 would come in the south and the Baltic. Already, on 3 May, the 3rd Ukrainian Front commander had been given the following order: you are charged with conducting operational *maskirovka* measures for the purpose of misinforming the enemy. It is necessary to show a concentration of eight–nine rifle divisions, reinforced with tanks and artillery, beyond the right flank of the front ... The false region of concentration should be animated,

showing the movement and disposition of separate groups of men, vehicles, tanks and guns, and the equipping of the region; anti-aircraft guns should be placed at the location of tank and artillery mock-ups, simultaneously designating the air defense of the entire region by the installation of anti-aircraft systems and patrolling by fighters.

The visibility and plausibility of the false objectives would be verified by observation and photographing from the air ... The period of conduct of operational *maskirovka* is from 5–15 June of this year.[82]

A similar order went out to the 3rd Baltic Front. In addition, the STAVKA ordered all *fronts* in the south to remain as active as possible and demonstrate the presence of the bulk of Soviet tank armies in that region. Prompted by these orders, limited objective operations occurred along the front lines in Rumania and southern Poland during May, to convince German intelligence that this was where the Soviets were placing their strategic priority.

Meanwhile the Soviets prepared to undertake the massive job of redeployment – concealed from German observation. A STAVKA directive of 29 May required that *front* commanders move all troops and equipment at night under strict light and march discipline. Daytime movement of small groups was permitted only during inclement weather or outside the range of enemy air observation. During pauses in troop movements, all forces were to be dispersed and camouflaged, and kept isolated from contact with the civilian population. In general, road movement was kept to minimum, and rail was used whenever possible. Of particular importance was the concealment of the relief of front line units. This was done at night as close to the time of attack as feasible without interfering with last-minute attack preparations.

All activities in the front lines were maintained at a constant and normal level to mask the choice of main attack sectors. Routine communications traffic continued, and all artillery units fired in normal pattern and intensity. Registration of forward deploying artillery units was done by single pieces already in the forward area according to a carefully planned schedule to maintain the air of normality. Reconnaissance occurred on a broad front and was limited to units already in the forward area. Soviet commands prohibited newly deployed units from conducting ground reconnaissance. Air army activity also continued at normal levels and air reconnaissance by new units was severely restricted.[84]

Throughout the planning phase the Soviets emphasized defensive measures in main attack sectors. They constructed false minefields;

improved defensive positions; and, as at Stalingrad, emphasized defense in all segments of the military press.

Rigorous command staff inspections daily enforced strict adherence to all required *maskirovka* measures. These included both air and ground inspection by members of *front* and army staff directorates. Representatives of operations sections of *fronts* and armies supervised regrouping and camouflage and verified the fulfillment of all aspects of the plan. They dispatched the results of their inspections at 2200 hours each day to the General Staff.[85] Marshal A.M. Vasilevsky, representative of the STAVKA for the 3rd Belorussian Front, reported:

> The front headquarters, staff, and political administration were giving serious attention to camouflage of rifle, tank, and artillery formations and other special troop units and all sorts of military cargoes arriving at the front. The officers of the front staff met the troops at the unloading station and escorted them to the region of concentration prescribed for them, requiring the strictest camouflage measures ... The troops' combat training was also periodically organized on well-equipped ranges and training fields in the rear, where divisions and special units earmarked for the penetration were sequentially and covertly withdrawn into second echelons.[86]

As the date of the offensive neared, *maskirovka* measures intensified. This included a major effort to simulate attack preparations in other regions of the front. On 16 June, the STAVKA ordered the 2nd and 3rd Baltic and 1st Ukrainian Fronts to:

> organize and conduct reconnaissance in force during the period of 20–23 June 1944 in a number of sectors of the front with detachments from a reinforced company up to a reinforced battalion in strength.[87]

This occurred simultaneously with similar reconnaissance measures in the actual attack region by forces of the 1st Baltic and 1st, 2nd, and 3rd Belorussian Fronts. Consequently, 60 advanced detachments operated at the same time along a front of over 1,000 kilometers, the most extensive use of reconnaissance up to this time.

The *front* commands responded to STAVKA guidance by undertaking major *maskirovka* programs at every level of command. These programs emphasized covert preparations for the operation and use of measure to disorient the enemy. The 1st Baltic Front on 30 May, published an extensive document detailing *maskirovka* measures and how to implement them to lower-level units.[88] The *front* also organized *maskirovka* on a territorial basis, with controllers appointed to oversee such work in each region. The *front* designated three distinct regions, at *front*, army, and troop level, each with distinct boundaries (generally measured from the front to the rear). The *front* chief of staff was responsible for *maskirovka* in army regions, and rifle corps commanders supervised such activities at the troop level.

Controllers had at their disposal special engineer units to assist in physical *maskirovka* preparations, special staffs to assist them, and traffic control units to assist in the efficient movement of arriving troop formation. In the case of the 1st Baltic Front, such organization was necessary to mask the forward deployment of a complete army (6th Guards) into a sector which had previously been occupied by only one rifle division (the 154th).

The 1st Baltic Front undertook its own plan to deceive the Germans as to the location of its main attack, by preparing for a surprise assault in a heavily wooded sector north-west of Vitebsk. It moved Sixth Guards Army with 12 rifle divisions, one tank corps and almost 100,000 men secretly over a period of three nights from the right flank of the *front* sector, a distance of 120 kilometers, into the sector of the 154th Rifle Division on the *front's* left flank.[89]

The 1st Belorussian Front undertook similar deception measures which required extensive and efficient *maskirovka* in order to succeed. The *front* planned to launch two main attacks to envelop German Ninth Army in the Bobruisk area. The first main attack was to occur from the Rogachev area westward (where the Soviets had attacked as recently as May 1944). The second would occur in the wooded and marshy area south of Bobruisk. The Soviets wanted the Germans to note some of the attack preparations at Rogachev, but hoped to keep the attack south of Bobruisk secret: a difficult task for the newly deployed army (the 28th) and a newly arrived tank corps (1st Guards), which would participate in the assault. The *front* developed an elaborate *maskirovka* plan (approved on 30 May) which included night movement, stringent controls over road movement, the creation of extensive false troop and tank concentrations, and deceptive artillery fire and reconnaissance procedures. According to the *front* commander, Marshal K.K. Rokossovsky:

> We required that staffs at all levels maintain constant control from the ground and the air over careful camouflage of everything associated with *front* forces. The Germans could see only that which we wanted to show them. Units were concentrated and regrouped at night, and railroad trains ran from the front to the rear in daytime with mock-ups of tanks and guns. In many locations, false crossings were prepared and roads built for

visibility. Many guns were concentrated on secondary axes, they conducted several sudden shellings, and then were transported to the rear leaving mock-ups in the false firing positions. The *front* chief of staff, General Malinin, was inexhaustible in this regard ...

The success of Soviet deception in the Belorussian operation can best be measured against the judgements of German intelligence, and the reaction of German Army Group Center before the attack. In general, the Soviet strategic *maskirovka* plan achieved its goals. Throughout May and June, Eastern Intelligence Branch of OKH clung tenaciously to its early May judgement that:

> the Soviet main effort would continue in the South towards the Balkans, where it would take advantage of the clearly shaky state of Germany's allies and finally establish the long-coveted Soviet hegemony in southeastern Europe. North of the Pripyat Marshes, the Eastern Intelligence Branch predicted the front would stay quiet.[91]

By mid-May the branch, the OKH in general, and the involved army groups also recognized the threat of attack on southern Poland, and adjusted forces accordingly. These high-level assessments continued even after signs of a Soviet build-up in Belorussia were detected in June. Eastern Intelligence dismissed such action in Army Group Center's sector as 'apparently a deception',[92] and German force dispositions continued to reflect these estimates.

After 1 June, Army Group Center noted some changes in Soviet force deployments but did little to alter their previous estimates or reconfigure the 3rd Panzer, 5th, and 9th Armies defenses. Increased attack indicators after 16 June 'aroused no excitement and only routine interest'.[93] A war journal entry of 20 June noted stepped-up partisan activity and said such activity, 'makes it appear that an early start of the offensive cannot be ruled out'.[94]

The complacency at army group and OKH level reflected the intelligence picture as these headquarters saw it as well as ingrained self-delusion. In the face of deteriorating German reconnaissance capabilities, the intelligence picture was inaccurate at best.[95] The Germans assessed that all six Soviet tank armies were deployed in the southern sector with only slight indications that Fifth Guards Tank Army was in the central sector. In reality, two full tank armies were in the central sector (2nd Tank Army and 5th Guards Tank Army). Intelligence failed to locate three armies which had formerly been involved in the Crimean operation (2nd Guards Army, 5th Army,

Coastal Army, two of them deployed after the offensive began) and also missed the redeployment of 28th Army (moved 200 kilometers from the south into the Bobruisk area) and of 6th Guards Army (into the region north-west of Vitebsk). The Germans noted the growth of Soviet frontal aviation strength both in the south and center, but determined that the main effort of long-range aviation (six of eight air armies) remained in the south. In general, German intelligence failed to detect the scope of Soviet reinforcement. By 22 June it had identified about 140 Soviet division equivalents and three tank corps facing Army Group Center. Actually, by that time, the Soviets had assembled 168 division equivalents, eight tank or mechanized corps, and two cavalry corps (which had significant armored strength within them) for use in the forthcoming offensive. The Germans assessed Soviet armored strength as between 400–1,100 tanks, far below the over 5,000 tanks the Soviets ultimately used in the offensive.[96]

Within the army headquarters of Army Group Center, indication of an impending Soviet attack were far clearer than at higher levels of command. By mid-June 'all four armies assessed enemy intentions to the effect that an attack was impending'.[97] After 19 June, 3rd Panzer Army regarded an attack as being possible at any time, although it incorrectly assessed that the main attack would occur south-east of Vitebsk. As late as 24 June, the second day of the Soviet assault, 3rd Panzer Army failed to identify 6th Guards Army as a participant although it had, by that time, identified two to three divisions of that army's 12 divisions (see maps 10–11). German 4th Army expected an attack at any time after 11 June, and on 19 June pinpointed the time of attack as being within two to three days. Fourth Army also correctly assessed the location of the Soviet main attack against its sector (see maps 12–13). German 9th Army after 13 June assessed an attack as pending and became more exact as the actual time of the attack approached. By 13 June 9th Army noted a Soviet build-up in both the Rogachev areas and the area south of Bobruisk. However, up to the time of the attack, it had failed to detect the threatening presence on its front of Soviet 28th Army, 1st Guards Tank Corps, or the Cavalry-Mechanized Group (see maps 14–15).[98]

Warnings of the impending attack sent by the armies to Army Group Center were heeded only after 20 June, when it began almost passively referring to a possible Soviet offensive. Although informed of this information OKH attached little importance to it. Earl Ziemke in his work, *Stalingrad to Berlin*, captured the essence of German intelligence problems when he explained that:

As the often-repeated slogan, 'nur keine Schema' implied, a

10. GERMAN 3RD PANZER ARMY INTELLIGENCE MAP
22 JUNE 1944

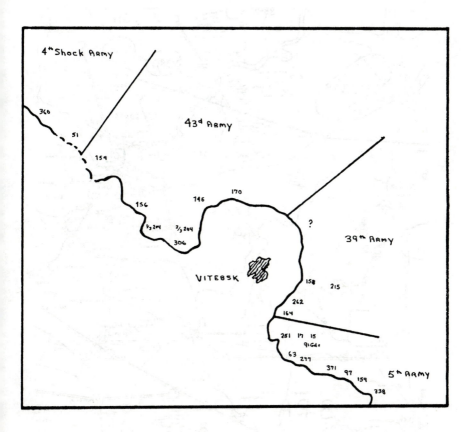

11. ACTUAL SOVIET FORCE DISPOSITIONS OPPOSITE
3D PANZER ARMY, 22 JUNE 1944

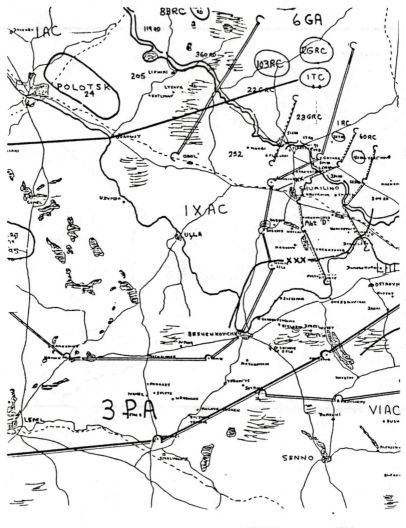

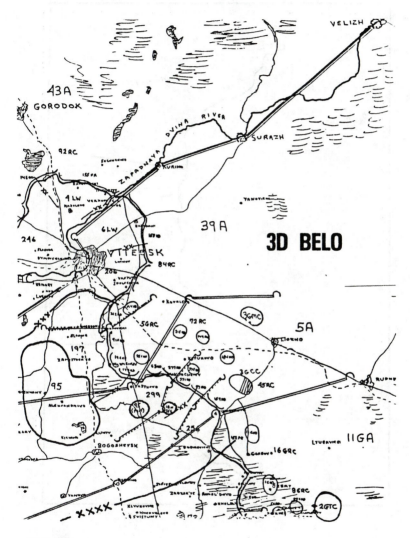

22, 6, 1944

12. GERMAN 4th ARMY INTELLIGENCE MAP, 11 JUNE 1944

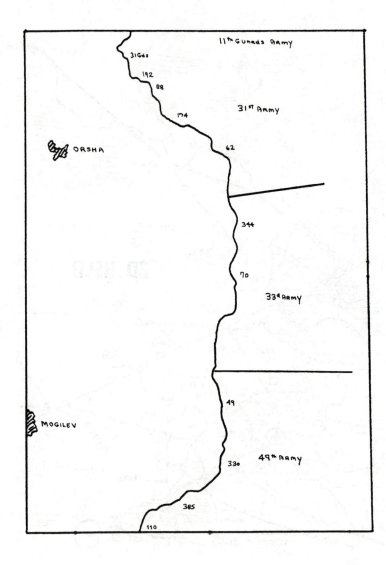

cardinal principle of German general staff doctrine was the avoidance of rigid or schematic tactical or operating conceptions. In June 1944 on the eastern front that rule was forgotten. To a Soviet deception, the German commands added an almost hypnotic self-induced delusion: the main offensive would come against Army Group North Ukraine because that was where they were ready to meet it.[99]

Soviet planning for and conduct of the Belorussian operation included the most ambitious *maskirovka* program they had ever attempted. It spanned all levels; strategic, operational and tactical. Its overall success depended on careful orchestration of measures implemented within each level. As a comprehensive program it was an unqualified success attested to most vividly by the ensuing 400–kilometer Soviet advance, which exceeded even Soviet expectations.

The German High Command and headquarters at virtually every level continued to reflect German contempt for the 'inferior Russians' and their underestimation of Soviet military capabilities. These attitudes, reinforced by faith in the reliability of their own intelligence, conditioned them to be victims of Soviet deception. The Soviet strategic *maskirovka* plan capitalized on German fears and misconceptions, blinding the German High Command right up to the time of the attack as to the focus of Soviet offensive intentions, thus clouding the timing of the offensive as well. Obviously, deception of the highest German levels of command rendered the actions of lower echelons virtually superfluous. Only a significant strategic redeployment of German forces could have matched similar Soviet deployments, thwarting or slowing the advance. There German strategic failure left Army Group Center exposed, vulnerable, and almost destined to suffer its ultimate fate.

At the operational and tactical levels, Soviet *maskirovka* was sophisticated enough to cover the vast scope of the attack preparations. The Germans detected few major redeployments of armies from other areas, and only noted separate tactical vestiges of the large-scale operational regrouping occurring within and between the four Soviet *fronts* making the attack. While the separate Germany army headquarters recognized the Soviet intentions to attack, and ultimately the general timing of the attack, they, like Army Group Center, appreciated neither the scope nor the strength of the impending assaults. In addition, neither Army Group Center nor the four armies anticipated the form the offensive that overwhelmed them would take.

The skill with which the Soviets planned and executed *maskirovka* at every level during the Belorussian operation showed how well Soviet

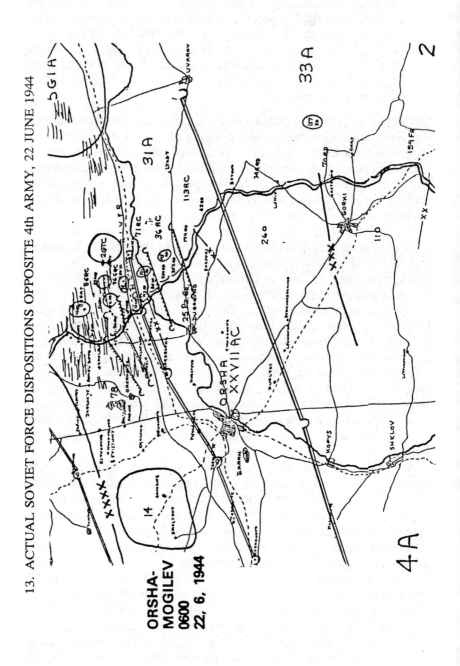

13. ACTUAL SOVIET FORCE DISPOSITIONS OPPOSITE 4th ARMY, 22 JUNE 1944

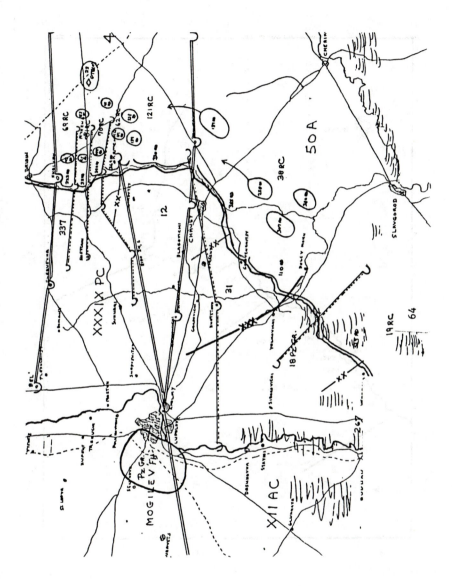

14. GERMAN 9TH ARMY INTELLIGENCE MAP, 12 JUNE 1944

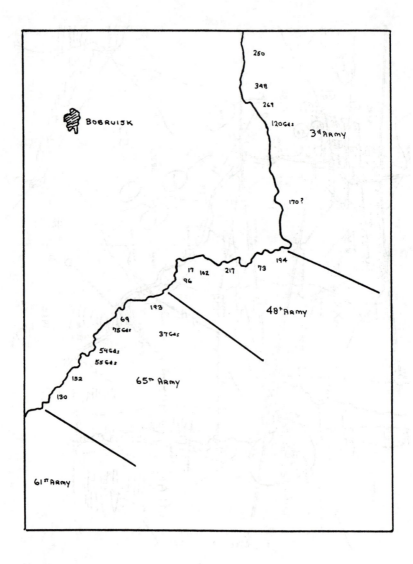

commanders and staff officers had digested the lessons of their earlier experience. Successful Soviet *maskirovka* and German self-deception accorded the Soviets a marked advantage which the Soviets capitalized on by destroying three German armies (28 divisions) and at least 350,000 men.

Manchuria, 1945

In August 1945 the Soviets conducted their geographically most challenging and extensive strategic operation of the Second World War. In response to the Allied request for Soviet assistance in the war against Japan, first made in 1944 and repeated in 1945, the Soviets at the Potsdam Conference (May 1945) committed themselves to operations against Japanese forces in Manchuria and on the Northern island possessions of Japan (the Kuriles and Sakhalin). There were about 700,000 Japanese troops in Manchuria facing an almost equal number of Soviet troops. An additional 300,000 to 400,000 Japanese in Korea might be expected to figure in the operation, with another 100,000 on Kurile Islands and Sakhalin.[100] A well-orchestrated Soviet attack would probably negate the requirement to engage those Japanese forces in Korea. On the basis of comparative strength, the Manchurian operation would be somewhat larger than that in Belorussia. Using Belorussia as a guide, Soviet forces in the Far East would have to be at least doubled in strength to more than 1.5 million. The Soviets did realize that Japanese armored weakness would permit Soviet armor superiority, making up for part of the lack in manpower. Thus, initial Soviet planning assessed the need for about 1.5 million men and least one tank army and one to two tanks or mechanized corps to defeat Japanese forces in the requisite time frame.

Several conditions delayed Soviet preparations for the operation, increased the importance of the Manchurian operation, and placed major significance on the factor of surprise and the role of *maskirovka*. The first reality was the size of the projected theater of operations (roughly 600 by 1,000 kilometers) and more important, the distance of the theater from European Russia. To raise Soviet force strength to over 1.5 million men would require moving almost 700,000 men over 9,000 kilometers along the umbilical cord of the Trans-Siberian Railroad from the European theater to the Far East. Even more significant was the necessity of moving large armored forces (one tank army and one tank corps) and the massive quantity of necessary equipment and supplies. To maintain strategic surprise this movement would have to be kept as secret as possible. Once deployed for the offensive, those forces would have to advance through the difficult and varied terrain of Manchuria to a dept of almost 900 kilometers. Terrain problems also

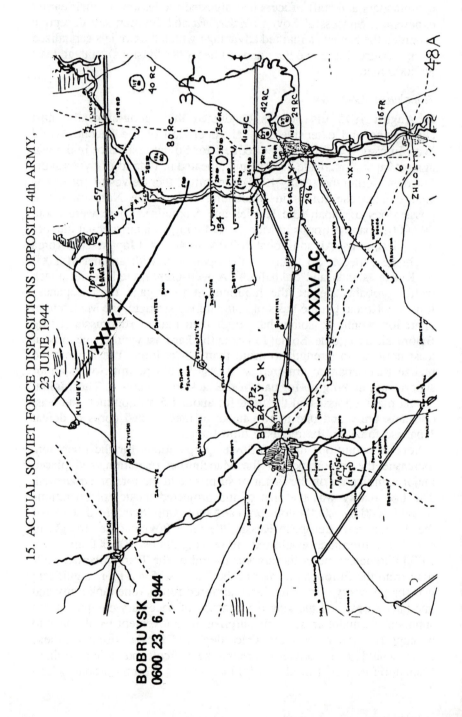

15. ACTUAL SOVIET FORCE DISPOSITIONS OPPOSITE 4th ARMY, 23 JUNE 1944

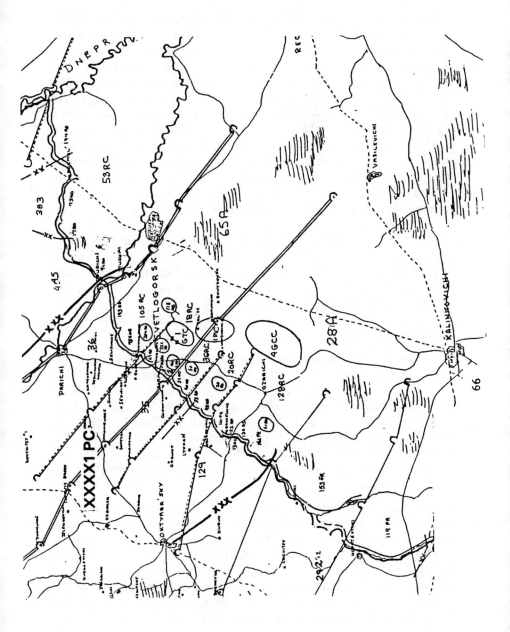

necessitated deceiving Japanese forces about actual routes of the Soviet advance.

The second reality was the degree of fanatical resistance the Japanese had displayed in earlier operations against US forces.[101] There was no reason to assume more passive Japanese reception of a Soviet advance into Manchuria. This made it necessary for skillful operations, using the best operational and tactical techniques developed in the western war. Thus, the Soviets had to send experienced forces and commanders to the Far East. The final reality confronting the Soviets on the very eve of the offensive was that of time constraints. American use of the nuclear bomb, and the possible ensuing Japanese collapse, made it imperative that the offensive should achieve its goals in a matter of days, rather than weeks or months. The Soviets determined that Manchuria had to be secured within 30 days and the main entrances into central Manchuria within one week. This was as much a political as a military necessity.

From virtually every perspective, *maskirovka* would make the difference between success and failure. To a greater extent than in the west, successful strategic *maskirovka* was imperative, while operational and tactical *maskirovka* had to be perfect if the overall operational plan was to be realized.

The Soviets understood the difficulty in masking their overall offensive intentions. General S.M.Shtemenko noted:

> Our striving for surprise in our operation was complicated very much by the fact that the Japanese had long and steadfastly believed in the inevitability of strategic surprise was hardly a practicable matter. Nevertheless, after pondering this problem, we returned more than once to the first days of the Great Patriotic War. Our country had also expected the war and prepared for it; however, the German attack proved unexpected. Consequently, it was not necessary to prematurely repudiate surprise in the current case.[102]

Surprise in the Manchurian operation depended first on maintaining the secrecy of the operational plan and the nature and scope of Soviet offensive preparations. Also, to an extraordinary degree, surprise would depend on the form of the attack, which had to be conducted in a manner *guaranteed* to pre-empt Japanese defenses or paralyse the Japanese command and control structure. This meant the use of unorthodox operational and tactical techniques, tested earlier but never before relied upon to such a major extent.

The first task was to secure planning for the operation.[103] The Soviets followed procedures developed in previous operations and severely restricted the number of planners and of planning documents. A Far East Command directive restricted full participation in planning to the *front* commander, the member of the *front* military council (political officer), the chief of staff, and the chief of the operational directorate. *Front* chiefs of troop branches and services participated in developing only their functional portions of the plan and were not familiar with overall *front* missions. The directive read:

> The army commander will be assigned missions personally and verbally, without the delivery of written directives from the front. The participation in the development of the army operational plan will be established on the same basis as within the front. All documentation concerning the plans of troop operations will be kept in the personal safes of the front and army commanders.[104]

The most sensitive aspect of offensive preparations was the problem of masking the extensive force and *matériel* build-up in the Far East. This effort would take considerable time to complete, and would rely on a limited transport network already highly vulnerable to Japanese observation. This concentration, regrouping and deployment of forces and *matériel*, and the movement of commanders and staffs required to lead the forces were carried out under the cloak of a host of *maskirovka* measures. High-level commanders and their staffs traveled to the Far East (normally by air) under assumed names, wearing bogus badges of rank, branch and service.[105] Movement by rail of *matériel* began as early as January 1945; and, whenever possible, the Soviets relied upon indigenous stocks and production to equip their forces. Movement of men and *matériel* occurred only at night under strict camouflage conditions. Hundreds of kilometers of artificial covers were built to physically mask the rail line from Japanese observations (especially along the Amur and Ussuri Rivers where the rail line was under direct observation of Japanese forces on the far bank).

During June and July the Soviets used 136,000 rail cars to move the requisite number of men and *matériel* to launch the offensive (22–30 trains per day).[106] While the Japanese noted the increased volume of traffic, Soviet camouflage probably concealed from Japanese eyes 50 per cent of the volume of men and *matériel* moved.

Once in the Far East, the *fronts* placed arriving units and *matériel* in widely dispersed camps and depôts in positions distant from the front, but accessible for quick deployment forward, needing only limited use of forward assembly areas and jumping-off positions. During these movements troops conducted exercises which made it possible for units to train, adapt to local conditions, and prepare for the attack while maintaining their concealment. One to two days before initiation of the attack, where necessary, forces moved into their initial positions, in which movement of any kind, food preparation, and wood-cutting were strictly forbidden. All newly arrived units maintained strict radio silence. Similar measures covered the extensive redeployment of forces already stationed in the Far East and Trans Baikal regions.[107]

The Far East command and the *front* headquarters published detailed directives and instructions concerning general and specific *maskirovka* plans to govern their forces. For example, the 1st Far Eastern Front (previously the Primor'ye group and 25th Army) issued extensive instructions calling for the creation of false troop concentrations, a decoy offensive sector, active defense preparations in other sectors, and activation of bogus reconnaissance. Troops performing these missions were not informed about the false nature of their activities.

Meanwhile, all activity in front sectors was kept at normal levels. The population carried on normal activities, military units followed usual routines, and radio traffic continued with no change. Newly arriving units moved only at night and rested in forests and villages out of the enemy's view. Where cover was unavailable (as in the steppes), tanks, vehicles and personnel dug in and concealed themselves with camouflage materials or nets. The Soviets prepared unit command posts in advance, either digging them in or using existing structures which blended in with the surroundings. All communications nets lines were dug in as well as artillery firing positions prepared in advance by specially designated engineer units. Though these and other measures did little to alter Japanese judgements about ultimate Soviet offensive intentions, they did conceal the timing, scope and location of the impending attack.

The extensive secrecy and *maskirovka* measures were but one aspect, albeit an important one, concerning preparations for the operation. Equally important were techniques used by the Soviets to surprise the Japanese regarding the form of the attack. Most of these techniques were by no means new, having been used on various occasions in the German war, when the Soviets had been able to judge their effectiveness. However, in Manchuria the Soviets used a wide array of these techniques on a grander scale than ever before.

As in 1939, Japanese attitudes toward likely Soviet performance conditioned the Japanese for being surprised.[108] The Japanese apparently stereotyped Soviet combat performance on German reports of how the Soviets had operated early in the war (1941–42). Thus, they underestimated the ability of the Soviets to employ armor skillfully and co-ordinate combined arms forces in poor terrain. They underestimated their logistical capability to effect and support large troop concentrations in terrain they (the Japanese) considered unsuited for large-scale military operations, particularly the areas adjacent to western Manchuria. The skill of Soviet combat performance far exceeded Japanese expectations.

The form and location of the Soviet attack at the strategic, operational and tactical levels also surprised the Japanese.[109] The Soviet's two-front strategic envelopment through both eastern and western Manchuria contradicted Japanese expectations and deployments. Soviet units routinely crossed terrain the Japanese considered impassable, leaving it virtually undefended. Moreover the Japanese were unable to counter the Soviets' conscious decision to use every possible avenue of approach in their attack. Soviet use of armor in first echelon at every level of command – initially, or shortly after the beginning of the attack – also caught the Japanese off guard. Having discounted the threat of armor in such difficult terrain, they could not deal with it. The Soviet tendency to bypass fortified positions confounded Japanese commanders and rendered most Japanese defenses useless.

Tactically as well, the Japanese were unprepared to deal with Soviet combat techniques. The Soviet use of small, task-organized assault groups with heavy engineer and firepower support clashed with the image of human waves of infantry in the assault. Perhaps most unexpected for the Japanese was Soviet reliance on forward detachments to probe Japanese defenses, bypass them, and attack deep into the Japanese operational rear. The Soviet commanders' display of initiative at all levels did not fit Japanese preconceptions of Soviet performance. In fact, the scope of Soviet use of rapid maneuver surprised and confused the Japanese, resulting in a general paralysis of their command and control. To a greater extent than at any time before, in Manchuria the Soviets followed the advice found in all of its earlier regulations, specifically to achieve *maskirovka* by 'employing methods of fighting that are new for the enemy and weapons unknown to him'.

Soviet *maskirovka* measures achieved marked success. Certainly in mid-1945, the Japanese anticipated that the Soviet Union would ultimately join the war against Japan. The Soviet attack when it did occur, however, 'caught the Japanese totally unprepared for an invasion they expected'.[110] In late January 1945, the Japanese Army Vice Chief of Staff predicted the Soviets would abrogate the Japanese–Soviet Neutrality Pact and enter the war against Japan in the latter half of 1945.[111] It happened in April. After the German surrender in May, the Japanese High Command (JSHQ) assessed that Soviet entry into the war was unlikely until the spring of 1946, when Japan would be closer to surrender. They conceded, however, that Soviet attack preparations could be complete by August or September 1945; but thought weather conditions in that period were not conducive for an attack.[112] All these assessments were based on a political judgment that Soviet war losses would force them to await an American invasion of Japan before they would join the war. Moreover, in August Manchuria was subject to heavy, often torrential monsoon rains which turned its few roads into morasses.

After Yalta, the Japanese estimated it would take at least three months after the German surrender for the Soviets to move necessary forces to Manchuria for an offensive. By July Japanese estimates of Soviet reinforcements put Soviet strength at about 1.3 million men. By August or September the Japanese estimated the Soviets would have 40–50 divisions.[113]

The Japanese did detect large-scale Soviet rail movements into the Far East. From February to August the Kwantung Army counted 800–1,000 trains of 40 cars each and deduced the movement of 20–25 Soviet divisions. Thus, Japanese intelligence 'underestimated between 30 to 50 per cent the forty Soviet divisions actually deployed eastward',[114] which caused them to believe 'that they still had time to prepare their defenses against the Soviet invasion in the spring of 1946'.[115] Interestingly enough, while undercounting military units and incorrectly estimating deployment regions, the Japanese kept a fairly accurate count of overall Soviet manpower strength in the Far East.

Based on these optimistic estimates, the Japanese were slow to implement changes in force disposition associated with their 1944 alteration of overall Kwantung Army planning from an offensive to a defensive posture. Many units had not completed their redeployment by the time of the Soviet invasion.

As in Belorussia, there was a dichotomy between intelligence assessments at lower level and high-level headquarters, with the lower-level taking a more realistic view.[116] At a 4 August conference at 3rd Area Army the Kwantung Army operations section said no invasion could be expected until September. If the attack did not begin then, the Kwantung Army believed it would probably begin in the spring. High-level optimism muffled warnings from below, starved lower level units of meaningful intelligence information on the Soviets, and stifled the war preparations of low level units. 'In short, the Japanese were unprepared strategically, operationally, or tactically for the massive Soviet blow which fell on 9 August 1945.'[117] The captured deputy chief of staff of the Kwantung Army, General M. Tomokatsu, declared that the specific dates of the entry of the USSR into the war remained unknown, despite the fact that the Kwantung Army had detected the

Soviet build-up. Hence, he declared that the declaration of war by the Soviet Union on 8 August was completely unexpected.[118] General Semizu, commander of Japanese Fifth Army, stated, 'We did not expect that the Russian army would go through the taiga, and the offensive of Russian forces from almost inaccessible regions proved a complete surprise for us'.[119] To a great extent, the combat performance of the Kwantung Army during the Manchurian operation attested to the degree of surprise the Soviets achieved by using new operational and tactical techniques enabling them to achieve objectives in half the time. An operation optimistically judged to last at least 30 days was in fact completed within 15 days.

Manchuria represented a sterling effort for the Soviets regarding the wartime use of *maskirovka*. More important, it was one of their few experiences of employing *maskirovka* in the initial stages of war and has therefore become a major focal point of study. Specifically, the Soviets have investigated the role of *maskirovka* in that increasingly sensitive period of the transition from peace to war.

Soviet *maskirovka* measures at the strategic, operational and tactical levels achieved greater success in Manchuria than in any previous operation. They were able to confuse the Japanese regarding the timing, scope, location and form of the offensive. Hence, Manchuria has become a textbook case for the Soviets on how to conduct strategic *maskirovka*. The time and special considerations of the offensive seemed to create conditions and requirements somewhat analogous to theater offensives in a modern nuclear context. That fact has prompted even more intense Soviet study.

V

REFLECTIONS ON SOVIET SECOND WORLD WAR MASKIROVKA EXPERIENCES

The experience of the Great Patriotic War vividly demonstrates that secretly prepared operations occur as a surprise for the enemy. Operational surprise continually stuns the enemy and deprives him of the capability of rendering organized resistance. However, operations in which all types of forces and weapons, possessing contemporary means of reconnaissance participate, are very difficult to hide from the enemy. It demands great skill, initiative, and creativity on the part of the organizers of the operation and impeccable fulfillment of all measures, spelled out in the operational *maskirovka* plan.[120]

These simple comments by Marshal G. V. Zhukov capture the essence of what the Soviets learned from their Second World War experiences with deception at the strategic, as well as the operational and tactical levels. The war broadened Soviet appreciation of the utility of *maskirovka* and generated an understanding of the immense complexity in undertaking such a task. It is significant that Zhukov used the present tense when describing the scope of those experiences. Soviet study of *maskirovka* today rests upon a foundation of the study of *maskirovka* in the past. To the Soviets, the scope, duration and complexity of combat in those four years of war have yet to be surpassed. Thus, a mastery of those experiences remains a prerequisite for sound study of deception in a contemporary context.

The Soviets derived from the war an understanding of the ubiquitousness of *maskirovka*, which simply reinforced their natural ideological tendency to avoid distinguishing between normal peacetime deception and wartime military deception. The events of August 1939 (Poland); May 1940 (France); and, in particular, those of June 1941 and August 1945 proved the unity of peacetime and wartime deception even to those in the military who had focused on *maskirovka* as primarily a wartime phenomenon. *Maskirovka*, before or during 'the initial period of war', emerged after Stalin's death as a major subject of Soviet concern made even more urgent by the likely quickened pace and enhanced destructive power of war in the nuclear age.

War experiences also proved the essential unity of deception relative to all levels of war, and all types of *maskirovka* employed. It was simply impossible to separate strategic, operational and tactical deception measures since all were inter-related and interdependent. While one could undertake tactical deception without planning great operational or strategic deception measures, it was impossible to do the reverse. Successful strategic deception depended entirely on the thoroughness of similar measures at the lower levels. In May and June 1944 the ability to deceive the Germans concerning overall Soviet strategic offensive plans depended on the successful secret redeployment of multiple armies and corps. That secrecy depended on the efficient conduct of movement security which in turn depended on the rather mundane requirement to hide the individual tank and vehicle from prying German eyes. Similarly the most elaborate deception plans would fall prey to sloppy camouflage or slipshod radio security. It was no good hiding major troop concentrations if they could be detected from analysis of radio traffic. Unimaginative reconnaissance techniques or artillery registration procedures could compromise the most carefully orchestrated *maskirovka* plan. It took failure, often on numerous occasions, for a talent for *maskirovka* to emerge. By the middle of 1944 that talent was evident.

Since it depended on the most extensive successful procedures and techniques, strategic deception took longest to master. Moreover, because of its broad focus it usually involved a wide geographical area and depended on skillful conduct of *maskirovka* measures by a vast array of units deployed in different sectors. Hence, its success depended not only on the skill of the high command, but also on the proficiency of the Red Army in general. Only after the extensive regulations and instructions on *maskirovka* generated by war experiences had been absorbed and mastered by lower-level units could the Soviet High Command expect to master strategic deception.

Soviet attempts at strategic deception during the Moscow operation were crude and limited in scope. Their purpose was simply to hide from German intelligence the scope and location of their counter-offensive, a task which involved the masking of movements and deployment of three relatively small armies. Soviet success in that endeavor resulted as much from the chaos of the general situation and fortunate bad weather as from Soviet skill at *maskirovka*. German failure to detect those large units was merely a continuation of earlier German failures, only now on a large scale. Throughout the summer and fall of 1941, the Soviets had continually surprised the Germans by their ability to mobilize and field a series of new reserve armies, many of which appeared in unexpected locations. As so often, this German failure resulted from the prejudice produced by their pre-war estimates of Soviet wartime mobilization potential. These estimates failed to predict the huge scale of Soviet mobilization, consequently, German intelligence neither expected nor detected the deployment of numerous reserve armies. In subsequent operations after December 1941 the Germans continued to miss the deployment of Soviet reserve armies. This recurring failure became a more serious problem throughout the war as those undetected armies became stronger and more numerous and German reserves dwindled.[121]

At Stalingrad in November 1942, the Soviets embarked on an even more deliberate attempt to conduct strategic deception. The plan involved several planned troop concentrations in other regions of the front (at Moscow, for example), as well as the usual practice of deploying masked forces into hidden concentration areas. While the threatened Soviet strategic feints had limited effect on German strategic deployments, the Soviet local redeployments and resulting secret concentrations worked well, producing the German disaster of

November 1942. Here the Soviets demonstrated markedly improved skills which paid significant dividends.

The 1944 Belorussian operation was the first occasion when Soviet strategic deception achieved virtually all of its aims. The elaborate measures undertaken to simulate hostile intent elsewhere distracted German attention and significant German forces from deployment into Belorussia. The ensuring Soviet strategic regrouping of forces progressed undetected by the Germans. Successful Soviet deception of the Germans regarding intent, scope and location of the offensive produced spectacular but utterly predictable Soviet results.

In August 1945 circumstances arose whereby the Soviets could apply their talents to a theater offensive against a nation with which they were not at war. Successful strategic deception of the Japanese in Manchuria proved that the techniques learned in four years of war could be applied to the opening phase of war. Soviet success with deception in Manchuria partially compensated for the similar deception of the Soviets in June 1941, providing another case for study in the post-war years.

From their war experiences with strategic deception the Soviets learned several valuable lessons. First, they learned that it is virtually impossible to conceal totally an intent to attack. This is true in the 'initial period of war' as well as during the course of war itself. That difficulty increases in direct proportion to one's strength relative to the enemy. Experience indicates, however, that it may not be necessary to mask intent. Successful masking of the scale, scope, location or timing of the attack can produce results as satisfactory as could be produced by covering one's intent. In fact there may be an advantage in not deceiving the enemy regarding one's overall offensive goal. Very simply, an expectant enemy tends to have a more active imagination. He is more receptive to false indicators, in particular if his intelligence collection is indiscriminate or inept.[122] A partially warned enemy can definitely be deceived regarding the other aspects of *maskirovka* such as the scale, scope, location and timing of the attack.

Of these four aspects, timing is the most difficult to mask. Yet even timing need not be masked perfectly to achieve its desired ends. Specifically, the enemy need only be deceived to the point when it is impossible for him to make necessary redeployments to thwart the attack. And, if deception works regarding offensive scope and location, even a small time miscalculation by the enemy can spell disaster, for a force can be struck in the midst of redeployment. Throughout the war the Soviets were satisfied if they deceived the Germans by a factor of at least several days. By 1943 they normally achieved this aim.

In the Soviet view, perhaps scale, scope and location were the most important and achievable aspects of strategic deception. Certainly these were more easily achieved than intent and timing. The results were usually sufficient to ensure defeat of the enemy even if he knew of the general time of the attack. In virtually every strategic operation the Soviets successfully deceived the Germans in scale and scope, even if the location was known. As the war progressed and the correlation of forces shifted significantly to the Soviets' benefit, their ability to mask their advantage improved. At Moscow, Stalingrad, Belorussia, and Manchuria enemy underestimation of Soviet strength progressively increased. By 1944 and 1945 Soviet *maskirovka* routinely confounded enemy intelligence, resulting in the enemy missing over 50 per cent of the Soviet offensive build-up and, hence, underestimating the Soviet force by at least 25 per cent. This, the Soviets learned, was sufficient enemy miscalculation to accord a huge, if not decisive, battlefield advantage.

At the strategic level, Soviet deception achieved increasing success as the war progressed. Strategic deception contributed significantly to the pace of Soviet victory, while providing a wealth of experience for Soviet theorist to analyse and draw upon in post-war years.

The greatest Soviet successes in deception were operational and tactical. Here the Soviets learned some significant lessons. First, *maskirovka* had to be an organized venture. The army as a whole had to be well trained in its conduct, and *maskirovka* measures had to be carefully co-ordinated on a centralized basis by the headquarters anticipating its use in an operation. Zhukov wrote:

> In the Great Patriotic War operational *maskirovka* produced good results, because it was planned, prepared, and carried out on the basis of the centralized direction of the *STAVKA*. The principle of organizing operational *maskirovka* remained the most important and was unswervingly fulfilled in all operations on all fronts.[123]

Throughout the war the STAVKA and General Staff supervised the education of the army in *maskirovka* measures, just as it did in other operational and tactical areas. It orchestrated the program for compiling, analysing, and disseminating information on *maskirovka*; developed the regulations, directives and instructions; and, more important, monitored the degree to which units absorbed and capitalized on that experience. Within operating headquarters chiefs of staff and operations sections performed the same function. *Maskirovka* became an integral part of Soviet operational planning. By

1943 the *maskirovka* plan was a distinct section of all Soviet operational plans, a portion accorded the highest concern.

Time was of primary importance in deception planning. Sufficient time was essential to develop *maskirovka* concepts successfully. Conversely, planners had to have a good grasp of the time needed to implement specific measures that would produce the desired effect. A careful balance had to be maintained between the sophistication of *maskirovka* measures and the time to implement them. Simple plans and measures often fit the circumstances better than elaborate schemes.

The Soviets paid particular attention to the size of forces and weapons used to produce the desired effect of *maskirovka*. Allocation of too many resources could detract from obtaining the very results that *maskirovka* was designed to produce. Accordingly, 'decoy' forces and weapons also had to be used in timely fashion or they would be unavailable to contribute their own weight to overall decisive combat.

Of critical importance to successful deception was the maintenance of secrecy around operational and tactical planning. Early in the war loss or careless transmission of planning documents had compromised Soviet operations in general, and *maskirovka* plans in particular.[124] Hence the Soviets surrounded planning with Draconian security measures that severely restricted the circle of planners and number of written planning documents.

Forces assigned *maskirovka* missions had to be well prepared to carry out their tasks. Often the Soviets solved this dilemma by not informing the units that their mission was in fact a feint. In other instances, actions had to be performed with the same care and vigor that was applied to usual offensive tasks. Forces engaged in *maskirovka* missions had to be provided with the requisite specialized support (engineers, for example) to perform their tasks. The complexity of these missions necessitated drafting separate detailed deception plans to ensure proper attention to every detail of the mission.

Maskirovka measures had to be tailored to meet special conditions of terrain, weather and equipment availability. The Soviets had to struggle against the ever-present tendency to apply fixed-pattern solutions to a wide variety of operational and tactical cases. What worked in the forested regions of north Russia would not necessarily work in the steppes of the Ukraine. Likewise the assignment of a unit which lacked bridging equipment to a mission of conducting a feint river crossing would have been folly. The Soviets circumvented this common problem by relying heavily on the use of dummy and mock-up equipment deliberately revealed to enemy observation.

One of the deadliest weaknesses of deception planning was lack of knowledge about what the enemy knew concerning one's own *maskirovka* techniques. While routine methods would probably achieve success against a new and unsuspecting enemy, they could spell disaster against an experienced one. The Soviets learned this on numerous occasions early in the war when rigid practices yielded predictable patterns which the Germans then capitalized on. Attempts at reconnaissance *maskirovka* designed to deceive the enemy as to the location of main attacks actually tipped off where the attack would occur (Middle Don, December 1942). From 1943 on, Soviet directives urged commanders to use imaginative, innovative and flexible techniques to preclude the establishment of predictable stereotypes. The same could be said of excessive or clumsy use of radio silence which, in fact, could be recognized as an indicator of impending offensive action.

Perhaps most important was the requirement that *maskirovka* measures capitalize on enemy perceptions, self-delusions, or misconceptions (essentially on his psychological state). This required subtlety in high-level planning and skill in low-level implementation. It also demanded imagination in the planning of deception and realism and plausibility in the execution of *maskirovka* plans. This exhortation to exploit the believable became a hallmark of Soviet deception. Even in 1941, and certainly in 1942, Soviet planners used this technique to good ends in their strategic planning. After 1943 the Soviets continued to do so at the strategic level, exploiting German and Japanese perceptions at the operational and tactical level with notable frequency.

All of these lessons exemplify the theme that education in wartime is an unending process. As their voluminous writings on war experience (both official and post-war works) indicate, the Soviets believe the quality of performance in war directly reflects the study of war. Their detailed study progressed until the end of the war, persisted throughout the post-war years, and goes on today; probably in the same organized fashion as before. Education in *maskirovka* has been and is a part of this process.

VI

IMPLICATIONS FOR THE FUTURE

The Soviets have consistently believed that the nature, means, and potential impact of *maskirovka* evolves in consonance with the changing conditions of changing times. This is consistent with, if not an inevitable product of, their dialectical view of history. Changes in national attitudes (political and social) and mores, although difficult to measure, are part of the dialectical process and have an effect on the atmosphere in which *maskirovka* is employed, and its effectiveness.

More easily understood is the effect that changing technology has on prospects of using *maskirovka*. It is in this area that the potential effects of *maskirovka*'s future use have been most pronounced. The introduction of new weapons systems, nuclear weapons, computer technology, and a wide variety of technological innovations has produced an enormous series of new problems for military planners to solve. The Soviets certainly consider the basic intent, method, technique, and perhaps the basic principles of *maskirovka* derived from a study of experience to pertain to the modern era. These basics must, however, be constantly and carefully reconsidered in the light of technological change, ensuring their continual utility in contemporary or future war. The Soviets have striven to keep abreast of those changes, as their post-war writings have indicated.

During the immediate post-war years, while Stalin retained the helm of the Soviet state, doctrine developed during the Second World War, in particular during its last two years, remained dominant in Soviet military art and science. As such, the subject of *maskirovka* remained an important aspect of war as defined in late wartime directives. As before, the Soviets studies *maskirovka* within the overall context of the nature and utility of surprise in war. During this period the Soviets characterized war as 'predominantly a war of maneuver, a war involving the exertion over long periods of time of great pressure, and a war which cannot be decided in a single crushing blow'.[125] This view argued against a nation's ability to achieve strategic decisions in one grand battle, hence relegated strategic deception to the function of helpful adjunct to the securing of advantage in the initial stage of a war (a means of achieving surprise) – the same role it had performed in the Second World War. In describing combat, the Soviets contended that:

> The mass saturation of armies with technical equipment has made it possible to give to operations a quality of maneuver, to give them an exceptionally decisive impact and an ability to move rapidly and in great depth. It has made it possible to carry out complicated maneuvers at the same time that the scale of operations themselves has continued to grow.[126]

The prospective quickening pace of war gave added importance to surprise. This description of combat at the operational and tactical level recognized both the promise and the complexity of successful *maskirovka*, but did not accord it the decisive role on the battlefield over other factors (such as correlation of forces).

After Stalin's death in 1953, Soviet military theorists, while continuing their studies of all aspects of battle, were free to investigate themes which could not be discussed while Stalin lived. Foremost among these was an investigation of the occurrences of June 1941, which permitted the devastating surprise German attack on the Soviet Union. Examination of this question became a catalyst for studying a broader question relating to the nature of the initial period of war and its relationship to success or failure. Obviously the question of deception (strategic) became central to this study. Ultimately the Soviets focused attention on other initial periods of war, including France in May 1940 and Manchuria in August 1945. The threatening presence of growing nuclear arsenals lent urgency, if not an entirely new dimension, to the study of this problem.

The first series of articles investigating the initial period of war appeared after 1959, the year that the Soviet *Military History Journal* began publication. In the ensuing years Soviet theorists analysed the theme by studying the conditions surrounding the events of June 1941. In these studies the topic of surprise and *maskirovka* played a large role, and obviously much of the work touched upon the relevance of those earlier experiences to the nuclear age. Soviet attitudes toward surprise and *maskirovka* before 1960 remained heavily rooted in judgements derived from the war experiences. Specifically, the Soviets considered surprise and *maskirovka* to be important factors in achieving offensive success, but not necessarily the only decisive factors. The Soviets developed a greater appreciation of the defensive aspects of *maskirovka* than before, particularly at the strategic level. They also developed a heightened respect for the impact of nuclear weaponry on modern combat.

After 1960, Krushchev's rise to power signaled a significant change in Soviet military theory. The Soviets accepted that indeed a 'revolution' had occurred in military affairs. Nuclear weapons and delivery systems took a pre-eminent position on the battlefield. Battlefield expansion now encompassed virtually the entire depth of warring nations. The new Soviet view was based on the premise that 'the massive use of nuclear rockets substantially alters the nature of war and methods for waging it; it imparts to war a drastically decisive and destructive character.'[127] As a consequence:

> the waging of war by the above-mentioned ways and means [nuclear] may fundamentally alter the former notions of the development of armed combat according to periods or stages of war. It simultaneously attests to the extraordinary increase in the role of *the initial period of war* ... the initial period of a contemporary nuclear-rocket war will obviously be the main and decisive period, and will predetermine the development and the

outcome of the entire war. Armed combat in this period will obviously be the most violent and destructive.[128]

By accepting this stark view of war, Soviet theorists were compelled to recognize the increased, even critical importance of surprise.

> The most probable and, at the same time, most dangerous means for the unleashing of a war by the imperialist bloc against the socialist camp would be a surprise attack. Soviet military strategy takes into account the features of a real aggressor and considers that in contemporary circumstances, even a large war might arise suddenly, without the traditional threatening period characteristic of the past.[129]

These views, written by the most articulate and thorough Soviet theorist of the 1960s, Marshal Sokolovsky, summed up Soviet fixation on strategic nuclear issues during the period. Consequently conventional operational and tactical concerns clearly became secondary to concerns for strategic nuclear war. The Soviets focused on questions of strategic surprise (and *maskirovka*) in a nuclear arena to the detriment of more traditional *maskirovka* concerns. The time factor became a pre-eminent Soviet concern along with their fixation on the issue of parrying (or achieving) a potential first strike. Thus:

> the main problem is the development of methods for reliably repelling a surprise nuclear attack as well as methods of frustrating the aggressive designs of the enemy by the timely infliction of a shattering attack on him.[130]

Behind these judgements rested a growing Soviet understanding of the consequences of strategic surprise derived from their by now extensive study of the circumstances of June 1941.

It is now clear that by the late 1960s, shadowed by Khrushchev's demise, the Soviets began to question their preoccupation with strategic nuclear matters. As a result of the emerging nuclear balance worldwide, the inevitable use of these weapons became less clear. Mutual inhibitions (political and moral) concerning their use emerged. There was growing evidence that perhaps defenses could be erected to deter their use, or lessen their effects.

The net effect of this complex and subtle Soviet reassessment was a slow but perceptible shift away from sole concern for nuclear war to a growing acceptance that war was possible in either a nuclear or conventional context. Sokolovsky's 1968 edition of *Strategy* showed evidence of this shift. Victory must be attained within 'the shortest possible time, in the course of a rapidly moving war'. He added:

> But the war may drag on and this will demand the protracted and

all-out exertion of army and people. Therefore we must also be ready for a protracted war and get the human and material resources into a state of preparedness for the eventuality.[131]

To his comments that nuclear war was likely to begin with a devastating surprise attack, he appended:

> However, the possibilities of averting a surprise attack are constantly growing. Present means of reconnaissance, detection, and surveillance can opportunely disclose a significant portion of the measures of direct preparation of a nuclear attack by the enemy ... Thus the possibilities exist not to allow a surprise attack by an aggressor.[132]

While qualifying his earlier statements about the nature of war, Sokolovsky did not definitely answer the question, 'What will be the nature of modern war?' Theorists did give a partial answer. While continuing to recognize the possibility for and dangerous consequences of nuclear war, they focused again on conventional operations within and outside nuclear context. They maintained an appreciation for surprise in a nuclear context, but also returned to the study of surprise – *maskirovka* – in a more traditional context within the scope of theater, front, or army operations. While the reality of nuclear war remained, the study's substance more often than not, was of conventional *maskirovka* techniques within a theater of operations.

An important 1972 work on operational art by Colonel Savkin exemplified this renewed concern with the operational level of war. He recognized the increased complexity and importance of surprise produced by the existence of nuclear weapons, but his judgements rested clearly within the context of Second World War experiences.

> The ways and methods of achieving surprise are very diverse. In 1954–1959 they were developed in great detail in the works of Soviet authors. Depending on the concrete conditions of the situation, surprise may be achieved by leading the enemy astray with regard to one's intentions, by secrecy in preparation and swiftness of troop operations, by broad use of night time conditions, by the unexpected employment of nuclear weapons and other means of destruction, by delivering a forceful attack when and where the enemy does not expect it, and by employing methods of conduct of combat operations and new means of warfare unknown to the enemy.[133]

This is a prescription for the requirements of *maskirovka*. Savkin artfully wove into his description all of the traditional elements of *maskirovka*. It was a restatement of appropriate passages of the 1944 regulations with the nuclear issue adroitly inserted within it. It represented a return to the more balanced appreciation of the potential nature of war evidenced in the period before 1960. According to Savkin:

> Thus, the appearance of new means of warfare has immeasurably broadened the possibilities of achieving surprise. However there is now new, albeit very sophisticated, technology which of itself is capable of having a surprise effect on the enemy. It is necessary above all to have a technically correct and tactically competent employment in order to deliver surprise attacks with any weapons. In other words, there is requirement for a scientifically based military theory providing the most expedient recommendations for the effective surprise employment of ever more complex means of warfare in an operation or battle.[134]

Savkin stated that, 'Other paths [exist] concerning the attainment of surprise along with searches for new weapons and their sophistication'.[135] These paths are: a secret build-up in numbers of available weapons, which may lead to surprise with their mass employment on the most important axes; a search for the most skillful and original method for the unexpected use of available weapons; and the employment of methods which are new or unexpected for the enemy in the organization and conduct of an operation of battle. All of these measures required successful *maskirovka*. Savkin liberally laced his analysis with Second World War examples, and reaffirmed, 'The experience in achieving surprise acquired by Soviet troops in the past war has largely retained its value and instructiveness. Therefore, one must not forget it, but study it attentively'.[136] For balance Savkin added the usual qualification: 'However, the critical use of experiences of past wars is far from sufficient. One must have a constant creative search for contemporary new methods of achieving surprise in an operation or battle'.[137] Savkin's description of war, markedly different from that of Sokolovsky, typified the renewed Soviet concern for a balance, traditional approach. That attitude has persisted and broadened since the early 1970s.

Parallel to the renewed Soviet concern with operational matters, military theorists have accelerated their study of the initial period of war. A plethora of articles were capped in 1974, when a major work was written by General S.P. Ivanov detailing the circumstances of May 1940, June 1941 and August 1945. He derived from those cases relevant lessons for contemporary theorists.[138] Ivanov's work concentrated on the conventional, but noted the heightened danger posed by nuclear weapons. Above all, Ivanov answered Sokolovsky's call to study the nature of war, providing a basis for current Soviet judgements on the initial period of war, and the role of surprise and *maskirovka* in particular. As a result of Ivanov's and other theorists' work, the Soviets now have a better understanding of the nature and dangers of the initial period of war. Thus:

> The experience of the Second World War underscores the tendency for the initial period of war to shorten ... It also underscores the tendency for an increased scale and decisiveness of combat operations, and the desires of warring sides to achieve considerable results in the initial period of war in order to be able to exercise greater influence over the future course of war.
>
> From the experiences of earlier wars it is clear that up to this time no one had fully achieved victory over the enemy in the initial period. However, the presence of nuclear weapons and large groupings of armed forces located in a high state of readiness, in the case of their surprise use at the present time, as in no earlier time, permits one to achieve in the very beginning of war those results which have a decisive influence on the course and even outcome of war.[139]

Having studied the changing nature of war in its initial phases, other theorists have pondered the role of surprise and *maskirovka* in this new context. According to M.M. Kir'yan, nuclear weapons could be used either at the beginning or during a war. Whether or not such weapons were used:

> The aggressor will try to unleash war by surprise. In this regard the development of the means of achieving strategic surprise is allotted exceptionally great attention. The experience of war has demonstrated that the aggressor, unleashing war by surprise, usually achieves considerable success.[140]

Kir'yan qualified this statement by noting elsewhere that: 'The development of the technical means of reconnaissance [such as radio-electronic] makes the achievement of surprise difficult'.[141] Consequently, he emphasized the importance of careful planning and execution of *maskirovka* measures if one sought to capitalize on surprise at all levels of war.

Contemporary Soviet theorists give surprise a dominant position in the litany of the principles of war, describing it as: 'unexpected action which leads to the achievement of success in battle, operations and war'.[142] Surprise, an exploitable and potentially decisive factor at all levels of war, 'consists of the selection of time, methods, and means of combat actions which permit the delivery of a blow when the enemy is least prepared to repulse it in order to paralyze his will for organized resistance'.[143] Surprise accords a force an advantage which, along with the exploitation of other factors, can produce victory. The stated prerequisite for achieving surprise today echoes earlier prescriptions for success. Specifically, surprise is achieved by:

- misleading the enemy as to one's intentions [disinformation]
- maintaining the secrecy of one's own plans
- hiding combat preparations
- the use of new weapons, techniques, and forms of combat
- correct choice of the direction of the main blow and correct timing for its delivery
- unexpected air, artillery, and armor attacks and the surprise use of all types of forces
- rapid maneuver and the decisive actions that forestall enemy response and countermeasures
- conduct of fraudulent actions and deception [dummies, false installations, etc.]
- skillful use of terrain, weather, time of year, and season.[144]

Maskirovka, in its broadest definition, directly applies to five of these nine prescribed measures and tangentially affects the success of all. The tone of these means remains markedly conventional and traditional.

Certainly modern technology has had an impact on deception as well. To the traditional means of *maskirovka* such as masking, camouflage, radio deception, feints, demonstrations, and disinformation have been added the more technical means of optical, radio-technical, sound, hydro-acoustic, and radio deception measures – each with a well-defined function and role in the overall deception of the enemy.

Throughout the Soviet military experience there has been a basic continuity in their treatment of military *maskirovka*. Certainly Soviet intent to use *maskirovka* has remained a constant. Lenin's remonstrance that, 'in warfare one does not inform the foe when an attack will occur', and 'one must try to catch the enemy unaware and seize the moment when his troops are scattered', seem to epitomize Soviet concerns for *maskirovka*.[145] The Soviets have long understood the inter-relationship of political (peacetime) and wartime deception, an understanding only heightened by recent study of the initial period of wars. Soviet study and conduct of *maskirovka* has been characterized by a practical concern, and much of their experience has focused on determining what can realistically be achieved in war by *maskirovka*, rather than what might be achieved in the ideal.

Throughout their experience, the Soviets have adhered to the dialectical approach. True to this methodology, they strive to understand both the factor of what has occurred (experience) juxtaposed against the imperative of what is occurring (changing technology), to arrive at a better understanding of what will occur in future war. (The dialectical process of understanding both thesis and antithesis to better comprehend the resulting synthesis.) Such a process demands a thorough understanding of past practices and implies that the best be retained today. A nation hoping to compete successfully with the Soviets in the military realm must understand the Soviet approach, what they study, and their conclusions from that study. In a dangerous world, this applies particularly to the realm of *maskirovka* or deception in war, lest we fall victim to history we have failed or been unwilling to comprehend.

NOTES

This paper was presented at the US Army College Conference on 'Intelligence and Military Operations', Carlisle Barracks, Pennsylvania 22–25 April 1986. The views expressed in this article are those of the author and do not reflect the official policy or position of the Department of Defense or the US Government.

1. This sharply clashes with Stalin's post-war pronouncements which belittled the effect of strategic surprise in the initial period of war. Stalin, of course, being himself association with the débâcle of June 1941, had reason to shun the subject. After Stalin's death the Soviets began intensive investigation of the events of June 1941 in particular – and strategic surprise in general. That investigation continues today.
2. I have used *maskirovka* and deception synonymously throughout this paper. Lesser included aspects of *maskirovka* are described by their own terms such as camouflage, disinformation, etc.
3. V.A. Yefrimov, S.G. Chermashentsev, 'Maskirovka' (Deception), *Sovetskaya voennaya entsiklopediya* (Soviet military encyclopedia), 5, (Moscow: Voenizdat, 1978), p.175. (hereafter cited as *S.V.E.*)
4. Ibid.
5. Ibid.
6. Ibid.
7. S.P. Ivanov, *Nachal'nyi period voina* (The Initial Period of War), (Moscow: Voenizdat, 1974), p.350.
8. For those not familiar with the dialectic, Marx derived his concept of the dialectic from the German philosopher Hegel, who argued that all historical development emanated from the operation of the dialectic which in essence described a process of inevitable change. According to Hegel all aspects of man's development were governed by a dominant ideal or spirit (*Zeitgeist*). In each distinct period of history all social, economic, and political institutions, as well as man's intellectual state, were products of and reflected that dominant spirit. Over time, Hegel maintained, counterforces emerged to challenge the dominant 'idea' in essence, an antithesis that began to struggle with the original thesis. This struggle of thesis and antithesis would ultimately produce a new dominant 'spirit', which would then become a new thesis with a whole new set of resultant institutions. A new antithesis would arise to challenge it and renew the process of change. Hegel implied that as this dialectic operated, each new synthesis would contain the best aspects of the old struggling

operated, each new synthesis would contain the best aspects of the old struggling thesis and antithesis. Hence, ultimately, perfection would result from this metaphysical concept of the nature of change.

Marx accepted the validity of the dialectical process but challenged Hegel's belief in the 'idea' [or 'spirit'] as the dominant element. Instead Marx turned Hegel's dialectic on its head. He argued that economic realities dominated man's development and all other aspects of that development (social, political, intellectual) were mere reflections of these economic realities. According to Marx, the key economic reality was the means of production and those who controlled them. Since primeval times those means of production had been ripped from mankind's grasp and passed from dominant class to dominant class in a dialectical manner. Ultimately, Marx argued, the alienation of man from the fruits of his labor would be complete. At that point, that very alienation would produce a new awareness among the exploited mass who would then rise in revolution; overthrow the capitalistic class; and restore to man (labor) the means of production (fruits of his labor), creating the end result of genuine socialism.

Marx specifically identified the stages of history which were in reality stages in the development of the dialectic, each with a dominant economic system (slaveholding, feudal, capitalistic), and described the inevitable end of the process, the last stage – socialism. Marx implied that by the end of the nineteenth century the world would be ripe for revolution and the creation of socialism. When early twentieth-century developments contradicted Marx's predictions, Lenin updated Marx by discovering a new stage of economic development, that of imperialism, or 'the highest stage of capitalism', which man would suffer through before revolution would occur. For contemporary Marxists and Marxist-Leninists, the dialectic process remains valid, although there are variations in tactics, methods of change, and the nature of the end (socialism).

9. For example, the use of secret rail movements to regroup large forces before major offensives against the forces of Admiral Kolchak and Generals Denikin, Yudenich and Wrangel.

10. For example, see M.V. Frunze, 'Osnovnye voennye zadachi momenta' (The fundamental military missions of the time), *Izbrannye proizvedeniya* (Selected Works), (Moscow: Voenizdat, 1984), p.93.

11. P. Mel'nikov, 'Operativnaya maskirovka' (Operational *maskirovka*), *Voenno-istoricheskii zhurnal* (Military History Journal), April 1982, 18 (hereafter cited as *VIZh*).

12. Ibid.

13. *Polevoi ustav RKKA, 1929* (Field regulations of the Red Army, 1929), (Moscow, 1929), translation by JPRS, March 1985, pp.4–5.

14. Ibid., p.41.

15. *Vremennyi polevoi ustav RKKA, 1936* (Temporary field regulations of the Red Army, 1936), (Moscow: Voenizdat, 1937), translation by Translation Section, the US Army War College, Washington, DC, September–October 1937, p.52.

16. Ibid., emphasis added by author.

17. M.R. Galaktionov, *Tempy operatsii* (Tempos of operations), (Moscow: Gosvoenizdat, 1937), reprinted in *Voprosy strategii i operativnogo iskusstva v sovetskikh voennykh trudakh (1917–1940 gg)* (Questions of strategy and operational art in Soviet military workd (1917–1940), (Moscow: Voenizdat, 1965), p.541. (Hereafter cited as *Voprosy strategii*).

18. For specifics, see I.F. Kuz'min, *Na strazhe mirnogo tryda (1921–1940 gg* (On guard for peaceful work), (Moscow: Voenizdat, 1959), p.212. The consequences of Soviet deception are vividly related in Edward J. Drea, *Nomonhan: Japanese–Soviet Tactical Combat, 1939*, Leavenworth Papers No. 2 (Fort Leavenworth, KS: Combat Studies Institute, US Army Command General Staff College, January 1981).

19. The Germans took note of Soviet failures as well.

20. A. Kononenko, 'Boi vo flandrii (Mai 1940 gg)' (The Battle in Flanders) (May

1940), *VIZh*, March 1941, 10, 20.
21. Ibid., 20, 22.
22. S.N. Krasil'nikov, *Nastupatel'naya armeiskaya operatsiya* (The army offensive operation), (Moscow: Voenizdat, 1940), reprinted in *Voprosy strategii*, p.490.
23. Ibid., p.493.
24. Ibid., pp.493–494.
25. Ibid., p.495.
26. Mandated in *Directive of the General Staff Concerning the Study and Application of War Experience, 9 November 1942*, No. 1005216, translated by US Army General Staff, G–2.
27. V. Matsulenko, 'Operativnaya maskirovka sovetskikh voisk v pervom i vtorom periodakh voiny' (Operational *maskirovka* of Soviet forces in the first and second periods of war), *VIZh*, January 1972, 12. (Hereafter cited as 'Operativnaya maskirovka ... v pervom i vtorom periodakh'.)
28. Ibid.
29. Such as the surprise Soviet use of the medium T-34 and Heavy KV-1 tanks in the initial stage of war. German intelligence had no knowledge of these tanks' existence and even when it was discovered, the Germans were slow to spread the word and take counter-measures. Introduction by the Soviets in late 1941 of the new multiple rocket launchers (the Katyushas) also came as a surprise for the Germans.
30. Growing Soviet numerical strength and the subsequent shift of momentum in the Soviets' favor permitted them to initiate operations over a wider expanse of front. This improved the capability of the Soviets to plan diversions. It did not, however, reduce the need for massive force regroupings. Hence it placed an even greater premium on masking large force redeployments.
31. G.K. Zhukov, *Vospominaniya i pazmysheniya* (Memoirs and reflections), (Moscow: Voenizdat, 1969), p.418.
32. The widespread Soviet self-deception detailed in V. Morozov, 'Pochemu ne zavershilos nastuplenie' v Donbasse vesnoi 1943 goda' (Why the offensive in the Donbas was not completed in the spring of 1943), *VIZh*, March 1963. See also D.M. Glantz, *From the Don to the Dnepr: A Study of Soviet Offensive Operations, December 1942–August 1943* (Carlisle, PA: US Army War College 1984), pp.122–224.
33. Matsulenko, 'Operativnaya maskirovka ... v pervom i vtorom periodakh ...,' pp.18–19. German 4th Panzer Army intelligence maps do not reflect the false unit location of *major* Soviet units. German force deployments, however, indicated a degree of Soviet success in deceiving the Germans with regard to the location of the Soviet offensive.
34. These, and subsequent maps are reproductions of photographs of the original German maps. The photographs are often difficult to read. The maps simple illustrate the description of German unit locations described in the text.
35. A thorough description of Soviet deception measures associated with the secret deployment of 3rd Guards Tank Army is found in V.A. Matsulenko, *Operativnaya maskirovka voisk* (Operational *maskirovka* of forces), Moscow: Voenizdat, 1975), translation by US Army Foreign Science and Technology Center, Charlottesville, VA, 1977, pp.98–103. (Hereafter cited as Matsulenko, *Operativnaya.*) The success of these measures is attested to by the intelligence maps of German 8th Army and 4th Panzer Army for the period 29 October–5 November 1943, some of which are reproduced in D. Glantz, 'The Kiev Operation, 3 November–24 December 1943', *1985 Art of War Symposium, From the Dnepr to the Vistula: Soviet Offensive Operations, November 1943–August 1944, A Transcript of Proceedings* (Carlisle, PA: US Army War College, 1985), pp.1–54. (Hereafter cited as 'The Kiev Operation'.)
36. P.P. Tovstukha, R.M. Portugal'skii, *Upravlenie voiskami v nastuplenii* (Command and control of forces on the offensive), (Moscow: Voenizdat, 1981), pp.80–81, outlines the form and content of formal *maskirovka* planning and the agencies

designated to accomplish it.
37. V. Matsulenko, 'Operativnaya maskirovka voisk v tret'em periode voiny'
    (Operational *maskirovka* in the third period of war), *VIZh*, June 1972, 29–30.
    (Hereafter cited as Matsulenko, 'Operativnaya maskirovka ... tret'em periode
    voiny'.)
38. *Nastavlenie po proryvu pozitsionnoi oborony* (Regulations for penetration of a
    positional defense), (Moscow: Voenizdat, 1944), p.147.
39. *Polevoi ustav krasnoi armii*, 1944 (Field regulations of the Red Army, 1944),
    (Moscow: Voenizdat, 1944), translation by the Office of the Assistant Chief of
    Staff G-2, GSUSA and published by JPRS, 1985, p.10.
40. Ibid., p.44.
41. Ibid.
42. Ibid.
43. Although the Soviets have written little on the specific deception plan associated
    with the build-up for the new offensive, German intelligence documents clearly
    indicate that they were unaware of the scope of Soviet preparations. See 'The Kiev
    Operation'.
44. This Soviet deception effort is covered in detail in A.I. Radzievsky (ed.),
    Armeiskie operatsii (Army operations), (Moscow: Voenizdat, 1977), pp.150–53.
    German 8th Army intelligence reports confirm this Soviet Failure. See also 'The
    Korsun–Shevchenkovskii Operation, 24 January–17 February 1944', *1985 Art of
    War Symposium, From the Dnepr to the Vistula: Soviet Offensive Operations,
    November 1943–August 1944, A Transcript of Proceedings*, (Carlisle, PA: US
    Army War College, 1985), pp.115–75.
45. For an account of deception in both operations see Matsulenko, *Operativnaya*,
    pp.134–67.
46. Detailed descriptions of *maskirovka* practices in the final year of war are found in:
    Matsulenko, *Operativnaya*, pp.179–217; Matsulenko, 'Operativnaya maski-
    rovka ... v tret'em periode voiny', pp.37–40; Radzievsky, *Armeiskie operatsii*,
    pp.147–50; I. Galitsky, 'Iz opyta operativnoi masirovki pri podgotovke nastu-
    pleniya fronta' (From the experience of *maskirovka* during the preparation of a
    front offensive), *VIZh*, May 1966; V. Matsulenko, 'Operativnaya maskirovka
    voisk v Vislo–Oderskoi operatsii' (Operational *maskirovka* in the Vistula–Oder
    operation), *VIZh*, January 1975.
47. Franz Halder, *War Journal of Franz Halder*, VII, typescript translated copy,
    (Carlisle, PA: US Army College, undated), pp.168–9.
48. Ibid., p.198.
49. Soviet preparations for the Moscow counteroffensive described in D.Z. Muriyev,
    Proval operatsii 'Taifun' (The failure of Operation Typhoon), (Moscow: Voeniz-
    dat, 1966), pp.142–159; A.M. Samsovov, *Porazhenie vermakhta pod Moskvoi*
    (Defeat of the Wehrmacht at Moscow), (Moscow: Moskovskii Rabochi, 1981),
    pp.247–258; *Bitva za Moskvu* (The Battle for Moscow), (Moscow: Moskovskii
    Rabochi, 1968), pp.1–97.
50. *Maskirovka* measures associated with the forward deployment of 10th Army are
    detailed in F. Golikov, 'Rezervnaya armiya rotovitsya k zashchite stolitsy' (A
    reserve army prepared to defend the capital) *VIZh*, May 1966.
51. Matsulenko, *Operativnaya*, pp.11–12.
52. Halder, p.184.
53. Ibid., p.188.
54. D. Muriyev, 'Nekotorye voprosy sovetskoi voennoi strategii v Moskovskoi bitve'
    (Some questions concerning Soviet military strategy in the battle of Moscow),
    VIZh, November 1971, 17.
55. A. Seaton, *The Battle for Moscow*, (New York: Playboy Press Paperbacks, 1971),
    p.198.
56. Halder, p.208.
57. Matsulenko, 'Operativnaya maskirovka ... v pervom i vtorom periodakh ...,':
    pp.14–15.

58. Soviet planning for the Stalingrad counteroffensive described in A.M. Samsonov, *Stalingradskaya bitva* (the Battle of Stalingrad), (Moscow: Izdetel'stvo Akademii Nauk SSSR, 1960), pp.438–63; *Stalingradskaya Epopeya* (The Stalingrad Epoch), (Moscow: Izdatel'stvo 'Nauka', 1968); K.K. Rokossovsky (ed.), *Velikaya pobeda na Volga* (Great Victory on the Volga), (Moscow: Voenizdat, 1965), pp.207–59.
59. A.M. Vasilevsky, *Delo vsei zhizni* (Life's work), (Moscow: Voenizdat, 1973), p.220.
60. *Dvesti ognennyhk dnei* (Two hundred days of fire), (Moscow: Voenizdat, 1968), pp.60, 62.
61. V. Matsulenko, 'Operativnaya maskirovka voisk v kontranastuplenii pod Stalingradom' (Operational *maskirovka* of forces at Stalingrad), *VIZh*, January 1974, 12 (hereafter cited as Matsulenko, 'Operativnaya maskirovka ... pod Stalingradom'). See also N. Orlov, G. Tvardovskii, 'Sposoby obespecheniya skrytnosti podgotovki operatsii i vnezapnosti deistvii voisk v gody voiny' (The means of securing secrecy in the preparation of operations and surprise in the operations of forces in the war years), *VIZh*, September 1981, 20.
62. Matsulenko, *Operativnaya*, pp.33–5.
63. E. Ziemka, *Stalingrad to Berlin* (Washington, DC: Center for Military History, 1968), p.46.
64. Ibid., p.48.
65. Matsulenko, *Operativnaya*, p.34.
66. Matsulenko, 'Operativnaya maskirovka ... pod Stalingradom', pp.13–14.
67. Matsulenko, *Operativnaya*, pp.32, 40.
68. K.K. Rokossovsky, *Soldatskii dolg* (A soldier's duty), (Moscow: Voenizdat, 1968), p.152.
69. *Dvesti ognennykh dnei*, p.139.
70. Ziemke, p.48.
71. Alan Clarke, *Barberossa: The Russian–German Conflict 1941–45* (New York: Signet Books, 1965), p.272.
72. W. Goerlitz, *Paulus and Stalingrad*, (New York: Citadel Press, 1963), pp.196–7.
73. Ziemke, p.48.
74. Ibid., p.49.
75. H. Schroeter, *Stalingrad*, (New York: Ballantine, 1958), pp.52–3.
76. Ziemke, p.49.
77. Matsulenko, *Operativnaya*, p.33.
78. Goerlitz, p.229.
79. Matsulenko, *Operativnaya*, p.113. The scale of redeployments covered in detail in N. Yakovlev, 'Operativnye peregruppirovki voisk pri podgotovka Belorusskoi operatsii' (Operational regrouping of forces during the preparation of the Belorussian operation), *VIZh*, September 1975.
80. Vasilevsky, p.415.
81. Matsulenko, *Operativnaya*, pp.117–18.
82. S.M. Shtemenko, *General'nyi shtab v gody voiny* (The General Staff in the war years), (Moscow: Voenizdat, 1968), pp.233–4.
83. V. Chernyeyev, 'Operativnaya maskirovka voisk v Belorusskoi operatsii', (Operational *maskirovka* of forces in the Belorussian operation), *VIZh*, August 1974, 12.
84. Matsulenko, *Operativnaya*, pp.115–16.
85. Chernayayev, p.13.
86. Vasilevsky, pp.424–5.
87. Matsulenko, *Operativnaya*, p.118.
88. Chernyayev, p.14. This article also reprints detailed tactical *maskirovka* instructions the 1st Belorussian front issued to all of its subordinate commands.
89. The scope of this redeployment detailed in Yakovlev, p.92, and in I.M. Chistyakov, *Sluzhim otchizne* (In the service of the fatherland), (Moscow: Voenizdat, 1975), pp.216–20. German Third Panzer Army intelligence maps clearly show the

Soviet 154th Rifle Division sector but up to 24 June do not evidence any awareness of the extensive Soviet redeployments into that sector. See p.223 for sample map.

90. K.K. Rokossovsky, 'Na napravlenii glavnogo udara' (On the direction of the main blow), *Osvobozhdenie Belorussii, 1944* (The liberation of Belorussia, 1944), (Moscow: Izdatel'stvo 'Nauka', 1974), p.143. For an army level view (65th Army) see P.I. Batov, *V pokhodakh i boyakh* (In campaigns and battles), (Moscow: Voenizdat, 1966), pp.405–16.

91. Ziemke, p.313.

92. Ibid., p.315.

93. Ibid.

94. Ibid., pp.315–16.

95. For an excellent overall assessment of German intelligence capabilities see H. van Nes, 'Bagration: Study of the Destruction of Army Group CENTRE during the Summer of 1944 as seen from the Point of View of Military Intelligence', *1985 Art of War Symposium, From the Dnepr to the Vistula: Soviet Offensive Operations, November 1943–August 1944, A Transcript of Proceedings,* (Carlisle, PA: US Army War College, 1985), pp.245–93. An OKH perspective is found in Graf von Kielmansegg, 'A View from the Army High Command (OKH)', *1985 Art of War Symposium,* 293–7.

96. Soviet order of battle and strength figures found in Samsonov, pp.741–85 and 'Belorusskaya operatsiya v tsifrakh' (The Belorussian operation in figures), *VIZh,* June 1964.

97. van Nes., p.267.

98. Ibid., pp.270–72.

99. Ziemke, p.316.

100. 'Kampanii sovetskikh vooruzhennikh sil na dal'nem vostoke v 1945 g (facti i tsifry)' (The campaign of the Soviet armed forces in the Far East in 1945: facts and figures), *VIZh,* August 1965, 64–74; Saburo Hayashi and Alvin Coox, *Kogun: The Japanese Army in the Pacific War,* (Quantico, VA: The Marine Corps Association, 1959).

101. In two months of fighting on Okinawa 110,000 American troops had suffered 49,000 casualties defeating about 60,000 Japanese.

102. Shtemenko, p.347.

103. Planning details found in L.N. Vnotchenko, *Pobeda na dal'nem vostoke* (Victory in the Far East), (Moscow: Voenizdat, 1971), pp.64–168.

104. Shtemenko, pp.354–5.

105. Ibid., pp.342–3. See also K.A. Meretskov, *Serving the People* (Moscow: Progress Publishing, 1971), pp.337–8; Chistyakov, 271–3.

106. M.V. Zakharov, (ed.), *Finale,* (Moscow: Progress Publishers, 1972), p.71.

107. Matsulenko, *Operatinaya,* pp.221–3.

108. Those Japanese attitudes portrayed in Drea, *Nomonham.*

109. A detailed account of Soviet operational and tactical techniques is found in D.M. Glantz, *August Storm: Soviet Tactical and Operational Combat in Manchuria, 1945,* Leavenworth Papers No. 8 (Fort Leavenworth, KS: Combat Studies Institute, 1983).

110. E.J. Drea, 'A Japanese Pearl Harbor: Manchuria 1945', (Fort Leavenworth, KS: Combat Studies Institute, 1984), manuscript, p.1.

111. E.J. Drea, 'Missing Intentions: Japanese Intelligence and the Soviet Invasion of Manchuria, 1945', *Military Affairs,* April 1984, 67.

112. Ibid., 67–8.

113. Ibid.

114. Ibid.

115. Ibid., 69.

116. Ibid., 70.

117. Ibid.

118. Matsulenko, *Operativnaya,* p.221.

119. Ibid., p.227.

120. G. Zhukov, 'Organizatsiya operativnoi maskirovki' (The organization of operational *maskirovka*), *VIZh*, May 1977, 48. (Hereafter cited as Zhukov, 'organizatsiya ... maskirovki'.)

121. The German ability to detect Soviet tactical units (corps and below) also deteriorated as the war progressed. From 1941 to early 1943, German intelligence could usually identify newly deployed Soviet divisions within 24 hours of their arrival in front line positions. By early 1944 the detection time lengthened to 2–3 days, and in late 1944 and early 1945 detection took 3–4 days, and often did not occur at all before a major attack. This deterioration testified to both reduced German reconnaissance capability and improved Soviet *maskirovka* at the lowest levels.

122. This should be of particular concern to contemporary intelligence agencies who tend to be inundated by voluminous but often uncollated and unanalysed data gathered by a variety of sophisticated technological collection means. Experience shows that too much information can be as confusing as too little, and it can paralyse operations by even the best analysts.

123. Zhukov, 'Organizatsiya ... maskirovki', p.48.

124. Soviet communications security was lax, particularly in 1941 and 1942; for example during the Khar'kov operation of May 1942. Although communications security remained poor throughout the war the limitations on the number of planners inhibited the work of German intelligence. By 1944 the Soviets actually capitalized on their communications problems by using radio traffic to give the Germans disinformation.

125. L. Vetoshnikov, 'Operativnoye isskustvo i ego mesto v Sovetskom veonhom isskustve' (Operational art and its place in Soviet military art), *Voennaya Mysl'*, April 1949, translation by Eurasian Branch, G–2, USAGS, p.9.

126. Ibid.

127. V.D. Sokolovsky, *Voennaya Strategiya* (Militar Strategy), (Moscow: Voenizdat, 1962, 1963, 1968), translation for the Foreign Technology Division, by H.F. Scott, p.200.

128. Ibid., p.211.

129. Ibid., p.193.

130. Ibid., p.218.

131. Ibid.

132. Ibid., p.288.

133. V.E. Savkin, *Osnovye printsipy operativinogo iskusstvo i taktiki* (The Basic principles of Operational Art and Tactics), (Moscow: Voenizdat, 1972), translation by the US Air Force, p.235.

134. Ibid., p.236.

135. Ibid.

136. Ibid., p.238.

137. Ibid.

138. Ivanov, *Nachal'nyi period voiny*.

139. M.M. Kir'yan, *Problemy voennoi teorii v sovetskikh nauchno-spravochnykh izdaniyakh* (The Problems of Military theory in Soviet Scientific Reference Publications) (Moscow: 'Nauka', 1985), pp.123–4.

140. Ibid., p.113.

141. M.M. Kir'yan, 'Vnezapost' (Surprise), *S.V.E.*., 2. 1976, p.163.

142. Ibid., p.161.

143. Ibid.

144. Ibid.

145. Savkin, p.230.

American Strategic Deception in the Pacific: 1942–44

KATHERINE L. HERBIG

In standard American histories of the Second World War in the Pacific it has been the Japanese who are credited with the ability and the will to deceive their enemies, not the Americans. Japan's surprise attack on Pearl Harbor, which humiliated the US and catapulted the country into the war, became the popular archetype for Japanese treachery. When the investigations of the Pearl Harbor raid held during and after the war revealed that the attack itself had been supported by a clever deception campaign, this only reinforced the stereotype. The Japanese had simulated radio traffic from their invasion fleet which falsely placed it in the coastal waters south of Japan, not headed north-west toward Hawaii. They had planted false clues to their own unpreparedness, such as sending Japanese soldiers ashore on leave just hours before their ships sailed. They had reinforced garrisons in Manchuria to suggest a northern target for their obvious military preparations instead of the true southern one, and they had prolonged their show of diplomatic negotiations in Washington.[1]

Yet it was the United States, not Japan, that perfected the more sophisticated capacity for deception in the Pacific War. Eventually the US adopted deception on a scale which helped to shorten the war and to save American lives. While strategic deception came to characterize American strategy by the war's end, Japan's attempts to deceive diminished over time. Taking a lead from the British, whose elaborate deceptions in Europe contributed to the Allied victory there, the Americans tried to deceive the Japanese about their every strategic move during the last two years of the war. With the relatively recent release of some of the records dealing with deception, it is possible to begin the study of this hitherto obscure chapter in American military history. This history helps to clarify how in fact the United States won the war in the Pacific and what an important part deception played in the American, not the Japanese, war effort.

The United States built its capacity for strategic deception from nothing when the war began into a large program led by a trained cadre of specialists at its end. Thinking deceptively did not come easily or naturally to most American military officers, whose training stressed ideas of mass and position derived from nineteenth-century European theorists. Arranging to meet the enemy with overwhelming force, not weakening him in advance with deception, preoccupied mid-twentieth century American strategists. To some extent deception remained suspect in American military circles throughout the war, and those who understood its potential and wished to rely more on it found themselves repeatedly justifying their views.

None of the American military services had deception planning agencies when the war in the Pacific broke out. Deception needed an institutional home before its supporters could build the organization they needed. Since strategic deception demands access to the highest levels of leadership, and the authority to manipulate actual as well as bogus operations, the obvious place for a deception agency for the Pacific war was in the burgeoning bureaucracy of the Joint Chiefs of Staff (JCS) in Washington. In the fall of 1942 at the urging of the British, a small agency was designated two tasks: military security, its primary role, and only secondarily, the co-ordination of deception activities for the Allied operation Torch, the invasion of North Africa that would take place in November 1942. Called Joint Security Control, the deception agency suffered from a schizophrenic mission both to protect secrets and to create them, and it fought bureaucratic rivals throughout the war for more power and discretion for itself and more scope for its deception projects.[2]

During the first 18 months of the war, while a deception oversight agency gradually evolved and began to function in Washington, US Navy and Army commanders and their staffs handled deception for themselves. Deception by Americans in the Pacific in 1942 and for most of 1943 was at an operational level, linked to a specific campaign or impending clash with Japanese forces, and intended primarily to have local or short-term significance. From the beginning deception played a part in the American effort to regain the initiative in the Pacific and then to sustain the drive to Japan itself. The operational deceptions of the first months became the base of experience on which the later strategic deception programs were built.

After Pearl Harbor the US Navy stretched its scarce forces thinly to cover commitments to defend Hawaii and the sea routes to Australia and New Zealand. Japan consolidated its hold on the East Indies by February 1942, brushing aside the initial Allied opposition in the short-lived ABDA (American British Dutch Australian) command. The US Navy dared not risk naval battles which endangered its few remaining aircraft carriers until others could be built to join them in the Pacific. The first American actions of the war were cautious raids on Japanese positions. In the unaccustomed and unenviable role of underdog, the navy overcame its distaste for deception. Fleet Admiral Chester W. Nimitz, Commander-in-Chief, Pacific Fleet and Pacific Ocean Areas (CinCPAC-CinCPOA) based in Hawaii, favored any means that promised to augment his meagre resources and get results.[3]

The chance for Nimitz's first engagement with the Japanese Navy, which would become the Battle of the Coral Sea occured in April 1942. Using intelligence reports from the navy's small but excellent cryptanalytic staff, the Combat Intelligence Unit at Oahu, Nimitz built deception into his plans. He would send a light cruiser, the *Nashville,* to the rich Japanese fishing grounds off the Kamchatka peninsula early in May. There he hoped the cruiser's presence would distract the Japanese as they prepared their projected operations against Tulagi and Port Moresby on the southern coast of New Guinea. The *Nashville* would be instructed to attack fishing boats and, more to the point, send radio signals designed to simulate a carrier task force. However, as the real US task force under Vice Admiral Frank Jack Fletcher prepared to intercept the Japanese invasion fleet in the Coral Sea early in May, the Kamchatka diversion did not materialize: the *Nashville* ran aground at Midway en route to the North Pacific, and had to return to Pearl Harbor for repairs.[4]

Warnings by navy cryptanalysts reading parts of the Japanese Navy's secret code in May tipped off Nimitz that the next Japanese target would be Midway.[5] He took the opportunity afforded by several weeks of advance warning to initiate various deceptions to guard his preparations to meet the Japanese at Midway. In the weeks before the battle the cryptanalysts put together where and when and even how many ships Japan would send to attack Midway early in June; Nimitz gradually had solid information and enough precious time to mass his three remaining carriers. The disparity of forces at Midway could have been crushing: Japan had 11 battleships, five carriers, 16 cruisers, and 49 destroyers against American forces with no battleships, three carriers, eight cruisers, and 14 destroyers.[6] Nimitz's carefully planned surprise and several pieces of luck gave the US its strategic victory over long odds.

Before he ordered Vice Admiral William (Bull) Halsey's Task Force 16 to leave the Solomon Islands in mid-May and to return at once to Pearl Harbor, Nimitz apparently sent Halsey secret orders: he should deliberately reveal himself to Japanese patrol planes attached to an invasion force headed toward Nauru and Ocean Islands, east of the Solomons in the Pacific. The Japanese duly reported sighting Halsey's two carriers on 15 May, after which the American task force turned and withdrew. The unexpected sighting provoked a flurry of response from the Japanese, who ultimately decided to call off their invasion of Nauru and Ocean as too risky with American carriers in the vicinity. Four days later Halsey set off for Pearl Harbor and then Midway, leaving the South Pacific temporarily without a US Naval presence. The sighting on the 15th, however, kept the Japanese nervous about the whereabouts of Halsey's carriers, in effect covering his departure, and leading into a radio deception scheme which began later in May.[7]

This plan called for simulating the presence of the carrier task force off the Solomons by using the communications and ships of the Commander of Naval Forces, Southwest Pacific, Vice Admiral Herbert Leary, based in Melbourne, Australia. Beginning on 25 May, two ships, a cruiser and a sea-plane tender, sent dummy radio traffic patterned on the recent battle in the Coral Sea as they steamed back and forth off the Solomons. Shore traffic was returned from Melbourne.[8] To Japanese traffic analysts, limited to radio as their only channel of information, it appeared that Halsey's carrier task force remained east of the Solomons where it had so recently been seen. This relatively simple deception paid handsome dividends a week later, 4 June, at Midway. Intelligence analysts of the Naval General Staff in Tokyo took note of the American radio traffic coming from the Solomons. They advised their invasion fleet commanders that US carriers remained in the South Pacific, a fact which implied, they claimed, that the Americans remained ignorant of Japan's intention to attack Midway. Even in the face of contrary evidence, after the Japanese forces already in the Pacific had monitored the tell-tale increase in radio traffic as Fletcher's task force left Pearl Harbor for Midway on 30 May, the Naval General Staff in Tokyo remained convinced that two American carriers were still off the Solomons and that the surprise attack on Midway was secure.[9]

In the event, Nimitz's ambush north-east of Midway caught the Japanese striking force by surprise. They lost four aircraft carriers and the battle of Midway. The United States gained one of its most important victories in the Pacific. According to Japanese historians of Midway, the US won as much because of Japanese intelligence failures as because of the admittedly brilliant American intelligence achievements. The sighting of Halsey's carriers, when 'confirmed' by the subsequent simulated radio traffic, misled intelligence analysts in Tokyo.[10] Even when Admiral Isoroku Yamamoto's main force, lurking west of the Midway striking force, caught the suspicious increase in radio traffic from Pearl Harbor on the 30th, they did not warn the commander who led the strike. They maintained their own radio silence instead. Admiral Nagumo was lulled to disaster at Midway, according to Fuchida and Okumiya, by the

Naval General Staff's persistent misestimate, maintained until the very eve of the battle and communicated to the advancing Japanese forces, that an American task force was operating in the Solomons area, strongly implying that the enemy had no suspicion of the impending Japanese attack on Midway.[11]

The deception supporting Midway was an excellent example of how a small-scale, locally planned and implemented deception could materially contribute to a victory which, in this case, had great strategic significance. After losing four carriers at Midway, Japan never resumed the offensive in the Pacific.

There was an ironic footnote to deception at the battle of Midway. Another American commander in a secondary theatre of the battle was misled by a lack of information and his own assumptions concerning enemy deception. On 3 June, the day before the main strike at Midway, a diversionary Japanese force attacked American installations in the Aleutian Islands. US cryptanalysts had determined from Japanese radio traffic that this target would prove to be a diversion. The North Pacific commander, Rear Admiral Robert A. Theobald, received word that analysis suggested that the Japanese would first bomb Dutch Harbor, and then attempt landings at Kiska, Attu and Adak Islands further west in the Aleutians. Admiral Nimitz did not share with his force commanders the secret cryptanalytic basis of this prediction, however, which made it harder for Theobald to believe it. Coupled with warnings from Nimitz himself that the 'Japanese are adept at the practice of deception', Theobald decided that the American intelligence scenario for the Aleutians must be based on Japanese radio deception because Dutch Harbor, the largest US base in the area, seemed to him the only worthwhile invasion target.[12] He therefore concentrated his small and aged naval force southeast off Dutch Harbor on 3 June, where they missed the Japanese bombing runs in the fog and could do nothing to oppose the actual landings later that day on Kiska and Attu, 500 miles to the west. While the Japanese suffered for underestimating American capacity for deception, Admiral Theobald suffered for crediting the Japanese with deceptions of which, in this instance, they were innocent.[13]

WEDLOCK: DECEPTION IN THE NORTH PACIFIC

After much wrangling, the Joint Chiefs of Staff finally agreed on a general policy for deception against the Japanese in September 1943. There must have been a feeling of anti-climax at Joint Security Control as September and then October slipped by and no proposals for strategic deception based on the hard-won policy arrived at the Pentagon from the Pacific. Reaction from the field to the new policy against Japan was a resounding silence. Admiral Nimitz's attention was focused on the impending invasion of the Gilbert Islands in November. This would be followed at year's end with assaults against the Marshalls. Thus the navy's long-awaited drive across the central Pacific was finally beginning. In the South Pacific Admiral Halsey was building on the conquest of Guadalcanal the previous February with attacks on islands in the Solomons, advancing toward the Japanese stronghold at Rabaul. General Douglas MacArthur's forces in the Southwest Pacific paralleled this line of advance as they continued to fight up the northern coast of New Guinea. No one, it seemed, had time to develop strategic deception plans.[14]

Finally JSC took the initiative. After roughing out an idea, they saw to it that Lieutenant General Simon Bolivar Buckner, Jr., Commanding General of the Alaska Department, received orders to develop such a plan. The Operations Plans Division (OPD) of the War Department General Staff sent Buckner the draft with a directive on 3 November 1943 asking for a deception plan for the North Pacific as soon as possible.[15]

Alaska had become an attractive site for deception operations because of recent turns in the military situation and because of decisions the JCS had reached during 1943. The Japanese had occupied the Aleutian Islands of Attu and Kiska early in June 1942 during the attack on Midway, and had held them for nearly a year. Not until mid-1943 could US forces be spared to reclaim two barren, isolated bits of American territory. The US Army's assault on Attu, begun on 11 May 1943, proved surprisingly difficult and slow as the Japanese bitterly defended the island. Expecting more of the same at Kiska on 15 August, American invasion forces were surprised to find the Japanese gone. During the landings and exploration of the uninhabited island, further embarrassments arose as jumpy American soldiers shot at each other, and some were killed. The Japanese had evacuated all their grateful troops by submarine in July after Kiska had been cut off from its supply routes, and they had not been detected in the fog.[16]

In the meantime the Joint Chiefs, meeting with their British counterparts at the Trident conference in May and the Quadrant conference in August 1943, had presented their decision to approach Japan from the south, building on the gains from the New Guinea and Solomon Islands campaigns, then adding the central Pacific threat. They abandoned for now earlier plans also to converge on Japan via the shorter northern route. Plans for a northern invasion had assumed the Soviet Union would need immediate relief in 1942 and that the Russians would enter the war against Japan.[17] When Soviet troops held Stalingrad and Russia did not declare war on Japan these assumptions collapsed, while experience in the North Pacific proved how intransigent the boggy terrain, heavy seas, habitual fogs and high winds of the region could be. A major invasion of the Kuriles from the Aleutians was postponed indefinitely in the fall of 1943, and became less likely as the months passed.[18]

Although the Japanese had had the same disheartening experience with the fierce Aleutians weather, they had built defensive bases in the Kurile Islands, which stretch like stepping stones between the northernmost home island of Japan and the Aleutian chain. From the size of their Kurile defenses it was plain that the Japanese felt somewhat vulnerable to attack from the north. If the US could play on this anxiety, and through deception create a threat in the Aleutians which provoked the Japanese to reinforce the Kuriles, this would weaken Japanese defenses elsewhere. A northern deception would generate a third plausible threat, one which might distract the enemy from the two actual lines of advance, Nimitz's across the central Pacific and Mac-Arthur's from the south-west.[19]

The objectives of General Buckner's deception had been outlined for him in the November directive: to deceive the Japanese about US plans for Alaska and the Aleutians by exaggerating current American forces and their activities there, and more specifically, to convince the Japanese of a build-up intended to invade the Kurile Islands. Tentatively this fictional assault was first slated for 1 August 1944. Following these guidelines, Buckner sent his plan, AD-JAPAN-44, to Washington on 9 January 1944. The plan suffered somewhat because it was the first American strategic deception of the Pacific War. Crucial details were left vague, particularly where co-operation from the navy would be necessary. The plan had no deception 'story' to outline what the target was supposed to believe and do, which would have tied the various measures together. Not surprisingly, the plan gave strategic control over the planning and execution of the idea to the army, largely to General Buckner himself.[20]

Admiral Nimitz responded early in February with recommendations for changes in Buckner's plan. Not surprisingly, he preferred to keep strategic control in the hands of the navy and himself, but he awarded tactical control over operations in Alaska to the army. Looking ahead to the evolving central Pacific campaign, Nimitz saw a way to sharpen the deception's impact by trying it to an actual operation. He suggested moving the fictional assault on the Kuriles forward to 15 June, D-Day for the invasion of Saipan in the Mariana Islands, the next major step toward Japan. The threat to invade from the north could then serve as cover for the Marianas' assault, codenamed Operation Forager, further south. The Joint Chiefs approved these suggestions and incorporated them in a revision which became JCS 705 on 17 February.[21]

The revised plan envisioned creating a fictional force of five American divisions and some 2,500 Canadian troops, plus headquarters and corps troops. They would appear to be staging for an invasion of two Kurile islands, Paramushiro and Shimushu, from five different bases in the Aleutians and Alaska.[22]

Co-ordination between the services advanced somewhat ater Nimitz and Buckner met in San Francisco on 14 March and when, a week later, a conference convened there between CinCPAC, JSC, and the Alaska Department. There they thrashed out just who was supposed to do what for Wedlock. They decided to portray the fictional infantry as a members of a reactivated Ninth Amphibious Force, and that an artificially enlarged Ninth Fleet would become Wedlock's naval arm. They agreed to set up a new Joint Communication Center on Adak to handle the rising volume of radio traffic that the deception would require. Since the navy's Communication Policy would guide the traffic, the navy would do the planning, create the call signs, and design a new joint cryptographic system especially for the deception. The army in turn would provide personnel, build the facilities, and handle the army traffic at the new Joint Center. The navy would control both naval and Joint communications. Nimitz's strategic control over the enterprise was reiterated, and General Buckner agreed to hold tactical responsibility.[23] With a mere ten weeks left to implement the deception before D-Day in the Marianas, those in charge of setting up a credible deception scrambled to meet their deadlines.

By the time Wedlock began officially on 1 April 1944, the central Pacific campaign had swept into the Marshall Islands. Early in February the Marines had occupied undefended Majuro and had invaded Kwajalein and Eniwetok. Later that month carrier raids destroyed most of the aircraft at Truk and at airfields in the Marianas. Advantages from the strategy of two converging advances were becoming clear. The Japanese had stationed their Combined Fleet in the South expecting to fight a climactic naval battle against the fleet supporting MacArthur's continuing drive along the New Guinea coast. This had drawn Japanese naval strength out of Nimitz's way for the Marshalls campaign. The navy's subsequent raid on Truk, intended primarily to neutralize Japan's potential to interfere in the Marshalls, also furthered the isolation of Rabaul from air support, helping MacArthur's operations.[24] If carefully timed, the two campaigns could continue to be mutually supportive. Unintentionally, one of Mac-

Arthur's leaps along the New Guinea coast was to help Nimitz surprise the Japanese on Saipan as much as, if not more than, the northern deception now taking shape in Alaska.

Admiral Nimitz further complicated the relationships between the actual and the deceptive Pacific campaigns on 22 March when he submitted his own deception plan for Operation Forager. He incorporated plan Wedlock, with its origins in JSC and the army, as a supportive and subsidiary phase of his own concept, yet his plan sought to deceive the Japanese in a different way.

In effect Nimitz proposed to recast the deceptive picture the Americans would show the Japanese. Instead of portraying Wedlock as a third independent offensive converging on Japan simultaneously with the two actual campaigns, Nimitz proposed that cover for Forager would focus on deceptive objectives closer to the lines of advance, namely Truk and targets in the Celebes. Wedlock should simmer in the background as an operation awaiting the results of the Central Pacific campaign, while further confusion was generated for the Japanese about the timing between the two campaigns. Nimitz would try to turn the enemy's head back and forth between Forager and Wedlock, minimizing Forager and exaggerating the threat from the north, but CincPAC's plan held out no hope that Wedlock could be made to appear the larger of the two.[25]

Nimitz's plan would generate more options through deception than Wedlock alone, options which would have to watched and factored into Japanese defensive planning. It also relied less on a single, untested strategic deception scenario. Too many options, however, could dilute the deceptive picture too far and generate suspicion. Even more serious, Nimitz's version demanded rapid shifts in the enemy's expectations and assumed that these could be orchestrated by deceptive signals and propaganda; there was no provision for delays, misinterpretations by the enemy, or the unexpected and accidental. Nor were there any plans to evaluate the results of the plan and make corrections based on feedback from the Japanese intelligence as it developed. Nevertheless, the Joint Chiefs of Staff found Nimitz's proposal 'in harmony' with the earlier plan Wedlock, and approved the deception plan for Forager.[26]

Then a snag arose. A colonel on MacArthur's staff wrote to the Pentagon protesting about Nimitz's plan to focus the enemy's attention on the Celebes Sea. Although MacArthur hoped to bypass this area and move into the Southern Philippines, encouraging the Japanese to concentrate in the Celebes Sea seemed too close to his intended operations for comfort. He doubted whether the Japanese would respond quickly enough to deception turning them back into the central Pacific to be out of his way on his left flank. And for good measure, the memo spelled out the skepticism for strategic deception in general held at Southwest Pacific headquarters. It concluded, 'I would like to point out that the deception policy of the Southwest Pacific has heretofore been one of saying nothing about further intentions and allowing the Japs to sweat it out.'

In response to this protest the JSC modified the plan to eliminate specific targets in the Celebes and all mention of MacArthur's future plans. This toned down but did not eliminate the south-west phrase of Nimitz's deception. No one would try to focus the enemy's attention on MacArthur's operation at times convenient for Nimitz. As events developed, no one needed to try.

While Nimitz's plan played down reliance on Wedlock, others in the navy had higher hopes. They expected Wedlock to support operation Forager in several significant ways. They would try to convince the enemy that the thousands of troops training and staging in the Hawaiian Islands for Saipan were actually destined for the Kuriles, after the initial invasion from the Aleutians succeeded. Although the rising volume of radio traffic generated by these preparations in Hawaii could not be concealed, they hoped to add enough deceptive traffic to suggest that the first object of attention would be the Kuriles. Commanders of the Forager invasion were to be hidden among commanders identified as assigned to invade the Kuriles. Most ambitiously, Wedlock might

> by its scope and continuity, create the appearance (1) that FORAGER is but one part of simultaneous or coordinated assaults against island objectives flanking the northern and southern approaches to Japan proper; (2) that FORAGER will appear as the lesser of the two threats to the enemy and that our traffic reflects in WEDLOCK the existence of a greater danger in the North Pacific area; (3) that continuing WEDLOCK through FORAGER's 'D' Day will maintain the picture of a campaign soon to be launched against the Kuriles, contingent upon the decision reached in FORAGER ... [28]

To make the Kuriles seem the largest invasion threat of early summer 1944, while the central Pacific campaign appeared headed for Truk, and MacArthur's next move remained mysterious - these were the intentions of American deception operations in the Pacific beginning in April 1944.

When the Japanese evacuated Kiska in July 1943, they gave up their last reconnaissance base in the North Pacific. Air reconnaissance was necessarily haphazard due to the region's foul weather, and heavy seas discouraged submarines from keeping stations off the Aleutians.[29] The Japanese were left only one direct channel by which to receive information about American activities in the North Pacific: radio communications. Since their cryptanalytic efforts had so far not broken into any high-level American secret codes, they were forced to rely on traffic analysis exclusively.[30] These circumstances helped the Americans in their deception, since by carefully manipulating information over this one channel they could largely control what the enemy learned.[31] Radio deception was the star performer in the Wedlock drama; visual deception, press releases, actual operations and information passed via special agents played supportive but secondary roles.

To set the stage, the army built a Joint Communications Center on Adak devoted to processing Wedlock traffic. By 15 April it began laying out deceptive radio patterns. Over the following months the center expanded into two large quonset huts and required, on the Army side, 18 officers and 40 enlisted men assigned solely to implement signal deception.[32] Also by the 15th the largely phantom Ninth Fleet had been reactivated and began sending and receiving messages from the very real Third and Fifth Fleets. Five numbered task forces of the Ninth Fleet received radio call signs and began sailing on make-believe errands.[33]

The army intended to 'show' enemy analysts five American infantry divisions and almost two Canadian divisions (some of whom were training in the Aleutians for another purpose) arrive at five garrisons. Then through radio traffic they would appear to board ships, form into two assault forces en route to the Kuriles, and sail toward Paramushiro and Shimushu. The ominous message for Japanese analysts would be that the troops had embarked and the ships were under way.[34] D-Day for the Kuriles continued to be the D-Day for Forager, 15 June.

The US Army Air Force also co-operated in Wedlock to simulate the necessary build-up of air strength an invasion would demand. Fake traffic from Patterson Field and real traffic in Wedlock's code between the Eleventh and Fourteenth Air Forces in the North Pacific suggested their co-ordination in the operation.

The directors of the Wedlock scenario used their supporting players to amplify the story sent out over the radio circuits. Press releases to US newspapers constituted one sure means, since it was clear to US intelligence from Ultra traffic that the Japanese often used the US press to verify their leads.[35] The press began stressing the advantages of the shorter northern route to Japan during Wedlock; newspaper stories speculated about what was happening in distant Alaska since Kiska had been seized, somewhat farcically, the previous August. When Admiral Nimitz and Lieutenant General Buckner had met in San Francisco in mid-March 1944 the press was encouraged to focus on the meeting as a portent for the future.[36]

Joint Security Control developed the means to put across information through 'secret channels' directly into Japanese intelligence headquarters. In addition to the access granted by the British to their extensive double agent network, the US also ran a successful controlled German agent network which JSC used to pass material relating to Wedlock, co-operating with the Federal Bureau of Investigation which handled the controlled double agents in the United States.[37] Military and naval attachés also helped JSC to tap agents in neutral countries such as Switzerland, Portugal and Argentina. In March 1944, JSC began a limited exchange of information on the Japanese Navy with the Russion Navy. JSC sent a list of items to be passed to the Russians and a list of requests to the US military attaché in Moscow.[38] In addition to the planned tidbits for controlled agents, JSC planted documents, rumors and indiscretions where Japanese uncontrolled agents were likely to find them.[39] Thick log-books detailing each piece of information, the date, and the means of its transmission piled up in the JSC files.

Via these channels Japanese intelligence received disquieting rumors and a healthy dose of true but harmless facts: the divisional numbers, dispositions, and probable (fictional) objectives of the five US divisions being 'sent' to the North Pacific; the fact that Canadian troops were active in the Alaska Theatre; schedules of supplies arriving in the area in growing numbers; new, ominous-sounding advances in technological design that would allow better use of the boggy terrain in the north; and frequent bulletins on impending major actions planned for these forces.[40]

Wedlock's plan called for air and naval bombing of the Kuriles to increase that spring and continue heavy until Wedlock's D-Day. Surface bombardments by COMNORPAC's fleet of six over-age cruisers and destroyers pounded Paramushiro and Shimushu in early February, March and mid-June, while navy bombers and the Eleventh Air Force bombed the Kuriles 'every day, weather permitting'.[41] Unfortunately the North Pacific weather often did not permit. Criticism of Wedlock later would note that there was probably not enough activity, especially not enough reconnaissance and bombing, of the area to support the threat being portrayed by other means. Accordingly the actual operations were called 'the weakest link' in the operation.[42]

Joint Security Control also loosed numerous straws in the wind toward Japanese intelligence. All US soldiers embarking through Seattle during the spring of 1944, including those destined for tropical atolls, received Arctic clothing and equipment and had to sign a pledge not to disclose this fact. Designers produced shoulder patches for each of the five phantom army divisions and sent 30,000 up to Alaska Department headquarters for distribution. When a Russian fishing ship put in at Adak on 29 April, the crew could see a large new building labeled 'Adak Reserve Depot', and the captain was treated to casual conversation about feverish activity in the Aleutians and a rapid turnover among civilian employees. Behind this Russian connection lay the assumption that the Japanese Navy could be boarding Russian ships and debriefing their crews for information as they returned home.[43]

Finally, early in June the army began rapidly building what appeared to be an airstrip at Holtz Bay on Attu, the westernmost Aleutian island. By the end of July the airstrip, anti-aircraft installations, dumps, supply depots, barracks, and control tower could be observed from the air. This dummy camp, code-named a Filbert, came complete with landing craft, which included ten fake craft diverted early in June from a shipment to Britain for the deception for operation Overload, the invasion of Normandy. Completed too late for Wedlock's D-Day, the Filbert would figure in the continuation of the Northern threat after 15 June.[44]

Japanese reactions to Wedlock would be studied in considerable detail in the last months of the war using ULTRA evidence, but during the weeks the deception ran JSC noted some encouraging signs. The Associated Press ran a story on 11 May which quoted a Radio Tokyo commentator who had credited the US with 'some hundred planes, naval forces and some five to six infantry divisions including paratroops and air-borne troops' ready to jump off from the Aleutians.[45] Soon afterwards Vice Admiral Frank Jack Fletcher told the AP that 'American bases in the Aleutians are established for an assault against Japanese homelands'. Fletcher apparently was not aware of the extent of the deception, for the Office of Naval Communications queried tongue-in-cheek to JSC, 'who is fooling whom?'[46] All support, however inadvertent, was welcomed. While thousands of Japanese troops in the Kuriles awaited a major US operation from the Aleutians, the deception seemed to be working.

While they waited, however, operations in the south-west Pacific in late May preoccupied Japanese strategists. Hard on the heels of the largest amphibious assault yet attempted by MacArthur's forces, at Hollandia on 22 April, the general's combined army, navy, and air force units assaulted Wakde Island in mid-May and Biak Island, still further up the New Guinea coast, on 27 May. MacArthur's goal in this phase of the campaign was to capture enemy airstrips which would be converted for American use to sustain his next leap up the coast, until his planes were in range to support the invasion of Mindanao in the southern Philippines.[47]

When he reached for Biak Island, MacArthur touched a sensitive nerve in the Japanese high command. The new Commander of the Combined Fleet, Admiral Soemu Toyoda, planned shortly to use land-based aircraft from Biak to support his Mobile Fleet in a projected battle with the American Task Force 58. This assumed that TF58 would continue to aid MacArthur's drive along New Guinea. During May Toyoda maneuvered to be ready for a showdown in the western Carolines with TF58. If Biak were in US hands, the Japanese would be denied this site for air support, and their opponents would enjoy it instead.[48]

The Japanese responded vigorously to this challenge. Discounting the likelihood of an invasion of the Marianas, they rushed hundreds of planes from airfields there down to New Guinea, and to the island of Halmahera nearby, to force MacArthur off Biak Island. The transfer of planes in early June occurred just days before the American assault on Saipan. Planes also flew into the south-west from Japan and from the Carolines. On 11 June, as the Japanese assembled a large naval force at Batjan in the Molucca Islands with which to reinforce their troops on Biak, word came of the American Fifth Fleet's preliminary bombardment of Saipan, and the Japanese turned their attention and their fleets northward instead. Their ships concentrated in the Philippine Sea, and the resulting carrier battle was to destroy virtually all Japan's remaining naval aircraft. Although Japanese troops on Saipan, a large, mountainous island, resisted for weeks, air defense of the island was weak after the transfer of planes for Biak and subsequent American bombing of Saipan's airfields.[49]

MacArthur's bid for Biak Island on 27 May thus helped the American deception effort to cover the Saipan invasion three weeks later. In Nimitz's mind this was what the two campaigns should be doing for each other, but the determined Japanese response in this case was a surprise.

Nimitz's deception plan for Forager had called for MacArthur's headquarters to control its radio communications to deliberately hide peaks of volume and precedence. While Wedlock inflated traffic in the north, the south-west was to deflate its traffic as much as possible.[50] This helped to keep the enemy guessing about the next American target, but the overall direction of MacArthur's advance was unmistakable. The Japanese believed that MacArthur's was the main American campaign. Before Forager the scale of the Central Pacific thrust was not clear to them; they treated it as a diversion to MacArthur's operation. The attempt to lull the enemy with radio deception did little for

MacArthur's fast-moving campaign in May 1944, because the Japanese focused on him as the greatest threat to their own strategic resources, especially oil, from the Dutch East Indies, and because they brought to the situation their own plans, which did not allow the loss of Biak Island. Ironically, while they fought for Biak, Task Force 58 steamed north to join the Fifth Fleet for action off the Marianas. Although the Japanese tried to use their interior position to shuttle assets back and forth, position did not compensate them for the size and number of US forces opposing them in the spring of 1944. The immediate threat from MacArthur in the south-west proved more salient to the Japanese than the deceptive threat built up for their benefit in the North Pacific.

Their forces would have stretched farther, however, if the Japanese had not been holding 70,000 troops in the Kuriles 'on constant alert' for an invasion from the Aleutians. Wedlock's most obvious achievement was to convince the enemy of an inflated American order of battle for the North Pacific which led them to tie up troops to oppose these phantoms.[51] Five extra US and two Canadian divisions, generated by radio deception, appeared in Japanese intelligence estimates in August 1944 that had not been in estimates six months earlier.[52] Ultra had monitored the persistent exchange of anxious warnings and inquiries by the Japanese about the raising activity in the North Pacific that spring. While the US withdrew 36,000, or one third, of its troops from the Alaska-Aleutian theatre and maintained its fleet of six ships and some 350 aircraft, the enemy credited them with 'powerful Army forces, surface vessels, submarines, aircraft, [carriers] and possibly amphibious forces'.[53] The numbers of the actual and the inflated estimates of troops can be compared in the following chart.

	January 1944	June 1944
Japanese troops in Kuriles	25,000	70,000
Japanese planes in Kuriles	38	589
American troops in Alaska	100,000	64,000
American planes in Alaska	347	373
Japanese estimates of American troops	100,000	400,000
Japanese estimates of American planes[54]	300	700

Only the highest expectations for Wedlock were disappointed as the deception unfolded. The Japanese did not brace specifically to repel an invasion of the Kuriles on 15 June, Wedlock's D-Day.[55] Nor did they, as the deceivers had hoped, rate the threat from the north as the primary one. They continued to react as if their most pressing concerns were the south-west Pacific and the new, still undefined move in the Central Pacific.[56] A naval message from Shimushu in the Northern Kuriles in May summed up the opinions held there. 'It seems very likely that there is some sort of positive plan for an attack in the NE area in the future (probably after the central and Southern operations are for the most part accomplished.)'[57]

Thus while the deception succeeded in convincing the enemy that the US did have menacing forces in the north, it failed to convince him that this menace was immediate or of primary importance. Rather than misleading the Japanese into reordering their priorities for the threats which faced them, the deception added another plausible threat to an already ambiguous situation.

Through a digest of intelligence based largely on Ultra excerpts, the 'Magic' Far East Intelligence Summary, put out by the Special Branch of Military Intelligence from mid-1943, one can trace the evolution of Wedlock's threat in Japanese eyes.[58] Japan's Northern Army, headquartered at Sapporo on the Japanese home island of Hokkaido, told Tokyo on 13 February, six weeks before Wedlock even began; 'In view of the present ...conditions, urgent measures have been taken throughout the northeastern area of operations.'[59] During March these defensive measures could be monitored in detail through Ultra. Radio traffic from Paramushiro documented a strengthening of that garrison. 'Plans for cannon emplacements and turrets, a "bomb-proof message center, direction-detector equipment and underground works"' were noted.[60] On 15 March the Imperial General Staff in Tokyo speculated that only a shortage of 'high speed [US] aircraft carriers' was delaying the 'projected operations against Hokkaido and the Kurile Islands'.[61] The Wedlock deception built on a known foundation of Japanese anxieties about the North Pacific.

In April as the padded radio traffic began, Japanese troops, supplies and aircraft continued to pour into the Kuriles. A new division and 134 planes had arrived in March, and now the newly formed 27th Army debarked from its transports at Northern headquarters. The air strength rose to over 500 planes by the end of May.[62] On 29 May the US intercepted a Japanese schedule of convoy escorts which expected another 9,600 troops to arrive in the Kuriles early in June.[63]

These Japanese soldiers could expect lean rations while on duty in the North Pacific. US attacks on Japanese shipping had already forced the Kuriles garrison at Paramushiro to reduce food rations by 30 per cent in mid-March, to 650 grams (some 23 oz) of rice per day. This level put the Kuriles in the worst category, 'very difficult supply', according to current Japanese surveys of their supply problems.[64] Some ships reached the Kuriles, however, for the Japanese Navy increased its forces from eight to 18 ships between January and June 1944.[65]

In the first week of June, while the contest for Biak Island drew planes and ships into the south-west, several more amphibious brigades of Japanese troops journeyed north to the Kuriles instead. Garrison forces there were reorganized and reinforced by fresh troops from Japan. On 2 June the Vice Chief of the Imperial General Staff demonstrated continuing concern for the north when he warned all Japanese attachés in Europe that

There has been steady progress in the enemy preparations for operations in the Alaskan and Aleutian areas. It is also suspected that they have recently reinforced some of their land and sea forces there. We want you to be particularly alert for information about this area.[66]

The Imperial Headquarters Naval Staff projected on 4 June that the Americans would attack using a two-pronged strategy: one attack group in the North Pacific would be co-ordinated with another large strike somewhere in the central Pacific, but they remained uncertain about the targets of these attacks. Bombardments by US naval forces in the Kuriles on 12 and 13 June reinforced Japanese expectations of an attack there sometime from the powerful American northern fleet, to which they credited battleships and aircraft carriers in addition to the actual cruisers and destroyers.[67]

Ultra interceptions document the patterns of Japanese beliefs about the North Pacific over the months of Wedlock, but it would be the enemy's actions, his shifting of forces and equipment to anticipate the next American move, that determined the contributions deception made to this phase of the war. The 70,000 Japanese troops and 500 plus aircraft in the Kuriles on 15 June when Americans hit the beaches at Saipan stayed in the Kuriles, waiting for a second blow in the north.[68] By diverting and holding significant enemy forces in a quiescent theatre, the first American strategic deception in the Pacific made a substantial contribution and lessened the costs of victory in the Marianas.

Wedlock became the most studied, most closely evaluated of the American strategic deceptions because it ran while the war continued. Its lessons about why and how to practise deception were still urgently relevant in mid-1945, until the atomic bombs brought the war to an abrupt end in August. Most of the wartime evaluations of Wedlock praised it, citing favorably its communications deception as proof of radio simulation's effectiveness. Some constructive criticisms were also offered. One study noted the absence of efforts to counter contrary intelligence which, through Ultra, implementers of the deception knew were influencing the enemy. Some blamed this gap on the lack of a written story of Wedlock, for without a scenario to work from the implementers of the deception were like film directors working without a script. A second factor seemed to be the newness of agent channels. JSC had been working with agents only since November 1943, and they did not trust their agents' credibility enough to push beyond a circumspect, inferential approach to passing information. To counter specific opinions would mean sending over some persuasive, high-level data, and they felt their agents were not yet well-placed enough for that.[69]

Unlike most of the evaluations, the Office of the Director of Naval Communications studied Wedlock's radio deception and found it seriously flawed. Their criticisms can readily be generalized to patterns in all sorts of deception and merit close attention for what they reveal about deception in general. The report's complaints focused on the various ways in which Wedlock's traffic patterns, call signs, destinations and timing advertised themselves as unusual and different from standard procedures throughout the Pacific.

For example, the code-words used to indicate classification in Wedlock's special joint code could not have appeared normal to alert analysts, because these indicators showed up only in North Pacific traffic; all the other joint codes were used throughout the Pacific. Worse, these new North Pacific indicators appeared simultaneously with the new temporary call signs, and since they were always used together, they tainted each other with doubt. Too much of the traffic came from the three designated deception stations and not enough from local Alaskan and Aleutian outposts and from other Pacific commands. Consequently high-level command traffic outweighed traffic from low-level commands, and the latter could be observed to maintain their typical levels of normal activity. 'As long as an increase in traffic is limited to high command channels and call signs,' the report chided, 'the danger of an imminent operation is not too great.'[70]

Further problems arose from the lack of sufficient ship-to-shore traffic to suggest the transporting of all the supplies, men and equipment a major operation demanded. The Adak Joint Communications Center fell into an unfortunate habit of sending its deceptive traffic to Pearl Harbor not at normal hours when the airwaves chattered with competing signals, but during quiet off-hours, when it was conspicuous. Finally, the traffic levels did not rise gradually during the winter and early spring 1944 (for good reasons, since during this period the deception plan was still being polished) so that when a sudden increase in traffic which had some suspicious qualities appeared, there were few clues in place to allay those suspicions. 'This winter traffic gave the true picture from which the false traffic could be subtracted. When the suspected traffic was subtracted from the whole, the remaining traffic was completely unchanged from what it had been for many preceding months.'[71]

How could a strategic deception which relied so heavily on a flawed communications deception have succeeded as well as it did? Part of the answer must lie with the chronically poor state of Japanese military intelligence, which declined with Japan's fortunes in the war. The Japanese made little headway against American codes, and they failed to put in place a reliable agent network. Their attachés in neutral countries gathered intelligence so amateurishly that the British despaired of them as reliable channels for planted information. Forced to rely on traffic analysis supplemented by information from American newspapers and magazines and prisoner interrogations, the Japanese were vulnerable targets for deception because they controlled relatively few channels.[72] When a significant threat appeared to be developing on their northern flank, even if the picture was clouded by contradiction and doubt, they had to watch it carefully and defend against it because they could not disprove it. The Japanese did not see through Wedlock. A post-war American report noted with satisfaction that 'there is no reason to believe that the enemy knows how or to what extent he has been deceived'.[73]

Another part of the answer may be that the communications deception in Wedlock was good enough, judging from its results, and this is a significant lesson in itself. The Office of Naval Communications, writing in October 1945, measured this deception against objective criteria and found it wanting in many details. Its criticisms outline by implication how the perfect radio deception should be run. Wedlock was far from perfect, and it fell short of its most ambitious goals in that the Japanese did not rank it the prime threat in the Pacific, nor did they brace for invasion of the Kuriles on 15 June. Yet even though mistakes were made in the communications scenario, and the weather prevented most of the air operations that were to lend authenticity, and the agents were new at their jobs, as for that matter were the deceivers, still this 'good-enough' deception reinforced Japanese anxieties about the northern invasion route so that they held sizeable numbers of troops and planes there which were needed when American Marines landed on Saipan. This suggests not that deceivers can be cavalier and still count on success, but that strategic deception can be a powerful weapon even if it is not run perfectly.

Although after the ostensible move to invade the Kuriles on 15 June was canceled the phantom troops sailed back to Alaska, the Wedlock deception did not abruptly end. For weeks before the invasion of Saipan Nimitz and his staff had been planning the next westward step after the Marianas were secured. Nimitz believed that the bases in the

Palau Islands for land-based aircraft and for fleet anchorage would be essential. He submitted a deception plan for the invasion of Palau, code-named Operation Stalemate, on 9 June. He intended to move into Palau on 15 September and he argued in his plan that this target would be as obvious to enemy strategists as it was to Americans. Room for deception could be found, Nimitz suggested, in the rapid timetable his plan presupposed. The Japanese would not expect another major invasion so soon after the Marianas campaign. Therefore he recommended continuing Wedlock through the summer by making it appear that the five divisions remained in the North Pacific and that the invasion had been postponed until mid-September, when the weather in the north would improve. The radio deception should proceed, along with more bombing and reconnaissance of the Kuriles, naval raids, and confirmations by propaganda and special means.[74] This plan became the basis for continuing deception in the North Pacific.

Joint Security Control asked for a conference to co-ordinate the new phase of deception. It began at Pearl Harbor on 10 July, with representatives from Nimitz's and MacArthur's staffs, the CNO's office, JSC, and the army in Alaska. They agreed that intelligence available thus far suggested the Japanese were reacting favorably to Wedlock, and that it could and should be continued. The next phase could not just re-enact the first phase, however, since repetition might endanger credibility. They agreed to generate a rising level of activity over the summer, to peak in mid-September without enacting a simulated invation.[75] They decided the continuation of Wedlock would be code-named Husband - a clever but arguably a potentially serious breach of code-name discipline.

Husband began in fits and starts. The finale of Wedlock had been left deliberately vague to allow for developments in the Marianas. When the invasion of Saipan took longer than anticipated, it delayed in turn assaults on Tinian and Guam and left Wedlock hanging fire. In addition to watching whether the Japanese tried to withdraw forces from the Kuriles to reinforce the Marianas (they did not), Nimitz co-ordinated his plans with MacArthur's operations in the south-west. There two further leaps westward from Biak Island, to Noemfoor Island early in June and to Cape Sansapor late in July brought MacArthur's forces to the northern tip of New Guinea. When intelligence officers in Alaska learned of Nimitz's proposals for Stalemate in mid-June, they hastily radioed him to point out that the ending for Wedlock had not yet been written. No plans covered a reactivation of the five divisions' call signs to suggest their return and a postponement of the invasion. Nimitz then authorized reactivating the call signs on a schedule calculated on average convoy speeds to show the divisions had sailed toward the

Kuriles then doubled back, to arrive at the closest base on 22 June.[76]

Implementation of Husband continued along lines laid down in Wedlock. CinCPAC's office scripted radio traffic to suggest 'sustained military activity'. The Ninth Fleet and the Ninth Amphibious Force appeared from their traffic to remain in the north and more ships appeared to sail north over the summer. The joint code continued to portray co-operation between army and navy. After a simulated fast-strike task force left Pearl Harbor for Alaska on 11 September and made a faked rendezvous with North Pacific naval forces a few days later, traffic fell to maintenance levels to suggest the forces remained in place.[77]

Objectives for Husband had been scaled down from Wedlock's earlier ambitions, so US deception planners could be pleased with the operation's less-than-sweeping results. Husband was scheduled to end 31 October 1944. Between 1 July and 1 November the Japanese increased their troops in the Kuriles by 10,000 to 80,000 but they withdrew all their ships and submarines and reduced their aircraft to 44 planes from a high of 589 on 15 June. They continued to believe in the phantom US forces in the north. A Japanese naval intelligence report captured on Leyte, dated 22 July, listed five American and two Canadian divisions and several Marine battalions in the North Pacific, plus 15 submarines operating from Dutch Harbor. There were in fact no submarines there.[78] Even better, in mid-August the enemy estimated over 1,000 US planes in Alaska and the Aleutians, when the actual figures hovered below 500. In the ten months of 1944, while planning and implementation of Wedlock and Husband proceeded, the Japanese doubled their ground forces in the north, the US halved theirs, and the Japanese persisted in listing four times as many US troops in their estimates of US northern forces.[79]

As the American invasion of the Philippines in October brought the war to Japan's inner circle of defenses, the North Pacific deception entered a quiet phase. Ultra revealed that the Japanese estimated only three divisions in the Alaskan-Aleutian area late in September 1944. A follow-up deception code-named (almost predictably) Bambino, sought to maintain the enemy's belief in those three fake divisions, at Attu, Amchitka and Adak, and to prevent the Japanese from seeing through the year-long tissue of deception, thereby jeopardizing the deception techniques themselves. Radio deception alone kept the three divisions 'alive' over the winter of 1944–45.[80]

Bambino's results justified the limited investment made in it: the Japanese continued to estimate between three and five American divisions in the north through January 1945, and they held their 80,000 troops in place. No ships or planes joined the northern Japanese garrisons, but enemy analysts maintained exaggerated notions of US naval and air strength opposing the Kuriles. In December Ultra intercepts revealed that enemy intelligence had decided no serious operations against the Kuriles would occur before spring 1945 due to predictably bad weather, and this feedback prompted JSC to suggest cancelling Bambino in favor of yet another follow-up deception.[81] The fourth and last North Pacific deception, a modest operation called Valentine, would begin early in 1945. In turn it helped support the largest, most sophisticated, and last American deception attempted in the Pacific, Operation Bluebird.

PERSISTENT ORGANIZATIONAL STRUGGLES

Wedlock was not merely the first American strategic deception in the Pacific; for many months it was the only one. During 1944, when no further plans were proposed by theatre planning staffs, Joint Security Control continued to argue, cajole and pressure the authorities to strengthen its hand, so that it could in turn generate more interest in and use of deception in the field. This struggle to educate the US military about deception's potential, and at the same time to rationalize its own organization, preoccupied Joint Security Control until the end of the war.

Already in November 1943 the agency had begun a campaign to be declared the inter-service and inter-Allied co-ordinating body for deception methods, information, training and devices. By this time deception in the European theatre had become widespread, although it was still considered an offbeat technique by many. Enough American and British officers had been exposed to it to produce a boomlet of demand for deception projects and paraphernalia. The problem, as JSC described it, was that no one was keeping track of what was being developed, decided and taught on deceptive techniques throughout the Allied military agencies. Nor was there an office to co-ordinate specifically between the US and Britain. The result had been a series of gaffes and delays, as more agencies plunged into the deception business without knowing what had already been done or what was afoot elsewhere. JSC provided the Joint Chiefs many telling examples in a report which documented the extent of enthusiasm and disarray in Allied deception research and development.

The British, for example, had already prefabricated mobile dummy tanks and other such devices for the North African campaigns late in 1942, and thousands of these dummy tanks, based on the British designs, had been produced in the US for the campaign in Sicily in mid-1943. Yet two months later officers from both the Commanding

General of the US forces in Europe and from the British Headquarters Middle East Force were in Washington seeking information on what dummy land vehicles might be available.[82]

Examples of overlapping efforts multiplied. For months the British Army and the US Navy developed, in parallel, devices for sonic warfare; the navy's were stronger and more compact, with greater volume and range, but the British version had better fidelity. Neither knew about the US Army's project, done in conjunction with a different, unsuspecting section of the US Navy, to produce a third version of a similar sonic device. Likewise, JSC reported, 'the US Navy, the Army Engineer Board, and the British in the Near East and the United Kingdom have all separately, and without the exchange of information undertaken the simulation of gunfire – with varied success'. When the British Chiefs of Staff sent an officer to Washington to brief the Americans on British developments in deception devices, the responsibility for deception oversight was so scattered that he spent 'three weeks in fruitless inquiry' before finding the agency to which he should speak.[83]

The co-ordination of information and communications policies and training had become similarly snarled during 1943. Army radio traffic in the US did not parallel the navy's and air force's traffic, so that normal patterns for one service could compromise the planned deceptive traffic of the others. Inter-Allied co-operation proved no better. When three American officers, one from each service, who were trained in signals deception, arrived in Algiers in May to engage in communications deception for the invasion of Sicily, they found a British signals, security and deception program already running which did not even include the facilities of US forces in North Africa, let alone participation by three Americans. On the one hand, no one was collecting information on what was available and then disseminating it to those charged with deception planning at the various theatre commands, but on the other hand, other agencies had stumbled upon the 'cloak-and-dagger' projects and were clamoring to be let in on the secrets. The welter of Allied bureaus, agencies and services involved in deception had grown into a wasteful and haphazard patchwork that threatened deception security. Joint Security Control must have proved its argument, because the Joint Chiefs of Staff soon designated JSC the co-ordinating agency for all deception-related developments.[84]

As the months passed without further deceptions to oversee, Joint Security Control tried to insert deception planning earlier into JSC's process for developing war plans. The Joint Chiefs had assigned their Joint Staff Planners the task of deception planning at the highest levels of strategy, and theatre-level command staffs the task of planning for their own theatres. In theory Joint Security Control entered the process only to implement what had been agreed upon by others. During 1944, however, it had become clear that in practice JSC served as a focus of interest and a clearing-house for information on deception which drew the agency's informal deception working group, the Special or Deception Section, into a leadership role on deception issues. Late in 1944 JSC proposed to ratify this informal practice with formal authorization. They asked the Joint Chiefs of Staff to charge the JSC Deception Section to write deception annexes for war plans as they were being considered by the Joint Staff Planners. In this way the deception objectives, and the requirements for implementing them, would be considered alongside the actual objectives of an operation; presumably better co-ordination would result, and more complex deceptions could be attempted. This suggestion won approval as well, giving Joint Security Control its first official role in deception planning.[85]

Since drafts of proposals to revamp and strengthen the deception organization were still being circulated by 22 August 1945, the deception section's struggles for independence and greater authority were not over when the war suddenly ended. The American high command never granted its deception agency the access to top-level commanders and the sweeping authority enjoyed by the London Controlling Section, a fact bitterly resented by US deception planners.

On another front Joint Security Control had better success encouraging the use of deception in the US military. To implement their new tasks of co-ordination and dissemination of information on deception – and to do so in the far-flung Pacific theatres in a timely fashion – JSC had proposed in mid-1944 an intensive month-long training session to produce a cadre of deception specialists. In a message to Admiral Nimitz and Generals MacArthur and Stillwell sent out on 5 August, the Joint Chiefs tried the art of gentle persuasion with an offer no one could refuse. Deception training would begin the following month for teams of three officers, one each from the army, navy and army air force. Once trained they would be assigned to each major Pacific theatre for 60–90 days on temporary tours of duty. Commanders could expect that these deception officers 'would have full knowledge of over-all and theatre deception planning, the co-ordination of deception activities on an inter-theatre and interservice basis, and the most recent developments on devices, techniques, and special tactical deception units together with the availability thereof'.[86] Commanders could either nominate three of their own staff members to proceed at once to Washington for training, or a team would be trained for them and assigned to their staffs. The determination to put more expertise in strategic deception at the theatre level, despite previous foot-dragging by the commanding officers, was clear.

After a month of intensive training in deception theory, techniques and devices, teams of three officers were sent out to various Pacific theatres to indoctrinate their staff officers. The reception given the new deception professionals on theatre staffs varied considerably. At CinCPAC–CinCPOA headquarters in Hawaii the team reported smooth progress and even enthusiasm for their proposals late in December 1944. Nimitz's staff had produced a theatre deception plan in November, had organized a deception group from their existing staff sections, and this group in turn had discussed their ideas with the chiefs of staff of the various forces in the Pacific. Fleet and unit level commanders expressed interest in what deception could do for them, although naturally they were most interested in tactical deceptions for their own impending operations. In particular the 10th Army and the 5th Fleet requested assignment of beach jumper units, trained in naval tactical deception, and special signal service companies to handle tactical level communications deception.[87] These developments encouraged the deception team to report that the Central Pacific was 'ready for the employment of strategic deception', although they admitted continuing problems in the distribution of information within the theatre and with the absence of a comprehensive strategic deception plan from the Joint Chiefs.[88]

JSC's cadres were received with more ambivalence at General MacArthur's headquarters in Brisbane. On the one hand MacArthur had already proved himself open to, even adept at using deception to lessen Japanese opposition as his forces fought up the northern coast of New Guinea. For the Hollandia operation in March and April 1944, MacArthur's staff had made good use of intelligence suggesting that the Japanese expected American forces next at Hansa Bay and Wewak, within range of land-based American air cover. By daring to substitute carrier-based air to support his surprise leap to Hollandia, MacArthur followed the best tradition of doing what the enemy assumes is impossible, or at least quite unlikely. SWPA forces undertook a co-ordinated deception to reinforce the erroneous Japanese impressions. They stepped up air attacks on the deceptive targets, dropped dummy parachutes, sent conspicuous reconnaissance planes overhead, staged PT boat runs in the area, and converged guerrilla intelligence teams on the deceptive targets. MacArthur's deception planners were rewarded for their pains with light opposition to the Hollandia invasion, most of the Japanese forces having stayed further east at the deceptive target sites. Captured Japanese intelligence estimates placed Hollandia third in probability after the two deceptive sites.[89] MacArthur's headquarters thus had only recently demonstrated facility with deception at an operational level.

Indeed, the theatre deception plan submitted by the JSC deception team during their three months in Brisbane was eventually adapted and parts of it appeared as MacArthur's tactical deception for the invasion of Luzon. The team's other recommendations, including the addition of staff officers who would concentrate on deception and the closer co-ordination with Washington's strategic deception plans, however, fell on deaf ears.[90] SWPA's attitudes toward participating in large-scale strategic deception can be read between the lines of a report by a member of CinCPAC–CinCPOA's deception team, Colonel J.A. Hilger, who met in Tacloban in December 1944 with two SWPA officers, Major General Chamberlain, chief of operations, and Major General Akin, communications officer. Colonel Hilger briefed them on proposals for plan Bluebird, which called for a deceptive invasion of Formosa and the south-eastern coast of China in the spring of 1945. General Akin ventured his firm opinion that 'long range deception will not work against the Japanese and nothing other than tactical or day-to-day deception is practical'.[91] He also refused to commit SWPA to the radio silences postulated in Bluebird because 'he deemed military necessity of communication greater than any advantage occurring from radio silence'. He also 'objected violently' to sections of the plan which suggested that CinCPAC–CinCPOA would control SWPA communications. In general the meeting encapsulated the jealousy of prerogatives typical in that theatre, its officers' skepticism about the value of strategic deception, and their lack of interest in closer co-ordination or co-operation with either Hawaii or Washington. As a parting shot, Chamberlain and Akin warned Colonel Hilger that if the US promised its Chinese allies an invasion, and then used the promise only for strategic deception, the Chinese would blame this 'double-dealing' on only one man, General Douglas MacArthur.[92] Apparently Joint Security Control would have to implement Bluebird without the wholehearted support of MacArthur's staff in SWPA.

The situation in the China–Burma–India theatre was even less encouraging. There Americans, wartime diplomats as well military commanders and staff officers, had to insinuate themselves into a British colony, the crown of the British empire, at a time when Indian nationalism was gathering strength in the struggle for independence. British policies and personnel naturally dominated the Indian and Burman areas of the theatre, to the discomfort of the Americans assigned there. Differences between the British and the Americans in procedures, values and style overlay conflicting political goals in the region: the British sought to maintain and extend their hold on

India, the Americans wished to dissociate themselves from British imperialism and identified quietly with the nationalist cause.[93] As a result, the US refused all British offers to create combined Allied staffs or committees in India, preferring parallel but separate staff structures which could maintain distance from British policies in India. Cordell Hull, the Secretary of State, expressed the American attitude when he urged US representatives in India to 'reject all overtures which would indicate to the public mind in India that American and British activities are identical, except in so far as prosecution of the common enemy'.[94]

In this context of teeth-gritted co-operation, the US deception effort in India remained small in size and in accomplishment. Not until late in 1943 did a deception section in India exist to represent US interests. It was run by a long-suffering Colonel E.O. Hunter who had both a sense of humor and an intelligent grasp of deception principles, but it was dominated by the British deception office which ran operations for the whole Far East, and which, at least to American eyes, was lavishly staffed.[95] Hunter's problems with the British, as well as with his own forces stationed in India, demonstrated the inter-Allied tensions there.

For example, in October 1943 Hunter mailed a forged intelligence report to China for delivery to a Japanese agent. A month later he retrieved the same report from the head of the British Secret Service in India: it had 'braved the Hump' into China, where US General Chennault of the 14th Air Force and his chief intelligence officer decided 'the British were better at that sort of thing' and had passed the report to them to deliver to the Japanese. The British in turn sent it back to India, without telling the Americans, for their Secret Service to 'have a look at it', despite its already having been cleared by the British Director of Military Intelligence in Delhi. Equally frustrating to Hunter, General Chennault's chief of intelligence had requested more copies of the report, 'as he had several channels he wished to try'. When Hunter explained that if multiple copies of a forged report reached Japanese Intelligence its bogus origins would become obvious, the intelligence officer 'said he had not thought of that angle'.[96] Hunter used this incident to press successfully for an independent US deception section, still closely co-ordinated with the British, but he wrote, 'it should not be necessary for us to ask them to do our work, particularly in a theatre like China where we have a considerable force while the British have none'.[97]

By December 1944, when the cadre of deception experts arrived in India to survey deception assets and to give briefings on deception developments in Europe, the complicated command relationships had shifted again: the India–Burma theatre was split off from China and the former no longer held operational status. The 'action' in deception had shifted to South-east Asia, which meant to SEAC's 'D' Division and, to a much lesser extent, to American staffs in the OSS, the navy, and the 14th Air Force in China.[98] The team concluded that there were not enough US staff, forces, or channels left in India–Burma to do independent deception. Radio channels were particularly weak because the Japanese did little radio monitoring of the area. They recommended that the American deception role in India–Burma therefore should be limited to liaison and support for the British in 'D' Division.[99]

The team similarly evaluated the potential for deception from China as low, but for different, even opposite reasons. In India the problem was a lack of US channels: no Japanese air reconnaissance, virtually no radio monitoring, and no independent American agents. In China there was a plethora of channels: the team reported that 'intelligence is readily and rapidly passed back and forth across the lines almost on a commercial basis. The enemy carefully monitors all radio traffic. He is particularly sensitive to air diversions'. The difficulty lay in the multitude of enemy agents rife throughout China. As an Ally the Chinese staffs could demand access to real Allied plans, and military security in China was so poor that 'any information given to the Chinese, even on the highest level, is assumed to be in the hands of enemy intelligence almost immediately'.[100] Therefore the team reluctantly concluded that no large-scale deceptions could be undertaken in China either.

Joint Security Control deception teams thus chalked up mixed results early in 1945 when they returned from their temporary tours of duty with the Pacific theatre staffs. At CinCPAC–CinCPOA's headquarters lasting progress had been made: a small deception staff was in place and a large new plan was ready for implementation. In the South-west Pacific, suggestions concerning deception from Pentagon 'outsiders' received low-priority handling. By January 1945 no deception staff *per se* had been designated, and SWPA's co-operation in Bluebird seemed problematic. Further east the war had already largely by-passed the CBI and SEAC theatres and British deception resources in 'D' Division were so adequate as to discourage even US deception partisans from proposing a competing US operation there. Joint Security Control turned its full attention in December 1944 to co-ordinating Bluebird, the finale of the American deception effort in the Pacific, with its organization considerably strengthened by its training and indoctrination campaign, but few felt that an ideal situation had yet been achieved.

JAPAN AS A DECEPTION TARGET: EVALUATIONS

A deceiver is often tempted to give himself too much credit for influencing his adversary's actions. He may do everything right: plan and generate his clues, transmit them to his opponent, and watch while the opponent does what the deception intended – and may still not deserve much of the credit. Deception can only be evaluated as a success if the victim has received, believed and acted on the basis of the deceptive information. From the deceiver's point of view, like looking through the large end of a telescope, he can see clearly what he did to influence his adversary, and he easily assumes that what he did caused his enemy's reactions. From the victim's perspective, however, the eyepiece end of the telescope, he sees many competing lines of intelligence, many sources, many estimates, and many unique, even accidental influences that went into making his strategic decisions; most likely his enemy's deceptions were only one of many factors causing the decision, if they affected it at all. To strive to evaluate a strategic deception objectively it is therefore necessary to examine events from the victim's perspective and to weigh how much effect deception seems to have had on his decisions and on his actions.

For the Pacific cases the frustrations attending such an examination are considerable because of the destruction of many Japanese wartime records during and just after the war, and the lack of translation from the Japanese of what does remain. Only a few histories of the Second World War by Japanese scholars have been translated into English, and even the volumes of the official war history series, still in process, are available only in Japanese. The comparative slighting of follow-up attention to deception in interviews conducted with Japanese war leaders by the US Strategic Bombing Survey in the months after the war adds another disappointment. What evidence is available as a basis for looking at US deception from the Japanese side, thought inadequate, must serve to make some preliminary statements and to frame some tentative conclusions. There may need to be substantial revisions in the face of new and better evidence.

Several factors converged to influence Japanese strategic planning late in the war. The nature of Japan's military intelligence system had an impact, as did some of the assumptions made and goals held by Japanese strategists irrespective of any deceptive information they received. The timing of when certain capabilities were lost that were crucial to acting in ways other than the US deception desired also shaped the result. American deception overlay and interacted with these other, indigenous influences.

The military intelligence system was the immediate target of deception and served as its essential conduit to the Japanese high command. The Japanese military was not well served by its intelligence system, despite the devotion of those who served in it, and this was largely the military's own fault. Japan gathered intelligence not with a unified system, but with three autonomous organizations each serving its own master: the army, the navy and the Foreign Office. Each intelligence organization worked independently, using its own sources to make its own evaluations and estimates for its service. The mechanisms for liaison, collaboration and exchange of information were rudimentary. The Chiefs of Army and Navy Intelligence met once a week when they briefed the Cabinet and then listened to each other's views. Subordinates shared information across services only haphazardly. Parochial loyalties undermined confidence in the competing service's intelligence, and differences of opinion between the army and navy intelligence estimates were typical and at times acrimonious.[101]

As a function intelligence did not rank high in the values of the Japanese military. Ambitious officers did not choose to work in intelligence, and most personnel assigned to intelligence received no special training. There was a chronic lack of personnel: full-time intelligence officers worked only at the General Staff and the major fleet command levels in the navy, and at the General Staff, area commanders' and army commanders' staff levels in the army. Lower levels could choose to designate intelligence duty to a staff member, often the communications officer, or could do without it.[102] Although before Pearl Harbor Japanese intelligence had been thorough and very useful to planners, the reputation of Japanese intelligence among its consumers soon declined until those charged with planning on operations staffs and the high command often ignored intelligence estimates and proceeded to act on the basis of their own sense of the situation.[103] Lieutenant General Suezo Arisue, Chief of Army Intelligence, admitted after the war that army officers typically felt that 'intelligence was not necessary'. Furthermore, as the war went on intelligence officers suffered the fate of Cassandra: because of their unwanted news that Japan was losing the war, they were ignored and information supporting their dire conclusions was discounted.[104]

Thus Japanese intelligence suffered from a lack of co-ordination in two directions: co-operation was minimal between the two services' intelligence agencies, and co-operation between the intelligence agencies and their own operations divisions was similarly inadequate. With 40 years of hindsight one can add that these problems, while more acute perhaps in Japanese intelligence, were not unique to it. Instances of them could also be found in the US, German and British intelligence systems during the war.

An intelligence system this fragmented could be an unpredictable wild card to an adversary trying to play out a strategic deception for its benefit. The ideal in a deception target's intelligence organization from the deceiver's point of view is one he can learn and chart the pathways of influence and information flow. The deceiver wants to depend on his target's organization to function reliably, but not to function well enough to unmask a deception. The Japanese organization was complicated and overlapping, and because it also had gaps, it could easily lose or ignore deceptive clues passed over for its perusal by deceivers. The organization missed some planted evidence simply because it did not have enough personnel to cover its enormous areas of responsibility. Secondary theatres like the Aleutians, scene of the Wedlock deception, got short shrift.[105] On the other hand, occasionally these deficiencies inadvertently helped the Japanese to detect deception. In a 1947 memorandum on the Japanese intelligence organization Admiral Thomas B. Inglis, former Chief of Naval Operations, noted that

in addition to ineffective regional coordination, it appears that there was no regular central direction from either Imperial Japanese headquarters or the respective ministries in Tokyo. Finally, as might be expected from the foregoing, there was much unwieldiness and overlapping. (It is interesting to note that duplication of effort, normally considered a defect, occasionally did enable the Japanese at the headquarters level in Tokyo to detect cases of deception against their field representatives on the part of the Allies, neutrals, or even some of their Axis colleagues.)[106]

Tantalizingly Inglis provides no details on these incidents, but he does suggest that the Japanese scored some victories in counter-deception despite, or because of, the inadequacies of their system. There is no evidence, however, of realization on their part of the major American strategic deceptions.

The inadequacies of their target's intelligence system probably limited how subtle American strategic deception against Japan could be, but they handicapped the Japanese even more, especially coupled with the steady loss of channels for the gathering of information which Japan suffered as the war progressed. The decline of air reconnaissance capability with the losses of planes and pilots, the decimation of naval forces, especially carriers, and merchant shipping, the inability caused by the naval losses to supply new cryptographic codebooks to its far-flung empire, the by-passing and consequent isolation of island garrisons and their observers, the lagging effort to develop radar and other electronic means of surveillance, the failure to crack high-level US codes, all resulted in a shrinking of available channels through which to gather information on the US. While in theory this also implied that there were fewer channels available to deceivers to pass along their clues, the American deceivers continued to control and use an adequate array of channels, and Japan proved the more vulnerable to deception because of its enforced reliance on limited and manipulable channels of information.

US interrogators of Japanese intelligence officers after the war compiled a list of sources which had been perceived as the most reliable and therefore rated most highly. Radio interception had been seen as the most fruitful source. The Japanese wrung much useful information from traffic analysis, but broke into few of the US codes with the exception of the merchant ships' BAMS code, which was passed along to them by the Germans.[107] Impending actions could often be deduced from specific increases in types of transmissions: air-to-ground and air-to-air transmissions would warn of an air strike, extra submarine transmissions could mean air strikes or landings. Radio direction finding also proved fruitful, and the monitoring of US news broadcasts and analysis of news items gleaned insights into performance and production schedules of aircraft, locations of units, and the participants at conferences on strategy. Based on their monitoring of conference schedules, the Japanese developed a theory that important US actions were heralded 20–30 days in advance by conferences between the commanders involved and the high command, and they could point to a consistent pattern of such incidents as evidence.[108]

US deception planners thus spent their resources wisely when they devoted a large measure of personnel and effort to radio deception, because their enemy was indeed monitoring this channel and relying on it to the best of his ability. Traffic analysis of radio transmissions served as the workhorse of intelligence in the Second World War; without a convincing grounding in it no intelligence appreciation was likely to be taken seriously. With the progressive curtailment of other channels, Japan relied even more on the airwaves, and radio deception probably assumed even more importance during the last deception, operation Bluebird, than in the earlier Wedlock.

Reports from Japanese attachés in foreign countries proved less reliable, and the attachés themselves steadfastly denied having generated military intelligence. Attachés in Sweden, Switzerland, Portugal, Spain, Argentina, Germany, and Russia were nevertheless mentioned in the post-war interviews as having supplied information, with the Swedish source reputed to have been the best.[109] US deceivers had tapped this channel with their agents who could feed deceptive information to Japanese attachés, and by mid-1945 the US intelligence mechanisms were fine-tuned enough to monitor through Ultra the planting of a clue with a Japanese agent, its transmission to Japan, and its retransmission via the circulars put out by Imperial Headquarters, to the field commands.

The Japanese Army rated the reports it received on operations from its field commands more highly than the navy, but both services used such information to determine the number and size of air strikes per day, ship bombardments, identification and composition of Allied forces observed, damage inflicted, Allied methods, and Allied reconnaissance attempts.[110] US deceivers felt that the operational substance of their deceptions was the most difficult to sustain given the chronic shortage of men and machines with which to accomplish all the deceptive activities called for on top of the operational necessities. Lack of large-scale and sustained activity undercut Wedlock's chances of masquerading as the main assault in the Pacific in mid-1944. This was an incremental loss, however, not a substantive one which would have 'blown' the deception.

Japanese intelligence took advantage of America's sprawling and independent-minded news media to monitor not only radio broadcasts but newspapers and magazines as well, and they were often satisfied with these as sources of intelligence. Purchased in neutral countries and shipped to Tokyo, analysts particularly prized *Time, Life* and *Newsweek*. If immediate transmission was important, attachés would relay information; otherwise it often arrived six months late.[111] Since US deceivers consistently used the unwitting news media to highlight deception themes, speculating on Alaska's importance or stressing a forthcoming conference the deceivers wished the Japanese to notice, at least part of this information furthered American strategic deception goals.

Remaining sources used by Japanese intelligence proved less effective to them for various reasons: air and submarine reconnaissance declined with the loss of submarines and planes and the reluctance of pilots to undertake reconnaissance missions; captured documents, which they could on occasion be gold-mines, became very rare with Japan in retreat after 1942; interrogation of prisoners yielded little of substance; and on the question of spies and agents the Japanese were evasive but admitted to buying information from international or nuetral agents.

Considerable American effort had gone into the orchestrating of agents to pass along clues and inferences through agent networks overseas or through the British double-agent system to Germany and thence on to Tokyo. Through Ultra the deceivers had monitored the transmission and receipt of these clues, but the varying reputations of agents, the divergences and contradictions inherent in agent information, and the inevitable wild gossip and rumors that were passed alongside good information must have reduced the Japanese intelligence system's reliance on agent information, at least when it was unsupported by other means.

The 'fit' between the Japanese intelligence system and the US deception campaign in the Pacific was close but not perfect. American deceivers played to their enemy's most important channels with deceptive information and backed up the main channels with as many others of lesser reliability as they could tap. Some mistakes and lost opportunities still slipped through: the failure to control the US merchant ships' coded transmissions, when as it turned out the BAMS code was the only American naval code the Japanese were reading; or the relative lack of effort put on manipulating the apparent patterns in US activities when these patterns proved to have been of great interest to Japanese intelligence analysts. For example, Japanese analysts predicted large-scale attacks on the basis of concentrations of submarines, concentrations of shipping in nearby staging areas, and crescendos of aerial bombing, but of these three indicators US deception only manipulated bombing patterns, and then often not widely enough to be really convincing.[112]

In May 1946, when US deception planners were able to read transcripts of the interrogations of Japanese communications intelligence officers, they indulged in some gnashing of teeth because they had not received this valuable feedback earlier during their implementation of the deception, even though prisoner interrogations had been available much earlier. 'It constitutes the ultimate irony,' one wrote, '[since] we knew from 1943 on that such interrogations were being conducted, but all attempts at persuading authority to make data available to us wholly failed.'[113] The refusal to share information which would have given valuable feedback on strategic deception was another lost opportunity apparently based on the continuing underappreciation of deception by some sectors of the American military establishment.

Deceivers hope that the false strategic picture they construct will be recognized by their enemy's intelligence sensors, interpreted as they intended, then transmitted to the enemy planners and ultimately on to the high command, where it will shape their strategic decisions. The enemy brings his own views to these decisions, however, and deceptions tend to work best if they play on the deception target's existing views rather than trying to shift or change them. Thus the 'mind-set' of the target is an importance element in deception planning. To gauge the assumptions the Japanese brought to their direction of the war in the Pacific during its last two years, US deception planners seem to have suffered from a lack of evidence on their opponents' expectations and hopes. In Joint Security Control planning documents and memoranda there is little proof that Americans had a 'feel' for their Japanese adversaries which would have allowed them to speculate in an informed way on how their deception targets were likely to respond to various deceptive scenarios. Unlike the British deception teams which included officers fluent in German who may even have lived in Germany and thus brought the necessary expertise mentally to put themselves in their enemy's shoes, the American deception organization does not appear to have benefitted from this sort of background.[114] There were too few Americans who had lived in Japan and learned the language for every agency which needed them to have them, and the relative inaccessibility of the Japanese language and culture to Americans, compared with those of Germany, was evident in the greater mental distance between Americans and their targets. Consequently, US deceivers made only cautious, generalized inferences about what their target was expecting that could be played upon in deceptions. Yet despite their understandable caution, US deception planners managed to plug their largest strategic deceptions right into the pattern of their target's expectations.

When Japan's initial campaign failed to knock the US completely out of the Pacific war and instead Japan was forced on the defensive, Japanese military leaders determined to hold on to as much of their empire for as long as they could, hoping to wear down the Americans' determination to fight until at last they left off and withdrew. During the last two years of the war, as it became apparent that Americans were committed to finishing the Pacific war, the Japanese fashioned a series of defensive perimeters along which they apportioned their remaining forces. Each perimeter was eventually breached and superseded by another closer to the homeland. The dispositions of the forces to defend these perimeters were decisions made by Japanese strategists playing off the need to protect vital resources in the south against the desire to contest the island chains that guarded the Pacific approaches from the west and north. Some of the same forces assigned to defend consecutively smaller perimeters were also reckoned by US deceivers to reflect the impact of their deceptions. If the Japanese had reinforced these areas to the levels they did for their own purposes, no matter what threat to them had been deceptively depicted, then deception cannot be credited with the result.

The Japanese decision to reinforce and strengthen the garrisons in the Kurile Islands, for example, was first taken in May 1943, after the

US invasion of Attu and the consequent isolation of the one remaining Japanese outpost in the Aleutians, at Kiska. With this last outpost cut off and about to be evacuated in June, Japanese strategists determined to make the northern Kuriles the first line of defense against an attack from the Aleutians. The Kuriles were to become the Northern anchor for the first, or outer defensive perimeter set in May 1943 in the 'Z' operation plan; the line of defense ran from there to Wake, the Marshall and Gilbert islands, through Nauru and Ocean Island, to Bismarcks. Troops, aircraft and anti-aircraft and coastal batteries were ordered north in a directive from Imperial Headquarters on 21 May 1943. Reinforcements complying with this order began that summer, but with the onset of winter weather and the demands of the Gilberts and Marshalls campaigns late in the fall, these preparations were delayed, until in February and March 1944 troops again began moving into the North from Hokkaido.[115]

From February until mid-June 1944 Japanese forces in the Kuriles rose from 25,000 to perhaps 70,000.[116] This renewed reinforcement coincided with the enactment of Wedlock by American deceivers, and thus the deception overlaid a reinforcement program for perimeter defense that the Japanese had decided on nearly a year earlier and which had been under way in fits and starts for months. The activities associated with the deception, including the small but persistent air raids on Kurile outposts starting in January 1944, the US Navy's bombardment of Paramushiro in early February, and communications intelligence that the Japanese understood as meaning that fresh American divisions were leaving the West Coast for Alaska, all added pressure on the Japanese to hurry to complete the strengthening of northern defenses. The deception did not generate the concern for the region itself, nor the determination to build up defenses there, but rather it reinforced the intentions the Japanese already had.

Could Japan have acted in ways which would have fulfilled the best-case scenarios of American deception planners? During Wedlock in January through June 1944 Japan still had the shipping available and the troops in reasonably accessible areas such as Manchuria to accomplish a major reinforcement of the Kuriles to brace for an invasion from the Aleutians. That it did not suggests that Wedlock was over-ambitious in its goals for the North Pacific as a plausible route for a primary invasion. Interviews with intelligence and operations officers just after the war and in the recent past established the general belief among Japanese strategists that the North Pacific could only be a secondary theatre, useful for feints or diversions, not a primary route. The execrable weather, particularly for the vital air operations, the absence of large islands in the Kuriles for staging and air bases, and the distance from the sectors on which Japan placed highest strategic value, in the oil-rich south, all argued in favor of this view.[117] Taking into consideration Japanese preoccupations and intentions, the strategic demands of being on the defensive, the shortcomings of the Japanese intelligence system, and the loss of means to act other than as the deception demanded, the US victory in the Pacific War still demonstrates the important role of the major US strategic deceptions. Strategic deceptions like Wedlock were not perfect, and their failings can be as profitably studied for lessons as their successes. They were good enough, however, to reinforce concerns for areas of secondary strategic importance, to generate additional reinforcements for these areas at the expense of reinforcing actual targets, and to waste flagging intelligence resources in sorting out superfluous scenarios from true ones. The US was winning the Pacific War regardless of its deceptions, on the basis of its much larger pool of economic and human resources. Strategic deception helped to reduce the cost in lives by directing and holding Japanese forces away from the Marianas and, later on during Bluebird, from Okinawa, when these important strongholds were invaded. The history of the Pacific War is the more complete for having written into the familiar story the little-known chapter on US strategic deception.

NOTES

This paper was originally presented at the US Army War College Conference on Intelligence and Military Operations, Carlisle Barracks, Pennsylvania, 22–25 April 1986. The views expressed in this article are those of the author and do not reflect the official policy or position of the Department of Defense or the US government.

1. Roberta Wohlstetter, *Pearl Harbor, Warning and Decision* (Stanford, 1962), pp.379–80; and 'Cuba and Pearl Harbor: Hindsight and Foresight', *Foreign Affairs*, 43 (July 1965), 691–707, 704.
2. JSC 79/4/D, 'Directive: Security Control for Military Operations', 26 August 1942, CCS 334 JCS (8–4–42) section 1, Record Group (RG) 218, Modern Military Records (MMR), National Archives (NA), Washington, D.C.; Vernon E. Davis, *The History of the Joint Chiefs of Staff in World War II*, vol. II: *Development of the JSC Committee Structure* (Washington D.C.: Historical Division, Joint Secretariat, Joint Chiefs of Staff, 1972,) pp. 330–31.
3. John B. Lundstrom, *The First South Pacific Campaign: Pacific Fleet Strategy, December 1941–June 1942* (Annapolis: Naval Institute Press, 1976), p. 84.
4. Ibid.
5. W.J. Homes, *Double-Edged Secrets* (Annapolis: Naval Institute Press, 1979), pp. 85–95.
6. Thaddeus Tuleja, *Climax at Midway* (New York: W.W. Norton & Co., 1960), pp. 51–52,62.
7. Ludstrom, *The First South Pacific Campaign*, pp. 156–9.
8. Ibid., p. 180.

9. Mitsue Fuchida and Masatake Okumiya, *Midway: The Battle that Doomed Japan* (Annapolis: Naval Institute Press, 1955), pp. 129–30.
10. Ibid., pp. 109–10.
11. Ibid., pp. 232–3.
12. David Kahn, *The Codebreakers. The Story of Secret Writing* (New York: Macmillan, 1967), p. 571.
13. Holmes, *Double-Edged Secrets,* p.97.
14. E.B. Potter and Fleet Admiral Chester W. Nimitz, eds., *Triumph in the Pacific* (Englewood Cliffs, NJ: Prentice-Hall, 1956). pp. 35–74 *passim.*
15. 'Deception Measures Against Japan, AD-JAPAN – 44', 9 January 1944, CCS385 Pacific Theatre (4–1–43) (sect. 2). RG218, MMR, NA.
16. Brian W. Garfield, *The Thousand-Mile War. World War II in Alaska and the Aleutians* (Garden City, NY: Doubleday, 1969), pp. 204–58 for the battle on Attu.
17. 'Campaign Against Japan via the Northern Route', JPS67, November 25, 1942, ABC 381 Japan (5–31–42) (sect. 1), RG165, MMR, NA.
18. Garfield, *The Thousand-Mile War,* pp.290–92.
19. Memo for Colonel [Newman] Smith, 'Summary of Radio Deception in Plan WEDLOCK', 6 October 1945, Strategic Plans Division Records Support Plans Branch, OP–607 (during the Second World War this was Navy Section, Joint Security Control, Cominch F–28), Operational Archives (OA), Naval Historical Center (NHC), Washington, D.C.
20. 'Deception Measures Against Japan, AD-JAPAN – 44', pp. 5–8.
21. 'OP30C–OUT–204', Navy Section, Joint Security Control, Overview and Evaluation of Wedlock, no date, not paged, copy obtained from U.S. Navy Chief of Naval Operations, OP–944, Pentagon, Washington, D.C.
22. Ibid., third page of draft.
23. 'Statement of Principles Agreed Upon in Conference at San Francisco, 23 March 1944, Regarding Plan Wedlock', 26 March 1944, U.S. Navy Chief of Naval Operations, OP–944, Pentagon.
24. Potter and Nimitz, (eds.), *Triumph in the Pacific,* p.102.
25. 'Chronology of PLAN WEDLOCK', 30 June 1944, U.S. Navy Chief of Naval Operations, OP–944, Pentagon.
26. Ibid.
27. Memorandum for Chief, Strategy and Policy Group, 'Comments on JPS 433/1 and JCS 806', 15 April 1944, ABC 381 Japan (15 April 43) (sect.4), RG165, MMR, NA.
28. 'Chronology of Plan Wedlock', 30 June 1944, U.S. Navy Chief of Naval Operations, OP–944, Pentagon.
29. American submarines had the same difficulties in the region. See the dispatch from COMNORPAC to COMSUBPAC and CinCPAC, 27 January 1944, reporting rapid deterioration of submarines on patrol in the northern Kuriles. Pacific Dispatches, 16 January 1944 – 31 March 1944, Dispatches and Records from the Chart Room of Cominch, U.S. Fleet, OA, NHC.
30. Kahn, *The Codebreakers,* pp.582–4.
31. For a discussion of the vulnerability of single channel systems, see R.V. Jones, 'The Theory of Practical Joking - An Elaboration', *Bulletin of the Institute of Mathematics and Its Applications* 11 (1975), 10–17.
32. 'Chronology of Plan Wedlock', p.2; 'Memorandum for Colonel [William A.] Harris', 30 January 1946, copy obtained from USN, CNO OP–944, Pentagon.
33. 'Chronology of Plan Wedlock', p.3.
34. 'Summary of Radio Deception in Plan WEDLOCK', 6 October 1945, p.4, OA, NHC.
35. 'AD-JAPAN–44', 9 January 1944, Headquarters ALASKAN DEPARTMENT, Office of the Commanding General, RG 218, CCS 385 Pacific Theatre (4–1–43) (sec. 2), MMR, NA, pp.13–14.
36. 'Résumé and Evaluation of AD-JAPAN-1944', no date, in F–28, Navy Section files of Joint Security Control, OA, NHC, p.12.

37. Don Whitehead, *The FBI Story. A Report to the People,* (New York: Random House, 1956), pp.197–98.
38. Dispatch from Joint Security Control to General Deane, Moscow, U.S.S.R., March 8 1944, Pacific Dispatches, 16 January 1944–31 March 1944, Dispatches and Records from the Chart Room of the Cominch, U.S. Fleet, OA, NHC.
39. 'Résumé and Evaluation of AD-JAPAN–1944', p.11.
40. Ibid.
41. 'AD-JAPAN–44', 9 January 1944, RG 218, CCS 385 Pacific Theatre (4–1–43) (sec. 2), MMR, NA, pp.15–16.
42. 'Deception Operations in Support of the Marianas, Palau and Philippines Campaigns', 8 June [1946 ?], p.4, OA, NHC.
43. 'AD-JAPAN–44', pp.17–18; 'Cover and Deception Operations in the Alaskan-Aleutians Area 1944–1945', 7 March 1945, from F–28 files, Navy Section JSC, OA, NHC, p.2.
44. 'OP 30C-OUT-204', evaluation report on WEDLOCK, no date, USN, CNO, OP–944, Pentagon, p.170.
45. 'Chronology of Plan Wedlock', marked p.1 (paging erratic).
46. Ibid.
47. Potter and Nimitz (eds.), *Triumph in the Pacific,* pp.76–8.
48. Ibid., pp.79–9.
49. Ibid., p.79; Vice Admiral Daniel E. Barbey, *MacArthur's Amphibious Navy* (Annapolis: U.S. Naval Institute, 1969), pp.202–3; United States Strategic Bombing Survey (USSBS), *The Campaigns of the Pacific War* (Washington, D.C.: Government Printing Office, 1946), see Appendix 79, 'First Mobile Fleet Classified No. 1048, (5 September 1944), Detailed Battle Report of AGO Operations', pp.241–2.
50. 'Summary of Radio Deception in Plan WEDLOCK', 6 October 1945, OA, NHC.
51. 'Deception Operations in Support of the Marianas, Palau and Philippines Campaigns', 8 June [1946 ?], OA, NHC.
52. 'OP 30-OUT-204', evaluation report on WEDLOCK, map following p.175.
53. Ibid., and p.174.
54. 'Military Cover and Deception (Strategic)', Enclosure A to CNO Serial 00087P30 of 5 August 1947, OA, NHC, p.8.
55. 'OP 30-OUT-204', evaluation report on WEDLOCK, pp.173–5.
56. Ibid.
57. Digest of intercepted Japanese message of May 17 1944 in 'Magic' Summary, Far East Series, Japanese Army Supplement, 1944, no. 2, SRS–72, 29 May 1944, MMR, NA, p.8.
58. Ronald Lewin, *The American Magic, Codes and Ciphers and The Defeat of Japan* (New York: Penguin Books, 1983), p.143.
59. Quoted Japanese message of 13 February 1944, in 'Magic' Summary, Japanese Army Supplement, 1944, no. 1, SRS 11, 29 February 1944, MMR, NA.
60. Digest of Japanese message of 7 March 1944, in 'Magic' Summary, 25 March 1944, MMR, NA.
61. Quoted Japanese message of 15 March 1944, in 'Magic' Summary, 28 March 1944, MMR, NA.
62. 'OP3OC-OUT-204', evaluation report on WEDLOCK, map following p.175.
63. Digest of Japanese message of 29 May 1944 in 'Magic' Summary, Japanese Army Supplement, 1944, no. 3, SRS–90 18 June 1944, MMR, NA.
64. Quoted Japanese message of March 18 1944, in 'Magic' Summary, Japanese Army Supplement, 1944, no. 2, SRS–42, April 17 1944, MMR, NA.
65. Memorandum for Colonel Newman Smith, 15 September 1945, 'Japanese Estimate of U.S. Strength-Accuracy Check on', quoting an earlier report ATIS no. 327 dated 4 March 1945, OA, NHC.
66. 'OP30C-OUT-204', evaluation report on WEDLOCK, p.169, and quoted Japanese message of 2 June 1944 in 'Magic' Summary, Japanese Army Supplement, 1944, no. 3, SRS–80, June 1944, MMR, NA.

67. 'OP 30C-OUT-204', p.174.
68. Ibid., p.175.
69. 'Deception Operations in Support of the Marianas, Palau and Philippines Campaigns', OA, NHC.
70. 'Evaluation of Wedlock Communications by OP–20–K [Director of Naval Communications]', October 1945, OA, NHC.
71. Ibid.
72. 'Japanese Naval Intelligence', The ONI Review, Vol.1.No.9 (July 1946), Office of Naval Intelligence, pp.36–40; [Ewen Montagu] 'Memorandum for Commodore Thomas B. Inglis [CNO]', London September 1945, USN, CNO, OP944, Pentagon.
73. 'OP30C-OUT–204', p.174.
74. 'Résumé and Evaluation of AD-JAPAN–1944', pp.14–15.
75. Ibid., p.16.
76. Potter and Nimitz (eds.), Triumph in the Pacific, pp.78–80, 'Résumé and Evaluation of AD-JAPAN 1944', pp.16–18.
77. Ibid.
78. Ibid., pp.22–24.
79. Ibid.
80. Ibid., pp.19–20.
81. Ibid., p.21.
83. 'Cover and Deception Plans Period November 1942 to November 1943. Report by Joint Security Control to study CCS 434/2', no date [November 1943 ?] JCS, Pentagon.
83. Ibid.
84. 'Recommendations to further the development and employment of planned deception in the war against Japan', Memo for Joint Staff Planners, Joint Security Control, 17 November 1944, CCS 385 Pacific Theatre (4–1–43) (sect.3), RG 218, MMR, NA.
85. Minutes, Joint Staff Planners, 181st meeting, 29 November 1944, and JPS 560/2, Joint Staff Planners, Deception in the War Against Japan, 30 November 1944, both in CCS 385 Pacific Theatre (4–1–43) (sect.3), RG 218, MMR, NA.
86. Text of Outgoing Messages, Number WARX 76573, Joint Chiefs of Staff 77500, August 5, 1944, with Enclosure, 'Deception in the War Against Japan, Report by Joint Security Control', CCS 385 Pacific Theatre (4–1–43) (sect.3), RG 218, MMR, NA.
87. 'Memo for Joint Security Control: Cover and Deception, Report of Progress, Central Pacific', 29 December 1944, by Captain P.E. McDowell, JCS, Pentagon.
88. Ibid.
89. U.S. Army, Far East Command, General Staff, Military Intelligence Section, 'A Brief History of the G-2 Section, GHQ SWPA and Affiliated Units', (Tokyo 1948), pp.25–28, Military History Institute, Carlisle Barracks, PA.
90. 'Memo for Joint Security Control ... Central Pacific', 29 December 1944, JCS, Pentagon, p.2; Memo for the Chief of Staff, The Deception Situation (Tab A), 27 October 1944, labeled 'Enclosure F', General Headquarters, Southwest Pacific Area, JCS, Pentagon, pp.16–27.
91. 'Conference Between Colonel Hilger and Representatives of General Headquarters, Southwest Pacific Area, at Tacloban--Report of', 17 December 1944, OA, NHC.
92. Ibid.
93. U.S. Department of State, Foreign Relations of the United States, 1943, The Conferences at Washington and Quebec, 1943, (Washington, D.C.: Government Printing Office, 1970), pp.424–6.
94. Ibid.
95. 'Organization of Deception Section', Memo by Col. Edward O. Hunter, 14 November 1943, in file name; 'To 312.1(1) China–India–Burma Theatre', JCS, Pentagon.

96. Ibid.
97. Ibid.
98. 'Report on Deception in CHINA and INDIA BURMA Theatres', Memo, December 30, 1944, Annexure A, p.1, in file name 'To 312.1(1) China–India–Burma Theatre', JCS, Pentagon.
99. Ibid., pp.1–2.
100. Ibid., p.1.
101. 'Japanese Intelligence', internal report based on United States Strategic Bombing Survey interviews written for Joint Security Control,n.d., OA, NHC, p.l; USSBS, (Pacific), 'Japanese Military and Naval Intelligence Division', April 1946 (Washington, D.C.: US Government Printing Office, 1946), pp.1–2.
102. 'Japanese Intelligence', p.1.
103. Ibid., pp.8–9.
104. Ibid., p.9.
105. Interview with Mr Kakuzo Oya, former Chief, Sixth Section, United States, Latin America, England and Southern Areas, Second Division, Intelligence, Japanese Army General Staff, on 9 October 1984 in Tokyo.
106. Thomas B. Inglis, 'Memorandum for Rear Admiral C.D. Glover, USN, on Japanese Intelligence Service in Latin America and Europe', 28 January 1947, in file 'Japanese Intelligence Organization', Series XXII, OA, NHC.
107. USSBS, 'Japanese Military and Naval Intelligence', pp.29–31.
108. 'Japanese Intelligence', p.4.
109. Ibid., pp.2–3; USSBS, 'Japanese Military and Naval Intelligence', p.36.
110. USSBS, 'Japanese Naval and Military Intelligence', pp.32–33.
111. Ibid., p.32.
112. 'Japanese Intelligence', p.7.
113. 'Memo for 20K, Subject: Attached Interrogation Report', 1 May 1946, addendum to USSBS Interrogation Number 431, Lt. Comd. T Satake, Communications Department, Naval General Staff, JCS, Pentagon.
114. See for example, Roger Fleetwood Hesketh, 'FORTITUDE: A History of Strategic Deception in North Western Europe, April 1943 to May 1945', excerpts in Donald C. Daniel and Katherine L. Herbig (eds.), Strategic Military Deception (New York: Pergamon Press, 1982), pp.233–42; J.C. Masterman, The Double-Cross System in the War of 1939 to 1945 (New Haven and London: Yale University Press, 1972), passim.
115. Interview with Mr Ichiki, Professor of Military History, National Defense College, Tokyo, on 11 October 1984, in Tokyo; USSBS, The Campaigns of the Pacific War (Washington, D.C.: Government Printing Office, 1946), pp.82–3.
116. Research in the War Diary of Army Imperial Headquarters by Professor Ichiki puts the figure at 60,000 for total Japanese troops in the Kuriles on 14 June 1944; U.S. estimates of the time were 70,000.
117. Ibid; interview with Mr Chikataka Nakajima, former Intelligence Officer, Combined Fleet Headquarters, Imperial Japanese Navy, on 8 October 1984 in Tokyo.

A German Perspective on Allied Deception Operations in the Second World War

KLAUS-JÜRGEN MÜLLER

Writing the history of intelligence operations is s tricky and hazardous undertaking. The writer is treading on slippery ground full of snares and delusions. First, there is a serious lack of sources; even four decades after the end of the Second World War a substantial portion of relevant sources still remain inaccessible to researching historians. Even more disastrously for historical research, there is good reason to assume that valuable information was never entrusted to, or was deleted from, the registry of any intelligence agency. Even after becoming accessible, the archives would not provide sufficient material to help or hinder the researcher. In the preface to his book on MI–6 Nigel West gives some telling examples.[1] Finally, the researcher has to rely largely on authors who belonged to the intelligence community. It is, however, obvious that writing one's own history is not the best way to be objective, no matter how hard one tries. Moreover, these writers are subject to lapses of memory after so long; this cannot be denied despite the wealth of interesting and valuable information they pass on to their readers.

Reading books written by former intelligence officers on the subject, one often gets the impression that some authors are obviously inclined to overestimate the effects of the activities they were involved in.[2] This is quite normal, not only because it is part of human nature, but also because these writers, having been *au coeur de la mêlée,* necessarily lack the proper perspective needed to write history. These deficiencies are usually increased by the limited number of sources available. Many examples can be found in the relevant literature on intelligence history to prove this, particularly when dealing with deception operations: Ewen Montagu states that Operation Mincemeat succeeded beyond all expectations.[3] General Ismay, in his preface to Montagu's book, expresses the same view in even more enthusiastic terms: deception activities destined to cover Operation Husky exceeded the wildest hopes of those who planned and executed them. According to Montague and Ismay, these operations induced the Germans to scatter their reserves all over Europe, thus preventing any effective defence of Sicily.[4] Other authors, also old intelligence hands, share this point of view. They have obviously influenced more than one professional historian to adopt this evaluation without further scrutiny.[5]

A closer examination, however, reveals that very often such an exaggerated evaluation of the effects of deception operations is not well founded, and therefore not very convincing. Even where these stratagems were 'bought' by those they were sold to, their effect at the strategic level was minimal in many cases. Deception at the tactical level, however, was very often successful. At the strategic level there are many examples of deception operations being less successful or even failures. In some instances deception is counter-productive.

Let us return to the methodological problems which are behind the deficiencies to which I have referred. Sometimes the conclusions some writers reached were drawn from inadequate sources. Montagu, for example, came to his optimistic evaluation of Mincemeat's effects by analysing a small number of captured German documents he happened to find.[6] But these originated either from subaltern *Abwehr* agents, diplomatic representatives abroad or from the *Seekriegsleitung*, which was by no means a decisive factor in the decision-making process at the highest level in Hitler's Germany. He never did systematic reasearch in the German Archives, nor did he ask how high-level decisions were made. From the methodological point of view it is grossly inadequate to analyse enemy documents collected at random and to base one's conclusion on such a meagre sample of sources. Yet this is how not a few of the memoirs and other books on deception have been written.[7] The obstacles in the way of establishing a cause–effect relationship are much more formidable than most people think. To assess the effect deception operations had on the strategic level and their impact on the German High Command, one has to reconstruct the decision-making process, which in Hitler's Germany was normally rather complicated. Background information has to be thoroughly investigated so that decisions behind actions may be verified as truly caused by a deception operation. Simply to confirm that some crack German divisions were sent to Greece instead of being used to defend Sicily is not at all a convincing proof of the success of deception operations. Yet this is just the kind of argument frequently used in those books.[8]

A closer look at how decisions were made in Hitler's Germany during the war will soon reveal that the process leading to such decisions was more complicated and influenced by more factors than simply fake information produced by Allied deception planners. An account, and especially an analysis isolating deception operation factors, inevitably misses the point. Deception history cannot really be written by dealing exclusively with intelligence operations. This approach leaves out factors essential for understanding intelligence itself.

ALLIED DECEPTION AND GERMAN PERCEPTION OF THE MEDITERRANEAN STRATEGY

Here are two examples of how difficult it is to asses the influence a deception operation had on the course of events, and how relative the effect really was.

My first example is drawn from the deception operations destined to cover Operation Husky, the invasion of Sicily, which misled the Germans as to the time and place of an Allied strategic landing operation in the Mediterranean. I have already referred to Lord Ismay's and Montagu's optimistic assessment of these operations (Mincemeat and Barclay). This evaluation is commonly shared by many writers.[9] The view is widespread, even among professional historians who have dealt with intelligence history, that the German High Command, almost without hesitation, fell into the traps set by Allied deception planners. Hitler and his generals were led to believe that the objective of the next Allied amphibious operation was to be the Balkans and Sardinia. The development of German forces was made accordingly, and new reinforcements were sent to these parts of Greece and Italy.

Cruickshank, although confirming that 'what was generally accomplished in the fields of cover and deception … may seem to be rather less dramatic than is suggested by some earlier accounts written without the benefit of the (archival) papers',[10] summarises his analysis by telling us 'that substantial German forces had been sent to the Balkans.[11] Another author maintains that as a result of the Allied deception measures 'two excellent infantry divisions in southern Italy … were sent not to Sicily but to Greece': and that on 'D-Day Sicily' seven German divisions were in Greece and only two in Sicily.[12]

Apart from the fact that such calculations cast no light at all on how German decisions were made, they distort the whole picture. The following analysis might contribute to correcting it.

1. The development of Luftwaffe forces gives a totally different picture. According to Hinsley,[13] the bulk of the Luftwaffe remained in the western Mediterranean around Sicily. At the beginning of July, of 1260 planes in the Mediterranean area, 990 were in the Central part, and a special *'Fliegerführer Sizilien'* had even been installed. In Sicily there were 300 fighters, compared with 70 in Sardinia.[14]

2. Two army divisions, one of them a Panzer division, were deployed in Sicily, compared with a single Panzer grenadier division in Sardinia and one brigade in Corsica. The great majority of German anti-aircraft artillery was stationed on both sides of the Messina Strait. The ostensible objective, Sardinia, had fewer garrisons than Sicily, where the German main force was garrisoned.[15]

3. As for the Balkans and Greece, the *main reason* for sending reinforcements there was not the possibility of an imminent Allied invasion, as suggested to the Germans by clever Allied deception planners, but (apart from general strategic considerations) the prospect of a probable Italian collapse. I will return to this matter later.

4. The deployment of German divisions as indicated by Mure is not correct. On both sides of the Straits of Messina the Germans had deployed two Panzer divisions and two Panzer grenadier divisions, whereas only one Panzer division was sent to Greece,[16] the bogus first object of an Allied operation. Some time later this division was withdrawn from that area. In contrast, an additional Panzer division (26th Panzer Division) was sent to the region north of Calabria in the first days of July. Another Panzer division was garrisoned north of Rome.[17]

5. It is methodologically unsound to compare the number of divisions in southern Italy with those being deployed in the Balkans. The build-up there (according to Hinsley from eight to 18 divisions) and Greece (from one to eight divisions)[18] must be compared with the respective build-up of a strategic reserve in northern Italy and southern France, destined to intervene in Italy in the event of an Italian collapse, plus the forces in southern Italy and on the islands. In northern Italy and southern France an operational body of troops was to be built under Rommel's command which – apart from the units already deployed in southern Italy and the Italian isles – included 11 divisions.[19]

All this shows that to get a correct picture of the deployment of German forces before Husky, it is not enough to refer to any units that happened to be identified by Allied signal intelligence or other means. It is necessary to rely on primary sources such as German military archives.

Many examples of inadequate methodological approaches to the complicated problems of intelligence history may be found. Cruickshank, for example, affirms (1) that 'tactical diversionary threats' kept substantial enemy forces many miles away from the Sicilian beachhead; (2) that captured German documents and interrogations of

MAP 1

'SCHWERPUNKT' – DEPLOYMENT OF AXIS FORCES

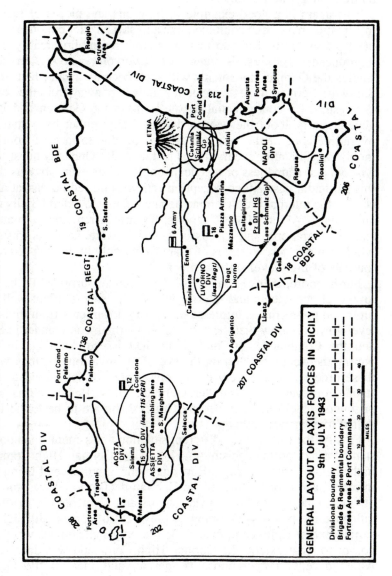

GENERAL LAYOUT OF AXIS FORCES IN SICILY
9th JULY 1943

Divisional boundary
Brigade & Regimental boundary
Fortress Areas & Port Commands

MILES

prisoners revealed that the assault forces had achieved complete surprise; and (3) that up to the last moment the Luftwaffe thought that Sardinia might be the object.[20]

This again is a good example of how bits and pieces of facts and information have been combined like a jigsaw puzzle (but one in which most pieces are missing so that no picture resembling reality can be reproduced). The rest is *guesswork*. Everyone who systematically studies the German documents will soon become aware, first, that in Sicily the German forces were deliberately kept away from the beaches – a result of a controversial debate[21] within the German and Italian general staffs about the way to defend Sicily: either by a static and overall defence of the whole coast-line or, due to lack of troops, by mobile warfare after enemy troops had landed.[22] One may question the wisdom and soundness of this decision. It is, however, obvious that in this particular case Allied deception activities played no part at all. Of course, the internal Italo-German debate on how to defend Sicily never appeared in Allied SIGINT reports, because it remained a matter of staff deliberations and discussions which were never entrusted to wireless messages. Vestiges of it are found only in the respective war journals of high-level staff members.[23]

Furthermore, there is the element of tactical surprise. To be sure, low-level documents and interrogations of prisoners might well have produced the recorded impression, but key documents from divisional level upwards show that the responsible German commander in Sicily and the Commander-in-Chief South had issued warnings in time, putting the troops on alert on the eve of the invasion.[24] It may be that these orders, for a variety of reasons, were not forwarded to some Italian, or even some smaller German, units. Hence, perhaps, the prisoners' assertions recorded by Cruickshank are to be found in the Allied intelligence archives.

Finally, the Luftwaffe's different situation assessment[25] had no substantial effect on the decision-making of the German High Command in the field of grand strategy. Here again, the importance of being well-informed about the nature of the German decision-making process is obvious. One has to know what factors and elements did or did not influence the process. The mere deployment of forces, although to a certain extent significant, cannot be the only indicator of whether or not, or to what extent, the German High Command was deceived by Allied deception operations. To get a valid idea of the German strategic decisions, motives and evaluation on which these decisions were based, one has to analyse thoroughly the whole decision-making process, which is by no means entirely reflected by the SIGINT material available in the Allied archives.

The German evaluation of the strategic situation and of the expected Allied operation, was not *decisively* influenced by Allied deception activities – even if some German authors also put forward this hypothesis.[26] Quite the contrary, it was determined by a multitude of factors: military, psychological, political, geographical and economic. Typically, the German way of making decisions was that they always tried to put all relevant factors and elements into a reasonable correlation and coherent frame of reference – a procedure which was deeply influenced by a specific kind of strategic thinking. According to the German military tradition of strategic thinking, which goes back to the days of Moltke and Schlieffen, the planners aimed at a quick and decisive operation – the destruction of enemy forces as quickly and as radically as possible by one decisive blow at the right place: the doctrine of *Vernichtungsschlacht*. This was thought to be necessary in view of the vulnerable geostrategic position of Germany, a land in the heart of Europe without strategic depth, or natural boundaries behind which an opponent's initiatives could be awaited.[27] No doubt, this specific pattern of thinking and perceiving reality decisively determined to a large extent the German evaluation of the strategic situation in the summer of 1943.

At the end of 1942, long before Mincemeat and other deception operations were launched, the German High Command started preparing studies on the possible evolution of the war in the Mediterranean.[28] It was quite clear that sooner or later the Allies would launch a strategic offensive against the southern flank of Hitler's Europe. Studies prepared in December 1942 and February 1943 had already dealt with possible Allied landings directed against the Italian islands which, in a second phase, could serve as a base for a large-scale strategic operation against the Italian mainland.[29] The German analysts soon became convinced that Sardinia was probably the target of the next Allied offensive. This island was the best starting-point not only for a strategic air offensive against northern Italy, but for a strategically decisive operation against the Axis powers. From Sardinia an amphibious operation could be launched against the Italian mainland eliminating Italy as a belligerent factor, and pushing the Germans back to the Alps, opening a way across the Appenine Peninsula into the Balkans to link up with forces operating in the Adriatic. Thus, they had a good chance of overthrowing the German position in the Balkans and the whole Mediterranean area. This could be a decisive step to win the war. Additionally, the Allies could launch a strategic air offensive by making use of airfields in northern Italy against the vital war industries in southern Germany. To German analysts, all the elements of the strategic situation at the beginning of 1943 pointed quite logically to Sardinia as the next objective of an enemy operation.[30]

All these studies, however, were purely theoretical, reflecting more how German planners themselves would proceed if they were in the position of their Allied counterparts, rather than presenting a well-founded analysis of Allied strategy. The main German intelligence agency, the *Abwehr,* was unable to provide reliable information on future Allied operations. On the other hand, they were inundated by contradictory reports on Allied strategic plans, in which almost all the places suitable for amphibious operations were mentioned.[31] The German High Command was well aware that the Allies were doing everything to deceive and mislead them. In February, the *Wehrmacht-führungsstab* (WFst) issued a warning in this respect.[32] Nobody in the *Führerhauptquartier* could really distinguish between real or fictitious information. This contributed considerably to weakening the effect of Allied deception measures. The German analysts and planners therefore had to rely on their own strategic ideas when anticipating future Allied operations. They had great difficulty envisaging an enemy strategy which did not aim at a decisive operation, but simply sought to achieve an amphibious operation against Sicily and the Toe of Italy. Would such a strategy not carry the risk of being forced to fight one's way up the Italian peninsula in a step by step campaign? Such a slow and costly strategic approach could never bring about a decisive victory.

It was therefore absolutely alien to German military thinking. In this perspective, an amphibious operation against Sicily was strategically unsound.

In these circumstances the documents found on the 'man who never was' provided no new aspects to the process of assessing the Allied intentions which the German High Command was desperately trying to explore. These documents had, therefore, only a temporary and complementary effect, if any, on the German High Command.

The information they contained was by no means the *decisive* factor which triggered the idea of an Allied landing operation in Sardinia. This hypothesis had been discussed since the end of 1942 on the basis of German strategic principles. Studies about reinforcing this island had also been made, as well as decisions to these ends, since the beginning of February 1943, long before the Mincemeat documents arrived at the *Führerhauptquartier.*[33] The discovery of the 'Man of Huelva' and the message he carried made no *lasting* and no decisive impression on Hitler and his planners. After a while they dropped the Sardinian hypothesis and came to the conclusion that all three islands were threatened, together with Calabria, the Dodecanese and the Peloponnese. But finally Hitler and the German High Command became more and more convinced that there was a much greater and

MAP 2
TARGETS OF ALLIED AIR ATTACKS IN ITALY,
10 OCTOBER 1943 – 9 JULY 1943

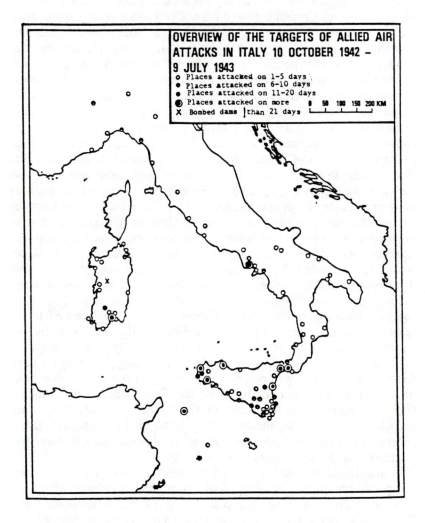

OVERVIEW OF THE TARGETS OF ALLIED AIR
ATTACKS IN ITALY 10 OCTOBER 1942 –
9 JULY 1943
o Places attacked on 1-5 days
● Places attacked on 6-10 days
● Places attacked on 11-20 days
◉ Places attacked on more
X Bombed dams |than 21 days

more imminent danger to Sicily.[34] This new evaluation could have been
produced by Allied air operations, which increasingly concentrated on
Sicily (see map 2), and by an intelligence report received by Hitler on 18
May from the SD, the intelligence agency of the SS, which explained:
'The enemy intention to land in Sicily is confirmed by the great interest

which the US War Information Office is showing in continuous reports by their European agents about the political and economic situation of the island and the attitude of the population'. Mussolini and General Roatta shared this point of view.[35] So Hitler seemed increasingly disinclined to swallow the bait the British deception force had offered him. To General Christian, one of his military aides, he remarked, after having read the SD report and the Huelva Documents, 'Christian, couldn't this be a corpse they have deliberately planted on our hands?'.[36] As we already know, the *Wehrmachtführungsstab* had warned some weeks before that the Allies were staging deception operations and disinformation activities. No doubt, there were obviously several changes in their assessment of the situation, also some divergencies in the evaluation of Allied plans among the different staffs, the *Wehrmachtsführungsstab,* the Naval High Command, the Luftwaffe, the C-in-C South, and the Italian military authorities. But the German High Command's interest focused more and more on Sicily. What then really became decisive for the German evaluation in view of an Allied landing operation and for the preparation of German counter-measures against it was that the German analysts managed to draw up a list of presumed Allied operational priorities. Thus, the last situation report of the OKW argued that the forces assembled in North Africa far exceeded those necessary for an invasion of Sicily and diversionary actions in Sardinia or Corsica. Part of these forces were, according to the German analysts, likely to be destined for a supplementary operation against Greece.[37] The Allies seemed to be planning, first, a main operation against Sicily, followed by an amphibious operation in Calabria cutting off Sicily, and after that a landing against Greece. Colonel Bevan, the leading genius of London Controlling Section, was not mistaken in supposing that at that time 'the Germans believed Sicily to be the likely target with Rhodes, Greece, Sardinia, and the south of France (in descending order of probability) as possible alternatives',[38] In the final analysis the Allied deception planners had obviously failed to convince the Germans that Sardinia was the next target and not Sicily.

In the light of sources quoted above, one may argue that the deception operations, at least, could have had a *relative* effect on German decision-making. Of course, the Germans reinforced the Sicily–Calabria region;[39] but on the other hand did they not feel obliged to scatter their rare reserves both in Italy/south of France *and* in the Balkans/Greece? The German decision-making process was, however, much more complicated. The predominant reason for the deployment of German forces had less connection with Allied deception measues than one tends to believe. In contrast to what is usually the main aspect in the books dealing with intelligence history – the question of where and when the expected Allied operation would take place – the decision-making process in Germany was far more influenced by two other important questions to which the 'where and when' question was definitely subordinated. First, there was the *imminent danger of Italian collapse and defection* and, second, directly connected with this eventually, there was the predominant problem of *securing the Balkans.*

Both problems were key elements of Germany's grand strategy in 1943. Hitler's strategic plan was to launch a strong, although limited, offensive against the Kursk Salient (Operation Citadel) immediately after the mud period ended (June).[40] This offensive was designed to deal such a heavy blow to the Soviet forces that they would henceforth be unable to carry out any strategically decisive operations. Strong German forces could then be transferred to the Mediterranean theatre of operations and repel any Allied invasion. Having achieved such a defensive victory on the strategic level, Hitler would have secured his *Festing Europa* (Fortress Europe) for a longer period.

Within this strategic context the two problems – securing the Balkans and keeping Italy in the war – became the essential preconditions for the continuation of the war by Germany.

The Balkans had been a major part of Hitler's concern since 1939, and in particular since 1941. As we know he had even risked the fatal postponement of the Russian campaign in 1941 to secure Germany's unrestricted command of this region, which became more and more a key position in Germany's strategy. The Balkans were not only the vital right flank of the Eastern Front; they were equally vital to Germany's war economy. Germany was dependent on the Balkans for 100 per cent of its chrome, 60 per cent of bauxite, 50 per cent of oil, almost 30 per cent of antimony and more than 20 per cent of copper.[41] The stability of the Balkans was of the utmost importance to the Reich for these reasons. The role played there by Germany's allies – Romania, Bulgaria and Hungary – could not be neglected by Berlin. All in all, the Chief of the *Wehrmachtführungsstab,* General Jodl, was absolutely right in pointing out that 'the command of the Balkans as a constituent part of the 'Fortress Europe' is vital for the conduct of war because of its strategic, economic and political importance,'[42]

Long before deception operations covering Husky were launched and even before the North Africa glacis was definitively lost, Hitler became increasingly worried about the Balkans. On 28 December 1942 he issued a *Führerweisung* dealing especially with the Balkans:[43] in this directive he gave orders 'to reinforce southeastern Europe like a fortress' *('festungsmässiger Ausbau Südost-Europas')* and created a new C-in-C South-east (Army Group E), to look after the security of this region, especially in the event of destroying the guerrilla forces there, to secure the coastline and organise its defence, not so much against an Allied amphibious operation, but against attacks launched from Turkish territory. The reasoning behind this was the threat of a political offensive by Western powers towards Turkey, which was becoming more and more sensitive to Allied pressure. Churchill made a strange proposal to the Turkish government for a new Balkan League, aligned against both the Soviet Union and the Axis powers.[44] Romania was inclined to put out discreet feelers for secret negotiations with the Allies. Hitler, knowing about these initiatives by intercepted messages, launched a diplomatic counter-offensive, having meetings with Marshal Antonescu (in January and April), with Admiral Horthy (in April) and, at the same time, exerting pressure on Hungary's military and political leaders.[45] Additionally he ordered fresh re-inforcements to be sent to the Balkans: a *Luftwaffen-Felddivision* in January, heavy artillery to the Dodecanese in February, an assault brigade to Rhodes in March, in May another *Luftwaffen-Felddivision* to the Isthmus of Corinth and a Panzer division (although not fully equipped) transferred from France to the Peloponnese.[46] A constant stream of reinforcements was indeed sent to the Balkans. In the spring Hitler gave orders to mount three successive operations in Yugoslavia, to annihilate the partisans and secure the bauxite mines of Mostar.[47] He sent Ribbentop to Rome to press the Italians into taking decisive action against the Cetniks in Yugoslavia.[48] The enemy should exploit neither the situation created by the partisans nor the psychological and political impact which military set-backs in Russia might have on Germany's allies in the Balkans.

If he lost the Balkans, he would lose his last allies, and the right flank of the Russian front would be dangerously exposed. Germany would lose considerable strategic depth, Romania's oil-fields, and the copper, bauxite, and chrome mines on which Speer's war industry depended heavily. The Balkans, therefore, had become one of the main sources of Hitler's concern even before North Africa was lost. After the fall of Tunis, however, the menace to the soft underbelly of Europe had increased considerably. The Balkan problem became more acute, but it was not the dire prospect of an Allied amphibious invasion which had created it. Consequently, the question of where and when the next Allied operation in the Mediterranean would take place remained a problem of secondary importance compared with the main strategic problems of securing the Balkans and keeping Italy in the war.

Allied deception operations, therefore, were not fundamental in Hitler's worries about the Balkans. They did not even play a major role in the German High Command's deliberations and decisions. This is particularly true where Mincemeat was concerned. In February, General Jodl had already warned that the Allies were trying to mislead the Germans by deception operations.[49] The Führer's conferences of May 1943 show very convincingly that the coming crisis in Italy and the internal situation in the Balkans were at the centre of all deliberations.[50]

Not by a single word did Hitler refer to the Mincemeat documents. An Italian crisis would have dire repercussions on the Balkans. Hitler was well aware of the interdependence of the Balkans and Italy. This is clearly shown in the minutes taken by one of his military aides, Captain Junge, during the Führer's conferences. Hitler told his staff that Italy might well defect voluntarily, or under Allied pressure, to the enemy camp. 'Italy in enemy hands ... (this) would lay open the western flank of the Balkans too!'[51] And on 19 May he explained to his generals, 'If we lose the Balkans, the consequences will without any doubt, be extremely serious.'[52] In this perspective the consequences of an Italian defection or collapse would be extremely dangerous, for large parts of the Balkans were Italian-occupied.

Thus at the conferences of May 1943, all Hitler's thoughts were concentrated on the vacillating position of the Duce, the unreliability of his Italian ally, and the possible effects an Italian collapse would have on the Balkans: 'If the Italian question becomes acute' – so he warned his generals in the strongest terms – 'it is of utmost importance to keep the Balkans, otherwise a catastrophe beyond any expectation will happen.' (' ... *eine uferlose Pleite entsteht ... wenn die italienische Sache kommt.'*)[53]

From the end of 1942 until May 1943, the main strategic problem became more and more clear to Hitler and his strategic planners: it was not so much a specific operational problem like the defence of Sicily, Sardinia or some Aegean islands: it was not even the question of when and where the Allies would launch their next invasion, but a question of grand strategy. The question that increasingly haunted Hitler was how to defend Europe's exposed southern flank in the event of an Italian collapse or defection, for Hitler's confidence in Italy's ability and willingness to carry on with the war after the loss of North Africa was totally shaken.[54]

Henceforth, the probable place of an Allied invasion was no longer the central concern. Sicily was where Hitler expected the next Allied landing operation to take place (not excluding secondary or diversionary operations elsewhere). The main problem, however, was what precautions to take in view of the overall consequences of an Allied strategic initiative: the collapse of Italy and the challenge to the Balkans.

The deployment of German forces in the Mediterranean was, at that time, *decisively determined* by these two eventualities. Any attempt to assess the effects of Allied deception operations simply by looking at the German order of battle in the Mediterranean theatre of war is misleading, therefore. The deployment of German troops cannot be explained as the result of any of the Allied tactics. The fact that only relatively few German forces were sent to Italy before Husky (although with a clear concentration of forces in Sicily) and that, compared with these forces, more troops were sent to the Balkans and Greece, was not a consequence of Allied deception measures but had quite different causes.

As the records of his conferences of 19 and 20 May clearly show, Hitler was extremely reluctant to send more troops to Italy. He was not even prepared to reinforce the troops in Sicily despite the imminent danger of an Allied invasion.[55] For a certain time he even tended to withdraw German divisions from the island, which was to be defended exclusively by Italian troops. Hitler was worried that his fine divisions might be trapped there in the event of an Italian collapse. Rommel – full of resentment and contempt for the Italian ally – shared and supported Hitler's point of view.

Instead of sending more troops to Italy, Hitler gave orders for a build-up of a strong intervention force in southern France and southern Germany and, very cautiously, to a certain extent in northern Italy.[57] On 18 May, he ordered Rommel to set up a skeleton staff of new Army Group B for what was, after all, the German occupation of Italy in the event of a collapse or defection by the Axis Power. Contingency plans were made for lightning action. The operation, called *Alarich* (the name of a king of the medieval Gothic Kingdom in Italy), was so secret that Hitler at first declined even to sign the OKW draft directive. A similar directive, called *Konstantin,* provided for filling the vacuum in Greece and Yugoslavia should the Italian army suddenly pull out as a consequence of an Italian collapse or defection.[58]

Hitler originally planned to send three of his most trusted and battle-hardened SS-divisions[59] to Italy; but owing to the postponement of the Kursk operation, they were still needed in Russia. He then decided to disband the forces assembled at the Hispano-French border of Operation Gisela (an intervention in Spain in the event of an Allied invasion there) and use them for Alarich.[60] His plan was to infiltrate four divisions by stealth into northern Italy, while 11–16 more were to follow under Rommel the moment Italy collapsed as a result of an Allied invasion. Ultimately, the Alarich forces totalled 11 divisions, among them four crack Panzer grenadier divisions and two elite parachute divisions. Hitler preferred to assemble the bulk of these forces outside Italy so as not to arouse Italian suspicion and to respect Mussolini's feelings. He was convinced that in doing so he ran no great risk. The excellent road and railway system in Italy would nevertheless enable the Alarich intervention forces to move in very rapidly.[61]

In complete contrast to the situation on the Italian peninsula, the communication system in the Balkans was bad.[62] Only one single railway line of limited transport capability was running via Saloniki to Athens: other lines of communication were running through partisan-infested regions of Yugoslavia and Macedonia. These communication conditions would not permit forces to rush in if an intervention became necessary. Troops had to be sent into the Balkans ready to cope with all eventualities, especially for a lightning action against the Italians occupying parts of this region. An additional reason for reinforcing the troops there was that Hitler had ordered three major operations against the partisan units to be launched between February and the beginning of May.[63]

Here we have the true reasons why Hitler decided to send reinforcements immediately to the Balkans and, to a lesser extent, to Greece. It was not because he took Allied deception operations particularly seriously. Although these activities coincided with the Allied deception operations, they were by no means directly connected or interrelated with them. The deployment of additional troops in the Balkans can be explained without reference to deception operations. Again, it is clear that correlating deception operations with troop movements does not provide sufficient proof of their supposed effect. Those who argue that the relatively small forces deployed in southern Italy from May to July, and the stronger reinforcements sent into the Balkans, proved that the Allied deception operations succeeded in drawing German forces away from the real target, obviously misinterpret the relevant facts. They even ignore the important fact that considerable forces had been built-up in southern France to intervene in Italy, not to defend the French coast. In particular, they fail to take into consideration the motives which the German High Command had for this kind of force deployment.

A similar example of an insufficient methodological approach is the interpretation which (according to David Mure) Colonel 'Galveston', one of the great masters of deception, gave when, shortly after Husky had started, he commented upon Rommel's transfer to Saloniki. Galveston attributed Rommel's being nominated C-in-C in Greece to the presumably successful Allied deception measures.[64] But the 'Desert Fox' was not sent to Greece the very day when Husky began, but eleven days later, and, more particularly, he was not sent because the OKW thought him the only general capable of coping with the presumed threat of an imminent invasion of the Peloponnese caused by the (fictitious) Allied forces in the Eastern Mediterranean. The whole story was much more complicated. First, Hitler intended to make Rommel C-in-C of all German forces in Italy, not Greece. But both the German ambassador in Rome, von Mackensen, and *Reichsmarschall* Göring protested,[65] believing this nomination would be counterproductive in view of Rommel's barely concealed contempt for the Italians. So Hitler decided to send Rommel to Greece. This was the true story of Rommel's nomination to command the forces in Greece. The marshal himself was well aware of what had happened behind the scenes. He wrote in his diary for 19 July: 'I learned that the Führer has been advised not to make me C-in-C in Italy as I am suspected of being hostile towards the Italians. I assume the Luftwaffe is behind this ... '[66] He was, at least partly, right, whereas Colonel Galveston was entirely mistaken. Galveston's interpretation is a classic example of the misleading *post hoc, ergo propter hoc* argument.[67]

This again shows that, in order to decide whether there were any effects of deception operations or not, one has to analyse the decision-making process (in this case the genesis of Rommel's transfer to Saloniki) and, moreover, to look very thoroughly at the relevant facts (in this case there was no chronological coincidence of Rommel's transfer and the beginning of Husky). Simply to combine some facts and to draw a conclusion from the combination seems insufficient, particularly when the facts have not been properly researched.

ALLIED DECEPTION AND GERMAN STRATEGY IN NORWAY

German reactions in the Mediterranean were, as we have already seen, predominantly determined by one single motive: the fear of Italy's imminent collapse and/or defection. As to the deception operations designed to pin down German forces in Norway or even to persuade the Germans to send reinforcements there, the picture presented by the sources is more complicated.

Usually, one looks almost exclusively on Operation Fortitude North and its diplomatic twin, Operation Graffham. According to Cruickshank Fortitude North had 'achieved its purpose and made a substantial contribution to the success of the Allied invasion of Europe', and with regard to Graffham he argues that although 'it is impossible to say what the effect of all this was on the Germans' it 'may have discouraged them from moving troops from Norway to France.[68] This assessment is based on the undeniable fact that Operation Overlord was entirely successful. Hence some writers quickly drew the conclusion that the deception operations designed to cover the invasion in Normandy had been equally successful. But the whole story of deception operations in the Norwegian theatre of war is much more complicated, and started much earlier than the preparation for Overlord.

Hitler's fear of an Allied invasion of Norway was initially caused by the British raid of 4 March 1941 against the Lofoten islands. It soon became a permanent obsession to the dictator. The effect this raid had on him can hardly be overestimated. The Germans had lost ten ships, more than 100 soldiers had been taken prisoner and many important military documents confiscated.

Hitler immediately (26 March 1941) issued a directive, 'Kampf-anweisung für die Verteidigung Norwegens', triggering a substantial flow of reinforcements to Norway. It was the British raid, not so much the improvised deception Operation Omnibus that persuaded Hitler that Norway was dangerously exposed to the threat of British invasion. In his directive he wrote: 'Following the example of the Svolvaer incident other British raids have to be taken into account for the future. As strong German forces are engaged in other theatres of war the British may be persuaded to mount large-scale landing operations, backed by their superior fleet, against Norway.[69]

This assessment coincided with Hitler's and the Naval High Command's conviction of the strategic importance of Norway, a point of view which had been a commonplace among the German naval elite since the First World War.[70] Norway offered not only excellent naval basis, in particular for submarines, thus protecting the German Navy from being bottled up in the Bay of Heligoland, but was also important in affording Germany an unhampered supply of Swedish iron ore.

When Hitler embarked upon his fatal campaign against Russia, Norway became even more important. This is shown by his directive of 7 April 1941, 'Weisung an den Wehrmachtbefehlshaber Norwegen über seine Aufgaben im Fall ''Barbarossa'' ', in which he emphasised once more that 'the most important task is the effective protection of the whole Norwegian area not only against raids, but also against serious landing operations which have to be taken into account for the summer period'. He continued: 'This task implies that the forces already in Norway may not be weakened: in some sectors, which are particularly exposed, e.g. the Kirkenes-Narvik area, they even have to be reinforced'.[71]

All this clearly shows how important Norway was in Hitler's view. There was no need for Allied deception operations to persuade Hitler to reinforce his troops there or to have them stay put. His own strategic assessment, coupled with British raids, had already convinced him to act accordingly. The British raid on Vagoy and Maloy on 27 December 1941 (Operation Archery) confirmed his anxiety.

Until April 1941, the number of forces in Norway had remained unchanged. Then as a consequence of the Svolvaer incident reinforcements were sent in. In June 1941 the original seven divisions in Norway had been reinforced by an additional four divisions. From then until March 1943, the equivalent of about 11–13 divisions were always garrisoned in Norway. Some of them were not removed from there until 1945, others were gradually replaced by worn-out divisions from Russia which were to be refreshed, re-equipped and re-trained in Norway. Generally speaking, one may say that the combat value of these troops was relatively low. With very few exceptions they were either garrison troops with limited or no mobility, or poorly equipped units composed of elderly soldiers, or of soldiers unfit for service at the Russian front. They were, therefore, only of limited capability and not ready to be sent into battle, except during extreme emergencies.[72] The number of coastal artillery troops had also been increased in accordance with Hitler's orders.

From the beginning of 1942 a phase of increased activity began in Norway. Fresh divisions were sent to this area, but the number of divisions remained constant. The British, however, got the impression through Ultra that troop movements were taking place in excess of defence needs.[73] Apart from simple rotation of troops, the only reinforcement was that the Norway Command started to build a makeshift tank unit (*Panzerverband z.b.V.* 40), which was later to become the 25th Panzer Division (a poorly equipped unit at that time).[74] During 1942 the troops garrisoned in Norway were frequently alerted. This was, however, not so much the effect of Allied deception operations such as Solo I, which, designed to cover the strategically important Operation Torch, was executed in August/early September 1942. Masterman, although in somewhat vague terms – 'they may have some effect' – tends to give credit for the success of Torch to such deception activities, in particular to Solo I.[75]

According to the German High Command's diary it was much more the constant threat produced by the Murmansk–Archangels convoys which were frequently misperceived by the Germans as an invading armada.[76] In mistaking these convoys for an invasion fleet the German High Command perhaps fell into a trap set by Allied deception planners. But there is no evidence in the German Archives to substantiate this hypothesis. The order to organise a Panzer unit, moreover, was given much earlier than Solo I came into being.

Nevertheless, in comparison with Western Europe, and despite the perceived threats, Norway was thought to be less threatened. That is why the C-in-C West had about 43 divisions at his disposal, compared with his fellow commander's 11 divisions in Norway.[77] Not even the construction or the improvement of the strategically important Highway No.50 running from the central part of Norway to Finland can have been triggered by Solo I, because orders to this end were already given in June 1942.

In retrospect, 1943 was a somewhat dramatic year concerning deception operations and their probable effects. Generally speaking there was clearly a strange discrepancy between the Germans' increasing nervousness and the Allies' pessimistic assessments at that time of the effects of their deception operations.

In the summer of 1943 the Allies started Operation Cockade, a number of deception activities destined to 'keep alive in the Germans' mind the possibility of cross-Channel operations from Britain'.[78] Tindall was part of this overall deception plan, and especially designed to contain German forces in Norway by feinting an operation against Stavanger. In assessing Tindall, Charles Cruickshank quotes from General Andrew Thorne's final report, where the officer responsible for the execution of the plan wrote 'that it had completely failed to interest the enemy'. Thorne concludes that 'judging by the lack of enemy air reconnaissance which this operation was designed to achieve, it would appear that the operation was failure'.[79] Cruickshank obviously came to the same conclusion which is based exclusively on British documents. Had he consulted the German archives he would soon have realised that, in contrast to General Thorne's assessment, the German evaluation was much darker in 1943.[80] Here we have a fine example of 'invented misperception'.

In January an attack by British MTBs (24–24 January) combined with a raid that caused losses among German troops manning the coastal defences had aroused anxieties about the probability of a larger operation. The coastal artillery in Norway was immediately reinforced. The *Wehrmachtführungsstab* discussed the situation on the highest level, with Hitler himself intervening.[81] The WFst stressed the impossibility of guarding the whole Norwegian coastline. Another small-scale operation in February led to further deliberation about how to strengthen the Norwegian bastion. Hitler ordered the build-up of a mobile reserve, more troops to be sent, and more artillery and small vessels to be allotted to the Norwegian command.[82]

On the other hand, it was quite clear that the German High Command thought that Western Europe was more threatened than Norway by a probable Allied landing. Despite the fact that in July the Home Fleet made some menacing movements simulating a landing against Norway in two feints,[83] Hitler considered transferring the only Panzer unit in Norway, the now fully equipped 25th Panzer Division, to France (13 August 1943). Repeated reports came in of increasing

Russian pressure being exerted on the Western Powers to open the long-promised Second Front. Together with information about a concentration of Allied forces in southern England, this information finally decided Hitler to send the 25th Panzer Division from Norway to France (18 August) as part of the reinforcements for the Pas de Calais section. Only one weak tank battalion and a bicycle regiment remained in Norway. Later, the remaining components of this unit were to be reinforced by a number of out-dated captured enemy tanks. This makeshift unit was to be called 'Panzer Division' for the sake of camouflage. A worn-out Panzer Division was to be transferred from the Russian front as soon as possible and amalgamated with the remaining units to form again a mobile force of substantial strength.[84] All this shows how stretched the German reserves were. The whole story suggests that on the one hand the Germans fell right into the trap laid by Allied deception specialists as the fictitious invasion forces in southern England were concerned: on the other hand, they perceived a threat to Norway – an effect which Tindall had been intended to produce, but in fact was produced by Allied raids or simulated landing operations. The British thought Tindall a failure, and it may be so: at the same time, however, the Germans felt the Norwegian bastion threatened, but did not react as the British deception masters wished. They neither reinforced Norway nor had their forces there stay put: they even transferred the only mobile unit to France. This is in my view a fine example of how complicated intelligence history can be.

The whole story has another paradoxical aspect. The 'Panzer Division Norwegen', was, before larger elements of it were transferred to France, mainly destined to deter Sweden from joining the Allies in the event of a successful amphibious landing operation in Norway. From April 1942 to August 1943, this unit had been built up, in spite of all shortages, and was now fully equipped and definitely superior to the Swedish tank forces.[85] After its transfer to the West, the C-in-C in Norway repeatedly asked for new troops to organise another tank force capable of continuing this mission. But the promised worn-out Panzer division from Russia never arrived. Thus, during a period when no Allied deception (or factual initiatives) had been executed to make the Germans think that Sweden was about to join the Allies, a relatively strong tank force was kept in Norway despite the terrible shortage of Panzer units in Russia. When the Allies really staged a deception operation to these ends in March 1944 (Graffham), a substantial German intervention force against Sweden was never built up again.

Between autumn 1943 and May 1944, the overall strength of German forces in Norway remained practically unchanged. Slightly more than 11–13 nominal divisions formed the forces for the C-in-C North.

Several times, a rotation of divisions took place.[86] Because of their immobility and their heterogeneous composition they were of only limited combat value. Since August/September 1943 no threat had been perceived. The *Wehrmachtbefehlshaber Nord* (C-in-C North) reported in his weekly situation report of 22 September 1943, that 'there are no indications for enemy operation in the near future'.[87]

In April 1944, the situation changed. On 3 April, the Department *Fremde Heere West* (MI Department, Western Armies) submitted a report confirming that a large-scale invasion was imminent. No other place was to be taken into consideration but the West. Allied offensives in northern Europe or in the Balkans were not acceptable to the Soviets. A landing on the Peloponnese could not be excluded as a diversionary action.[88] The German analysts were well aware that gigantic deception operations were taking place to mislead them about the place and time of the imminent invasion of Europe. There were, for example, some indications of operations against Denmark and Sweden – obviously a reflex of Graffham which was mounted in March 1944. But the Germans did not swallow this bait. On 19 April 1944 the *Fremde Heere West* told their military and political master that, for a number of reasons, such operations were highly unlikely. At best one could expect a smaller diversionary operation,[89] but this was thought improbable. Thus, the effects of Fortitude North were not much better than that of Graffham. Although the *Fremde Heere West* concluded that an attack on Norway could not definitely be excluded, as the Allied forces in Scotland and Iceland had been reinforced, no additional German troops were sent to Norway. The forces there were put in a state of readiness. The chain of command was reorganised to be more effective, and some new defensive positions were reconnoitred.[90]

In May 1944 the euphemistically so-called 'Panzer Division Norwegen' had to be transferred to Denmark to be amalgamated with other tank units being sent to the eastern front as the 25th Panzer Division.[91] Just before the invasion in Normandy took place, the German forces in Norway had been reduced: obviously, Allied operations in this area were no longer expected. The Allied deception operation designed to prevent the Germans from moving reserves to France or Russia in the weeks leading up to Overlord came to nothing. The tank units were withdrawn from Norway and, after a period of refitting and training sent to the eastern front, as, according to the OKW-Diary,[92] the German western front had already reached a state of readiness at the beginning of April. Allied deception operations before Overlord therefore did not seduce the Germans into sending more troops to Norway. Between October 1943 and May 1944 only one division (89th Infantry Division) was sent to Norway, but only to relieve one of the other divisions there (214th Infantry Division), which was being withdrawn.[93] One cannot, therefore, confirm Wheatley's assessment that 'Hitler's reaction to Graffham was to order two new divisions to be sent to Norway' (as Field Marshal Keitel is said to have told his Allied interrogators after the war). No additional 'thirty thousand men were standing on their flat feet in Norway with no worthy purpose, when we [the Allies] launched OVERLORD'.[94] Considering that the Panzer Division Norway was withdrawn in May one cannot agree either with the opinion expressed by Charles Cruickshank that 'the effect [of Fortitude North] was to halt the further depletion of their garrisons in Norway and Denmark, thus restricting the reinforcements in northern France from these countries'. Also, no 'additional first class division was sent to Norway.[95] His conclusion that 'it ... seems certain – at least as certain as it is possible to be in this realm of make-believe – that FORTITUDE NORTH achieved its purpose and made a substantial contribution to the success of the Allied invasion of Europe' seems therefore slightly exaggerated.[96]

Both historical examples – of Italy and the Balkans in 1943, as well as of Norway in 1941–43 – can teach us a fine lesson: that deception history is more complicated than we are normally inclined to believe. Intelligence history, and especially deception history, can, therefore, only properly and effectively be studied in a larger context, for intelligence history is more than simply the history of intelligence operations.

NOTES

This paper was originally presented at the US Army War College Conference on Intelligence and Military Operation, Carlisle Barracks, Pennsylvania, 22–25 April 1986. The views expressed in this article are those of the author and do not reflect the official policy or position of the Department of Defense or the US government.

1. N.West, *MI–6. British Secret Intelligence Services Operation 1909–1945* London: 1983), p.XIV.
2. This point is stressed by the Hesketh Report 'Fortitude. A History of Deception in North Western Europe, April 1943 to May 1945', p.VIII: 'It is always tempting for those who set out to deceive and who see their objects fulfilled, to claim the credit for their attainment when, in fact, the motive force lay in another quarter.'
3. E. Montagu, *Der Mann, den es nie gab* (Zug, 1975) [English edition: *The Man Who Never Was]*, p.201.
4. Ibid., p.8.
5. Cf. as example: W. Hubatsch, *Kriegstagebuch des Oberkommandos der Wehrmacht (Wehrmachtführungsstab) 2. Halbband III/6* (München, 1982), C. Darstellender Teil: Die deutsche Wehrmachtführung im Kulminations jahr des Krieges, verfasst von Walther Hubatsch*, p.1614; and M. Handel, *Military Deception in Peace and War* (Jerusalem Papers on Peace and War 38) (Jerusalem, 1985), p.15.
6. Cf. his documentary annex containing telescripts from the Navy's High Command

cables exchanges between the German ambassador to Spain and his political master. Some other documents of minor importance are also cited in his text.

7. D. Mure, *Practice to Deceive* (London, 1977), p.103.

8. Although Charles Cruickshank, *Deception in World War II* (Oxford, 1970), p.59, says quite correctly: 'It is difficult to decide how far deception contributed to the success of the Allied invasion of Sicily', he follows, in fact, the same pattern of arguing in that he states that because of the deception operation 'substantial German forces' had been sent elsewhere instead of reinforcing the Italian islands, in particular Sicily.

9. Cf. for example J.C. Masterman, *The Double-Cross System in the War of 1939–1945* (New Haven and London, 1972), pp.136–7.

10. Cruickshank, op.cit Introduction (s.p.) and p.59.

11. Ibid., p.59.

12. Mure, op.cit p.103.

13. F.H. Hinsley *et al.*, *British Intelligence in the Second World War. Its Influence on Strategy and Operations*, Vol.III, part I, (London, 1984), pp.81–2.

14. Cf. the excellent study based on the German military archives by J. Schröder, *Italiens Kriegsaustritt 1943. Die deutschen Gegenmass nahmen im italienischen Raum: Fall 'Alarich' und 'Achse'* (Göttingen 1969: Studien and Dokumente zur Geschichte des Zweiten Weltkriege, Vol.10), p.138.sq.

15. A. Kesselring, *Soldat bis zum letzte Tag* (Born, 1953), p.220.

16. It was the 1st Panzer-Division which after having been severely battered in Russia, was being reorganised and re-equipped in France. At the time when it was dispatched to Greece it was the only combat-ready tank unit available among all other reserve units of the German Army. In the relevant English literature it is frequently referred to as the best German Panzer Division; it was, however, only the best of the reserve divisions. Compared with active front line divisions, it had not yet full combat strength (e.g. no assault guns, only 83 tanks compared with 99 of the SS-Leibstandarte: cf. H. Heiber (ed), *Hitlers Lagebesprechungen. Die Protokollfragmente seiner Militarischen Konferenzen 1942–1945 (Stuttgart, 1962)*, pp.212 and 216). According to KTB/OKW VI p.1051, it got its heavy tank battalion only in September (cf. also *Hitlers Lagebesprechungen*, p.212).

17. Cf. Schröder, op.cit pp.120–25 and KTB/OKW (cf. note 4), 6/p.764.

18. Hinsley, op.cit p.80.

19. Cf. Schröder, op. cit., pp.187–8 and KTB/OKW (cf. note 4), 6p.771 and 782 sq. Cf. also p.

20. Cruickshank, op. cit., p.59.

21. This debate anticipated the famous controversy on the employment of tank units in France between Rommel and Geyr v. Schweppenburg in 1944.

22. Cf. the report of the commanding German Officer there: F. von Senger and Etterlin, *Krieg in Europa* (Berlin 1960), pp.153–91 and Schröder op. cit., p.158, who gave the best analysis on the Battle of Sicily, and Kesselring, op. cit., p.215 sq.

23. On which Schröder in particular is basing his analysis.

24. Cf. KTB/OKW 6/p/755: troops in Sicily had been put on alert 18:40 hours on 9 July 1943 (cf. also Schröder, op. cit., p.163 sq. and Kesselring, op. cit., p.222). This was five hours after the convoy had been sighted sailing north from Malta, but 15 hours before the landing started (at 8:30 hours on 10 July) (Cf. KTB/OKW 6,p.1029 and 765 sq.).

25. Cf. Schröder, op. cit., pp.111–16.

26. Cf. Schröder, op. cit., p.113; W.Warlimont, *Im Hauptquartier der deutschen Wehrmacht 1939–1945* (Bonn, 1964), p.334 sq. and the material collected in KTB/OKW, Vols.5 and 6.

27. The best analysis of German strategic thinking is Y.L. Wallace, *Das Dogma der Vernichtungsschlacht* (Frankfurt, 1967), who quotes an article of General v. Rabenau in which Schlieffen's strategic principle has been brilliantly condensed: 'Schlieffen's point was the annihilation of the enemy by concentrating all forces in one point, the decisive place. In concentrating the forces he consciously was

running the risk of dangerously weakening his position in other places.' (Ibid., p.373).
28. Cf. Warlimont, op. cit., p.334 sq. and Kesselring, op. cit., p.217.
29. Schröder, op. cit., p.117; OKW/KTB 6/1430 ('Verstärkung der Abwehrkraft im Mittelmeerraum': v.12 May 1943). Cf. equally D. Irving, *Hitler's War* (London, 1977), pp.443 sq., 461 sq.
30. It is interesting to note that initially the British Chiefs of Staff and also the Joint Intelligence committee equally favoured an operation against Sardinia: Hinsley, op. cit., p.6; in Casablanca, however, the Allied leaders decided that Sicily, Corsica and the Balkans were to be the next target.
31. Schröder, op. cit., 114 sq. and Irving, op. cit., p.461 sq.
32. Hinsley, op. cit., p.120 n.
33. Cf.KTB/OKW 5/pp.108, 131, 178, 182 sq. 235.
34. The document ML 1955 CO (printed in the appendix) was, quite obviously, a consequence of the Huelva incident. It was, however, no operational directive or order, but simply an intelligence situation report destined to inform the C-in-C South and South-East of the most recent intelligence gatherings. Two days before, on 12 May, however, the OKW had already issued orders to reinforce the defences in Greece and on the Italian Islands (KTB/OKW 6,p.1429 sq.). These precautionary measures could possibly have been caused by the Huelva documents; but, on the other hand, at least one of these directives refers to a *'Führer-Weisung'* of 13 April, 1943. All this clearly indicates the merely temporary and relative effect of the Huelva documents.
35. F.W. Deakin, *Die brutale Freundschaft. Hitler, Mussolini und der Untergang des italienischen Faschismus* (Stuttgart/Hamburg, 1964), p.404. [Engl. edition: *The Brutal Friendship,* London, 1962].
36. Quoted in Irving, op. cit., p.517.
37. KTB/OKW, 6/763 (Situation report OKW/SFST of 9 July, 1943); situation report of C-in-C. South of 5 July 1943: p.752.
38. Cruickshank, op. cit., p.59.
39. KTB/OKW 5/p.466 sq. and Schröder, op. cit., p.116 sq.
40. It actually took place in the beginning of July (5–11 July, 1943); Cf. Schröder op. cit., p.51 sq., 185 sq. Hitler had postponed Operation Citadel in case the Italian generals and politicians were staging a mass defection while his back was turned and he was occupied by the operation at the Russian front.
41. Cf. OKW/KTB, 6/p.1612 sq.
42. Ibid.
43. W. Hubatsch(ed), *Fuehrerweisungen: Hitlers Weisungen für die Kriegführung* (Frankfurt, 1962), Weisung no.47, p.176 sq. Cf. also KTB/OKW 6/p.1612 sq.
44. Cf. Irving, op. cit., p.491.
45. A Hillgruber(ed). *Staatsmänner und Diplomaten bei Hitler,* Vol II. (Frankfurt, 1970); Cf. also A. Hillgruber, *Hitler, König Carol und Marschall Antonescu* (Wiesbaden, 1954).
46. Cf. KTB/OKW 6/p.1614, 5/14, 5/230 Cf. also Schröder, op. cit., p.176. As to the 1st Panzer Division, see note 16 above.
47. Cf. KTB/OKW 6/p.1612 sa. 5/196, 215 sq. 240, 255.
48. Irving, op. cit., p.493 (Ribbentrop and Mussolini met late in February).
49. Cf. note 32.
50. Heiber (ed), *Hitlers Lagebesprechungen;* conferences of 19, 20 and 21 May 1943, pp.205–250. During these conferences Hitler did not refer by a single word to the Huelva documents.
51. Quote in Irving, op. cit., p.519.
52. Heiber (ed). op. cit., p.205.
53. Ibid., p.231.
54. All the relevant sources have been analysed by Schröder, op. cit.
55. Heiber (ed), op. cit., pp. 224, 228.
56. Ibid., p.228 and Schröder, op. cit., 176 sq. cf. also Heiber (ed) op. cit., p.237.

57. Schröder, op. cit., p.176.
58. Cf. Schröder, op. cit., pp.176–95 and OKW/KTB 6/ 1606 sq. 1612 sq. 1561 sq.
59. Cf. Irving, op. cit., p.521, Heiber (ed), op. cit., p.207.
60. Cf. Schröder, op. cit., p.179 sq.
61. Heiber (ed), op. cit., p.207.
62. Cf. OKW/KTB 5/p.1612 sq. and Heiber (ed), op. cit., pp.217 and 219.
63. IKW/KTB 6/p. 1613 and 5/pp.168 and 694.
64. Mure, op. cit., p.103.
65. OKW/KTB, 6/p. 805 (July 19, 1943): 'Auf Vorstellungen des Reichsmarschalls und des deutschen Botschafters Rom hin wird dagegen von der Absicht, dem Duce den GFM Rommel als deutschen Oberbefehlshaber anzukündigen, Abstand genommen'. Cf. also OKW/KTB 6/p.815. In contrast to what Mure (op. cit.) wrote, Rommel's HQ was not in Athens, but in Soloniki.
66. Quoted in Irving, op. cit., p.540.
67. D. Mure later corrected the version printed in his book: it was his own interpretation rather than that of Colonel Galveston (D. Mure to the author, April 1986).
68. Cruickshank, op. cit., pp.113 and 137.
69. Cf. OKW/KIB I/346 and 247 (entries of 6 and 8 May 1941); according to this about 160 coastal batteries were to be installed in Norway in addition to the already existing ones.
    OKW/KTB 2/1007 sq. The Kampfanweisung begins with the sentences: 'Nach dem Vorgang von Svolvaer ist auch in Zukunft mit dem Versuch englischer Handstreiche gegen die norwegische Kuste zu rechnen. Die Bindung starker deutscher Kräfte und anderen Fronten kann überdies den Engländern den Anreiz geben, gestützt auf die überlegene Flotte, grössere Landungsunternehmungen gegen Norwegen anzusetzen'.
70. Cf. the books of Captain GN Edward Wegener which had a tremendous influence in the German strategic thinking in the inter-war period, especially in the Navy: cf. C. – A. Gemzell, *Raeder, Hitler und Skandinavien. Der Kampf für einen maritimen Operationsplan* (Lund, 1965).
71. OKW/KTB 2/1011.
72. Cf. OKW/KTB 6/1559.
73. Cf. Hinsley, Vol.II p.95.
74. OKW/KTB 2/388: Gliederung Norwegen' (28 April, 1941); cf. also OKW/KTB 4/ 1298 sq: 'Führerbefehl vom 13. September 1942 betr. Ablösung abgekämpfter Divisionen aus dem Osten,' esp. No.8: 'Insbesondere können ... 3 Infanteriedivisionen ... aus Norwegen ... gegen drei abgekämpfte Divisionen aus dem Bereich der Heeresgruppe Nord ausgetauscht werden'.
75. Masterman, op.cit., pp.109–10.
76. OKW/KTB 3/125 Und 4/1262 sq.: OKW-Weisung v. 14. December 1941 betr. Küstenverteidigung. 4/1271; 4/1292; between January and May 1942 a strong German Task Force, the *Tirpitz, Admiral Scheer, Admiral Hipper* and *Prinz Eugen* together with destroyers and 20 U-boats, were concentrated in Norwegian waters. (OKW/KTB 3/124. Cf. also Hinsley, op.cit., Vol.II, p.175, 480).
77. Cf. the order of battle of the German Army 1942: OKW/KTB 4/1253–1399. esp. 1398.
78. Cruickshank, op.cit., p.61 sq.
79. Ibid., pp.80–2.
80. Cf. Hinsley, op.cit., Vol.II, p.526: Although the ENIGMA had by then established that the German anxiety about Allied landings in Norway was again on the increase, the OIC was unaware that the main reason why she (the *Tirpitz*) was retained in Trondheim was Hitler's obsession with the defence of Norway.'
81. OKW/KTB 5/79.
82. OKW/KTB 5/129.
83. Hinsley, op.cit., Vol.II, p.252.
84. OKW/KTB 6/944, 976, 1037; 983: 'Sobald die Ostlage es erlaubt, soll eine abgekäpfte Pz-Dv. aus dem Osten nach Norwegen zugeführt werden.'. Cf. 6/1075

22 September 1943 the WFST issued an order to the C-in-C North to equip the Panzerdivision 'Norwegen' with bicycles and trucks so that the unit could be regarded as a mobile force (6/1129).

85. It took about a year and a half to equip the unit fully (OKW/KTB 8/Nachtrag IV/1, B p. 27 sq. and 37: evaluation of the Swedish Army by the WFst.
86. Cf. notes 71 and 81; cf. also OKW/KTB 7/918 (forces deployed in Norway); 7/117 sq.
87. OKW/KTB 6/1129.
88. OKW/KTB 7/297 sq.
89. OKW/KTB 7/297 sq.
90. OKW/KTB 7/913.
91. OKW/KTB 7/918 and 8/27 sq. also 7/913.
92. OKW/KTB 7/299: 'Die wesentlichen Massnahmen zur Verstärkung der drei Fronten des OB West waren bereits im Winter 1943–44 durchgeführt. *Daher hatte der Westen bereits Anfang April seine volle Verteidigungsstärke erreicht.* Da der erwartete Angriff sich wider Erwarten noch hinauszögerte, konnte die Zeit genützt werden, um die Abwehrkraft des Westen noch weiter zu steigern'. According to this timing on the German side, the planning of Fortitude North's scenario was entirely mistaken: cf. Cruickshank, op.cit. p.100: 'If the Germans were taken by Fortitude North, they might lay their plans for the defence of France on the assumption that the Allied cross-channel attack would come six weeks later than was actually intended.'
93. According to the OKW/KTB 6/731 and 7/918 the following movements of troops were made between 7 July 1943, 1 May 1944, and 16 September 1944.

	Total
Div.at July 43: 196./214./280./230./270./199./14.Lw/702./ ./269./274./710./	12
Div.at Oct.43: 196./214./280./230./270./199.14Lw/702./ /295./269./274./710./	13
Div.at May 44: 196.***/280./280./270./199./14.Lw/702./295./274./710./PzN*/89.**	13
Div.at Sept.44: –/–/280./230./270./199./14.Lw/702./295./269./274./710./	10

* transferred in May
** transferred in June (14 June 44)
*** transferred in July (2 July

94. Dennis Wheatley, *The Deception Planners* (London, 1980), p.179.
95. Cruickshank, op.cit., p.113; no reference could be found of a division transferred to Norway in the middle of May.
96. Cruickshank, op.cit., p.113.

The Success of Operation Fortitude: Hesketh's History of Strategic Deception

T.L. CUBBAGE

In February 1949 Colonel Roger Fleetwood Hesketh of the British Army put the finishing touches to the preface of one of the most remarkable historical manuscripts of the Second World War. Fifty copies were printed and stamped TOP SECRET. Colonel Hesketh's manuscript, 'FORTITUDE: A History of Strategic Deception in North Western Europe – April, 1943 to May, 1945', is the definitive history of how the deception operation Fortitude South was accomplished by a handful of *Abwehr* double agents under the control of Britain's MI5 in support of the deception operations plans of Ops (B) at SHAEF. The manuscript has remained unpublished for far too long. It needs to be known and talked about.[1]

But first a word about Colonel Hesketh. Born in July 1902 and educated at Eton and Christ Church, Oxford, he joined the Duke of Lancaster's Own Yeomanry in 1922. Called to the Bar in 1928, he practiced law until 1939. He served in the British Army from 1939 to 1945.[2] After the war Colonel Hesketh spent three years preparing the official history of Fortitude which was part of Bodyguard, the theater-wide deception operation.[3]

In 1976, after the disclosures concerning controlled agents and their use for counter-espionage and deception purposes by J.C. Masterman in *The Double-Cross System in the War of 1939 to 1945* (1972), Hesketh's manuscript was declassified, and the author duly received official clearance for publication.

The purpose of this article is to review Roger Hesketh's manuscript and to recall its existence to the attention of the intelligence and military history communities. Certainly no history of intelligence, deception or surprise in regard to the D-Day invasion of Normandy can be complete without reference to this critical source document.

Perhaps the best way to describe it is simply to let the reader see Hesketh's own Preface.[4] 'FORTITUDE: A History of Strategic Deception' begins with four lines from the *Essay on Vainglory* by Francis Bacon.[5] It continues:

In his report to the Combined Chiefs of Staff on the operations in Europe of the Allied Expeditionary Force, General Eisenhower remarked: 'Lack of infantry was the most important cause of the enemy's defeat on Normandy, and his failure to remedy this weakness was due primarily to the success of Allied threat leveled against the Pas-de-Calais. This threat, which had proved of so much value in misleading the enemy as to the true objectives of our invasion preparations, was maintained after 6th June, and it served most effectively to pin down the German Fifteenth Army east of the Seine while we built up our strength in the lodgement area to the West. I cannot overemphasize the decisive value of this most successful threat, which paid enormous dividends, both at the time of the assault and during the operations of the two succeeding months. The German Fifteenth Army, which, if committed to battle in June or July, might possibly have defeated us by sheer weight of numbers, remained inoperative during the critical period of the campaign, and only when the break-through had been achieved were its infantry divisions brought west across the Seine – too late to have any effect upon the course of victory.' This report seeks to explain why the Germans were persuaded to make such a fatal miscalculation. The interrogation of senior German commanders and the examination of captured documents have revealed with remarkable clarity the causes of our success.

FORTITUDE was the code name given to a series of deceptive operations carried out in support of the invasion. The present narrative opens with the appointment of General Morgan as Chief of Staff to the Supreme Commander Designate in April 1943 and is continued until the end of the war with Germany.

A variety of methods were employed to deceive the Germans. Some succeeded, others failed. It has not been thought necessary to spend a great deal of time in examining the methods which did not achieve their object. These have been studied in so far as it enables us to understand why they failed.

Where the ground has already been covered in an existing report, and this applies mainly to the technical aspects of deception, repetition has been avoided, a reference to the relevant report [by J.C. Masterman and others] being given.

It is always tempting for those who set out to deceive and who see their objects fulfilled, to claim the credit for their attainment when, in fact, the motive lay in another quarter. Every effort has been made to complete the chain of cause and effect so that the reader can judge for himself to what extent the Germans were influenced by the action of Allied deceivers and to what extent they were impelled by other considerations. At all times the writer has kept before him the boast of Æesop's fly as he sat upon the axle-tree. – R.F. Hesketh, February 1949.[6]

It is appropriate at this point to put strategic deception in North-West Europe into an organizational context.

At the Symbol Conference held at Casablanca in January 1943, Prime Minister Churchill and President Roosevelt decided that the Combined Commanders' planning staff organized early in 1942 should be increased by the addition of American personnel and that the entire staff should operate under the direction of a Supreme Commander, or a deputy until the Supreme Commander was appointed.[7] The enlarged staff was established in April 1943. Lieutenant-General Frederick E. Morgan of the British Army took charge of the staff as the senior planner with the title of Chief of Staff to the Supreme Allied Commander (Designate). Morgan named his staff COSSAC, after the initials of his title, and on 17 April 1943 the first COSSAC meeting was held. Its task was simply to plan and execute 'a full scale assault against the Continent in 1944, as early as possible'.[8]

When General Morgan's COSSAC staff was set up in April 1943, a section was formed within the G–3 staff, known as Ops (B), under the command of Lieutenant-Colonel John V.B. Jervis-Reid, to deal with deception. At the same time Lieutenant-Colonel Roger F. Hesketh was posted to Ops (B) and given the task of dealing with any part of deception operations which would be implemented by the controlled leakage of information – a process called 'Special Means'.[9]

As General Morgan at COSSAC had no troops of his own, he was obliged to enlist the help of the appropriate fighting service or other outside agencies for the execution of any deception plan. For controlled leakage, all the information which COSSAC wished to pass to the Germans was co-ordinated both with the W Board and the London Controlling Section.[10]

The W Board was an informal committee established in July 1940. Its members were the Army Director of Military Intelligence (DMI), the Director of Naval Intelligence (DNI), the RAF Director of Intelligence (D of I), the head of B Division of MI5, and the Lord President of the Council (who dealt with the civilian affairs). Although not a true member of the Board, John Cavendish-Bentinck of the Foreign Office (head of JIC), met with it for co-ordination purposes as required.[11] The purpose of the W Board was to approve information for relay to the Germans via controlled agent channels. Concerned initially with data to be used for counter-espionage purposes, the

Board later also passed on the question of whether particular agents would be used for deception purposes.[12] During the course of the war, the W Board met only 15 times, usually on a quarterly basis.[13] On 26 September 1940 the Board established the W Section as a working group to handle the detail work of the Board.[14]

In January 1941 the W Section was reorganized and renamed the Twenty Committee (also known as the XX – or Double-Cross Committee).[15] Still a sub-committee of the W Board, it included representatives from the War Office, Home Forces, Home Defence Executive, Air Ministry Intelligence, NID, MI6, Turner's Department in the Air Ministry (dummy airfields and targets), and MI5 (which provided the chairman and also the secretary).[16] Its function was to act as the clearing house for all the true and false information that was being passed to the Germans through *Abwehr* double agents acting under the control of the British.[17] The Twenty Committee met regularly, usually on Wednesdays, first at Wormwood Scrubs (headquarters of MI5) and later in the basement of the Admiralty Citadel.[18] The Committee met first on 2 January 1941, and last on 10 May 1945, holding some 226 meetings during the course of the war.[19]

At the start of the war the Inter Service Security Board was responsible for British deception planning. In October 1940 Colonel Oliver Stanley was appointed Controlling Officer for Deception and in April 1941 Colonel Stanley and his deception planning function was transferred to Prime Minister Churchill's Joint Planning Staff (JPS).[20] In June 1942 the deception planning function was reorganized, renamed the London Controlling Section (LCS), and placed under the command of Colonel John Henry Bevan.[21] The new LCS continued to serve as part of the JPS in the Prime Minister's underground headquarters at Whitehall.[22] In addition to Bevan and his deputy, Colonel Ronald Wingate, there were seven others on the LCS staff.[23] Working directly with the Prime Minister and the Combined Chiefs of Staff (CCS),[24] the LCS controlled British deception world-wide and was responsible for theater-wide deception plans which were approved by the CCS.[25]

Subordinate to LCS was the Twist Committee, an operational group whose task it was to work both with the Foreign Office and the B Department of MI5 to implement those parts of the various LCS deception plans that had to be put across by the controlled leakage of information.[26]

As it turned out, the only deception operation sponsored by COSSAC was Cockade in the fall of 1943.[27] During that effort, Colonel Hesketh would convey COSSAC'S requirements to the Twist Committee who then decided what agent or other channel would convey the misinformation to the Germans and saw that it was dispatched accordingly.[28]

General Dwight D. Eisenhower was President Roosevelt's appointee for the post of the Supreme Commander, and although some of his staff had been in London for several weeks, it was not until mid-January that the official appointment was signed and the COSSAC planning staff became part of the Supreme Headquarters Allied Expeditionary Force (SHAEF). The new Supreme Commander was told that he should 'enter the Continent of Europe [in May 1944] and .... undertake operations aimed at the heart of Germany and the destruction of her armed forces'.[29]

At the same time COSSAC was absorbed into SHAEF, Ops (B) was enlarged and divided into two subsections: one dealing solely with physical deception; the other – 'Special Means' – concerned with controlled leakage. Colonel Noël Wild who had served as deputy commander of 'A' Force in Cairo under Brigadier Dudley Clarke (the officer in charge of deception throughout the North Africa and Mediterranean campaigns), became head of Ops (B).[30] Colonel Jervis-Reid acted as his deputy, and continued to serve as head of the physical deception subsection. Colonel Hesketh also remained in charge of the Ops (B) Special Means subsection.[31]

Meanwhile, Colonel Bevans at LCS, realizing that the bulk of the controlled agent operations would now be focused on the implementation of the Fortitude deception plan, and not on the counter-espionage effort, decided that the right course would be to abolish the Twist committee and allow Ops (B) to work directly with the B1A section of the Security Service. This section of MI5 was in charge of the management of the controlled enemy agents – the so-called 'double agents' – which were by then proving to be the most effective channel for controlled leakage of information to the Germans.[32] The LCS continued to serve as the channel for co-ordinating with the W Board all the deception efforts requiring the use of diplomatic channels; similarly, the Twenty Committee continued to oversee the release of true information.[33]

In the field of deception an important change of command and control was brought about by the Fortitude directive issued by General Eisenhower on 26 February 1944. The Joint Commanders (General Bernard L. Montgomery, Admiral Bertram H. Ramsey and Air Chief Marshal Trafford L. Leigh-Mallory) became responsible for the detailed planning of Fortitude South. In practice this meant that Montgomery's 21st Army Group would do the basic planning in co-ordination with the naval and air services.[34] Shortly thereafter General Andrew Thorne, GOC Scottish Command, was given planning responsibility for the army's share of Fortitude North.[35] Thus, from late February until mid-summer, when SHAEF resumed undivided control of Fortitude South, the basic function of Jervis-Reid's physical deception staff in Ops (B) was to co-ordinate the plans of the Joint Commanders concerning the Pas-de-Calais sector of France with those of GOC Scottish Command concerning Norway.[36]

Meanwhile, General Eisenhower at SHAEF retained full control of the implementation of both aspects of the Fortitude plan by the use of Special Means. The function of Ops (B) Special Means was to adapt the plans concerning France and Norway to suit the needs of the controlled agent channels made available to SHAEF, and through these double agents, to plant the details of the deception story on the Germans.[37] The division of deception responsibility demanded the closest co-operation between SHAEF and 21st Army Group, for whereas Montgomery had charge of the conduct of the Fortitude South operation as a whole, the Special Means subsection was solely responsible for the day-to-day implementation of all controlled leakage. Accordingly, every real or notational troop location or movement that Ops (B) wished to pass to the Germans first had to have the approval of 21st Army Group. During the weeks that preceded the D-Day invasion, a dispatch rider from the Special Means subsection – usually Roger Hesketh's brother Cuthbert – travelled almost daily between SHAEF headquarters at Norfolk House and Southwick Park near Portsmouth, where General Montgomery's 21st Army Group was headquartered. In that manner the requirements of Ops (B) were cleared with G(R) – or R-Force – the deception staff at 21st Army Group under the control of Colonel David I. Strangeways.[38]

When the Fortitude directive was approved in February 1944, SHAEF already had prepared and issued a plan for Overlord, but soon after the Joint Commanders had taken charge, the original Overlord planning document was superseded by a new plan embodying certain important changes. This in turn led Montgomery's Chief of Staff, Major General Francis de Guingand, to advocate changes in the Fortitude directive, principally the plan to add greater weight to the post-assault phase – the deception concerning the landing of the notational First United States Army Group (FUSAG), under Lieutenant General George S. Patton – with the object of holding the *Wehrmacht* units within the *Armeeoberkommando* 15 sector in the Pas-de-Calais as long as possible after the D-Day invasion. This key change formed the basis for the post-invasion deception that the Special Means subsection was to pass to the Germans via the controlled agents.[39]

During the three months immediately preceding the Normandy invasion, the Special Means subsection of Ops (B) consisted of Colonel

Roger Hesketh (its head), Major Christopher Harmer who was seconded from MI5, Major Cuthbert Hesketh, formerly with the MI Liaison at the War Office, and Phillis White, a civilian supplied by MI5 who acted as secretary for the staff and kept the special registry.[40]

Once Ops (B) Special Means had established its direct link to B1A and the Special Means plan had been co-ordinated and approved by 21st Army Group, the next step in the controlled leakage process was to decide which of the B1A agents were best suited for each particular task within the plan. As soon as a choice was made, the agent's B1A Case Officer would come across from his office at St. James's Street to Norfolk House for a meeting to decide on the general sense of the message to be sent to the Germans. Then the Case Officer and the agent would translate the message into the particular report and idiomatic style of the agent, and at the appropriate time the message would be sent by the agent's Radio Officer via wireless transmitter or, in some instances by a secret ink letter in the agent's handwriting.[41]

As it turned out, practically the whole of the Special Means cover plan was passed to the Germans by two controlled agents: 'Garbo' (the Spaniard Juan Pujol-Garcia) and 'Brutus' (the Polish air force officer, Wing-Commander Roman Garby-Czerniawski).[42] In practice one of the Special Means officers was closeted at Norfolk House almost every day with Tommy Harris and Hugh Astor, the Case Officers who ran Garbo and Brutus.[43] It was during those long daily sessions that the details of the plot and agent story lines were finalized – it was one thing to decide on the misinformation that Ops (B) wanted to send to the Germans, and quite another to decide how the controlled agent could logically obtain it. Thus, credit for the total controlled leakage effort must be given in equal measure to the staff of Ops (B) Special Means and the Case Officers of B1A.[44]

Ops (B) did put a certain amount of information over through the agents Tate and Freak, but for reasons which Hesketh admitted he did not understand, very few of their messages found their way into the German intelligence summaries.[45] In March 1944 the agent Tricycle also made a useful contribution to the deception effort when he delivered to his *Abwehr* agent handlers in Lisbon a false Order of Battle which the OKH intelligence staff at *Fremde Heere West* ultimately accepted as genuine. However, the reaction of the Germans to the other lesser agents, such as Bronx, Mullett, Puppet and Treasure, was minimal.[46]

In late June Ops (B) was enlarged so that its Table of Organization provided for two operating centers: one in France and one in London.[47] While Ops (B) continued to churn out plans and send misinformation to the Germans via the controlled leakage channels well into 1945, the days of strategic deception came to an end toward the end of July 1944. Thereafter, the deceptions were of a tactical nature and often *ad hoc.*[48]

The story of the Special Means strategic deception effort might have ended there – fortunately it did not. After the war, Colonel Roger Hesketh and his brother Cuthbert began work on the SHAEF Ops (B) post-action report that became the detailed Hesketh manuscript. Their research efforts included the interrogation of senior German officers. In March 1946 both Hesketh brothers went to the Bridgend Prisoner of War Camp in South Wales and interviewed *Generalfeldmarschall* Gerd von Rundstedt, *Oberbefehlshaber West,* and *General der Infanterie* Günther Blumentritt, *Chief d. Gen.St., Ob. West.*[49] In April 1946 Cuthbert Hesketh went to Nuremberg and interrogated *Generalfeldmarschall* Wilhelm Keitel, *Chief Ob.Kdo. d. Wehrmacht, Generaloberst* Alfred Jodl, *Chief d. Wehrm. Führungsstab i. Ob.Kdo. d. Wehrm.,* and *Oberst* Friedrich-Adolf Krummacher, *Abwehr Verbindungsoffizier d. Wehrm. Führungsstab.* Cuthbert Hesketh came away from these interviews with the firm conviction that the message from Garbo transmitted at seven minutes past midnight on 9 June 1944, literally changed the course of the Battle for the Beachhead.[50] More will be said about the Nuremberg interviews later, but first a look at the text of the TOP SECRET letter dated 18 April which Cuthbert sent to Roger Hesketh is in order:

> I saw Keitel last night. He agreed that the halting of *SS Pz.Div. 1* would have been an *OKW* decision as they were very hesitant and nervous about moving anything from the P. de C. at that time. He could not however recollect the incident, nor could he say for certain what the *'bestimmte Unterlagen'* [definitive evidences] were. He suggested that it might have been air recce of shipping movements on the South Coast, or some other report from the *Kriegsmarine* or *Luftwaffe.* When he saw the *RSHA* message [,i.e., the GARBO report,] he as good as said, 'Well, there you have your answer.' He read through the comment at the end [of the message] and explained to me that it would have been written by [*Oberst*] Krummacher and that it exactly represented the frame of mind of the *OKW* at that moment, which was such that the *RSHA* report in question would have had just the effect of persuading them to countermand the move of those forces. He added, 'This message proves to you that what I have been telling you about our dilemma at that time is correct.' Later he said 'You can accept as 99% certain that this message was the immediate cause of the counter[manding] order' .... [51]

The Garbo message shown to Keitel was one received at OKW over the RSHA *Mil. Amt.* teleprinter at 2230 hours.[52] Translated it reads:

> *V-man* Alaric network ARABAL reports on 9th June from [his post in] England:
>
> After personal consultation on 8th June in London with my agents [D]onny, Dick and Dorick, whose reports were sent today, I am of the opinion, in view of the strong troop concentrations in South-East and Eastern England which are not taking part in the present operations, that these operations are a diversionary manoeuvre designed to draw off enemy reserves in order then to make a decisive attack in another place. In view of the continued air attacks on the concentration area mentioned, which is a strategically favourable position for this, it may very probably take place in the Pas-de-Calais area, particularly since in such an attack the proximity of the air bases will facilitate the operation by providing continued strong air support.[53]

When he saw the message, *Oberst* Krummacher underlined in red on the message form the words 'diversionary manoeuvre designed to draw off enemy reserves in order to make a decisive attack in another place', and added at the end of the page: 'Confirms the view already held by us that a further attack is to be expected in another place (Belgium?)'. The message then was shown to Jodl who initialed it at the top with his green ink, and underlined the words 'in South-East and Eastern England'. A green ink hieroglyph in the data box at the upper left hand corner of the message form signifies that Jodl considered the message to be of sufficient importance that it should be shown to the Führer. The letters *'erl'* (i.e., *erledigt* or 'done') in pencil to the right of Jodl's hieroglyph shows that the message was seen personally by Adolf Hitler.[54]

The implication of the Garbo message is explained in Chapter XXIII, The Invasion Through Enemy Eyes, of the Hesketh manuscript.

> On 8 June, in view of the growing Allied strength in the bridgehead, the remainder of the *OKW* armoured reserve was released, and at half-past ten on that evening an order was issued by *Ob. West* stating that *SS Pz.Div. 1, Pz.Regmt. Großdeutschland* of *Pz.Div. 116* and certain other troops would with immediate effect come under command of *Ob.Kdo. H.Gr. B.* Further, *Oberbefehlshaber H.Gr. B* was to earmark two *Infanteriedivisionen* in the Pas-de-Calais for employment in the Normandy bridgehead. The Daily Situation Report from *Oberbefehlshaber H.Gr. B* stated that the *SS Pz.Div. 1* was now 'moving out of its present area in the district East/North East of Bruges'.[55]

and:

At half-past seven on the morning of the following day, 10th June, *Ob. West* issued an order which read as follows: 'As a consequence of certain information, *Ob. West* has declared "a state of *Alarmstufe II*" for *Armeeoberkommando 15* in Belgium and Northern France (for Netherlands Command if *Ob.Kdo. H.Gr. B* thinks fit). The move of *SS Pz.Div. 1* will therefore be halted and it will go into the area previously occupied by *Luftfelddivision 19*'. The *SS. Pz.Div. 1,* together with *Pz.Div. 116,* both of which had already started for Normandy, now converged on the Pas-de-Calais, while in the whole of the *A.O.K. 15* area every German soldier and man is standing by night and day for defence.[56]

It is undeniably clear that 'certain information' had a profound effect on the German decision-making on 10 June.

What had occurred between 2200 hours on 8 June and 0730 on 10 June to cause such a complete reversal of plan at the *Berghof?* It is clear that, from the moment of the first landing the Führer and his entourage were in a highly undecided frame of mind about whether the Normandy beachhead was the *Schwerpunkt.* Their fear of a second landing was based chiefly on their belief in the existence of the notional FUSAG under General Patton in South East England. On 8 June, under intense pressure from *Ob.Kdo. H.Gr.* and from *Ob. West,* the OKW agreed to release armored formations from the *Armeeoberkommando 15* area. Then some report had reached them at the *Berghof Führerhauptquartier* which caused a change of mind.[57]

Three *Abwehr* messages compete for the honor of being the one decisive mind-changing piece of evidence. Roger Hesketh makes a convincing case that it was the Garbo message of 9 June that convinced Hitler and the OKW of the imperative need to countermand the orders designed to reinforce *Armeeoberkommando 7* in the Normandy area by bringing the strong mobile reserves south out of the *Armeeoberkommando 15* area in the Pas-de-Calais sector. Continuing in Chapter XXIII, he lays out his proof.

However, first a word must be said about how the *Abwehr* reports reached the OKW. By June 1944 all reports from the still existing field elements of *Amt Ausland/Abwehr* went direct to the *RSHA Mil. Amt* in Berlin which, in turn, would circulate summarized versions by teleprinter to the OKW and other interested headquarters (Ob. West was usually included). At the OKW, *Oberst* Krummacher, was the liaison officer between *RSHA* and the OKW. If he thought an incoming message was of sufficient importance he would show it to *Generaloberst* Jodl who initialed it. In his turn, if Jodl thought the Führer also should see it, then Jodl put a different kind of mark on it and added, if Hitler had seen it, either *'erl' (erledigt)* or *'hat K' (hat Kenntnis)*. As it turned out, three *Abwehr* messages passed through *Oberst* Krummacher's hands during the critical time period which might have influenced the thinking of Hitler and Jodl. With this background the reader can better weigh the evidence that Roger Hesketh marshals in favor of the Garbo message being the *Abwehr* report that turned the tide of history.[58]

Hesketh continues his presentation of the evidence:

> The first [*Abwehr* message] came in at 1335 hours on 9 June. It concerned an intercepted wireless message from London to an Allied organization in Brussels of which the Germans had gained control. The message contained two code phrases: *'Message pour la petite Berthe'* and *'Salomon a sauté ses grands sabots.'* The first code phrase was alleged by the German Intelligence to mean that a landing would take place 'the day after to-morrow at the latest' and the second that the invasion fleet had already started. The *Abwehrstelle* forwarding the message commented that the Allies must have known that this network was under German control and that in consequence it was probably deceptive, but the senior headquarters through which the message passed expressed the view that the Allies had not had time to discover that the organization had been penetrated and that it must in consequence be taken at its face value .... Krummacher did not think it of sufficient importance to show to Jodl.[59]

Accordingly, discounting this message, Hesketh continues:

> The second message came in on 9th June at 1910 hours [from the uncontrolled agent Josephine in Stockholm] ... as follows: 'Very reliable *V-man* reports regarding invasion situation early on 9 June (time of report the night of 8 June): General opinion, according to statements of War Office spokesman to English and American journalists afternoon of 8 June (conference takes place thrice daily), is that conditions for Allied landing troops have improved. Impression shared in authoritative British military circles. According to statements by Harrison, an absolutely clear picture on the British side cannot yet be given as the critical period for the invading troops is only just beginning. Strength so far employed is also described by him as considerable, greater than was originally intended. In his opinion and according to information from other sources a second main attack across the Channel directed against the Pas-de-Calais is to be expected ... British public very optimistic. But views in political circles more cautious. In Conservative circles the danger of too heavy losses is

continually emphasized, whereas the Labour Party and other
Left-wing movements are very satisfied with the beginning of the
invasion.' It is marked '*sofort*' [urgent] in Krummacher's handwriting and was seen by both Jodl and the Führer.[60]

Hesketh explains:

As [the second message] ... was the work of an uncontrolled
agent it will be necessary to explain very shortly a new development in their technique which was becoming evident at this time
and was causing us a good deal of embarrassment [in London].
The evidence of Most Secret Sources [the ISOS decip*ers of the
Abwehr transmissions] was beginning to make the conclusion
almost irresistible that the uncontrolled agents, or at any rate
the two most highly regarded ones – OSTRO in Lisbon and
JOSEPHINE in Stockholm – had acquired some knowledge of
the FORTITUDE story. It is true that a second attack on the Pas-
de-Calais following after the Normandy invasion might have been
guessed at by any intelligent but uninformed person as the likely
sequence of future events, but there were too many similarities of
detail to allow us to attribute this development to chance. We now
know that Dr Krämer [a German journalist living in Stockholm
who ran the fictional agent Josephine] had in fact access to
Abwehr documents. This also was very probably true in the case
of [Paul Fidrmuc, a German-Czech businessman in Lisbon who
ran the fictional agent] OSTRO, though this point has not been
proved. It was through these documents that Dr Krämer read
successive instalments of the FORTITUDE story and handed
them to the Germans a second time with his own embellishments.
The effect, mainly unfortunate, of this practice upon our own
efforts to deceive will be considered in greater detail in a later
chapter [concerning Arnhem]. All that need be said here is that if
this particular message of JOSEPHINE contributed in any way to
the issue of the countermanding order we [at Ops (B)] may
perhaps be allowed to claim a part of the credit since [Dr Krämer]
... was taking his cue from us and basing his appreciation on the
assumed presence of FUSAG on the South East of England, a
force which he himself had done nothing to establish in the
German mind.[61]

Accordingly, and on the basis of further proof which follows, Roger
Hesketh discounts the probability of the scales being tipped by the
Josephine message. His argument in favor of the Garbo message
follows:

The third and last message arrived at [the *Berghof* at] 2220 hours on 9 June .... [Earlier,] at seven minutes past midnight on 9 June Garbo began to send his great message, the transmission continuing without a break until nine minutes past two in the morning. Having announced that agents 7(2), 7(4) and 7(7) had arrived in London and delivered their reports, Garbo proceeded to give a full list of the major formations, real and fictitious, in Sussex, Kent and East Anglia. This, in effect, was a summary and a recapitulation of the reports of the previous days. He also referred for the first time to landing craft on the rivers Deben and Orwell .... [T]he message concluded thus: 'From the reports mentioned it is perfectly clear that the present attack is a large-scale operation but [it is] diversionary in character for the purpose of establishing a strong bridgehead in order to draw the maximum of our reserves to the area of operation and to retain them there so as to be able to strike a blow somewhere else with ensured success. I never like to give my opinion unless I have strong reasons to justify my assurances, but the fact that these concentrations which are in the East and South East of the Island are now inactive means that they must be held in reserve to be employed in the other large-scale operations. The constant aerial bombardment which the area of the Pas-de-Calais has suffered and the strategic disposition of these forces gives reason to suspect an attack in that region of France which, at the same time, offers the shortest route for the final objective of their illusions, which is to say, Berlin. This advance could be covered by constant hammering from the air forces since the bases would be near the field of battle and they would come in behind our forces which are fighting at the present moment with the enemy disembarked in the West of France. From [agent] J(5) I learnt yesterday that there were 75 divisions in this country before the present assault commenced. Supposing they should use a maximum of 20 to 25 divisions, they would be left with some 50 divisions with which to attempt a second blow. I trust you will submit urgently all these reports and studies to our High Command since moments may be decisive in these times and before taking a false step, through lack of knowledge of the necessary facts, they should have in their possession all the present information which I transmit with my opinion which is based on the belief that the whole of the present attack is set as a trap for the enemy to make us move all our reserves in a hurried strategic disposition which we would later regret.'[62]

Garbo's message was received at his control, *Abwehrstelle Madrid,* and

sent on to RSHA Mil. Amt in Berlin. There it was summarized and sent
to *Oberst* Krummacher at the *Berghof Führerhauptquartier* at 2220
hours in the abbreviated form noted above. Included with the message
was this comment by RSHA Mil, Amt:

> The report is credible. The reports received in the last week
> from the ARABAL (GARBO) undertaking have been con-
> firmed almost without exception and are to be described as
> especially valuable. The main line of investigation in future is
> to be the enemy group of forces in South Eastern and Eastern
> England.[65]

Hesketh's narrative continues:

> Later, when the other two messages came to light these two were
> put before Keitel and Jodl. They both dismissed the message
> containing the code phrases to the sabotage organization in
> Brussels as being of little importance. Jodl did so largely on the
> ground that the hieroglyphics proved that Krummacher had not
> thought it of sufficient importance to show to himself. They both
> thought that the other two must have had a decisive influence.
> Jodl gave a slight preference to JOSEPHINE. Keitel on the
> other hand held to his original view. 'I am personally still of
> the opinion that [the] message [from GARBO] ... played the
> decisive rôle, [the one from JOSEPHINE] ... had the second
> place in importance ....' Whatever the relative importance of the
> three messages, they both agreed that GARBO's message, as it
> came in last of the three, must have tipped the balance. There is,
> however, yet one more pointer in GARBO's favor. It will be
> remembered that his messages came through Madrid, while those
> of JOSEPHINE came from Stockholm. Attached to the OKW
> War Diary were a number of appendices, one of which con-
> tained copies of important documents relating to the Normandy
> invasion which were received from day to day at the *OKW*. On
> Jodl's instructions the *OKW* War Diary was preserved ... , but
> unfortunately, . . . the appendices were destroyed ... so that we
> have only the bare headings. Of the four 'invasion' documents
> included for 10 June one is entitled 'News from Madrid' *(Nach-
> richt aus Madrid)*. There is no corresponding heading entitled
> 'News from Stockholm'. It is natural to suppose that any message
> which [supported a countermand order which] altered the course
> of a campaign should have been thought worthy of inclusion in an
> appendix to the War Diary.[64]

Thus, Hesketh concludes:

Taking the evidence as a whole, the reader probably will agree that GARBO's report decided the issue. But whatever view one may take it must always be remembered that no message would have spurred the Germans to action on the morning of 10 June had they not already been convinced of the presence of FUSAG beyond the Straits of Dover. And the establishment of that force on either side of the Thames Estuary had been the combined achievement of [both] GARBO and BRUTUS.[65]

In my view, Hesketh has established his case in favor of the Garbo message beyond a reasonable doubt.

More could be written on how the false FUSAG Order of Battle was built up, and on many other aspects of the deception efforts that preceded and followed the Normandy invasion, but limitations of space prevents saying more now. The anecdote focused on here is the one which illustrates the critical pay-off of the efforts of Ops (B) Special Means. The rest of Hesketh's great history must await the publication of his manuscript as a book.

Much has been written in recent years to the effect that surprise is the great force multiplier, and that a little deception goes a long way. That is only half the story. Roger Hesketh's manuscript brings out the fundamental truth which is: Good intelligence – the truth, timely told – is the real force multiplier. Without good intelligence, properly used, one can never hope to plan and execute a good military operation – let alone a good deception operation. Without very good intelligence, properly analysed, one can never defend against deception or avoid surprise. Surprise is not a free good. It has to be bought and paid for with a proper deception plan that is grounded on reliable intelligence about what one's adversary is thinking. It would be tragic if Hesketh's teaching on this point were lost to present and future generations of intelligence and deception scholars. It is to be hoped that we shall soon have the opportunity to read the published edition of this unique historical record.

NOTES

1. In its official printed form the Hesketh manuscript bears all of the hallmarks of a book, but throughtout this review we shall refer to it as the 'Manuscript'.
2. *Who's Who in England, 1986–1987* (London: Marquis Press Ltd., 1986)
3. Plan Bodyguard was approved by the Combined Chief of Staff on 20 January 1944, and sent to SHAEF for the purpose of planning on 22 January. C.C.S. 459/2, 20 January 1944, Plan 'Bodyguard', with enclosures, and Memorandum for the Supreme Commander, Allied Expeditionary Forces, 22 January 1944, subject: 'Overall Deception Policy for War Against Germany'. Record Group 331, Records of SHAEF, File No. 381 *Bodyguard*, Modern Military Records Branch, National Archives, Washington, D.C. For the Fortitude plan, see SHAEF (44) 13, 23 February 1944, PLAN 'FORTITUDE', Record Group 319, Records of the Army Staff, Cover and Deception, File No. *ETO Exhibit G, 'Operations in Support of Neptune' (B) 'Fortitude North'*, Entry 101, Folder No. 8, Box 1, MMRB, NA, Wash., D.C.; SHAEF (44) 21, 26 February 1944, Subject: Plan 'FORTITUDE' (NEPTUNE), Record Group 319, Records of the Army Staff, Cover and Deception, Fine No. *ETO Exhibit G, 'Operations in Support of Neptune' (A) 'Fortitude North'*, Entry 101, Folder No. 7, Box 1, MMRB, NA, Wash. D.C.; SHAEF Ref No: – N.J.C./00/261/33, n.d., Subject: Part I COVER PLAN – FORTITUDE SOUTH, with Appendix 'B' (Naval) and Appendix 'D' (Air Plan), Record Group 319, Records of the Army Staff, Cover and Deception, File No. *ETO Exhibit G, 'Operations in Support of Neptune' (C) 'Fortitude North'*,Entry 101, Folder No. 9, Box 1, MMRB, NA, Wash. D.C.; SHAEF/18209/Ops (b), 3 June 1944, Record Group 381, Records of SHAEF, File No. *Fortitude*, MMRB, NA, Wash. D.C.
4. The Conclusion to the Hesketh manuscript can be found in its entirety at pages 233–42 of Barry D. Hunt 'An Eyewitness Report of the *Fortitude* Deception: Editorial Introduction to R.F. Hesketh's Manuscript', in Donald C. Daniel and Katherine L. Herbig (eds), *Strategic Military Deception* (Elmsford, New York: Pergamon Press, 1981), pp.224–42.
5. In *Essay on Vainglory*, Francis Bacon wrote:

    It was prettily devised of Aesop: 'The fly sat upon the axle-tree of the chariot-wheel and said, "What a dust do I raise!" ' So are there some vain persons that, whatsoever goeth alone or moveth upon great means, if they have never so little hand in it, they think it is they that carry it.

    Roger Fleetwood Hesketh, 'FORTITUDE: A History of Strategic Deception in North Western Europe – April, 1943 to May, 1945', (MS prepared for Ops (B) SHAEF, London, February, 1949, 259 pages), Preface. Hereafter referenced as Hesketh, 'Manuscript'. A copy of the manuscript is in the custody of this author.
6. Hesketh, 'Manuscript', Preface. The referenced reports are: (1) 'The Double-Cross System of the War of 1939–1945', by J.C. Masterman, printed by M.I.5 in September 1945; (2) 'Historical Record of Deception in the War Against Germany and Italy', held by L.C.S., M.O.D.; (3) 'History of G(R) 21 Army and H.Q. 'R' Force', dtd. April 1945; (4) 'Notes on Wireless Deception for Operation OVER-LORD 32/Security/15(Signals 9)', dtd. August 1944; (5) '''R'' Forces Wireless Activity 1st November 1944 to February 1945', n.d.; (6) 'Organization of the Twelfth Reserve Units', n.d.; (7) 'C.L.H./A/160–70/44, dtd. 7 July 1944, Naval Operations NEPTUNE, Radio Deception', n.d.; and (8) 'Operation QUICK-SILVER THREE – 'BIG BOB', May to September 1944', dtd. 3 November 1944.
7. Gordon A. Harrison, *U.S. Army in WW II – Cross-Channel Attack* (Washington: Office of the Chief of Military History, US Army, 1951), 47, citing CSC 169, Organization of Command, Control Planning and Training for Cross-Channel Operations, 22 January, 1943.
8. Harrison, *Cross-Channel Attack*, 49–51, citing Memorandum, Morgan for Br.

COS, Cross-Channel Operations, 21 March 1943, Annex to COS(43)148(O), 23 March 1943.

9. Roger Fleetwood Hesketh, 'Introduction, Part I', n.d., 2. Several years after his 1949 manuscript was completed, Hesketh prepared two short introductory notes which contain an organizational history of the deception units in Great Britain. As these notes were not part of the original document, they are referred to hereafter under the description of 'Introductory Notes, Part I' or 'Part II'.

10. Hesketh, 'Introductory Notes, Part I', p1.

11. Ewen Montagu, *Beyond Top Secret Ultra* (New York: Coward, McCann & Geoghegan, 1978), pp.61–2, 105.

12. Ibid., pp.40, 140, 148.

13. Ibid., pp.53–4.

14. Ibid., p.41.

15. Ibid., J.C. Masterman, *The Double-Cross System in the War of 1939 to 1945* (New Haven, CT: Yale University Press, 1982), p.10.

16. Montagu, *Beyond Top Secret Ultra*, p.62.

17. Hesketh, 'Introductory Notes, Part II', p.1

18. Montagu, *Beyond Top Secret Ultra*, pp.48, 50.

19. Masterman, *The Double-Cross System*, p.62.

20. Charles Cruickshank, *Deception in World War II* (New York: Oxford University Press, 1979), p.34; Masterman, *The Double-Cross System*, p.107; David Mure, *Master of Deception: Tangled Webs in London and the Middle East* (London: William Kimber & Co. Limited, 1980), pp.83–4.

21. Masterman, *The Double-Cross System*, p.107; Cruickshank, *Deception in World War II*, p.35.

22. Jock Haswell, *The Tangled Web: The Art of Tactical and Strategic Deception* (Wendover, UK: John Goodchild 1983), pp.94–5.

23. Ibid., p.94. In addition to Bevan and Wingate, there were Squadron-leader Dennis Wheatley, Majors Neil Gordon Clark, Derrick Morley and Harold Peteval, and Commander James Arbuthnott, R.N. They were ass..ted by Sir Reginald Hoare from the Foreign Office and Professor Androde, Presid:nt of the Royal Sociey, the science adviser. Dennis Wheatley, review of Anthony Cave-Brown, *Bodyguard of Lies*, 121 *RUSI* (Journal of the Royal United Service Institute for Defence Studies, September 1976, 87–8.

24. Haswell, *The Tangled Web*, p.95.

25. Montague, *Beyond Top Secret Ultra*, pp.133–4.

26. Hesketh, 'Introductory Notes, Part II', p.1.

27. Ibid. For Cockade, see Cruickshank, *Deception in World War II*, pp.85–7; John P. Campbell, 'D-Day 1943: The Limits of Strategic Deception', *Canadian Journal of History* (1977), pp.208–37; Campbell, 'Operation Starkey 1943 – 'A Piece of Harmless Playacting'?' (paper presented at the Intelligence and Military Operations Conference, U.S. Army War College, Carlisle Barracks, PA, April 1986). See above, pp.92–113.

28. Hesketh, 'Introductory Notes, Part I', pp.1–2; 'Introductory Notes, Part II', p.1.

29. Albert Norman, *Operation Overlord, Design and Reality* (Harrisburg, PA: The Military Science Publishing Co., 1952), p.70; Mary H. Williams, *U.S. Army in WW II – Special Studies, Chronology 1941–1945* (Washington: Office of the Chief of Military History, U.S. Army, 1960), p.163. The issuance of the Combined Chiefs of Staff directive did not come until 12 February 1944. General Eisenhower was informed two days later when he arrived in England. On 15 February he issued his first official order as Supreme Commander. That order created his staff and signified General assumption of the command of SHAEF. Harry C. Butcher, *My Three Years With Eisenhower* (New York: Simon and Schuster, 1946), p.491.

30. Hesketh, 'Introductory Notes, Part I', p.2. Mure, *Master of Deception*, pp.18, 242–3.

31. Hesketh, 'Introductory Notes, Part I', p.2.

32. Ibid. The leakage of information, both true and false through the covert use of diplomatic channels was another, albeit far less effective, means of controlled leakage.
33. Hesketh, 'Introductory Notes, Part II', p.2.
34. Hesketh, 'Introductory Notes, Part I', p.2.
35. Ibid.
36. Ibid., pp.2–3.
37. Ibid., p.3.
38. Ibid.
39. Ibid. Appendix V of Hesketh's 'Manuscript' is the part of the Outline Plan for Special Means, SHAEF/24132/4/SM/OPS, dtd. 6 May 1944, detailing in chronological order the movement of every formation involved in the operation. The purpose of such an outline was to provide Ops (B) with a framework within which the movement of the controlled agents, real and notional, could be made to synchronize with those the real and imaginary troops which Ops (B) wished to be brought to the attention of the Germans. The outline also served to correlate the date of the agent's messages. Ibid, pp.3–4.
40. Hesketh, 'Introductory Notes, Part I', p.4: 'Introductory Notes Part II', p.4.
41. Hesketh, 'Introductory Notes, Part I', p.4.
42. Ibid. The 13 pages of Appendix XIII in Hesketh's 'Manuscript' lists the content and the date of approximately 150 Ops (B) messages sent by *GARBO, BRUTUS, TATE, FREAK, and PANDORA,* all of which found their way into either the *OKH Lagebricht West* or the *Ueberblick des Britischen Reiches* between 1 February and 18 December 1944. In that period both Garbo and Brutus account for about 65 each. See also Juan Pujol and Nigel West, *Operation Garbo: The Personal Story of the Most Successful Double Agent of World War II* (New York: Random House, Inc., 1985), pp.5, 7, 146.
43. Hesketh, 'Introductory Notes, Part I', p.4. 'Introductory Notes, Part II', p.4.
44. Hesketh, 'Introductory Notes, Part I', p.4.
45. Hesketh, 'Introductory Notes, Part I', pp.4–5. Hesketh notes that out of a total of 208 passages in the OKH *Lagebricht West* and the *Ueberblick des Britischen Reiches* whose inclusion can be attributed to the work of B.1.A. controlled agents, 91 came from Brutus, 86 from Garbo, but only 11 from Tate.
46. Hesketh, 'Introductory Notes, Part I', pp.4–5. Masterman, *The Double-Cross System*, p.159–61. The Germans were paying attention to certain other agents and this was a source of concern at SHAEF. According to Masterman (p.161).

> In the autumn of 1943 ... we became aware that certain Germans in the [Iberian] Peninsula, notably OSTRO, were in fact giving information to the Germans which, as they declared, came from their agents in England. In fact these agents were notational, and their reports were constructed from rumor aided by invention and surmise. To us, however, they seemed in the highest degree dangerous. Not only was it possible that OSTRO reports would gain more credence in Berlin than the reports of our own agents, but it was not impossible that OSTRO might by a fluke give the exact area of the attack on the Continent, and thus destroy the deception plan ... [A] variety of schemes were put forward for the elimination of OSTRO. They did not succeed.

According to Roger F. Hesketh: 'On the 31st May, 1944 [Paul Fidrmuc, a German-Czech businessman in Lisbon, known to the *RSHA Mil. Amt* as agent] OSTRO, gave a correct forecast of the invasion. There is no evidence to show that his message was based on anything more solid than his own imagination'. Hesketh, 'Manuscript', Conclusion, 173, fn 1. According to Albert Speer, the Führer made pointed reference to the 'correct' agent report at the mid-day conference at the *Berghof* on 6 June:

> Hitler seemed more set than ever on his preconceived idea that the enemy was trying to mislead him. 'Do you recall? Among all the many reports we've received

there was one that exactly predicted the landing site and the day and the hour. That only confirms my opinion that [this landing in Normandy] is not the real invasion yet'.

Speer, *Inside the Third Reich: Memoirs by Albert Speer*, Richard and Carla Winston, trans., (New York: Macmillan Company, 1970), 354.

47. According to J.C. Masterman: 'The 212 Committee was formed in August 1944 by Twenty-first and Twelth Army Groups on the model of the Twenty Committee. The objects of the [212] Committee, which was afterwards taken over by SHAEF, were to approve traffic for controlled agents, to direct the deception policy governing the traffic, and to authorize the use of controlled agents for particular operations. The [212] Committee ran all double-cross agents on the Continent and continued to operate successfully until the conclusion of hostilities. Meanwhile, the old system continued in this country', Masterman, *The Double-Cross System*, p.167.

48. Hesketh, 'Introductory Notes, Part I', p.5. In the five pages of Chapter XXXII in the manuscript Hesketh recounts the efforts made to provide a cover plan for Operation Market, the airborne attacks directed at the capture of the bridges between Arnhem and the Belgian frontier. He also tells of the messages from the fictional agent Josephine being sent to Berlin by Dr. Krämer, the German journalist residing in Stockholm. Ibid, 'Manuscript', pp.102, 146–7, and Appendix XIV, pp.245–6.

49. Hesketh, 'Introductory Notes, Part I', p.5. The results of that interview became the basis for Chapter XXII of the manuscript entitled 'German Opinion in May'.

50. Hesketh, 'Introductory Notes Part I', P.5. See also, Masterman, *The Double-Cross System*, p.157–8.

51. Hesketh, 'Introductory Notes, Part I', pp.5–6.

52. On 18 February 1944, Hitler had removed *Admiral* Wilhelm Canaris from his post as head of *Amt Ausland/Abwehr*. That began the long process of absorption of the *Abwehr* headquarters into the *Reichssicherheitshauptamt* where it became RSHA Mil. Amt under the control of *Obergruppenführer SS* Ernst Kaltenbrunner. Gilles Perrault, *The Secret of D Day* (Boston: Little, Brown & Co., 1965), p.65; Chester Wilmot, *The Struggle for Europe* (New York: Harper & Brothers, 1952), p.188.

53. Hesketh, 'Manuscript', p.iii. The actual message from RSHA Mil. Amt to OKW, RSHA/Paris, and Ob. West reads:

V-ALARIC UNTERNEHMEN ARABAL MELDET 9. JUNI AUS ENGLAND: .. NACH PERSOENLICHER RUECKSPRACHE AM 8 JUNI IN LONDON MIT MEINEN AGENTEN JONNY, DICK UND DORICK, DEREN MELDUNGEN HEUTE UEBERMITTELT, BIN ICH AUF GRUND DER STARKEN TRUPPENBEREITSTELLUNGEN IN SUEDOST UND OSTENGLAND, DIE AN AUGENBLICK-LICHTEN OPERATIONEN NICHT BETEILIGT SIND, DER ANSICHT, DAS DIE OPERATIONEN ABLENKUNGSMANOEVER SIND MIT ZWECK FEINDLICHE RESERVEN AUF SICH ZU ZIEHEN, UM DANN ENTSCHEIDENEN STOSS AN ANDERER STELLE ZU FUEHREN. DIESES KOENNTE UNTER BERUECK-SICHTIGUNG DER FORTGESETZTEN LUFTANGRIFFE AN DER HIER FUER STRATEGISCH GUENSTIGEN LAGE DES ER-WAEHNTEN BEREITSTELLUNGSRAUMES SEHR WOHL IN DER GEGEND PAS DE CALAIS ERFOLGEN, INSBESONDERE DA BEI EINEM SOLCHEN ANGRIFF DIE NAEHER GELEGSNEN LUFT-STUETZPUNKTE FORTGESETZEN STAERKSTE UNTERSTUET-ZUNG DURCH LUFTSTREITKRAEFTE EINES SOLCHEN UNTER-NEHMENS ERLEICHTERN WUERDEN.=
RSHA, MIL. AMT, BR B NR 9495/44 ....

The message was put on the teleprinter at RSHA in Berlin at 1850 hours and was received by *Oberst* Krummacher at the OKW liaison office at the *Berghof Führerhauptquartier* near Berchtesgaden at 2220 hours.

54. Hesketh, 'Manuscript', p.iv.
55. Ibid., p.100.
56. Ibid. '[T]he movements of at least four divisions, and perhaps six, were effected by the counter order'.
57. Hesketh, 'Manuscript', p.101.
58. Ibid. The notation *'erl'* translates as 'done' and *'hat K'* as 'he is aware'.
59. Hesketh, 'Manuscript', p.101.
60. Hesketh, 'Manuscript', pp.101–102. Harrison is a fictitious Air Marshal to whom Josephine attributed much of his most sensational intelligence. It is possible that he was thinking of Air Marshal Harris, but mistook the name. Ibid., p.102.
61. Hesketh, 'Manuscript', pp.101–102. According to David Irving Krämer was the Counsellor of the German Legation in Stockholm. David Irving, *Hitler's War 1942–1945* (London, 1977), p.842. Dr Krämer ran two agents, Josephine and Hektor. Both are seen by the British as 'uncontrolled' and it is most probable that they were purely fictional agents – the notional produce of Krämer's fertile journalistic imagination. It has been established that Krämer's motive was pecuniary and he used the supposed needs of his agents to get money from the *Abwehr* – money he pocketed for himself. Ibid., p.102, fn. 19. In intelligence jargon, Dr Krämer was a 'papermill'.
62. Hesketh, 'Manuscript', pp.102–103.
63. Ibid., p.103.
64. Ibid., p.104.
65. Ibid.

Notes on Contributors

Michael I. Handel is Professor of National Security Affairs at the US Army War College, Carlisle, Pennsylvania, and co-editor of *Intelligence and National Security*. His published works include *The Diplomacy of Surprise: Hitler, Nixon, Sadat* (1981) and *Weak States in the International System* (1981), as well as numerous monographs and articles. In 1986 he edited a book on *Clausewitz and Modern Strategy*.

John P. Campbell is an Associate Professor of History at McMaster University, Hamilton, Ontario. His current interests are intelligence and deception during the Second World War and Combined Operations, and he has published articles in the *Canadian Journal of History*, the *Journal of American History, RUSI Journal for Defence Studies* and others.

Thomas L. Cubbage II is a Senior Counsel in the Phillips Petroleum Company. In 1965–71 he served in the Military Intelligence Branch of the US Army, reaching the rank of Major. He was an intelligence collection operations officer in Vietnam, and later the Middle East Current Intelligence analyst in the Pentagon. He is now working on a book about the factors leading to failures in the estimative process and the apparent inevitabiity of surprise.

David M. Glantz is Director of Research at the Soviet Army Studies Office, Fort Leavenworth, Kansas. He is the author of *August Storm: The Soviet Strategic Offensive in Manchuria, August 1945* (1983), *August Storm: Operational and Tactical Combat in Manchuria, August 1945* (1983) and *The Soviet Airborne Experience* (1984). He is completing work on Soviet offensive operations and use of deception in the Second World War.

Katherine L. Herbig is Adjunct Research Professor at the US Naval Postgraduate School, Monterey, California. Her research has centred on strategic deception and she is the author of a number of books and articles. With Donald C. Daniel she co-edited *Strategic Military Deception* (1982).

Klaus-Jürgen Müller is Professor of Modern and Contemporary History at the University of the Bundeswehr and at Hamburg State University. He was (1981–86) President of German Committee on the History of the Second World War and is a member of the Commission Internationale d'Histoire Militaire Comparée and of the Institut d'Histoire des Relations Internationales Contemporaines. His published works include *Das Heer und Hitler* (1969), *Armee, Politik und Militär in Deutschland 1933–1945* (1979), *General Ludwig Beck – Generalstatschef des deutschen Heeres* (1980), *Macht-bewusstsein in Deutschland am Vorabend des Zweiten Weltkrieges* (ed. with F. Knipping, 1984), *Deutscher Widerstand 1933–1945* (ed. 1986).